Seventh Edition

The Economics of Poverty and Discrimination

Bradley R. Schiller

The American University

Prentice Hall, Upper Saddle River, New Jersey 07458

Acquisitions Editor: *Leah Jewell*
Associate Editor: *Gladys Soto*
Editorial Assistant: *Kristen Kaiser*
Editor-in-Chief: *James Boyd*
Marketing Manager: *Patrick Lynch*
Production Editor: *Maureen Wilson*
Managing Editor: *Dee Josephson*
Manufacturing Buyer: *Diane Peirano*
Manufacturing Supervisor: *Arnold Vila*
Manufacturing Manager: *Vincent Scelta*
Composition: *Impressions Book and Journal Services, Inc.*
Cover Image: *Diana Ong, SuperStock, Inc.*

 Copyright © 1998, 1995, 1989, 1984, 1980, 1976, 1973 by Prentice-Hall, Inc.
A Simon & Schuster Company
Upper Saddle River, New Jersey 07458

Library of Congress Cataloging-in-Publication Data

Schiller, Bradley R.
    The economics of poverty and discrimination / Bradley R. Schiller.
  — 7th ed.
        p.   cm.
    Includes bibliographical references and index.
    ISBN 0-13-675083-4
    1. Poor—United States.   2. Poverty—United States.
  3. Discrimination—United States.   4. Economic assistance, Domestic—
  United States.   I. Title.
  HC110.P6S27   1998
  305.569′0973—dc21   97-32093
                                                                 CIP

Prentice-Hall International (UK) Limited, *London*
Prentice-Hall of Australia Pty. Limited, *Sydney*
Prentice-Hall Canada, Inc., *Toronto*
Prentice-Hall Hispanoamericana, S.A., *Mexico*
Prentice-Hall of India Private Limited, *New Delhi*
Prentice-Hall of Japan, Inc., *Tokyo*
Simon & Schuster Asia Pte. Ltd., *Singapore*
Editora Prentice-Hall do Brasil, Ltda., *Rio de Janeiro*

Printed in the United States of America

10   9   8   7   6   5   4   3

Contents

Preface

The principal impetus for this new edition was the Congressional passage of historic welfare reforms in 1996. The Personal Responsibility and Work Opportunities Reconciliation Act of 1996 terminated the program (AFDC) that had been the centerpiece of the U.S. welfare system for sixty years. In place of that federal entitlement, Congress created a block grant to distribute welfare funds to the states. Congress established new rules that sharply limit access to welfare for immigrants, nonworking adults, and longer-term recipients. At the same time, however, Congress gave the states much broader leeway to decide who gets welfare, how much they get, and under what conditions. Since July 1997 the states have been developing their own adaptations of the new welfare model. A primary goal of this edition is to describe the new Temporary Assistance to Needy Families (TANF) program and show how it fits into the nation's multilayered welfare system.

A second impetus for this new edition arises from the renewed battle over affirmative action. The gender and race preferences that have been the staples of affirmative action have come under intense assault. California's proposition 209 was not only a barometer of public opinion but also a threshold for the dismantling of gender and racial preferences. This edition re-examines the arguments for and against affirmative action; then it traces the development of equal opportunity policy through key court cases, legislation, and events.

This seventh edition also provides the most recent data on poverty and the maze of related public programs. Once again, an effort has been made to incorporate the latest research findings from diverse disciplines, including economics, sociology, political science, gerontology, and public health. Although my own training in economics gives a unique structure and perspective to the text, the discussion ranges far beyond the conventional boundaries of academic disciplines. This is particularly evident in expanded discussions of the urban underclass, the increasing feminization of poverty, the renewed IQ controversy, and the behavioral constraints on welfare reform. A review of the table of contents will confirm the breadth of the inquiry and the thoroughness of this revision.

The central focus of the text continues to be on the phenomenon of poverty, with discrimination examined as a potential contributing cause. The text begins with a conceptual discussion of poverty and inequality, highlighting the differing views of causation. Three distinct causal perspectives are introduced in Chapter 1, namely Flawed Character, Restrictive Opportunity, and Big Brother. These competing "explanations" of poverty and inequality are referenced throughout the text in order to accentuate disparate views of why poverty persists and what role public policy should play.

Chapter 2 tries to quantify the dimensions of poverty. The seemingly mundane task of counting the poor has become increasingly controversial, as evidenced by the National Academy of Science's 1995 report and the ensuing debate over poverty standards and census methods. Chapter 2 summarizes the key dimensions of this debate and emphasizes how our perceptions of poverty depend on the yardstick used. Data for 1995 are used to illustrate both the official poverty count and the impact of various adjustments.

Chapters 3–10 address the major causes of poverty. Each chapter focuses on a cluster of related causes, drawing on a broad range of research. Points of controversy are emphasized and analyzed in the context of the best available evidence. The intent is not to advocate one point of view but to encourage critical thinking on central issues in the poverty debate.

The more prominent policy options for eliminating poverty are examined in the final five chapters. Welfare reform gets a lot of attention, in keeping with the historic 1996 reforms. Chapter 11 reviews the motivations for those reforms and discusses their implementation and impact. Chapter 12 is devoted to social insurance programs. In addition to Social Security and Unemployment Insurance, the chapter includes an extended description of child-support enforcement and assurance. In each case, the theoretical and historical foundations of the policy option are reviewed, with an eye toward assessing its antipoverty potential.

The potential of unemployment and training policies to reduce poverty is examined in Chapter 13. The debate over whether economic growth creates "good" jobs or "bad" ones is reviewed, as are a host of skill-training programs. The impact of the Earned Income Tax Credit (EITC) on labor supply and income is also assessed in Chapter 13.

The renewed debate over affirmative action is the central focus of Chapter 14. The discussion reviews the history and experience of equal opportunity initiatives in both employment and education. The inherent conflict between affirmative action and reverse discrimination is examined in the context of legal milestones and the California and Texas experiences.

The ultimate objective of this book has not changed through seven editions. Its goal is to lay the foundations for a clearer understanding of poverty and discrimination and for a keener perspective on related public policy. Until we know why people are poor, or what kinds of programs are effective in combatting poverty and discrimination, we cannot expect these problems to disappear.

Teacher's Manual

Prepared by Steven Rock of Western Illinois University, the Teacher's Manual for this edition offers a brief synopsis of each chapter, a set of true/false and discussion questions, and some lecture suggestions. The Teacher's Manual is available on request from your Prentice Hall sales representative.

ACKNOWLEDGMENTS

As with previous editions, I have benefitted from the feedback of students and instructors who have used this text. I am particularly grateful for the detailed reviews provided by M. Neil Browne, Bowling Green State University; Steven M. Rock, Western Illinois University; and Nirvikar Singh, University of California—Santa Cruz. I am also grateful to the many personnel at the U.S. Bureau of the Census and the U.S. Bureau of Labor Statistics who provided the data—much of it unpublished—to update this edition. Finally, I would like to thank Maureen Wilson, my production editor at Prentice Hall, who has shepherded several editions of this text through the production process.

Bradley R. Schiller
The American University

CHAPTER

Views of Inequality and Poverty

A merica is a very rich nation. With only 5 percent of the world's population, America produces more than 20 percent of the world's output. While over half of the world's population struggles along with less than $1,500 per year in per capita income, the average American enjoys well over $25,000 in annual income. The typical American family has a kitchen outfitted with a microwave oven, a conventional oven/stove, and a refrigerator with built-in freezer. In Indonesia, Ethiopia, Kenya, Haiti, and Pakistan most families don't have any appliances and often no kitchen at all. The running water, hot showers, and indoor toilets that are taken for granted by the average American citizen are still considered luxuries by most people in the rest of the world. While Americans consume 3,600 calories a day and pursue exercise and diet programs to work the fat off, one-fifth of the world's population struggles to get enough food just to maintain body weight and support light activity (2,600 calories per day, according to the World Health Organization). With one doctor for every 500 people, Americans fret over the health care "crisis." In Ethiopia there is only one doctor for every 88,000 people, and life expectancy is only 48 years (versus 76 years in the United States). Few people around the world associate the word *poverty* with America.

THE CONTINUING CONTROVERSY

Within the United States, however, poverty is still an issue of intense concern. As rich as America is, its abundance is not shared equally. Some people have so little, in fact, that we consider them to be poor. They include the homeless persons who wander the streets, the welfare families who crowd into substandard housing, the farm workers who can't afford indoor plumbing, and the aged who need public assistance to provide food and shelter.

Too Little Assistance?

To many observers, such impoverishment in a land of evident abundance is unacceptable. Since we have enough income and wealth to assure everyone a decent standard of living, it is argued, we have a social and a moral obligation to do so. From this perspective, continuing poverty is a symptom of societal failure—the failure to use our wealth to assure a socioeconomic structure that is equitable and accessible to all. Those who view poverty in this way demand that we reslice the economic pie so that everyone has at least an "adequate" piece. They want to eliminate not only poverty, but also reduce the inequalities that keep some people in million-dollar mansions and others seeking shelter in abandoned cars.

Or Too Much?

Not everyone shares these views. Many people are convinced that America's so-called poverty problem is greatly exaggerated. Relatively few Americans, they say, experience real impoverishment. The so-called poor often own their own homes, and a car, and have a television, modern plumbing, and a microwave oven as well. If they need more food, they can get food stamps; if they are sick, they get free medical care (Medicaid or Medicare), and the government provides housing at little or no cost.

Many people argue not only that we have *already* fulfilled our obligation to the poor, but that we have perhaps provided *too much* help to people at the bottom of the income ladder. In a market-based economy incomes tend to reflect how much people produce. In 1996, Michael Eisner made over $200 million—$78,000 an *hour*—as chief executive officer of the Walt Disney corporation. In that same year, 30 million American households had incomes of less than $20,000. Maybe that wasn't fair or equitable, but it might have been an efficient way to slice the pie. Michael Eisner has led his company's efforts to develop new movies, plan a new theme park, and market Disney-brand clothes and toys. Judging by Disney's sales success, these were the kinds of goods and services American consumers wanted. By supplying them, Eisner helped raise the American standard of living. In other words, Michael Eisner increased the size of the pie. He took a large slice, but still left enough for everyone else to enjoy a bit more as well. By dangling such huge rewards, a market system encourages people to produce more output.

The situation at the bottom of the income ladder looks far different. Among the so-called poor there were 6 million families that worked only sporadically, or not at all. They contributed little or nothing to the nation's output of goods and services. To the extent that people *choose* not to work, why should the rest of society be obliged to take care of them? It is even possible that *helping* the poor may actually *discourage* them from working. If society offers a "free" slice of the pie to people who don't work, why should other people work hard for similarly sized slices? The provision of welfare benefits, food stamps, free medical care, and subsidized housing may destroy the *incentive* to work. The combination of higher taxes on the rich and more assistance to the poor may end up shrinking the size of the pie we are attempting to reslice.

Equity and Efficiency

Are economic incentives and notions of equity really so incompatible? Even if the market incentives were so important to our economic prosperity, must the slices received by the poor be so small? And those served to the rich so large? Would Michael Eisner have worked just as hard for, say, only $20 million? That would have left a lot more pie for the hungry and homeless. In other words, couldn't we *redistribute* incomes somewhat more equally, without impairing our production of goods and services?

Other critics of the existing inequities go even further, questioning the whole relationship between income and contributions to output. The market does *not* reward people, they argue, in relationship to their ability and effort. Some people command high incomes because they have the "right connections," "inside information," or other insulation from the competitive forces of the marketplace. At the other end of the income distribution, many people are forced to accept low incomes because they are "locked out" of good jobs, schools, and neighborhoods. In other words, the market *discriminates,* giving some people better opportunities than others.

CAUSES AND CURES

These contrasting explanations of inequality are mirrored in arguments about the causes of poverty. The presence of millions of poor people in the midst of the world's richest country begs explanation. Are the poor "left out"—excluded from access to the social and economic systems that assure most Americans a comfortable living? Or are the poor simply shiftless and lazy—with no desire to contribute to society or their own personal welfare?

Flawed Characters

People tend to have very firm ideas about what causes some people to be poor and others rich. To many it is simply a question of flawed characters. From this perspective, poverty is regarded as the natural result of individual defects in aspiration or ability. In colonial times, this perspective was aptly summarized by the puritanical Humane Society, which concluded that "by a just and inflexible law of Providence, misery is ordained to be the companion and punishment of vice." In more modern times, theories of sin and immorality have not fared well, and there now exists a general reluctance to ascribe to the laws of Providence the misery of the poor. Instead, we speak in terms of "motivation" or "work ethic": Poverty is thought to result from insufficient amounts of either. According to this view, modern poverty originates from flawed characters, much as in puritanical times.

A theoretical foundation for the Flawed Character argument can be found in the economic concept of *human capital*. Everyone starts out with a certain set of abilities. The critical question is how much those abilities are developed and expanded via later *investments*. Going to school and doing assigned homework represent an investment of time that will increase a person's productive capabilities. A retail clerk who takes night classes in accounting expects to get better job opportunities as a result of such efforts. A software writer who spends weekends examining new program codes expects her increased knowledge to result in superior products. A father who reads books to his children every night is making an investment in his offspring's human capital. In all such cases, the investments in human capital are expected to generate a later payoff in the form of better jobs and higher incomes.

The human capital theory implies that people who get ahead are those individuals (and families) that make the necessary investments. By implication, those who don't make it—the poor—have only themselves to blame. They chose to watch MTV rather than do homework. They didn't want to give up evenings or weekends for special classes. Or they chose to watch television rather than read to their kids. They ended up poor because they didn't invest enough time, energy, or money in the development of their own human capital. They might even be part of a cultural underclass that disparages such investments, focusing instead on more immediate gratifications.

There are three essential links in the human capital explanation of flawed characters. The first is the assumption that human capital is rewarded in the marketplace. If college graduates don't make more money than college dropouts, then investments in college don't pay. There must be consistent and tangible payoffs to human capital investment if we expect people to make such investments.

The human capital model also assumes rational *choice*. People need to know what their options are and be able to choose from among them. If they voluntarily make the wrong choices, their poverty is understandable.

Finally, the human capital interpretation of flawed characters depends on the existence of pervasive opportunity. From this perspective, anyone who wants to move up the income ladder can do so by making the required effort—the human capital investment.

The Flawed Character argument applies both to jobs and schools. In the labor market, people who do not find good jobs are assumed to lack sufficient initiative or diligence. To the extent that they are less able, as measured by education, skills, or ability tests, their disadvantage is to be explained by earlier lack of motivation in school. Individuals who do not work hard in school end up failing in the job market as well. Thus, the Flawed Character perspective sees individuals as in full control of their socioeconomic status.

Restricted Opportunity

An alternative explanation of poverty claims that impoverishment may result from forces beyond the control of the individual. According to this argument—the Restricted Opportunity argument—the poor are poor because they do not have adequate access to good schools, jobs, and income. They are discriminated against on the basis of race, sex, or income class. As a result, they can't get the education, the jobs, or the housing they need to get ahead. Even government services are denied them. They don't get adequate police protection; they get few tax breaks; and they are denied more mainstream public services (e.g., transportation service, street repair, public facilities). In the face of these external barriers, no amount of work ethic or effort assures escape from poverty.

The Restricted Opportunity argument denies a critical premise of the Flawed Character argument. If individuals don't have an equal opportunity to acquire education, then their lack of human capital isn't so easily explained by poor choices they might have made. Likewise, if the achievements of minority workers are rewarded less in the marketplace, the incentive to invest in their human capital is diminished as well.

Restrictions on opportunity need not originate in overt discrimination. One of the most rapidly growing segments of the poverty population is single mothers and their children. The failure of absent fathers to provide financial support for their children handicaps a mother's ability to raise the children or secure employment.

A basic implication of the Restricted Opportunity argument is that only the provision of improved opportunities would assure a reduction in the number of people we count as poor. The improved opportunities may entail improved access to quality education, better enforcement of child-support obligations, new job openings, or expanded health- and child-care assistance.

Big Brother

There is a third view of poverty that falls between these two extremes. This view—the Big Brother argument—blames the government for destroying incentives for stable families and economic self-sufficiency. From this perspective, poor people are not inherently flawed. Rather, the government perverts their perspectives and behavior through high taxes, welfare benefits, racial quotas, and other public policies. These policies, though intended to help the poor, actually destroy work incentives and create what George Gilder has called a "blight of dependency."[1]

The availability of welfare benefits, for example, may discourage people from working. Long hours working at low wages may look decidedly unattractive when the government offers the option of welfare benefits for those who do not work. Decisions to get married, to have a baby, or to move to another community may also be influenced by the kinds of public assistance the government offers. By *curtailing* welfare benefits and related services, the government might encourage people to make greater efforts on their own. Charles Murray suggests that the total elimination of welfare programs would ultimately change both the culture and the behavior of the poor in ways that promote financial independence.[2]

Self-Interest

While examining these different views of poverty, we must be mindful of how they appeal to self-interest. The Flawed Character argument, for example, appeals directly to the psychological needs of the middle-class majority. If the poor are poor because of flawed characters, then the nonpoor must be nonpoor as a result of nonflawed characters. (Otherwise, how are we to explain the superior position of the latter class?) Hence, the Flawed Character argument implies a psychological pat on the back for the nonpoor. Adam Walinsky made note of this same phenomenon when he observed that ego satisfaction requires each of us to ascribe the status of "those above us" to luck and the status of "those below us" to character and ability.[3] Thus, the Flawed Character argument not only explains poverty, but justifies the position and privileges of the nonpoor as well. To deny the Flawed Character argument is tantamount to questioning the status of the middle and upper classes.

Economic interests are also concealed in the Flawed Character argument. A basic implication of this argument is that society is already doing everything it can to help the poor. The poor have only themselves to blame for not taking advantage of the opportunities society offers. There isn't any need for more antipoverty programs or the taxes that pay for them. To the harassed taxpayer who equates higher taxes with more money for "the bums on welfare," the Flawed Character argument is economically appealing.

---

[1]George Gilder, *Wealth and Poverty* (New York: Basic Books, 1981), p. 12.

[2]Charles Murray, *Losing Ground* (New York: Basic Books, 1984).

[3]Adam Walinsky, "Keeping the Poor in Their Place," *New Republic,* July 4, 1964.

The Restricted Opportunity argument likewise derives support from unspoken biases. Some people are simply convinced that society is to blame for all social ills, that individuals are forever innocent and blameless. As a consequence, they are not inclined to collect or even examine evidence that might fault individuals for their own plight. This type of bias is often referred to as "bleeding heart liberalism." Often, this liberalism may be buttressed by economic interests (e.g., university researchers and public employees who benefit from expanded social programs and budgets).

The Big Brother argument also appeals to identifiable interests. The principal implication of the Big Brother view is that the government is trying too hard to take care of people's needs. By doing less, the government would foster greater private initiative and ultimately eliminate more poverty. In the process, of course, government spending and taxes would be reduced—a goal many people desire for its own sake. Also, if the government were to cut back on affirmative action and related activities, many white males and others would reap direct gains. Hence, there are political and economic interests wrapped up in the Big Brother argument that go beyond its antipoverty effectiveness.

Knowing our potential biases does not settle the controversy about the causes of poverty. But awareness of them may help engender just a bit more objectivity as we try to sort out the various arguments about poverty and inequality. At least we know that the deck may be stacked before the game begins.

Policy Implications

Which view of poverty we ultimately embrace will have a direct bearing on the public policies we pursue. If we conclude, for example, that people are poor because they cannot find decent jobs, our antipoverty efforts are likely to focus on the creation of more and better jobs. On the other hand, if we believe that people are poor simply because they are lazy, we are likely to provide fewer jobs and services. We may instead try to change the behavior of the poor with sanctions (e.g., work *requirements* rather than incentives).

Some people reject the notion that society's antipoverty efforts should be predicated on the causes of poverty. An ethical obligation to help everyone maintain a decent standard of living may supersede concern about who is to blame for poverty. A related argument is that a minimum standard of living is necessary for the exercise of one's rights to liberty and self-determination. To assure everyone those rights, society must offer universal access to basic living standards.[4]

Even if we accept an *ethical* obligation to help the poor, we may still be concerned about the *efficiency* of our antipoverty efforts. If people cannot find decent jobs because they lack basic skills, then the provision of more and better jobs will not eliminate much poverty. If welfare mothers can't find child care, then creating more training programs won't increase their employment very much. In such cases misperceptions of the causes of poverty would result in expensive failures for antipoverty policy. Hence, it is important that our public antipoverty policies be based on informed perceptions of the nature and causes of poverty.

---

[4]See Lesley A. Jacobs, *Rights and Deprivation* (New York: Oxford University Press, 1993), for an elaboration of this perspective.

Historical Perspectives

Different historical phases of antipoverty activity in America illustrate this interdependence of causal perspectives and policy prescriptions. As noted earlier, poverty was viewed in colonial times as a curse on those of disreputable character. Impoverishment was seen as the companion to and punishment for vice. Accordingly, early antipoverty prescriptions focused on religious training, corporal punishment (to drive out sin), and physical expulsion. Very little was done to help the poor become more self-sufficient or even to alleviate their suffering.

It was not until the depression of the 1930s that many people seriously began to question the Flawed Character proposition that poverty resulted from sin and slovenliness. The march of unemployed and poor men—Coxey's Army—on Washington, DC, in 1934 helped stimulate fresh perspectives on the origins of poverty. But it was not until 15 million Americans simultaneously experienced unemployment in the depths of the Great Depression that the Restricted Opportunity perspective on poverty took hold. Only when millions of otherwise responsible and industrious individuals fell abruptly into joblessness and poverty did the American public begin to view poverty as being outside the control of the individual. Awareness grew that poverty might be the consequence of social and economic forces rather than of immorality and vice.

From one point of view, our experience with depressions and poverty may have been too brief. With the passage of time and the return to prosperity, poverty lost its middle-class constituency, and people became less generous toward the poor. When everyone else is prospering, poverty becomes suspect. In good times, most observers again question the ambition, motivation, ability, and the entire cultural orientation of the poor.

In 1961, President Kennedy proclaimed that "a rising tide lifts all boats." As he saw it, a rapidly expanding economy would virtually eliminate poverty and dependency. But welfare caseloads continued to increase even during the economic expansion that began in 1962. People began to wonder about the character of the poor. Middle-class concerns about flawed characters were clearly reflected in the following editorial from the Tulsa, Oklahoma, *Tribune*:

> Relief is gradually becoming an honorable career in America. It is a pretty fair life, if you have neither conscience nor pride. The politicians will weep for you.
> The state will give a mother a bonus for her illegitimate children, and if she neglects them sufficiently she can keep enough of her AFDC payments to keep herself and her boyfriend in wine and gin.[5]

When economic growth faltered in the mid-1970s, Americans viewed the problems of the poor in a more charitable light. President Carter emphasized the restricted opportunities facing people in poor neighborhoods and pushed for better schools, guaranteed jobs, and more training opportunities.

During the economic expansion of the 1980s, public sentiment shifted again. From 1981 to 1989 over 20 million new jobs were created and average incomes rose sharply. By the end of the expansion (1989) it appeared that nearly everyone who

---

[5]Quoted in Edgar May, *The Wasted Americans* (New York: Harper and Row, 1964), p. 7.

wanted a job had one: "Full" employment was deemed to have been achieved. In the midst of such a strong economy, how could anyone remain poor unless his or her character was flawed? President Reagan urged compulsory work programs that would prevent people from getting a "free ride" from taxpayers. In 1990, over 90 percent of Americans attributed poverty to "lack of effort" by the poor themselves.[6] The Big Brother theory of poverty also attracted more attention. A spate of new research and books suggested that public welfare programs were responsible for undermining incentives for family stability, work effort, and saving. It was not lack of opportunity but flawed characters and flawed handouts that were perpetuating poverty and welfare dependence.

The debate over the causes of poverty continues. The problems of welfare and poverty in the 1990s are said to be different from those of earlier decades. A surge in both unwed mothers and divorce has feminized poverty. International competition and technological change have displaced millions of workers. Jobs for low-skilled workers have disappeared especially fast. Cultural norms have changed as well, reducing commitments to work and family.

Have all these changes really altered the nature of poverty? Most Americans aren't sure what to think. As President Clinton observed in 1993, "No one likes the welfare system as it currently exists." On the one hand, most Americans favor help for the poor. On the other hand, they distrust people who receive welfare assistance. In other words, poor people do warrant assistance (restricted opportunity) but once they receive it they somehow become unworthy (flawed character). As Professor John Tropman has observed, most Americans view acceptance of welfare tantamount to "giving up." Accordingly, those who accept welfare deserve punishment in the form of hostility and stigma.

Current American attitudes toward poverty are best described as ambivalent. "On the one hand, government and individuals alike decry poverty and devise programs geared to eradicate or eliminate it. On the other hand, the poor are disliked and perhaps feared."[7] The disquieting suspicion that external social and economic forces are at the root of poverty continues to stir the public conscience. At the same time, however, the egocentric conviction that the poor are less deserving still lingers. Only as unemployment rates reach crisis proportions—as in the early 1980s—does the former perspective clearly gather significant strength. Even then, however, President Reagan was careful to draw a distinction between the "truly needy" and those who could get by if they wanted to.

Against this background of uncertainty about the causes of poverty, it is not surprising that public policy is ambivalent and often ineffective. Tax laws are "reformed" to reduce inequalities one year, then revised to promote work and investment in another year. The historic welfare reforms of 1996 likewise both punished welfare dependency by imposing time limits and work requirements (the Flawed Character view) and attempted to expand opportunities for self-sufficiency with increased child-care and medical assistance (the Restricted Opportunity view). Such carrot-and-stick com-

---

[6]Lawrence Bobo and Ryan Smith, "Antipoverty Policy Affirmative Action, and Radical Attitudes," in *Confronting Poverty,* eds. S. Danziger, G. Sandefur, and D. Weinberg (Cambridge, MA: Harvard Press, 1994), Table 1.

[7]John E. Tropman, "The Image of Public Welfare: Reality or Projection?" *Public Welfare* (Winter 1977).

binations are perhaps inevitable. So long as the causes of poverty remain the subject of intense debate, we cannot expect consistent policies, much less substantial success. Even if we shared a consistent vision of the causes of poverty, conflicting goals and priorities might necessitate compromises and inconsistencies.

Before reaching any policy conclusions, however, we should at least try to sort out the various arguments. Which explanations of poverty make the most sense? To answer this central question, we will first look at the dimensions of poverty and then examine their causes. Once this foundation is set we will be in a position to evaluate current antipoverty policies and to suggest new ones.

INEQUALITY

The poverty debate is often treated as a self-contained issue. In reality, however, it is hard to isolate discussions of poverty from broader concerns about inequality. The $200 million that Disney's chairperson made looks like an awful lot of money even from a middle-class perspective. Indeed, income differences between the truly rich and the middle class dwarf distinctions between the middle class and poverty. Can we really address the problems of poverty without examining the sources of such inequality?

Explanations

The various theories offered to explain poverty can be tested in the broader context of inequality. The same forces that consign one person to poverty may push someone else to a low but not a poor position in the distribution of income. Human capital theory, for example, suggests that everyone's income reflects individual choices about investments in education and training. Accordingly, the Flawed Character argument may explain not only distinctions between rich and poor, but also much more detailed gradations in income.

Restricted Opportunity perspectives may also be relevant. Differences in opportunity (e.g., "Old Boy" networks, affluent school districts) may be as instrumental in creating class divisions as in explaining pockets of poverty.

The Big Brother argument is also germane to broader inequality concerns: Government taxes, expenditures, and regulations rarely affect everyone equally. The hand of government may push some people up the income ladder while pushing others down.

Public attitudes toward inequality, like those concerning poverty, also tend to mirror cyclical changes in the economy. When the economy is booming, individual incomes tend to rise. People have confidence in the future and many harbor hopes of "striking it rich." There is little resentment of those who have already acquired wealth and little political pressure to reslice the economic pie.

When the economy slumps, however, perceptions change. People who lose their jobs or have wages cut suddenly feel cheated by the system. The conviction spreads that rich people have rigged the market to assure that only they can succeed. The political pressure to reslice the economic pie increases.

Equity versus Efficiency

Equity and efficiency are also key issues in the inequality debate. The opportunity to strike it rich can serve as a tremendous incentive to seek out new and better ways of producing goods and services. Why else would people give up weekends and evenings to write new software or design new apparel? Or give up current job opportunities in order to attend graduate school? Or explore for new deposits of oil or gold? The essence of the Horatio Alger ethos is that the market will provide handsome rewards to those who try a little harder (or get lucky). Even if inequalities spur efficiency in production, however, they may be so large that they violate our notions of equity.

DIMENSIONS OF INEQUALITY

Most of the debates about inequality and poverty focus on money incomes. The terms *rich* and *poor* are used synonymously with high and low incomes. Money incomes are not the only standard of well-being, however.

Income versus Wealth

Income refers to the amount of money receipts a person collects in a year. Most income comes in the form of a paycheck. In addition to wages and salaries, households also get income in the form of dividends and interest, rent, and capital gains from the sale of property. Much of the income Michael Eisner received in 1996, for example, came from capital gains on the sale of stock options that Disney had given him; only $750,000 of his $200 million income was paid in salary. Although retired people do not receive paychecks, they may get monthly pension checks as well as interest payments and stock dividends.

The common characteristic of all forms of income is that they represent a *flow* of receipts received during some period of time. This contrasts with wealth, which represents a *stock* of value. The value of accumulated possessions (e.g., home, stocks and bonds, a farm or business) measures one's material wealth.

A person can be "rich" in one of these dimensions but "poor" in the other. A star athlete, for example, may command a huge salary but have little accumulated wealth. By contrast, a farmer may own thousands of valuable acres but earn little income in a particular year.

The distinction between income and wealth raises some preliminary questions about notions of inequality and poverty. Two individuals with identical incomes may have vastly different asset portfolios. Should we be worried about people who have low incomes but great wealth? This question is particularly relevant to many retired persons who have relatively modest incomes from pension benefits, dividends, and interest but own homes, savings accounts, stocks, bonds, and retirement funds. Because assets can be converted into income by selling them, people with assets have some discretion in determining how much income they receive in any year. The possession of wealth also provides economic security and creditworthiness that may compensate for income.

Transitory versus Permanent Income

The ability to convert wealth into income also raises a question about the time frame used to assess inequalities. A farmer who has a bad harvest may receive little income in one year. The farmer may still possess valuable land, however, and have a reasonable expectation of a much better harvest next year. In this case, the farmer's low income in a single year is not representative of his or her economic status. To assess the true economic circumstances, we might want to consider not only the farmer's wealth, but also his or her average income over a period of years.

A graduate student in law or medicine raises similar problems for characterizations of inequality. The typical graduate student subsists on a budget that resembles poverty standards. Yet, students have the expectation of earning exceptionally high incomes after graduation. When assessing the degree of inequality, should we consider only the income received while in graduate school or take a longer view of economic status? If we were to take a longer view, we would recognize that graduate students are acquiring human capital that, like physical capital, can be converted into future income.

Incomes fluctuate from year to year for lots of reasons. When the economy stumbles into a recession, millions of workers experience brief periods of unemployment that reduce their incomes below normal. So long as the spell of unemployment is brief, the temporary decline in income may have no lasting consequences. While unfortunate, such transitory declines in income may be of little consequence for the longer-term economic welfare of an individual. In fact short-run *expenditure* patterns may change very little when income declines. Stocks of consumer goods, accumulated savings, other wealth, and credit provide shock absorbers against transitory income changes. As a result, expenditure patterns tend to be more equal than annual incomes.[8] The distinction between expenditure levels and income levels is particularly striking when poor families are compared to nonpoor families. Nonpoor families have average incomes that are six times those of poor families, yet their expenditures are only three times larger than those of the poor.[9] Accordingly, the distinction between transitory incomes and more permanent measures of economic status should be considered in characterizations of either inequality or poverty.

Life-Cycle Dynamics

When viewed over a period of time, individual incomes also exhibit a pattern of change associated with age. When young people first enter the labor market, their wages are usually quite low and their hours erratic. As they gain education and experience (human capital), their wages increase. Indeed, incomes tend to rise substantially during the first 20 years or so of labor-market participation. As a result, middle-aged workers typically have much higher incomes than younger workers. Wage growth tends to slow in later years and often declines as older workers reduce their work activity.

These life-cycle patterns create substantial inequality across age groups. Workers in their peak earning years will tend to cluster at the top of the income distribution, while younger and older workers will gravitate to the lower rungs of the income ladder. Accordingly, much observed inequality may be no more than a reflection of typical

---

[8]Susan E. Mayer and Christopher Jencks, "Recent Trends in Economic Inequality in the United States: Income versus Expenditures versus Material Well-Being," in *Poverty and Prosperity in the U.S.A. in the Late Twentieth Century,* eds. Dimitri Papadimitriou and Edward Wolff (New York: St. Martins, 1993), pp. 121–203; also Daniel T. Slesnick, "Gaining Ground: Poverty in the Postwar United States," *Journal of Political Economy* (February 1993), pp. 1–38.

[9]Maya Federman, et al., "What Does It Mean To Be Poor in America?" *Monthly Labor Review* (May 1996), pp. 3–17.

age-earnings cycles. Should such life-cycle inequality merit the same concern as the inequality among individuals of similar age? Do we want to reduce inequalities across age cohorts? At a minimum, life-cycle dynamics add an important dimension to interpretations of observed inequality.

Public Provisions

Even when perceptions of inequality are adjusted for wealth holdings, transitory fluctuations, or life-cycle dynamics, they may still fail to capture the full dimensions of economic status. Income and wealth provide access to goods and services sold in the marketplace. Lots of goods and services are provided by the public sector, however. Public schools, libraries, parks, and roadways are available to everyone without explicit payment. Accordingly, private income and wealth do not completely determine how many goods and services one consumes.

The provision of public goods and services complicates perceptions of inequality in at least two ways. International comparisons of inequality are distorted by the varying public provisions in different countries. A nation that offers universal health services, day care, or college scholarships has less economic inequality than another country with fewer such provisions but an identical distribution of market incomes.

Perceptions of *changes* in inequality or poverty are also affected by the public provision of goods and services. As the welfare state has expanded in size and scope, people have become less dependent on market incomes. Medicare, for example, tends to mitigate income inequality among people over the age of 65. Forty years ago, the availability of health care for aged persons was more conditioned on income and wealth. Money still matters, but much less so since the federal government established subsidized health care for the aged. As a result, even an unchanged distribution of income over time might conceal a trend toward greater equality of living standards.

Social Equality

A full measure of inequality would take into account not only the *material* dimensions of life but its *social* dimensions as well. As Mickey Kaus has emphasized, *money* inequality is more palatable if *social* equality is preserved. Social equality implies that people share access to public amenities and responsibilities regardless of economic status. Access to justice, to police protection, to voting polls and civic liberties must be unconditioned by income or wealth. Similarly, everyone must have an equal likelihood of serving on juries or fulfilling other civic responsibilities.

Social equality also implies the absence of class stratification. People from all income classes should be able to interact, not only in schools and courthouses, but in the entire spectrum of social and civic activities. Where such access and equality prevail, money inequality has less social significance.

Kaus laments that a reduction in social equality has made money inequality less bearable. The end of the military draft, for example, not only eliminated a mechanism of social class mixing but also made military service income conditioned. Young people from low-income backgrounds are more likely to volunteer for military service, while "rich kids" pursue college and civilian careers. Cutbacks in funding for public schools, parks, and other public amenities also made income and wealth more important determinants of economic welfare. Even the observance of public holidays on Mondays and

Fridays has torn the threads of social equality. Midweek holidays tend to foster local community celebrations, whereas three-day weekends encourage out-of-town travel and class separation. Kaus proposes that we reverse these trends, thereby making money inequality less important.

Happiness

Kaus's emphasis on social equality is an appropriate reminder of the maxim that "money can't buy happiness." The political scientist Robert Lane pursued this question more directly by examining the relationship of economic status to self-reported levels of satisfaction. He concluded that the maxim has merit: Income and happiness are not well correlated. The things that bring daily happiness to people—friendship, family, work—are largely unrelated to income.[10] Accordingly, income inequalities may tell us little or nothing about differences in well-being. Perhaps we focus on them simply because they are so visible.

Professor Lane did make an exception for poor people. For people at the lowest rungs of the income ladder, Lane observed that additional money did increase the level of happiness. This suggests that money can buy happiness at least for those in poverty. Even at the low end of the income distribution, however, Charles Murray reminds us not to confuse poverty with unhappiness.[11]

Whose Happiness? Units of Observation

Much of the discussion about dimensions of inequality and poverty is grounded in concern for the well-being of individuals. As a society we have proclaimed that individuals should have the right to the pursuit of happiness, and much of our social policy represents an effort to guarantee that right. Most people don't live as single individuals, however; they live in families. This complicates our analyses of well-being and related measures of inequality.

Suppose for the moment that the well-being of individuals was our primary concern. How should we apportion a family's income or wealth among its members? We could divide the family's income by the number of family members and identify its *per capita* income. Implicit in this calculation is the assumption that family members share equally in the household's income and wealth. There is also a normative implication that each family member's welfare is fairly represented by the average income so computed.[12]

If we computed income and wealth distributions on a per capita basis we would be ignoring the economies of scale of larger households. A four-person family doesn't require four kitchens; the entire family shares one. As a result, a single individual living alone will have higher *per capita* rent expenses than will individuals who live in a family. A family can also benefit from specialization of labor: Rather than having to do everything for oneself, family members can specialize and perform household tasks more efficiently. What all of this means is that a lone individual with an income of

---

[10]Robert E. Lane, "Does Money Buy Happiness?" *The Public Interest,* 113 (Fall 1993), pp. 56–65.

[11]Charles Murray, "What's So Bad About Being Poor?" *National Review,* October 28, 1988, p. 36.

[12]For a discussion of the theoretical basis for characterizing the welfare of households, see Julie A. Nelson, "Household Equivalence Scales: Theory versus Policy?" *Journal of Labor Economics* (July 1993), pp. 471–493.

$15,000 per year is not as well off economically as a member of a family with the same per capita income. Accordingly, income and wealth distributions computed in per capita terms may not accurately reflect the economic circumstances of individuals.

Family-based distributions pose similar problems. Should the size of a family be factored into distributional measures? If not, then equality of family incomes would imply that smaller families were better off economically than larger families.

Changes in family size and composition also affect historical trends in inequality. Families are much smaller today than they were a generation ago. Single-parent families are also more common. These demographic changes tend to lower average family income and make the distribution less equal.

All of these considerations underscore the difficulty of operationalizing the concept of inequality. When debates about inequality turn to "the facts," many compromises have to be made about both the importance of various dimensions of inequality and the household units to which they apply.

POVERTY: DRAWING A LINE

All of the difficulties that cloud perceptions of inequality affect the identification of poverty as well. Should poverty be defined in terms of money? To some observers poverty is just as much a state of mind as it is a state of one's pocketbook. The Kentucky backwoods family is sometimes seen not as impoverished but as enjoying the rich benefits of a bountiful and uncluttered natural world. Henry Thoreau would have us idealize such individuals, not try to help them.

Alternatively, lots of people feel poor even though they may possess substantial income and wealth. Just not being able to buy everything one desires, or having less income than one's neighbor, can make one feel poor. These sociopsychological perspectives do not provide us with a very useful definition of poverty, however. When we speak of poverty in America, we envision families who don't have enough income to provide minimally acceptable standards of food, shelter, and clothing.

But where are these people in the income distribution? If we want to know how many people are poor in our society, we have to be willing to draw a line that separates the poor from the nonpoor. Without such a line, we would not know whom to help or be able to determine how successful such help is in reducing poverty.

Any attempt at drawing a poverty line will have to confront all of the inequality issues outlined previously. The distinction between transitory and permanent incomes, life-cycle dynamics, changing family composition, the public provision of goods and services are all relevant phenomena to measures of poverty. Even if we are able to resolve all these complexities, we will still have to confront two very different approaches to identifying a poverty line. The first approach seeks an *absolute* standard of deprivation, while the second relies on *relative* standards of adequacy.

The Absolute Approach

The absolute approach to defining poverty begins with the concept of minimum subsistence, that is, some bundle of goods and services that is regarded as essential to the physical well-being of a family unit. Those who do not possess the economic resources to obtain these goods and services are considered poor. In the most severe conception of the absolute approach, this bundle of economic goods and services consists of the minimum caloric intake essential to human existence, and perhaps some form of shelter. Additional frills are tacked onto this basic diet according to the generosity of the analyst.

This, of course, is the fundamental problem with the absolute definition of poverty. Once the bare-bones, life-sustaining minimum caloric diet has been exceeded, there is no agreement as to how many additional frills can be included in the definitional bundle of minimum goods and services. In the 1930s no one felt particularly poor if he or she did not possess electric lights. Yet, today, a family without electricity will most likely be considered poor. So we include a provision for electricity in our minimum poverty-defining budget. But consensus is far more difficult to achieve on a television, much less on a VCR, a CD player, a car, or a six-pack of beer. How many of these items will we include in a poor family's budget? Our answer will determine where to draw the poverty line.

A British survey conducted in the 1980s asked people to identify items that were absolutely necessary for subsistence. The list included not just a "damp-free home" and "three meals a day for children" but also a much longer list that included a television, a car, a video, and a pack of cigarettes every other day.[13] People who did not have three or more items on this list were deemed to be poor.

In principle, a list of absolute necessities should change very little over time. The concept of minimum needs should also have universal applicability. In reality, neither condition is fulfilled with absolute standards. People's perceptions of what is absolutely necessary for subsistence is conditioned by the array of goods and services available and prevailing living conditions in their own society. Notice in Figure 1.1 how American perceptions of how much money is needed to "just get by," "to live in reasonable comfort," and to "fulfill all your dreams" has changed over time.

There is also a question of who should draw the absolute poverty line. Should experts in nutrition and physiology define subsistence standards? Or should a cross-section of society be consulted, as in the public-opinion surveys? Faced with all these complexities, many observers have suggested an alternative approach to defining poverty, one that depends on relative standards.

The Relative Approach

As a practical matter, the absolute approach to defining poverty is vague and subject to the views of those formulating the yardstick. The relative approach is simply more explicit about this subjectivity. In essence, it states that a person is poor when his or her income is significantly less than the average income of the population. For example, we might say that a person or family with less than one half of the average income is poor. By defining poverty in these terms, we not only avoid the need to define absolute needs, but also put more emphasis on the (in)equality of incomes. This broader perspective underscores the relationship between our views of poverty and our perspectives on the fairness of the entire distribution of incomes.

There are just as many relative measures of poverty as there are absolute ones. Perhaps the most extreme version of relative measures is one that defines poverty as

---

[13]J. Mack and S. Lansley, *Breadline Britain, 1990s* (New York: HarperCollins, 1991).

Question: Thinking about the needs of you and your family, how much income per year would you say you and your family need to live in reasonable comfort? How much income per year do you feel your family would need just to get by? And how much income per year would you say you and your family would need to fulfill all your dreams? (median response)

Income you and your family need

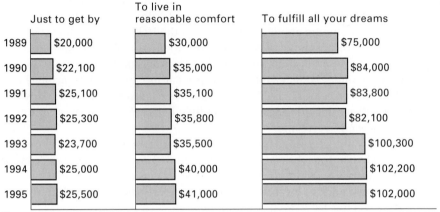

Source: Roper Starch Worldwide.

FIGURE 1.1   Increased Expectations

the low end of the income distribution; for example, anyone in the lowest fifth (or tenth, or third) of the distribution is regarded as poor. From this perspective, poverty will persist as long as inequality does.

Table 1.1 illustrates the basic distinction between absolute and relative definitions of poverty in another way. The table compares the income distributions in 1993 and 1935–36, with incomes in both categories expressed in 1993 dollar values. Note, for example, that 2.4 percent of all American families earned less than $3,000 in 1993, 4.8 percent less than $6,000, and so forth. Only 8 percent of American families earned more than $75,000. Note also that incomes were much lower in the 1935–36 period, even after adjusting for inflation (expressing amounts in 1993 dollar values). In the middle of the Depression 1 out of 9 families earned less than $3,000, and 1 out of 4 survived with less than $6,000 per year.

Suppose we wanted to compare the number of Americans who were poor in 1993 with the number who were poor in 1936. Franklin Roosevelt spoke of one-third of the nation as being "ill-housed, ill-clad, ill-nourished." Apparently he regarded an income of about $9,000 as a threshold of poverty (see Table 1.1). By Roosevelt's definition, only 8.3 percent of the American population was poor in 1993. From an historical perspective, then, we could conclude that the incidence of poverty in the United States had declined markedly over a period of 60 years.

But what would we conclude about the course of poverty between 1936 and 1993 if we had instead applied the relative concept of poverty to the comparison? If we consistently regard the lowest fifth of the American income distribution as poor, then by definition we would find that 20 percent of the population was poor in 1936 and continued to be so in 1993.

TABLE 1.1   Cumulative Family Income Distribution, 1993 and 1935–36 (in 1993 dollars)

Percentage of Families with Income Less than:	$3,000	$6,000	$9,000	$12,000	$15,000	$30,000
1993	2.4	4.8	8.3	12.5	16.8	39.7
1935–36	10.9	25.6	38.7	53.5	63.7	77.6

Source: U.S. Bureau of the Census.

This example illustrates the basic weaknesses of the relative measure of poverty. First, it perpetuates poverty in the statistical sense that some fixed proportion of the population is always regarded as poor. Poverty will always exist if the lowest fifth of the income distribution is regarded as poor. Second, a relative measure of poverty alone says nothing about the quality of life for the people at the bottom of the income distribution. Yet we want to know not only how many people are in poverty but also how desperate their situation is. In a similar vein, we may want to know how much money poor families need to reach an acceptable standard of living.

An improved measure of relative poverty, which has been suggested by Victor Fuchs, meets at least the first objection to relative definitions. By his definition, those with incomes less than *half* of the national median are poor. In 1993, for example, the median family income was just under $38,000. Thus, according to the "Fuchs point," families with less than $19,000 (half of the median) should have been considered poor. The advantage of the Fuchs point over simpler relative definitions is that it distinguishes the elimination of poverty from the elimination of inequality. The simpler relative definition precludes the elimination of poverty until complete equality of incomes is attained. The Fuchs point, by contrast, creates the possibility of eliminating poverty by merely *reducing* inequality, that is, narrowing but not wholly eliminating income differences.

There is nothing sacred, of course, about the use of one-half the median as a relative standard of poverty. We could just as easily have chosen to define poverty in relative terms as one-fourth, one-third, or three-sixteenths of the median income. There is as much subjectivity involved in defining the Fuchs point as there is in defining absolute minimum standards of poverty. In reality, one's choice of a *relative* standard is likely to be influenced by the *absolute* standard of living implied, just as the choice of an absolute standard is likely to be affected by the degree of inequality and the general standards of living we observe.

Professor Morton Paglin of Portland State University has raised another troubling issue.[14] With whom, he asks, should we compare our incomes? A young family with children has different needs and income sources than an older couple living in retirement. Should both households be treated equally when computing the median income? Or should relative incomes be measured only in comparison with families of similar size and age? In the former case, older couples and single-parent households will be most likely to appear poor. By the latter standard, however, more equal proportions of each population subgroup would be classified as poor.

---

[14]Morton Paglin, "The Measurement and Trend of Inequality: A Basic Revision," *American Economic Review* (September 1975).

In view of the conflicting measures of poverty, it is tempting to abandon the search for a poverty line. But this is neither necessary nor appropriate. We need an acceptable definition of poverty in order to identify people we desire to help and to measure our success in helping them. The search for a poverty line is analogous to the search for highway speed limits. No one really believes that all speeds in excess of 55 miles per hour are somehow dangerous and all speeds less than 55 miles an hour are somehow safe; the realities of highway driving are much more complex. Yet, we use 55 miles per hour as a convenient gauge of highway safety. The same is true of our poverty line. On the continuum of misery and human happiness, we cannot pretend that there is some point below which people are unhappy or poor and above which people are content. But, like highway speed limits, we do need a cutoff point—the poverty line.

In searching for the poverty line, we cannot conclude that one approach to defining poverty is inherently better than another. Instead, we will simply note that the contrast between relative and absolute measures of poverty highlights a basic policy issue. Is our primary policy concern the misery of those who command low incomes, or are we concerned with the unequal distribution of incomes? Though income distribution and poverty are intrinsically related, they can be approached separately.

SUMMARY

Inequality and poverty are subjects that generate impassioned debates. The debates begin with truly basic questions about the *dimensions* of inequality and poverty. What degree of inequality is "too much"? How low a level of income implies poverty? Is income the only criterion for measuring poverty and inequality, or are other dimensions of inequality more important?

The debate over *causes* of poverty and inequality is even more intense. Do flawed characters relegate people to poverty? Or do restricted opportunities prevent poor people from moving up the distribution of income? And what role does the government play? Do government programs facilitate income mobility or does Big Brother create barriers and disincentives that keep people in poverty?

Inequality is a complex notion that is not adequately reflected in a single dimension. Money incomes, for example, are an incomplete index of well-being, as they do not represent wealth, access to publicly provided services, or maybe even happiness. The significance of any given level of income also depends on how representative it is of longer-term economic status.

Poverty refers to those individuals at the bottom of the income distribution who don't have enough income to satisfy basic needs. The definition of basic needs is conditional, however, on societal perceptions of both absolute and relative deprivation.

FURTHER READING

Arthur, John, and William H. Shaw, eds., *Justice and Economic Distribution,* 2nd ed. Englewood Cliffs, NJ: Prentice Hall, 1991.

Inhaber, Herbert, and Sidney Carroll, *How Rich Is Too Rich?* New York: Praeger, 1992.

Katz, Michael B., *The Undeserving Poor.* New York: Pantheon, 1989.

Kaus, Mickey, *The End of Equality.* New York: Basic Books, 1992.

Piachaud, David, "The Definition and Measurement of Poverty and Inequality," in *Current Issues in the Economics of Welfare,* eds. Nicholas Barr and David Whynes. New York: St. Martins, 1993.

Sen, Amartya, *Inequality Reexamined.* Cambridge, MA: Harvard University Press, 1992.

Spicker, Paul, *Poverty and Social Security: Concepts and Principles.* London: Routledge, 1993.

Starr, Roger, "*The Other America* Revisited," *The Public Interest* (Fall 1995), pp. 107–121.

CHAPTER

Counting the Poor

2

Before deciding what to do about poverty, we need to know how many people are poor. As we observed in Chapter 1, this is not a simple task. To measure the extent of poverty, we need to draw a line somewhere along the income distribution, then count the number of people who fall on the "poor" side of that line.

In this chapter we take a brief look at the distribution of income, then examine the official government line that separates the poor from the nonpoor. As we will see, the official poverty line is far from perfect. It does provide, however, a consistent and well-established foundation for defining the empirical parameters of poverty. It will allow us to determine how many people are officially counted as poor in America and identify who they are.

THE DISTRIBUTION OF INCOME

Before attempting to count the number of poor people, it will be useful to know what the broader distribution of income looks like. As noted in Chapter 1, the shape of that distribution—and our own positions in it—may influence our judgments about who is poor and who is not.

All national statistics on income are collected in annual household surveys conducted each March by the U.S. Bureau of the Census. The annual surveys of roughly 60,000 households are supplemented every ten years by a complete census of all American households. Estimates of the distribution of income are based on people's responses to the Census surveys. Although smaller, more specialized surveys are conducted, the Census data are regarded as the best available and as the source of all official poverty counts. These data are also used to portray the distribution of incomes.

Figure 2.1 depicts the distribution of income for American families in 1995.[1] In that year, the average American family had an annual income of roughly $51,000. This

---

[1] *Family* refers to two or more persons related by blood or marriage who live in the same household. A *household* refers to one or more persons occupying a household unit. There are more households than families and their average income is lower.

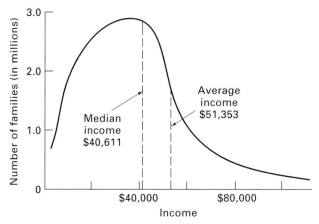

Source: Approximated from U.S. Bureau of the Census (1995 data).

FIGURE 2.1 The Frequency Distribution of Family Incomes

was five times higher than the average income in the rest of the world. Moreover, American incomes keep increasing nearly every year, making us a little bit richer over time.

Not every family received $51,000 in 1995. Figure 2.1 emphasizes how the *average* income was actually distributed. The curve has the shape of a slightly disfigured bell. Most families have incomes near the center of the bell; this is the broad middle class. The bell also has two tails, one of which extends far to the right. Although relatively few families reside at either end of these tails, they represent the lowest and highest incomes.

The continuous distribution of income depicted in Figure 2.1 is often summarized in categorical classes such as the middle class, upper class, and so on. The boundaries of such classes are vague, however. More precision is achieved by creating proportionate classes, wherein each class contains a certain percentage of the population. For this purpose, the population is often grouped into *quintiles* (five classes of equal size) or *deciles* (ten classes of equal size).

Table 2.1 depicts the quintile distribution of income that emerges from Figure 2.1. The quintiles are ranked from one to five, based on income. The first quintile contains the fifth of the population that received the highest incomes in 1995. To be in this top quintile, a family needed at least $72,261 of income. On average, each of these high-income families had roughly $120,000 of income, which was more than twice the average for the entire country ($51,353).

At the other end of the income distribution is the lowest quintile—the fifth of the population receiving the lowest incomes. Families in this lowest quintile in 1995 had less than $19,070 of income. On average, these families had incomes of only $11,265.

The inequality of income evident in Table 2.1 can be summarized in a couple of ways. We can observe, for example, that the average income of families in the top quintile is ten times larger than the average income of the lowest quintile. We may also note the relative *shares* of *total* income received by each group. The top fifth of the recipients gets 46.5 percent of total income. In other words, nearly half of everything we produce in a year goes to the top 20 percent of families. By contrast, the 20 percent of the population in the lowest quintile gets only 4.4 percent of all income (output).

TABLE 2.1   The Quintile Distribution of Family Income (1995)

Income Quintile	Mean Income	Percent of Total Income
1: $72,261 and over	$119,453	46.5
2: $48,986–72,260	$ 59,457	23.2
3: $32,986–48,985	$ 40,637	15.8
4: $19,071–32,985	$ 25,955	10.1
5: $0–19,070	$ 11,265	4.4
Average	$ 51,353	100.0

Source: U.S. Bureau of the Census.

THE OFFICIAL POVERTY LINE

Although Figure 2.1 and Table 2.1 offer convenient summaries of the distribution of income, they do not tell us who is poor. While we could designate everyone in the bottom quintile as poor, there is no particular justification for such a designation. Why not call the bottom decile poor, or the bottom ventile?

As discussed in Chapter 1 there are two general approaches to drawing a line that separates the poor from the nonpoor in the distribution of income. The absolute approach relies on some standard of minimum needs; the relative approach gauges poverty in terms of distance from the average income.

The official government measure of poverty uses the absolute approach to defining poverty. This has required the government to identify the minimum amount of money required to sustain a family. For 1995, the government decided that a family of four needed a minimum of $15,569 to purchase basic essentials (an amount equal to roughly $16,800 in 1998). But before we look at who is poor according to this definition, or what conditions give rise to such poverty, we should first take a closer look at how that figure was obtained. One of the problems with not being poor is that it is difficult to comprehend just what it means to be poor. Hopefully, a short review of our current definition of poverty will help increase that comprehension.

The Concept of Minimum Needs

In order to state that a specific amount of money income is required to keep a family out of poverty, one must have a firm notion of just how much that money will buy. That is, the identification of a poverty measure denominated in dollars logically begins with a standard of living denominated in essential goods and services. That task is not easy, particularly in view of the very different opinions people have about just what goods and services are essential. But let us suppose that we really could be coldly scientific and single out such goods.

We may begin to assemble an inventory of minimum needs by determining the absolutely basic ingredients of human subsistence; presumably, everyone will agree that our poverty measure should include at least these components. Such a list includes minimum food, clothing, shelter, and fuel requirements as determined by appropriate experts. To this list of basic minimums we may choose to include means of transportation, some recreation, and whatever additional goods and services we deem appropriate, if not absolutely essential. The sum total of our efforts, assuming consensus can be achieved, is a shopping list of what we consider to be essential goods and services. Those persons who cannot obtain all the items on our list will be considered poor, those who can as not poor.

Suppose for the moment that nutritionists, physiologists, and other assorted scientific experts could actually detail the minimum subsistence requirements we have outlined. Such a list might be like the one in Table 2.2. Note that each functional requirement is expressed in its generic measure. To this list of social and biological minimums we might add additional food, clothing, or entertainment, depending on our sense of generosity. In this way we could construct a complete specification of what we deem to be the minimum acceptable (or poverty) standard of living.

But consider carefully the list we have compiled. To begin with, how are we to translate 2,471 calories into more familiar staples, such as peanuts, bananas, and chewing gum? As anyone who has ever dieted well knows, there are an infinite number of ways in which a person can consume the requisite number of calories. Or consider the clothing requirement. The specification "4 pounds" tells us nothing at all about the appropriate type of clothing or even whether we should shop at Saks Fifth Avenue or at a Salvation Army store. Similar problems arise with every item on our list.

As if this vagueness were not a serious enough problem, let us return to the generic specifications. Though there is some conceptual foundation for speaking of minimum food, shelter, clothing, or fuel requirements, there is no firm basis for specifying what these minimums are. People do survive on varying amounts of calories; the warming and protective value of clothing cannot be adequately gauged in pounds; and the need for shelter varies enormously. Consequently, any claim to scientific precision, even in the generic specifications of a poverty standard, is pretentious and misplaced.

While the specification of a poverty standard is an imprecise endeavor, it is not necessarily useless. If we could identify a list of goods and services that most people regarded as minimum needs, we would have a common basis for measuring poverty. That would greatly facilitate discussions of how much poverty exists and what policy options to pursue.

Units of Measure

The achievement of consensus on an absolute poverty standard is facilitated by translating generic standards into dollars. In a market economy the ability of an individual to obtain needed goods and services is determined by his or her purchasing power.

TABLE 2.2 Hypothetical Minimum Needs

Category	Amount
Minimum food requirements	2,471 calories per day
Minimum fuel requirements	37 kilowatt-hours
Minimum shelter requirements	180 square feet
Minimum clothing requirements	4 pounds
Minimum transportation requirements	7 miles

Accordingly, we may be able to simplify our poverty standard by expressing that measure not in terms of a list of necessary goods and services but instead in terms of the purchasing power required to obtain those same goods and services. The necessary conversion requires that we price all the goods and services on our list, then add their prices up to determine the amount of money involved. That total is our gauge of poverty, for it represents command over the goods and services we have specified.

Not only is such a summary measure convenient, but it also facilitates the compromise that produced the standard itself. Suppose, for example, that Mr. Blixen believes that 1,437 calories and 1.57 pounds of clothing are the absolute daily minimum needs of one person. You, on the other hand, contend that 2,113 calories and 0.86 pound of clothing are necessary. Given your respective resolutions, you and Mr. Blixen are unlikely to reach a compromise on the generic specifications of minimum needs. However, what if current market prices indicate that your "needs" require $4.37 to fulfill, while Mr. Blixen's budget is $4.35 per day. In monetary terms, it is obvious that you are not far away from a potential compromise and that agreement on the generic components of a minimum budget might be postponed indefinitely.

Although we need the food, shelter, and other items on our shopping list daily, it is not necessary to have the right amount of cash every day. Shopping each day for the minimum requirements of shelter, fuel, clothing, and food would be extraordinarily inconvenient, if not downright impossible. Our real interest lies in ascertaining that a person has an adequate *flow* of cash so that he or she can acquire the basic necessities as the need arises. Hence, the poverty standard should incorporate the basic needs of an individual for a particular span of time and be expressed in terms of the amount of income needed during that period of time to make the required purchases. Whether that individual then elects to shop monthly, weekly, or daily is immaterial.

The best single indicator of a person's purchasing power over a period of time is income. But here, too, there are complications. Income is not the sole determinant of purchasing power. Two other factors, assets and credit, can render a person's command over goods and services much larger than his or her current income. Where credit is available, goods and services can, in effect, be borrowed. No current income is necessary, just a promise to make repayment when time and circumstances permit (or when the creditors demand).

A similar situation holds true with assets. Here again, a person may acquire goods and services without an income, in effect by trading one good for another. In the most common instance, a person may sell a particular asset to acquire a desired commodity. Or the asset may be traded for the commodity or the features of credit and wealth may be combined at a nearby pawnshop.

Finally, many people obtain goods and services directly without payment of cash or even a promise to pay (credit). The government has assumed an increasing responsibility for providing basic goods and services to people directly, especially if they have insufficient income or assets. Food stamps, for example, allow one to "buy" groceries with coupons ("stamps") rather than money. Food-stamp recipients, therefore, need less cash income to achieve any particular minimum standard. Likewise, families that live in public housing or receive free medical care enjoy a standard of living higher than their money income suggests. Money incomes have become a less reliable index of living standards, especially at the low end of the income distribution.[2]

Despite these limitations, money incomes are the single best index of a family's living standard, and it is the yardstick the government uses for measuring poverty. We first look at the official poverty index, then reexamine some of its limitations.

Poverty Thresholds

We are now in a position to identify what may be called a poverty line. We have established the process by which an absolute poverty line may be formulated; all that remains is to apply the process. Charles Booth, an English sociologist, used the same process to establish one of the first poverty lines in 1890. Booth identified the goods and services necessary to maintain a family in what he called a "state of chronic want." He then priced those commodities and concluded that a weekly income of approximately 24 shillings or less was necessary to achieve the condition he described. At about the same time, American economists estimated that from $400 to $600 per year was necessary to attain this condition in the United States.

Since Booth's time our standards of living have grown enormously. The number of proposed poverty lines has grown also, each varying with the circumstances of the time and the perspectives of the architect. While it is not necessary to review the history of those poverty lines, each of which had significance in its own time, it is instructive to examine two of the most influential formulations.[3]

The CEA Line

In 1963, the President's Council of Economic Advisers (CEA) officially sanctioned a poverty line of $3,000 per annum for a typical American family. The rationale behind the Council's poverty-line estimate was similar to that which we have already outlined. The Council accepted the notion that food requirements constitute the foundation of any poverty budget. Accordingly, they set out to determine the minimum nutritional requirements of a typical American family. The U.S. Department of Agriculture indicated that three minimally adequate meals a day would cost the typical family of two adults and two children exactly $2.736 a day.

The Department of Agriculture's estimates seemed to offer a convenient solution to the problem of defining at least the nutrition content of an absolute standard of poverty. But what about other minimum needs? The Council adopted a pragmatic if not entirely compelling approach to their estimation. They simply looked at how much people *spent* on food and nonfood items. Consumer studies indicated that low-income families spend approximately two-thirds of their incomes on nonfood items. Using this

---

[2]In-kind income is not limited to poor families; middle-class families benefit from subsidized public schools, job-related fringe benefits, special tax advantages, and an array of other noncash ("in-kind") forms of income. If all in-kind benefits were added up—not just those the poor receive—the poor might actually appear relatively worse off than their money incomes imply.

[3]An historical review of attempts to define poverty is provided by Gordon M. Fisher, *From Hunter to Orshansky: An Overview of (unofficial) Poverty Lines in the United States from 1904 to 1965* (Washington, DC: U.S. Department of Health and Human Services, Office of Assistant Secretary for Planning and Evaluation, October 1993).

TABLE 2.3 The CEA Poverty Budget, 1963

Food budget	$2.736 per day × 365 days	=	$ 998.64
Nonfood budget	2 × food budget	=	1,997.28
Total budget			$2,995.92

observation as a benchmark, the Council then multiplied their basic food budget by three to determine how much total income a poor family needs. The results of their calculation are depicted in Table 2.3. The Council then rounded off the total budget estimate to the $3,000 figure. Using this measure, the Council decided that there were 33.4 million poverty-stricken persons in America in 1963.

Michael Harrington once warned us "not to allow statistical quibbling to obscure the huge, enormous, and intolerable fact of poverty in America."[4] This is a warning we must take seriously, especially when millions of families may be involved. Accordingly, we would do well to overlook some of the imperfections in the Council's estimation procedures and concentrate on the mass of poverty they identified. Whether the true size of the poverty population in 1963 was then 33 million, 33.5 million, or even 35.23 million would not seem to be of much consequence.

But one glaring error in the Council's estimation procedure doomed it to obsolescence. To appreciate the nature of the Council's error, let us look at three families from the 1963 income distribution.

The husband in Family 1 is 37 years old and supports six children and a pregnant wife on his income of $3,200 a year.

Family 2 consists of a soon-to-be-retired couple, both in their mid-sixties. The wife does not work and the husband's earnings amount to $2,800 per year. They own their home, having made the final mortgage payment last Christmas.

Family 3 consists of a struggling graduate student, his working wife, and their three-month-old child. They both work at the college carry-out store in their spare time. Their combined earnings, including overtime and tips, amounts to $2,400 a year.

How did these three families place in the Council's census of poor Americans? Family 1, consisting of eight and one-half persons, was officially classified as nonpoor. Families 2 and 3 were counted as poor, as their incomes were under the $3,000 limit. But how many people would be willing to accept the Council's classification of these families? Family 1 is clearly desperate, while Family 2 is living a quiet and perhaps comfortable life. Our graduate-student family is not exactly affluent, but they are not desperate on $200 a month.

The source of the Council's error should be obvious at this point. The Council calculated a poverty budget for a typical family of two adults and two children. But not all families consist of four persons, nor do all four-person families have consistently typical needs. Clearly, the Council's definition of a poverty line had to be adjusted for varying family size. The possibility that families of the same size might have different needs due to age, location, or family structure also had to be considered.

---

[4]Michael Harrington, *The Other America* (New York: Macmillan Company, 1962), p. 10.

The SSA Index

These basic refinements of the Council's poverty line were undertaken by Mollie Orshansky of the Social Security Administration (SSA). She first adjusted for family size, then for varying family needs based on whether the family lived on a farm, whether the family included two parents or one, and the number of children. Using these four variables, she identified 124 family types and meticulously calculated an appropriate poverty budget for each one.

For the "typical" family of four identified by the Council of Economic Advisers, the SSA poverty budget and the Council's own budget were very similar. The SSA adjustments, however, counted many more large families and fewer smaller families as poor due to different family needs. Our earlier examples illustrate the difference. Ms. Orshansky found that Family 3, the struggling graduate student and his wife and child, needed only $2,275 for a minimum budget. Hence, they were not counted as poor under the SSA Index. Family 2, the soon-to-be-retired couple, required a minimum of only $1,855 and was living quite comfortably on their income. Family 1, however, with eight persons, needed at least $5,100 per year to meet essential needs and was classified as poor by the Social Security Administration index.

The Current Poverty Index

Despite the considerable sophistication of the 1963 Social Security Administration poverty index, it was not presented as either perfect or static. It was recognized that as prices and living standards continued to rise, the SSA poverty lines would require repeated upward adjustments.

The official poverty index now in use has been revised to account for the rising prices of goods and services, but not for our steadily increasing standard of living. According to Ms. Orshansky's earlier calculations, an average family of two adults and two children required a minimum of $3,130 in 1963. In 1995, after 32 years of inflation, that index stood at $15,569. We are saying that it cost $15,569 in 1995 to buy those goods and services that cost $3,130 in 1963. The increased dollar amount of the official definition does not imply in any way an increased standard of living for the poor. It adjusts only for rising prices. Because consumer prices have quintupled since 1963, the dollar value of the poverty line must be increased by a like percentage if the bundle of minimum needs is to be affordable by a poor family. Even since 1995, the poverty threshold has crept up with general inflation. Notice in Table 2.4 how the 1998 poverty standard for a family of four ($16,846) is higher than the 1995 standard ($15,569). The increased poverty threshold reflects two years of inflation. If we wanted to increase the standard of living of those whom we define as poor—and not many affluent persons are so inclined—then we would have to raise the index by more than the inflation adjustment.

A current poverty line that adjusts only for changing prices leaves the standard of living of the poor unchanged. But the income and living standards of the rest of the population will continue to advance as the American economy grows. Hence, poverty lines adjusted only for inflation imply a growing disparity between the status of the poor and that of the rest of the population. Like any absolute poverty line, the official poverty thresholds imply increasing *relative* poverty over time.

TABLE 2.4   Poverty Thresholds

	Poverty Standard	
Size of Family	*1995*	*1998*
One member	$ 7,783	$ 8,400
Two members	9,933	10,748
Three members	12,158	13,155
Four members	15,569	16,846
Five members	18,408	19,917
Six members	20,804	22,510
Seven members	23,552	25,483
Eight members	36,237	28,424

Source: U.S. Census Bureau, with author projection to 1998.

Despite the limitations of current poverty line adjustments, we will adhere to present standards. Accordingly, a 1998 income of less than $16,846 will qualify a family of four for inclusion in our head count of the poor. The application of this standard to other family sizes is summarized in Table 2.4.

Enumeration of the persons below either the 1963 or the updated poverty line is a simple and straightforward task. Unfortunately, the clinical nature of the statistical operation tends to impress the observer very little with the real impoverishment that the numbers represent. Consequently, it is worthwhile to dwell for a few moments on the standard of living that a poverty budget implies.

The austerity of the poverty budget was well described by B. Seebohm Rowntree, an English sociologist, in 1901. The essence of his description is still valid today.

> A family, living upon the scale allowed for in this estimate, must never spend a penny on railway fare or omnibus. They must never go into the country unless they can walk. They must never purchase a half-penny newspaper or spend a penny to buy a ticket for a popular concert. They must write no letters to absent children. They must never contribute anything to their church or chapel, or give any help to a neighbor that costs them money. They cannot save, nor can they join sick or Trade Union, because they cannot pay the necessary subscription. The children must have no pocket money for dolls, marbles or sweets. The father must smoke no tobacco and drink no beer. The mother must never buy any pretty cloths for herself or for her children, the character of the family wardrobe as for the family diet being governed by the regulation, "nothing must be bought but that what is absolutely necessary for the maintenance of physical health, and what is bought must be of the plainest and most economical description."[5]

That Mr. Rowntree's description of poverty living remains appropriate can be seen by looking more closely at the current poverty budget. A budget of $16,846 per year may sound generous. It allows only $3.85 per person for food each day, however. That is $3.85 for breakfast, lunch, dinner, and any snacks—an amount less than what

---

[5]B. Seebohm Rowntree, *Poverty: A Study of Town Life* (London: Longmans, Green & Company Ltd., 1901).

one lunch costs in most places. This means that the homemaker must plan, buy, and prepare a nutritious meal for a family of four for less than four dollars. When even hamburger costs over two dollars a pound, it is pretty clear that this poverty family is not eating either very well or very much. And if they have aspirations to eat out on occasion, their only hope is to save money by eating lots of hot dogs and boiled eggs at home.

You may respond that this is a gross exaggeration of how the poor live. You may even know of a poor person who eats steak. And in a sense you are right. We have described how a poor family would act if they spent only their food allowance on food. In fact, poor families do not follow our carefully budgeted allowances. They tend to forgo other items and spend some of their nonfood allowance money on better and more palatable meals with maybe even an occasional beer. And it is this process that comes closest to describing what it means to be poor. Every day a poor person or family must choose between an adequate diet of the most economic sort and some other necessity because there is never enough money to have both. Consequently, some of the poor eat steak and walk around with holes in their shoes.[6]

It is interesting to contrast what is officially regarded as a poverty income to what Americans generally believe is required to make ends meet. Gallup polls periodically ask a cross-section of Americans: "What is the smallest amount of money a family of four (husband, wife, and two children) needs each year to get along in this community?" In 1995, the median answer was $25,500 (see Figure 1.1). Historically, the public's view of minimum needs is always well above official poverty thresholds.[7] Quite clearly, most Americans do not believe that the poverty standard is enough, that is, that families really could get by for long on the government's definition of minimum needs. It is nevertheless true that poor families must find a way to cope. Indeed, most poor families command even less income than the official standard. For these families, even having the opportunity to choose between steak and shoes would seem like affluence.

If the prospect of existing for a short time on a poverty budget or less is not disquieting enough, consider the prospect of subsisting at that level into the indefinite future. A poor family must not only adjust to a subsistence budget but must also be prepared to remain at that standard of living. That is why a more affluent person cannot adequately grasp the significance of poverty by adopting a subsistence budget for a brief time. The affluent person knows that such an experiment can and will be terminated shortly. The poor person possesses no such luxury. As reported by Robert Hunter on a similar experiment by Tolstoy, "poverty is not the lack of things; it is the fear and the dread of want. That fear Tolstoy could not know."[8]

Let us then be clear about what our poverty index implies. The line we have drawn separating the poor from the nonpoor does not indicate what is enough—it only asserts with confidence what is too little. As Hunter observed in 1904, "to live up to the standard . . . means no more than to have a sanitary dwelling and sufficient food and

---

[6]Descriptions of how people cope with poverty-level budgets are provided in Mark Rank, *Living on the Edge* (New York: Columbia University Press, 1994); Carol Walker, *Managing Poverty: The Limits of Social Assistance* (London: Routledge, 1993); and Jonathan Freedman, *From Cradle to Grave: The Human Face of Poverty in America* (New York: Atheneum, 1993).

[7]See Denton R. Vaughan, "Exploring the Use of the Public's Views to Set Income Poverty Thresholds and Adjust Them Over Time," *Social Security Bulletin* (Summer 1993), pp. 22–46.

[8]Conversation quoted in Robert Hunter, *Poverty* (New York: Macmillan Company, 1904), p. 1.

clothing to keep the body in working order."[9] Those who fall below the line are un-questionably poor by contemporary standards, even though they might appear well-off by historical or international standards.[10] Nevertheless, many of those who have in-comes above our standard cannot be regarded as rich or even as moderately well-off. While we will concentrate our discussion on those persons we have defined as poor, it is important to remember that there are a great many more people whose standard of living is only marginally higher than that of the poor.

THE NUMBER OF POOR PEOPLE

With the official poverty index, the task of counting the number of poor people is straightforward. The U.S. Bureau of the Census does a household survey every March. In that survey they ask people how much income they received in the previous year. By comparing the reported income with the poverty index, the Census Bureau determines who is poor and who is not.

When the Census Bureau first counted the number of poor people in 1963, it con-cluded that 36 million Americans—one out of every five people in the United States—were poor. The widespread poverty convinced Presidents Kennedy and Johnson to start a "war on poverty." As Michael Harrington observed at the time, the number of poor Americans was simply unconscionable.

The Official Poverty Count

Figure 2.2 updates the poverty count. The top half of the figure shows the number of persons counted as poor each year. The poverty population shrank from 36 million in 1963 to a low of 23 million in 1973. Since then, the poverty population has grown so much that there were as many poor people in 1995 as in 1963.

The Poverty Rate

The increase in the size of the poverty population is hard to fathom, particularly in view of the growth of the American economy since 1963. Before examining that anomaly more closely, however, it will be helpful to put the raw numbers into context. Since 1963, the general U.S. population has increased by over 80 million persons. In view of this growth, changes in the number of poor persons are more appropriately gauged in per-centage terms. The lower half of Figure 2.2 does this by illustrating the official poverty *rate.* In 1963, the poverty rate was just under 20 percent with one-fifth of the U.S. popu-lation counted as poor. The poverty rate fell to a low of 11.1 percent in 1973 then started rising again. Despite the post-1973 growth in the poverty population, however, the offi-cial poverty *rate* in 1995 (13.8%) was significantly below that of 1963 (19.5%).

---

[9]Ibid., p. 7.

[10]Robert Rector of the Heritage Foundation has pointed out that today's poverty thresholds allow a lifestyle equal to that of the *average* American family in the 1950s. For international comparisons, see Timothy M. Smeeding, "Why the U.S. Antipoverty System Doesn't Work Very Well," *Challenge* (January/February 1992), pp. 30–35, and McKinley L. Blackburn, "International Comparisons of Poverty," *American Economic Review* (May 1994), pp. 371–374.

A. The Number of Poor Persons

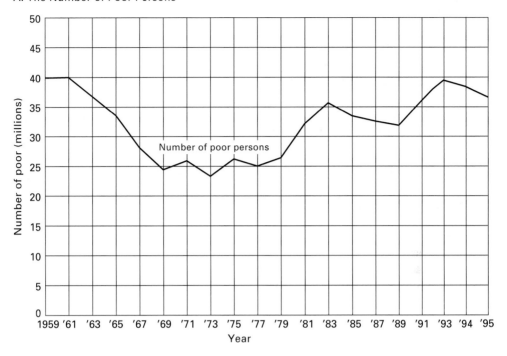

B. The Poverty Rate

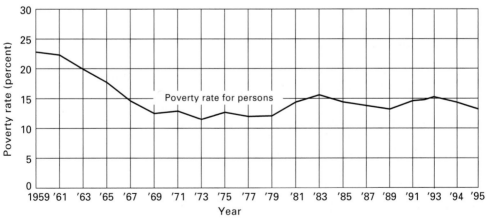

Source: U.S. Bureau of the Census.

FIGURE 2.2   The Official Poverty Count

How Poor?

The poverty count tells us how many people fall below the official poverty index but not *how far* below it they are. This is a critical issue. If most poor people were only a few dollars short of the poverty line, the poverty problem would be much less serious. If people have fallen far below the poverty line, however, it may take much more effort to pull them up.

The aggregate poverty gap refers to the total amount of the income shortfall experienced by poor people. In 1995, the poverty gap amounted to $80 billion. Although huge in absolute terms, the aggregate poverty gap amounts to only 1 percent of total U.S. income.

The aggregate poverty gap implies that the average poor person has an annual income that is roughly $2,200 below the official poverty threshold. There is great variation, however, in the size of that income deficit. The income deficit is much larger for single-parent families headed by women ($1,830 per person) than for two-parent families ($1,427). It is larger still ($3,762) for the 8 million poor individuals who don't live with their families.[11]

MEASUREMENT PROBLEMS

Figure 2.2 provides the official government portrait of poverty in the United States. Few people are satisfied with that portrait, however. Liberals argue that the official poverty line is too low. They also contend that the Census Bureau fails to count everyone whose income falls below even that standard. They believe poverty is more widespread than Figure 2.2 suggests.

Conservatives scoff at the notion that the government undercounts the poor. The reverse is true, they say. The official poverty count does not take all income into account and ignores completely a household's assets. The Census Bureau also relies on personal survey responses that may conceal some income. As a result, the official numbers vastly exaggerate the number of poor people and understate the achievements of the war on poverty. As far back as 1973, Professor Martin Anderson of Stanford's Hoover Institution asserted, "The war on poverty has been won, except for perhaps a few mopping up operations."[12] According to his reading of the data, there were only a few million people still poor in America ten years after the official poverty counts began. Robert Rector of the Heritage Foundation echoes that appraisal today, claiming that the extent of poverty is only a small fraction of the government's official count.

In-Kind Income

The major deficiency of official poverty statistics is that they count only a family's *cash* income. Yet, all families receive some "in-kind" income. Most low-income families, for example, receive food stamps, Medicaid, Medicare, or subsidized housing. Instead of

---

[11]For a measure of poverty that reflects the distribution of income deficits, see John L. Rodgers and Joan R. Rodgers, "Measuring the Intensity of Poverty Among Subpopulations," *Journal of Human Resources* (Spring 1991), pp. 338–361. For historical trends, see Mark Littman, "Poverty in the 1980s: Are the Poor Getting Poorer?" *Monthly Labor Review* (June 1989), pp. 13–18.

[12]Martin Anderson, *Welfare* (Stanford, CA: Hoover Institution Press, 1975), p. 37.

giving poor families the cash needed to buy groceries, health care, or housing, the government provides these goods directly. As a result, low-income families don't need as much cash income to maintain a given standard of living; in-kind transfers substitute for cash income.

The in-kind income offered to low-income families can be substantial. A family of four can get food stamps worth nearly $2,000 a year and housing subsidies of similar size. Medicaid can eliminate another major cash expense. Hence, a family with $16,000 of *cash* income might actually have a *total* income far above the official poverty line ($16,846 in 1998). However, the Census Bureau ignores the in-kind income and includes such a family in its poverty count.

Figure 2.3 indicates how serious the neglect of in-kind income might be. Over seventy percent of the female-headed families officially classified as poor on the basis of their cash income get food stamps. Thirty percent of these same families get housing assistance, and over half use Medicaid to pay doctor bills. The value of these in-kind benefits raises the living standard of these families nearly fifty percent above the level of their cash income. Two-parent poor families get a similar "boost" from in-kind benefits.

The poverty count would clearly be quite different if both cash and in-kind incomes were taken into account. Table 2.5 illustrates how great a difference a fuller accounting of real income might make. If the value of food stamps, housing subsidies, health care (Medicaid and Medicare), and other in-kind transfers were added to cash incomes, the poverty count would fall by 25 percent. In 1995, over 9 million people officially counted as poor would have been reclassified as nonpoor. If the Census Bureau also took into account home ownership with the resulting need for less rent money, the poverty count would have declined even further.

The neglect of in-kind transfers in official poverty counts distorts not only the size of the true poverty population but also trends in poverty rates. The major in-kind

FIGURE 2.3   In-Kind Income of Poor Families

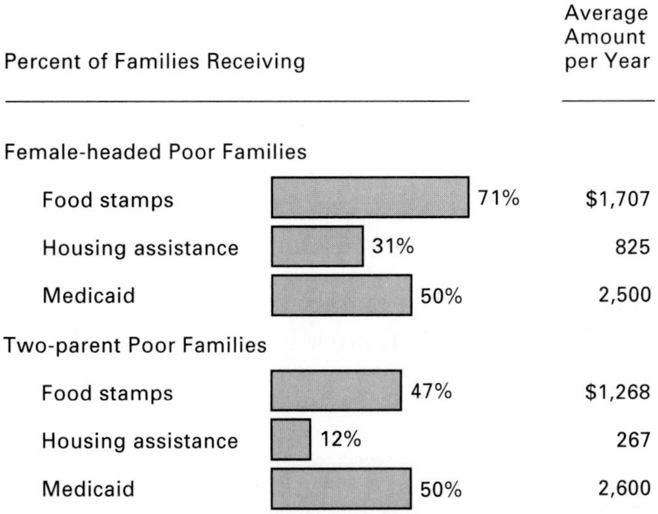

Percent of Families Receiving		Average Amount per Year
Female-headed Poor Families		
Food stamps	71%	$1,707
Housing assistance	31%	825
Medicaid	50%	2,500
Two-parent Poor Families		
Food stamps	47%	$1,268
Housing assistance	12%	267
Medicaid	50%	2,600

Source: U.S. Congress, Committee on Ways and Means, *1996 Green Book.*

TABLE 2.5 Alternative Poverty Counts (1995)		
Income Counted	*Number of Poor Persons*	*Poverty Rate*
1. Cash income only (official poverty line)	36.4 million	13.8%
2. Cash, in-kind transfers, and tax credits	27.2 million	10.3%
3. Cash, in-kind transfers, and rental value of owned home	24.8 million	9.4%

Source: U.S. Bureau of the Census.

transfer programs were first created in the mid-1960s. They grew enormously in scope and benefits throughout the 1970s. Accordingly, the distortion in the poverty count originating from in-kind benefits has grown over time.[13] This growing distortion has given an upward bias to the trend in poverty rates (Figure 2.2b).

Although it is evident that the official poverty counts are exaggerated by the neglect of in-kind transfers, the corrected estimates are subject to criticism as well. Not all in-kind transfers represent an improved standard of living. The amount of medical assistance a person receives, for example, depends on how sick one is. Accordingly, it isn't appropriate to regard a person as nonpoor just because he or she receives a lot of in-kind medical assistance (Medicaid or Medicare).

There is also a problem in assigning dollar values to in-kind benefits. Is a dollar's worth of food stamps really the equivalent of a dollar bill? Food stamps aren't accepted everywhere and can only be used to purchase food. There's also a stigma attached to using food stamps. Hence, a dollar bill is more highly valued than a dollar's worth of food stamps. If food stamps are to be counted as income, they should be discounted to reflect their lesser worth.

The same kind of problem affects housing subsidies. The government may spend $800 a month on a public housing apartment. The tenant might be able to find better housing, however, if provided with only $700 in cash. What is the in-kind assistance worth: $800 or $700? These kinds of valuation problems limit the Census Bureau's ability to include in-kind transfers in its official poverty count.

Underreporting

The official poverty count is also distorted by underreporting of income. The tendency of survey respondents to underreport their incomes has been documented repeatedly. People may fail to disclose all their income because some of it comes from illegal sources; because they fear higher taxes or welfare reductions; or because they simply forget infrequent payments (e.g., casual labor, dividends, and interest). According to a 1992 University of Michigan study, $2,000 of income per person goes unreported in the United States. Poor people may be particularly prone to underreporting. According to some estimates, poor families *spend* more than *twice* as much income as they report *re-*

---

[13]The availability of in-kind transfers, savings, and owner-occupied housing help explain why consumption-based measures of poverty indicate more poverty reduction than income-based measures; see D. T. Slesnick, "Gaining Ground: Poverty in the Postwar United States," *Journal of Political Economy* (February 1993), pp. 1–38.

ceiving. Moreover, the gap between expenditures and reported income continues to widen.[14] To the extent that poor people engage in such underreporting, their poverty is substantially exaggerated in official accounts.[15]

Income Mobility

A third criticism of the official poverty count is that its time horizon is too short. Consider these two possibilities. The first family enjoys a middle-class lifestyle throughout the year. But the family head was laid off from work for three months due to a back injury and yearly income fell by 25 percent. The temporary loss of a paycheck lowered the family's current income below the poverty threshold for the year. By drawing on savings and credit, however, the family was able to maintain its middle-class lifestyle. After the injury healed, the family's income recovered as well.

Should this family be counted as poor? The 25 percent drop in income was clearly a temporary setback. The same kinds of transitory earnings losses occur when plants close, people move, or the economy falters. These transitory events cause some family incomes to dip below the poverty standard. If income recovers quickly, though, there is likely to be little change in living standards. Consumption levels may be maintained by drains on accumulated savings or by borrowing. Even if living standards do drop briefly, the exposure to poverty may be very limited. Should the census of poverty be restricted to those who are poor *throughout* the year or should it include everyone who experiences even a temporary episode of poverty? The official Census survey counts everyone with low annual income and, therefore, includes many families whose permanent income and lifestyle exceed poverty standards. In reality, three out of five families that fall into poverty in one year are out of poverty in the following year. Only one out of 10 families stays in poverty for five years or more.[16] This kind of *income mobility*—year-to-year variations in income—is common among poor and nonpoor families alike.[17]

---

[14]Susan E. Mayer and Christopher Jencks, "Recent Trends in Economic Inequality in the United States: Income versus Expenditures versus Material Well-being," in *Poverty and Prosperity in the U.S.A. in the Late Twentieth Century,* eds. Dimitri B. Papadimitriou and Edward N. Wolff (New York: St. Martins, 1993), pp. 132–136. A more general exploration of survey measurement error is contained in John Bound, Charles Brown, Greg J. Duncan, and Willard Rodgers, "Evidence on the Validity of Cross-Sectional and Longitudinal Labor Market Data," *Journal of Labor Economics* (July 1994), pp. 345–368.

[15]For data on actual expenditures and assets of poor and nonpoor families, see Maya Federman et al., "What Does It Mean To Be Poor In America?" *Monthly Labor Review* (May 1996), pp. 3–17.

[16]Peter Gottschalk, Sara McLanahan, and Gary Sandefur, "The Dynamics and Intergenerational Transmission of Poverty and Welfare Participation," in *Confronting Poverty,* eds. S. Danziger, G. Sandefur, and D. Weinberg (Cambridge, MA: Harvard University Press, 1994). See also Ann Huff Stevens, "The Dynamics of Poverty Spells: Updating Bane and Ellwood," *American Economic Review* (May 1994), pp. 34–37; Mary Corcoran, Greg Duncan, Gerald Gurin, and Patricia Gurin, "Myth and Reality: The Causes and Persistence of Poverty," *Journal of Policy Analysis and Management* (December 1985), pp. 516–536.

A technique for isolating persistent poverty is proposed in Joan R. Rodgers and John L. Rodgers, "Chronic Poverty in the United States," *Journal of Human Resources* (Winter 1993), pp. 25–54.

[17]For more general descriptions of income mobility, see Bradley R. Schiller, "Relative Earnings Redux: Youth Mobility in the 1980s," *Review of Income and Wealth* (December 1994) and "Relative Earnings Mobility in the United States," *American Economic Review* (December 1977); Greg Duncan et al., *Years of Poverty, Years of Plenty* (Ann Arbor, MI: Institute for Serial Research, 1984); Peter Gottschalk, "Earnings Mobility: Permanent Change or Transitory Fluctuations?" *Review of Economics and Statistics* (August 1992); Jonathan R. Veum, "Accounting for Income Mobility Changes in the United States," *Social Science Quarterly* (December 1992), pp. 773–785.

The Uncounted Poor

Although in-kind benefits, underreporting, and income mobility all imply that the official poverty count is too high, there are other reasons for thinking it might be too low. The most obvious reason is that the Census Bureau doesn't count everyone. The Census surveys are directed at *households* and so fail to identify or include people without a fixed address. This means that the entire *homeless* population is excluded from annual surveys.[18] Hence, some of the lowest-income individuals are left out of the poverty count.

Because the homeless aren't counted in household surveys, no one knows how many of them there are. Estimates range from several hundred thousand to as many as 3 million. Christopher Jencks estimates that the homeless population peaked at around 400,000 in 1988.[19] Virtually all of these homeless individuals are destitute and thus properly should be included in a full count of the poor.

The official poverty count excludes not only the homeless but also poor individuals who reside in institutions. An aged person who resides in a public hospital or nursing home is not in the Census survey. The household surveys also exclude prison inmates. Since poor people have higher rates of morbidity and incarceration, the omission of institutionalized persons from the Census survey may understate both the *number* of poor people as well as the poverty *rate*.[20]

Another group that Census surveys miss are those poor people who live with relatives. An aged person without adequate resources of his or her own may be compelled to live with relatives. If the living arrangement is dictated more by economic necessity than by familial affection, the element of free choice is compromised. Furthermore, the unwanted relative may not share equally in the household's income or wealth, as Census Bureau statistics would imply. In this case, the aged resident of the household may be living in disguised poverty.

Professor Paul Leigh of San Jose State University has emphasized another downward bias in Census procedures. The Census Bureau surveys only *living* persons. This imminently practical approach would not seem to affect poverty statistics. Professor Leigh points out, however, that poor people tend to die at younger ages than nonpoor people.[21] Hence, the observed poverty *rate* is biased downward at older ages.

Latent Poverty

Besides failing to count many people who are manifestly poor, the Census Bureau also ignores those who are kept out of poverty only by government assistance. Remember that the official poverty count is based on the ratio of cash income to family needs, without regard to the source of the income. For many families, the most important

---

[18]An exception is that portion of the homeless population residing in permanent shelters.

[19]For descriptions of the homeless population see Brendan O'Flaherty, *The Ecomonics of Homelessness* (Cambridge, MA: Harvard University Press, 1996); Christopher Jencks, *The Homeless* (Cambridge, MA: Harvard, 1994); Martha Burt, *Over the Edge: The Growth of Homelessness in the 1980s* (Washington, DC: Urban Institute, 1992); also Martha Burt and Barbara Cohen, "Differences Among Homeless Single Women, Women with Children, and Single Men," *Social Problems* (December 1989), pp. 508–524.

[20]As much as one-third of the population over age 85—nearly 1 million individuals—lives in an institution; see Daniel B. Radner, "Economic Well-Being of the Old Old," *Social Security Bulletin* (Spring 1993), p. 4.

[21]J. Paul Leigh, "Distribution of Lifetime Income Allowing for Varying Mortality Rates Among Women, Men, Blacks, and Whites," *Journal of Economic Issues* (December 1992), pp. 1191–1220.

sources of income are income transfers such as Social Security benefits, welfare checks, and unemployment benefits. Without these income transfers, people now counted as nonpoor would be classified as poor. In 1995, over 20 million individuals were kept out of poverty with cash income transfers. Since these individuals are so dependent on income transfers rather than market incomes, they might also be included in a more complete enumeration of deprivation. Charles Murray has called these transfer-dependent individuals the *latent* poor; they would be poor in the absence of government help.

Too Low a Threshold?

One final critique of the official poverty count goes back to the basic standard used to define poverty. As noted earlier, the poverty thresholds are updated each year only for rising prices. Over time, however, average living standards rise as well. In real (inflation-adjusted) terms, the average American today has twice as much income as in 1963 when the official poverty lines were developed. However, the real value of the poverty line hasn't increased at all. As a result, the poverty standard is much further below average income levels today than it was when originally designed.

One consequence of rising living standards is that people now spend a smaller fraction of their incomes on food. Recall that the official poverty line was based on a minimum food budget and the observation that people spent one-third of their income on food. Today, American households allocate less than one-fifth of their budgets to food purchases. Were the same methods used to construct poverty lines today, the food-cost multiplier would be five, not three. With that higher multiple, the 1998 four-person poverty threshold would be closer to $28,000 than to $17,000 and a lot more people would be regarded as poor.

The official poverty standards have also failed to recognize changes in family structure and work patterns. The increasing incidence of single-parent families and the increased labor force participation of women have changed the structure of the typical household. With those changes has come a greater need for paid child care and more expenses related to work and transportation. Were poverty lines tailored to the actual expenses of different family types, many more single-parent families would be counted as poor.[22]

Popular opinion on what constitutes an adequate income appears to reflect these concerns about the adequacy of the official poverty standard. In 1963, the prevailing view of the level of income that was adequate to "get along" was close to the official poverty line. Today, however, the public's view of minimum needs exceeds the official poverty line by a wide margin.[23]

The Call for Revision

It is evident that the official poverty lines do not command universal acceptance. On the contrary, both liberals and conservatives are dissatisfied with official standards and urge major changes. To address these concerns, the National Academy of Sciences

---

[22]Specific budgets and poverty rates for single-parent families are estimated in Trudi J. Renwick and Barbara R. Bergmann, "A Budget-Based Definition of Poverty," *Journal of Human Resources* (Winter 1993), pp. 1–24.

[23]An historical comparison of official and popular poverty standards is provided in Denton R. Vaughan, "Exploring the Use of the Public's Views to Set Income Poverty Thresholds and Adjust Them Over Time," *Social Security Bulletin* (Summer 1993), pp. 22–46.

undertook a comprehensive review of the official poverty thresholds. After two and a half years of study, the Academy panel concluded in late 1994 that major changes were needed in the official poverty standards and offered a variety of recommendations for that revision. Since any revisions change both the perceived scope of the poverty problem and the implied policy agenda, the Academy's recommendations set off a highly political debate.

CHARACTERISTICS OF THE POOR

While the debate over the official poverty line continues, the need for statistics on the poverty population persists. Our ability and even our willingness to develop antipoverty policies are dependent on some sense of who the poor are and their numbers. Although poverty profiles are dependent on the poverty standards employed, we need a common starting point for empirical analysis. The official poverty index provides that foundation. It has the advantages not only of familiarity but also accessibility, since virtually all government data on poverty are based on the official index.

In some countries poverty is so pervasive that profiles of the poor are largely unnecessary. In the United States, however, poverty is an affliction of a minority of the population. Accordingly, middle-class people may have relatively little contact with the poor. As a consequence, perceptions of who is poor are likely to rely on chance observations and unfounded stereotypes. This is an inadequate basis for public policy.

To formulate intelligent policies to combat poverty, we need to know not only how many persons are poor but also whether they are young or old, infirm or employed, and whether they live in Abbeville, Louisiana, or Littleton, Colorado.

A complete statistical profile of the poor would demand considerable effort and patience. In addition, such an array of statistics might smother any meaning the numbers might possess. Therefore, we will examine the composition of the poverty population only as it relates to three major characteristics: age and family status; geography and residence; and labor force status. We will observe also the racial makeup within each category.

Age and Family Status

Table 2.6 provides a brief profile of the poverty population. Notice in particular the striking differences between the number of people and poverty rates among demographic subgroups. For example, there are a great many more poor whites (16 million) than poor blacks (10 million). But the poverty *rate* among blacks (24.3 percent) is three times higher than among whites (8.5 percent). The same kinds of differences in poverty numbers and rates are evident for Hispanics. Accordingly, we may say that blacks and Hispanics face a far greater likelihood of being poor, although they still comprise a minority of the poor. Persons of Asian extraction have a poverty rate (14.6 percent) much closer to that of whites.

Another striking disparity in poverty rates exists between two-parent and single-parent families. The incidence of poverty in single-parent families is far higher than in two-parent families. The incidence of poverty is particularly high in families where the single parent is female.

TABLE 2.6 The Poverty Population, 1995

Group	U.S. Population	Persons in Poverty	Poverty Rate (percent)
All Persons	363,733,000	36,425,000	13.8
Race:			
White	190,951,000	16,267,000	8.5
Black	33,940,000	9,872,000	29.3
Hispanic	28,344,000	8,594,000	30.3
Asian	9,644,000	1,411,000	14.6
Family Type*			
Two-parent	109,921,000	8,887,000	8.1
Single-parent			
Male	8,903,000	1,715,000	19.7
Female	29,233,000	13,096,000	44.8
Age:			
Over 65	31,658,000	3,318,000	10.5
Under 18	70,566,000	14,665,000	20.8

Note: Refers to families with children under 18.

Source: U.S. Bureau of the Census.

Since the 1970s the number of female-headed households in the United States has increased greatly. This growth in the number of female-headed families, together with the high poverty rate of such families, led to an increasing feminization of poverty. In 1963 only one out of four of *all* poor people lived in female-headed households. Today one out of three poor people reside in female-headed families.

Table 2.6 also indicates that poverty is far more prevalent among the young than the old. While one out of eight older persons lives in poverty, more than one out of five children are so impoverished. Children alone comprise almost 40 percent of all poor persons in the United States. We might well reflect on how equitable such a distribution of poverty is and what kind of preparation for adulthood an impoverished childhood provides. Will poor children become poor adults? If so, we may confidently predict that poverty has a great future in this country.

Geography and Residence

In an increasingly urban nation, it is not surprising to find a high proportion of poor families in metropolitan areas.[24] Seventy-five percent of the poor population lives in metropolitan areas, most of them in the central city. In general, the residential distribution of poor families resembles the residential distribution of all families. However, there does exist a tendency for the poor to be overrepresented in large central cities and in rural areas and underrepresented in suburban communities.

The racial distribution of poverty among metropolitan and nonmetropolitan areas is very similar; that is, poor whites are just as likely as poor blacks to reside in

---

[24]The term *metropolitan* essentially refers to cities of at least 50,000 and their surrounding communities.

metropolitan locations. However, a marked racial difference is apparent within metropolitan areas. While poor whites are likely to be found in either central cities or suburban communities, poor blacks and Hispanics are much more concentrated in the cities. It is important to note, though, that the high number of poor minorities in central cities is a result of the greater degree of urbanization among the minority populations rather than a higher likelihood of poverty in the cities. Indeed, black or Hispanic people in a rural area are more likely to be poor than their counterparts in an urban metropolis.

Nonmetropolitan areas include smaller cities, rural communities, and farms. While nearly one-fourth of all the poor live in such localities, very few poor persons actually live on farms. Farm poverty is a serious problem in the sense that the incidence of poverty among black and Hispanic farmers is very high (34 percent for blacks and 47 percent for Hispanics), but because the entire U.S. farming population is relatively small, poor farmers constitute only 2 percent of all the poor. Here again we must distinguish between the incidence of poverty among a particular group and the prevalence of that group within the entire poverty population.

Because the economic resources and social conditions of different regions in the United States vary tremendously, it is important to know the geographic location of the poor. Slower economic growth or less opportunity in a region is likely to create a regional concentration of poor families and require special programs. Were the poor all concentrated in Appalachia, for example, targeted antipoverty policies would be appropriate.

It is apparent from Table 2.7 that the South contains a disproportionate number of poor persons.[25] Less than a third of the total U.S. population lives in the South, but 40 percent of the poor reside there. This excess of poverty results not only from a high concentration of blacks in the South, but also from the fact that the South is simply poorer and less urban than any other region.[26] A southern resident, regardless of race, is more likely to be poor than his or her northern counterpart. In both the North and the South a black person is roughly three times as likely to be poor as a white person.

TABLE 2.7   Regional Distribution of the Poor

Region	Number of Poor Persons (thousands)	Poverty Rate (percent)			
		Total	White	Black	Hispanic
Northeast	6,428	12.5	9.9	30.8	36.5
Midwest	6,795	11.0	8.6	30.7	21.3
South	14,448	15.7	12.2	28.5	30.4
West	8,717	14.9	13.8	28.0	29.4

Source: U.S. Bureau of the Census (1995 data).

[25]The Census Bureau includes the following states in its definition of the South: Alabama, Arkansas, Delaware, District of Columbia, Florida, Georgia, Kentucky, Louisiana, Mississippi, Maryland, North Carolina, Oklahoma, South Carolina, Tennessee, Texas, Virginia, West Virginia.

[26]The official poverty index ignores regional differences in the cost of living. Since costs are lower in the South, measured poverty may be exaggerated. See National Academy of Sciences, *Measuring Poverty: A New Approach* (Washington, DC: National Academy Press, 1994).

Labor Force Status

The geographic and family characteristics of the poor are important considerations in the formulation of antipoverty policies. Their primary value, however, is to identify the potential of the poor to participate in national employment and income-generating policies. In a market economy the relationship of individuals or their families to the labor market is the prime determinant of their income. Furthermore, society's willingness to provide for the poor is materially affected by whether the poor are thought to work or at least seek work. Accordingly, the last characteristic we observe is the labor force status of the poor.

To be "in the labor force" signifies that a person is either employed or actively seeking employment (unemployed). Also included in this category are persons who are temporarily not working because of illness, bad weather, vacation, or a labor-management dispute. All these people are regarded as idle only momentarily, with visible prospects of returning to work. Their regular work may be full-time or part-time (less than 35 hours per week), and it must be monetarily compensated. Volunteer work is regarded as activity outside the labor force.

Being "out of the labor force" means essentially that a person does not fall into one of the foregoing categories. These persons are keeping house; attending school; unable to work because of age or disability; or, if otherwise able to work, are not actively seeking employment. The inactivity of the last group may result from a desire for leisure or the fact that employment prospects are too dim to merit job hunting.

It is widely believed that the poor are essentially a lazy lot. While we examine this contention in considerable detail in later chapters, Table 2.8 provides a preliminary perspective on the employment behavior of the poor. This table indicates what percentage of poor household heads in families with children worked at some time during the year.

The right column of the table confirms that working is what keeps most families out of poverty. Over 90 percent of all nonpoor householders (household heads) work at least part of the year. This is as true for single-parent families as for two-parent families,

TABLE 2.8 Work Experience of Family Head

	Percent Who Worked During the Year	
Families	*Poor*	*Nonpoor*
Two-parent Families		
White	80	97
Black	65	94
Hispanic	83	96
Female-headed Families		
White	51	95
Black	48	92
Hispanic	40	90

Source: U.S. Bureau of the Census. (Data refer to families with children under age 18 in 1995.)

and for all ethnic/race groups. Simply put, virtually every nonpoor family has at least one working member.

Work experience is decidedly less common in poor families. Even within the poverty population, however, the great majority of two-parent families are active in the labor market. Work experience is less prevalent among single-parent families: Less than half of all single mothers work at all. Racial differences are evident only among two-parent poor families where black fathers demonstrate substantially lower labor force commitment.

Table 2.8 indicates that most poor families have some job activity, even though their work experience is much less than nonpoor families. In later chapters we will focus on two crucial questions: (1) Why are any people who work poor? (2) Why don't poor families work more?

Similarities and Differences

The statistical profiles of the preceding sections are not intended to dull one's senses nor to obscure the many problems of the poor. Rather, they are offered as a backdrop to the analytical discussions that follow in later chapters. If any general impressions are possible, we might say that the statistical profiles of the poor are not markedly different from those of the rest of the population. For the most part, the poor population is a little younger, more southern, more often black and Hispanic, and less attached to the labor force than is the rest of society. Nevertheless, the poor, like the larger society, consist primarily of whites, of younger families with children, of urban dwellers, and of labor force participants. There do exist important distinguishing demographic characteristics, but they must not be allowed to conceal the basic similarities between the poor and nonpoor populations.

The demographic characteristics we have reviewed here by no means provide a complete description of the poor. Among the more obvious omissions in our profile are education, family size, and health. These characteristics are discussed in later chapters, where a more complete examination of the traits previously described is also found. But our profiles are incomplete in another important sense. We deal in this book almost exclusively with measurable, or at least observable, phenomena. Thus, we may report how old, white, or employed the poor are, or whether they live in cities or suburbs. What we are unable to do is relate how oppressed, politically isolated, or hostile the poor may be. In *The Other America,* Michael Harrington argued that today's poor are "more isolated and politically powerless than ever before." Although we are not in a position to evaluate that statement, we must recognize that such forces may be critical considerations in the lives of the poor.

SUMMARY

Incomes are distributed so unevenly that the top quintile (fifth) of all families has ten times as much income as the lowest quintile. Poverty is not officially defined in relative terms, however; an absolute standard of minimum needs is used. According to that standard, more than 36 million Americans were classified as poor in 1995.

The official poverty count is exaggerated by the neglect of in-kind income transfers (e.g., food stamps) and underreporting of income. The poverty statistics also include many people who experience only brief income losses and otherwise enjoy higher standards of living.

There are also downward biases in the official poverty count. The homeless population, people in institutions, and people living together out of economic necessity are not counted. In addition, there are millions of latent poor people who are kept out of poverty only by government assistance. Finally, if the poverty index itself were updated to today's living standards and family circumstances, many more individuals would be counted as poor.

The official poverty population is a bit younger than a cross section of America and includes higher proportions of minority and single-parent families. Poor families also have substantially less work experience than the nonpoor.

FURTHER READING

Federman, Mary, et al., "What Does It Mean to be Poor in America?" *Monthly Labor Review* (May 1996), pp. 3–17.

Fisher, G. M., "The Development and History of the Poverty Thresholds," *Social Security Bulletin* (Winter 1992), pp. 3–14.

Karoly, Lynn A., "The Trend in Inequality Among Families, Individuals, and Workers in the United States: A Twenty-Five Year Perspective," in *Uneven Tides: Rising Inequality in America,* eds. Sheldon Danziger and Peter Gottschalk. New York: Russell Sage, 1993.

Mayer, Susan E., and Christopher Jencks, "Poverty and the Distribution of Material Hardship," *Journal of Human Resources* (Winter 1989).

National Academy of Sciences, *Measuring Poverty: A New Approach.* Washington, DC: National Academy Press, 1995.

Ruggles, Patricia, *Drawing the Line: Alternative Poverty Measures and Their Implications for Public Policy.* Washington, DC: Urban Institute, 1990.

U.S. Bureau of the Census, *Poverty in the United States,* Series P60. Washington, DC: U.S. Government Printing Office, annual.

———, *Money Income of Households, Families, and Persons in the United States,* Series P60. Washington, DC: U.S. Government Printing Office, annual.

CHAPTER

Labor Force Participation

3

T he most obvious reason people are poor is that they don't earn enough income. Indeed, the most salient difference between poor households and nonpoor households is their attachment to the labor market: Over 90 percent of non-poor households earn income in the labor market. By contrast, only one out of two poor households earns any income. Not working—or not working enough—is a compelling explanation for poverty.

Unfortunately, the strong correlation between work and income raises as many questions as it answers. Do poor people *choose* not to work? Do they prefer idleness and even impoverishment to the rigors of the workplace? Are there simply not enough good jobs to go around? In other words, what *causes* the low level of labor force participation by the poor? Are Flawed Characters to blame? Or do Restricted Opportunities prevent poor people from fulfilling their employment and income ambitions? What role does the government play in determining the number or types of jobs available and who gets them?

In this chapter we examine in greater detail the workforce behavior of the poor. Our objective is to determine how often they work, as well as how often they *look* for work. In subsequent chapters we examine the incomes of the working poor and explore some of the reasons for this (non)work behavior.

INCOME SOURCES

The attachment of the poor to the labor market can be measured in many ways. The most direct way is simply to ask how many poor households receive *any* income from wages and salaries. This at least tells us whether *anyone* in the household worked at *anytime* during the year. An even more telling figure is the percentage of *total* household income derived from wages and salaries. This figure tells us the extent to which poor people depend on labor-market income as opposed to other income sources.

Two-parent households have a much better opportunity to participate in the labor market. Although many single-parent households do work, their labor force participation remains much below that of two-parent households. Because of this gap, we will examine two-parent and single-parent female-headed families separately. In both cases, the emphasis is on the *differences* in income sources of poor and nonpoor families. We confine our attention to families with children (under 18)—a category that encompasses about two-thirds of the poverty population.

Two-Parent Families

Table 3.1 summarizes the sources of income for two-parent families. The most striking observation is the overwhelming incidence of earnings. Virtually all (99.1 percent) nonpoor two-parent families earn some wages. Although two-parent poor families are less likely to have wage and salary income, their incidence of earnings is also substantial (79.1 percent).

There are huge differences between poor and nonpoor families in the receipt of *non*labor income. The largest difference occurs with interest and dividends: Only 23 percent of poor families get any interest or dividends, as compared with over 70 percent of all nonpoor families. This gap in dividend and interest income is easily explained by the greater assets of nonpoor families. The average American household owns net assets of roughly $50,000. Those assets held in the form of bonds and savings accounts generate interest income, while stock holdings pay dividends. Since poor people own relatively few assets, they are less likely to receive interest or dividend income. Note, however, that one-fifth of all poor families receive at least *some* nonlabor income from these sources.

Few two-parent families with children receive any income from Social Security or private pensions. This is simply a reflection of their relatively young age. As we will observe in Chapter 5, older Americans depend heavily on Social Security and pension benefits.

Also shown in Table 3.1 is the receipt of cash and in-kind welfare. Not surprisingly, poor families are likely to get welfare benefits; nonpoor families are not. The most prevalent source of welfare income for two-parent families is food stamps, which

TABLE 3.1   Income Sources of Two-Parent Families*

	Percent of Families Receiving Income	
Income Source	*Poor*	*Nonpoor*
Earnings	79.1	99.1
Interest, dividends	23.2	73.8
Pensions	1.3	4.1
Social security	8.5	6.0
Welfare:		
Cash benefits	25.2	3.4
Food stamps	49.3	3.8
Housing assistance	11.7	1.2

*Families with children (1994 data).

Source: U.S. Bureau of the Census.

half of these poor families get. Even some nonpoor families get food stamps, cash benefits, and housing assistance. These nonpoor families are typically "near poor," with incomes just a bit above the official poverty threshold. Some may be a bit higher up the income ladder but have slipped briefly into poverty at some time during the year.

Importance of Sources Figure 3.1 looks at the sources of income from a different perspective. Rather than looking at how many families receive *any* income from each source (Table 3.1), this table indicates *how much* income each source provides. The question of "how much" is answered in two ways. The first answer indicates the *percentage* of total family income coming from each source, that is, the extent to which families depend on various sources of income flows. The second dimension of Figure 3.1 reveals the dollar amount of income from each source.

Notice first in Figure 3.1 the huge gap between the average incomes of poor families ($11,124) and nonpoor families ($57,384). These incomes include the value of both food stamps and housing assistance. Hence, the gap between poor and nonpoor would look even larger without these in-kind benefits (not to mention *cash* welfare).

Figure 3.1 underscores the striking difference in the relative importance of various income sources. Income from working (wages, salaries, and self-employment) accounts for only 64 percent of total income for poor two-parent families but over 90 percent for

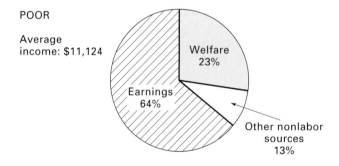

POOR

Average
income: $11,124

Welfare
23%

Earnings
64%

Other nonlabor
sources
13%

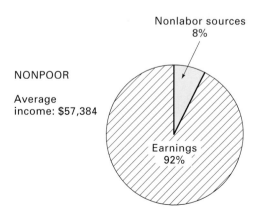

Nonlabor sources
8%

NONPOOR

Average
income: $57,384

Earnings
92%

Source: U.S. Bureau of the Census (1994 data).

FIGURE 3.1 Relative Importance of Income Sources for Two-Parent Families with Children

nonpoor families. Welfare provides a big chunk (23 percent) of the income of poor families, while Social Security and unemployment insurance provide another 8 percent. The contrasts in Table 3.1 and Figure 3.1 are striking. These statistics tell us that the huge income gap between poor and nonpoor two-parent families is almost completely explained by differences in labor-market earnings. Nonpoor two-parent families are much more likely to work (Table 3.1) and to earn more income when they do (Figure 3.1). The problem, then, is that poor families don't work enough, or are paid too little. Nothing else comes close to explaining their relative income status.

Female-Headed Families

Female-headed poor families have entirely different patterns of income than two-parent poor families. In general, the female-headed families have far less earned income and rely heavily on various forms of welfare. Yet, even among female-headed families there are vivid contrasts in labor-force activity between the poor and nonpoor.

Table 3.2 depicts the percent of female-headed families receiving various income flows. Most noteworthy is the high percentage of *nonpoor* families with earnings. The incidence of earnings for nonpoor female-headed families (95.3 percent) rivals that of nonpoor *two*-parent families (Table 3.1) and greatly exceeds the frequency of earnings for poor female-headed families. Most female-headed families stay out of poverty by working; those without earnings are apt to be poor.

Two-thirds of poor female-headed families receive cash welfare benefits. Food stamps (71 percent) and housing assistance (31 percent) are also common for this poverty subgroup. Only about one out of six nonpoor female-headed families receives any welfare.

The significance of earnings in distinguishing the poor from the nonpoor is strikingly apparent again in Figure 3.2. Nearly 80 percent of the income of nonpoor female heads comes from their own work effort. By contrast, poor women in identical household situations earn less than 30 percent of their family's total income.

TABLE 3.2   Income Sources of Female-Headed Families with Children

	Percent of Families Receiving Income	
Income Source	*Poor*	*Nonpoor*
Earnings	52.6	95.3
Interest, dividends	11.3	52.1
Pensions	1.0	4.3
Social Security	9.9	16.3
Child support	29.0	47.8
Welfare:		
Cash benefits	61.8	15.4
Food stamps	70.9	16.6
Housing assistance	30.8	7.3

Source: U.S. Bureau of the Census (1994 data).

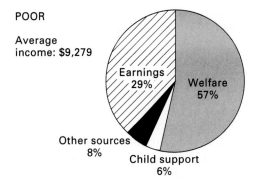

POOR

Average
income: $9,279

Earnings 29%

Welfare 57%

Other sources 8%

Child support 6%

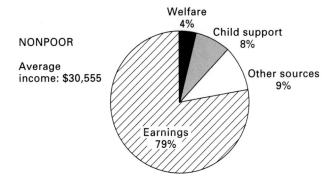

Welfare 4%

Child support 8%

NONPOOR

Average
income: $30,555

Other sources 9%

Earnings 79%

Source: U.S. Bureau of the Census (1994 data).

FIGURE 3.2 Relative Importance of Income Sources for Female-Headed Families with Children

Welfare benefits are clearly the economic mainstay of poor female-headed families. They get over half of their income from welfare checks, food stamps, and housing assistance. If Medicaid were included, their dependence on the welfare-system would be even more complete.

Child-support payments also augment the income of both poor and nonpoor female-headed families. Nonpoor mothers are much more likely (48 percent) to receive child-support than poor mothers (29 percent). In either case, however, the child support payments are relatively small, as Figure 3.2 confirms. The problems and potential of child support are discussed more fully in Chapter 6.

LABOR FORCE STATUS

The foregoing figures and tables highlight the importance of earned income as the primary determinant of poverty status. Good earnings keep families out of poverty; a lack of wages causes families to be poor. This simple observation is as valid for single-parent families as it is for more traditional two-parent families. Although single-parent families earn much less income than two-parent families—and women less than men—what keeps both single mothers and two-parent families out of poverty is work.

Although the outcomes of the labor market are clear, the mechanisms that produce these outcomes are less evident. Why do poor families have such low earnings? Do they work less? Are they paid less?

A convenient way to start answering these questions is by classifying people according to their labor force status. The labor force includes not only all people who are working for pay, but also people who are actively looking for jobs. Hence, both employed persons and unemployed persons are counted as labor force participants. Nonparticipants are people who are neither working for pay nor actively seeking paid employment.

Figure 3.3 suggests how important labor force participation is in determining poverty status. For each family type, the poverty rate is shown both for families whose head participates in the labor market during the year and for those headed by nonparticipants. In every case, the poverty rate more than doubles if the household head is a nonparticipant.

The extent of participation in the U.S. labor market is illustrated in Figure 3.4. In mid-1997 the total U.S. population numbered 270 million. Only half of the population participated in the labor market, however. Of these, 129 million were employed and another 7 million were actively searching for jobs.

The Nonparticipants

People who don't participate in the labor market obviously run the risk of poverty. But the link between poverty and participation is not that simple. Almost half of the nonparticipants are children under the age of 16. Few people expect them to work and

FIGURE 3.3 Poverty Rate, by Labor Force Status of Household Head

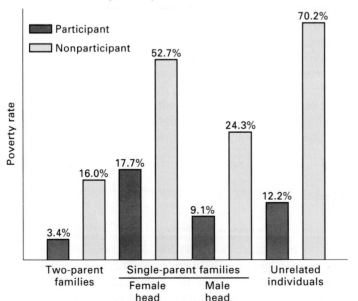

Source: U.S. Bureau of Labor Statistics (1995 data).

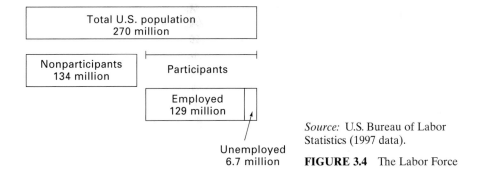

Source: U.S. Bureau of Labor Statistics (1997 data).

FIGURE 3.4 The Labor Force

child-labor laws forbid them to work in most cases. Their income depends on the labor force status of their parents, not their own participation.

Another 22 million individuals are retired. Up until recently, many older people were forced to quit working by mandatory retirement provisions. After such rules were struck down, however, older people still had an incentive to quit working. Social Security and private pensions offer significant income in retirement, giving older individuals an opportunity to enjoy more leisure without enduring poverty. Many older Americans also retire for health reasons or because they confront discrimination in job opportunities.

Eight million of the labor force nonparticipants are full-time students over age 16. Like children and retirees, they must largely depend on their families or savings for income support. Another 10 million individuals are either institutionalized, sick, or disabled.[1]

This leaves two groups unaccounted for among the nonparticipants. One group consists of the 23 million women who describe themselves as homemakers. The other are the 6 million individuals who have other reasons for nonparticipation.

The 23 million women who are classified as homemakers include the nearly 2 million nonworking single mothers whose families are in poverty. They also include another 2 million married women whose families could move above the poverty threshold if they worked outside the home. This is not to say that all women—much less all mothers of young children—should work. The point is instead that there is an element of individual *choice* here. Nearly 60 percent of women with preschool children work regardless of whether they are married or single. Hence, the presence of children can't be viewed as an insurmountable barrier to labor force participation. Most mothers in fact choose to work or at least decide that they need the extra income that comes from market employment.

Labor force nonparticipation is much less common among adult men. Yet, in many cases, such nonparticipation is even more difficult to explain. Why do these men

---

[1]Disabilities are themselves not completely objective. Donald Parsons has shown that labor force withdrawal of prime-age males is related to the availability of disability benefit payments. See Donald O. Parsons, "The Decline in Male Labor Force Participation," *Journal of Political Economy* (February 1980). For an alternative view, see John Bound, "The Health and Earnings of Rejected Disability Insurance Applicants," *American Economic Review* (June 1989), pp. 482–503.

fail to participate in the labor force? Is it because they prefer idleness and impoverishment, or because they are physically unable to work or locate a job? A U.S. Department of Labor study suggested that a good many such persons were "dreamers and drifters who were able to adjust both financially and psychologically to nonworker status." No data were available, however, to support that allegation. More recent studies have shown that very few men with family responsibilities desire to "dream and drift" rather than work. Many have not looked for jobs because they are convinced that no employment opportunities are presently available for them. Here again, however, causation is not cut and dry. People may *choose* not to try very hard before concluding that there aren't any jobs available. People counted as nonparticipants may also be involved in illegal or other "underground" (unreported) activities that bring in enough income to shun mainstream jobs.

The phenomenon of nonparticipation is not a permanent state. Labor force status changes over time along with marital, child-rearing, and economic conditions. Indeed, a salient characteristic of the poor is their extraordinarily high rate of mobility between different labor force statuses. The poor are constantly moving in and out of the labor force and from employment to unemployment. A poor person out of the labor force one week may well be working or looking for a job the next week.

To note that nonparticipation is likely to be a temporary condition is not tantamount to denying its causal importance for poverty. On the contrary, we have observed that nonparticipation is a condition that many poor heads-of-household experience. In later chapters we examine the causes of this nonparticipation in more detail.

Unemployment

Labor force participation is not a guaranteed ticket out of poverty. Figure 3.3 shows that participants are much less likely than nonparticipants to be poor. Nevertheless, millions of people who do participate in the job market remain poor. One reason for this is unemployment. People participate in labor markets by either working for pay *or* actively seeking a job. Those who aren't working but who are actively looking for a job are counted as unemployed.

Just because someone is looking for work doesn't mean he or she is poor. In 1997, for example, more than 7 million people were unemployed at any time. An even larger number—over 20 million—experienced at least a brief spell of unemployment. Millions of these job searchers, however, were students seeking summer jobs or graduates looking for their first permanent job. Many were middle-class women returning to the labor force after their kids entered school or left home. In such circumstances, unemployment may not be accompanied by economic hardship, much less poverty. Even mainstream workers who are involuntarily laid off or displaced are likely to stay out of poverty if other family members work or if they find new jobs soon. Unemployment may still cause financial and emotional pain in such cases, but it doesn't necessarily cause poverty. All told, less than one-fifth of the families who experience unemployment have incomes below the poverty standard.

The *duration* of unemployment is an important determinant of its poverty consequences. Half of the people who experience unemployment stay unemployed less than five weeks. Less than one out of ten unemployed persons remains jobless for as long as six months. Only these long-term unemployed individuals are likely to suffer substantial economic losses from joblessness.[2]

Although unemployment does not necessarily lead to poverty, it is apparent that joblessness afflicts many poor families. As Table 3.3 indicates, 17.6 percent of all families experiencing unemployment are poor. This amounts to nearly half of all poor families. Hence, we may conclude that one-half of all poor families experience at least some direct income loss as a result of unemployment. The most vulnerable families are those headed by women; the poverty rate soars to 42.6 percent when the female head experiences unemployment.

THE PROCESS OF ECONOMIC DETERIORATION

Just how unemployment leads to poverty is evident when the relationship is viewed over time. Whereas a few days or a week of unemployment will not significantly diminish a family's income, several weeks of joblessness will begin to undermine a family's economic foundations. Accordingly, we expect to see more and more people slip into poverty as the duration of unemployment status lengthens. This process is confirmed by Table 3.4, which portrays the various methods families use to meet expenses as the duration of unemployment increases.[3]

TABLE 3.3 Poverty Rates among Labor Force Participants by Family Type and Unemployment Experience

	Poverty Rate of Households with At Least One Labor Force Participant and	
	With No Member Unemployed During Year	With at Least One Member Unemployed During Year
All families	6.1	17.6
Two-parent families	4.4	11.4
Single-parent families		
Male-headed	5.8	21.7
Female-headed	17.0	44.1
Persons living alone	9.3	35.3

Source: Paul O. Flaim, "Unemployment in 1982: The Cost to Workers and Their Families," *Monthly Labor Review* (February 1984).

---

[2]The relationship between unemployment and economic hardship is also discussed by the National Commission on Employment and Unemployment Statistics in *Counting the Labor Force* (Washington, DC: U.S. Government Printing Office, 1979).

[3]For a closer look at the experiences of people unemployed for an extended period of time, see Walter Corson and Mark Dynarski, *A Study of Unemployment Insurance Recipients and Exhaustees* (Princeton, NJ: Mathematica, 1990), and U.S. Congress, Committee on Ways and Means, *1994 Green Book,* Section 7 and Appendix F.

TABLE 3.4   Methods Used by Families to Meet Living Expenses, by Duration of Unemployment (percent distribution)

Method	Duration of Unemployment	
	5 to 26 Weeks	*27 Weeks or More*
Used savings	49.1	39.9
Borrowed money	23.7	18.8
Moved to cheaper housing	8.8	12.0
Received help from friends	18.0	22.5
Received public or private charity	14.7	31.9

Sum of percents is more than 100 because many families resorted to more than one method.

Source: Adapted from Stanley Lebergott, ed., *Men Without Work* (Englewood Cliffs, NJ: Prentice-Hall, Inc., 1964), p. 144.

Government-provided unemployment insurance ("UI") benefits help cushion the income loss that accompanies unemployment. However, not all unemployed workers get UI benefits and those who do don't get them indefinitely. To get any benefits, a worker must have a history of employment and have been laid off (not fired for cause or voluntarily quit). Even then, benefits are only about a third of prior wages and typically available for a maximum of 26 weeks (Congress often extends their availability to 39 weeks in national recessions).[4] When benefit eligibility ends, economic distress increases. A Congressional Budget Office study revealed the following spread of poverty among long-term unemployment insurance recipients.[5]

9 percent of all long-term unemployment insurance recipients were in poor families prior to receiving unemployment insurance benefits.

19 percent were poor while receiving long-term benefits.

34 percent of those who remained jobless when unemployment insurance benefits ran out were in poverty.

In Table 3.4, the income sources of short-term and long-term unemployed families are compared. It can be seen, for example, that among the short-term (up to 26 weeks!) unemployed, 49 percent of the families have savings from which to draw in order to meet their everyday living expenses. As the duration of unemployment surpasses 27 weeks, however, the number of families with savings or available credit declines. As unemployment continues and families become more desperate, they begin to sell their homes, seek aid from friends, and, most striking of all, fall back on public or private charity.

---

[4]The unemployment insurance program is examined more closely in Chapter 12.

[5]Congressional Budget Office, *Family Incomes of Unemployment Insurance Recipients and the Implications for Extending Benefits* (February 1990) and *Displaced Workers: Trends in the 1980s and Implications for the Future* (February 1993).

SUBEMPLOYMENT

While it is clear that unemployment constitutes a direct and increasingly serious threat to a family's economic welfare, we have not yet completely described the dimensions of that threat. So far, we have considered only the immediate income loss to those families who suffer unemployment. There are indirect effects as well, however.

Discouraged Workers

When unemployment rates are high in a particular area, job seekers are apt to become increasingly frustrated in their efforts to secure employment. Jobs are scarce and available to only a select few. Faced with one employment rejection after another, job seekers are likely to give up the search. This erosion of confidence was expressed by a young man who described his search for a job as follows:

> I'll tell you, man, I go to Catholic Charities, to the youth center, down by the employment people—a couple of weeks ago I try to buy a job—I talk to social worker . . . you go from place to place, you know, and you get tired. I guess you get bored. Guys say no work, no nuthin', and then you say, "to hell with it. Let the job come to me."[6]

Not surprisingly, this young man is called a *discouraged worker*. Because he no longer seeks work actively, he is not counted as among the unemployed; he belongs to the ranks of the nonparticipants previously discussed. Yet it is clear that the two categories are not wholly separable. The extent and likely duration of unemployment in an area has a significant effect on the size of the nonparticipating population. Accordingly, many discouraged workers must be counted among the casualties of unemployment.

No one knows the exact number of discouraged workers among the poor. We do know, though, that a household head cannot maintain both a discouraged status and a family for long. The family must eat, and the head of the household will be compelled to locate some work, any work, just to keep body and soul together.

Discouragement is not limited to household heads. In families with both a mother and a father present, high rates of unemployment are most likely to affect the mother's labor force participation. Where unemployment is prevalent, a wife's chances for employment are likely to be even smaller than her husband's. Hence, the family may decide that her job search is fruitless and that her productivity will be highest in the home. Unfortunately, in withdrawing from the labor force—giving up the search for paid employment—the wife markedly increases the family's chances of becoming poor. Working wives are one of the surest escape routes from poverty.

Considerable statistical attention has been directed recently toward the phenomenon of discouraged workers. As a result, the U.S. Department of Labor estimated that in 1997—a year of low unemployment—there were roughly 400,000 persons at any time who wanted a job but were not looking for work because they felt their search would be in vain. A much larger number of people were out of the labor force for this reason at some time during the year.

---

[6]Quoted in Edgar May, *The Wasted Americans* (New York: Harper and Row Publishers, 1964), p. 60.

Underemployment

Another indirect hardship resulting from unemployment concerns the type and amount of work people undertake when jobs are scarce. As noted, the head of a low-income family, facing a dismal labor market, may have to accept whatever employment wages are available. The work may not fully utilize either his or her time or talents and is likely to be menial. But the person accepts the work as a temporary measure while waiting for better employment opportunities to emerge. A person who is in this situation is *underemployed*. That is, the person is at work (hence not unemployed) but not working to capacity. Commonly, the underemployed work full-time at menial jobs or part-time at any job, while seeking more or better employment. In 1997, the U.S. Department of Labor estimated that close to 4 million people were involuntarily employed on a part-time basis. Most of these workers had seen their hours cut because of slack work; the rest had not been able to find full-time jobs. Millions more were underemployed because the full-time jobs they had located paid wages below their usual experience. All of these manifestations of underemployment worsen markedly when the national economy slips into a recession.

Subemployment

The phenomena of unemployment, discouragement, and underemployment combine to form the concept of *subemployment*. Taken as a whole, the distressing impact of subemployment on a family's finances is reasonably clear. Very few families have enough economic resources to maintain themselves in the face of these forces for long. What is not so obvious is that the social foundation of the family, as well as its economic foundation, may suffer from the impact of these phenomena. Can we expect the father in a low-income family to gain self-respect or familial admiration as his employment prospects and income diminish? Do we anticipate a Charles Dickens kind of increased solidarity as the family begins to sink into impoverishment?

It is more reasonable to expect intrafamily tensions to mount along with economic distress. In fact, studies show that both divorce and child abuse increase when fathers are out of work. According to one study, children of unemployed fathers are three times as likely to be abused than children of employed fathers.[7] These kinds of effects are difficult to measure but are potentially of greater social significance than lost wages alone.[8]

Poverty Implications

As the list of direct and indirect consequences of unemployment grows, the crushing burden of nonemployment on the economic status of the poor becomes apparent. Table 3.5 offers a summary assessment. The top panel (A) contrasts the work experience of all adults in poor and nonpoor families. Less than half of all poor adults work at all, whereas over 80 percent of nonpoor adults do so. If only household heads

---

[7]This and other studies are reported in U.S. Congress, House Committee on Education and Labor, "Hearings on the Impact of Unemployment on Children and Families," January 31, 1983.

[8]We should also note that an involuntary change in status from employed to unemployed may have serious and long-term effects on a person's self-perception and social behavior. See Mary Merva and Richard Fowle, *The Effects of Diminished Economic Opportunities on Social Stress, Heart Attacks and Crime* (Washington, DC: Economic Policy Institute, 1992).

TABLE 3.5 Work Experience of Adults Living in Families

		Poor	*Nonpoor*
A.	All persons aged 16–64	13,510,000	125,962,000
	Didn't work at all	54%	18%
	Worked year-round, full-time	14%	54%
	Worked less than year-round, full-time	32%	28%
B.	Householders in families with children	5,845,000	30,217,000
	Didn't work at all	43%	6%
	Worked year-round, full-time	22%	76%
	Worked less than year-round, full-time	35%	18%
C.	Married fathers in families with children	1,918,000	23,769,000
	Didn't work at all	24%	3%
	Worked year-round, full-time	40%	85%
	Worked less than year-round, full-time	36%	12%

Source: U.S. Bureau of the Census (1995 data).

(*householders*) are considered (panel B), a similar gap in work experience is apparent: Whereas 94 percent of the nonpoor householders work, only 57 percent of poor householders work. Year-round, full-time work is rare among poor householders (22 percent) but common (76 percent) among the nonpoor. Panel C shows that the same discrepancy in work activity applies to fathers in two-parent families.

The message of Table 3.5 is clear: Millions of American families and unrelated individuals are in poverty because they don't work, or they don't work enough. If all poor families participated in the labor market at the same rate as nonpoor families and were equally likely to find jobs in the market, the poverty population would be a small fraction of its present size.[9]

THE QUESTION OF CAUSATION

The tremendous significance of subemployment on the extent and depth of poverty is apparent. However, we have not really resolved the question of causation. The evidence we have reviewed only confirms that subemployment is a major correlate of poverty; it does not tell us why so many poor people work so little.

Do the Poor Really Try?

When we seek to explain why so much subemployment exists among the poor, we may fall back to our earlier distinction between the Flawed Character, Restricted Opportunity, and Big Brother perspectives. On the one hand, it may be the case that the poor

[9]Current spells of joblessness may also lower future employment and income prospects; see Ronald D'Amico and Nan L. Maxwell, "The Impact of Post-School Joblessness on Male Black-White Wage Differentials," *Industrial Relations* (Spring 1994), pp. 184–205.

are not serious or persistent enough in their job search activity. They may be unrealistic in their employment demands or simply too lazy to go out and secure available work. On the other hand, the subemployment of the poor may result from no fault of their own; perhaps it is simply a reflection of the fact that few decent jobs are available for them. A third possible explanation might take into account the work disincentives imposed by government programs, especially the prohibitions on working associated with receipt of unemployment or welfare benefits.

Liberal analysts emphasize the restricted opportunities that poor people confront. David Ellwood, for example, sees in Table 3.5 (panel B) that most poor mothers and fathers do work at least part of the year. Ellwood argues that this work effort—even though often only part-time or part-year—suggests that the poor are willing to work. He notes that the actual employment rates of these families rise and fall with the strength of the general economy. Finally, he observes that the reasons poor adults give for not working more appear legitimate. As Table 3.6 shows, most poor adults who don't work at all during the year blame their joblessness on illness, disability, or on homemaking responsibilities. Poor adults who participate in the labor market only part of the year give similar explanations. This leads Ellwood to conclude that circumstances rather than attitudes keep poor people from working more.[10]

TABLE 3.6   Reasons for Nonparticipation Given by Poor Adults

Reason for Nonparticipation	Work Experience During Year	
	None	*Some*
A. All adults		
Ill or disabled	18%	13%
Retired	3%	1%
Home or family reasons	44%	35%
School or other	23%	39%
Could not find work	13%	12%
B. Householders in families with children		
Ill or disabled	20%	18%
Retired	1%	—
Home or family reasons	55%	46%
School or other	10%	24%
Could not find work	13%	12%
C. Fathers in families with children		
Ill or disabled	48%	29%
Retired	2%	1%
Home or family reasons	4%	9%
School or other	14%	36%
Could not find work	32%	26%

Source: U.S. Bureau of the Census (1992 data).

---

[10]For further details, see David T. Ellwood, *Divide and Conquer* (New York: Ford Foundation, 1987).

Conservative critics question both the accuracy and legitimacy of these explanations. They note that it is easier—and more socially acceptable—to blame one's joblessness on a lack of job vacancies than to admit to a preference for staying at home. In their view, explanations for not working given by the poor should be treated with a grain of salt. Even if true, the responses given in Table 3.6 obviously entail an element of choice, as noted earlier. Finally, conservatives are struck by how few nonworking poor adults even claim that a shortage of job opportunities kept them from working. Only one out of eight householders who spend time outside the labor force during the year say they "could not find work."

Nathan Glazer is among those critics who sense a certain irresponsibility on the part of the poor. He perceives that at "the heart of the crisis is a massive change in values which makes various kinds of work that used to support families undesirable to large numbers of potential workers today."[11] In other words, the jobs are there but the poor simply refuse to take them. Glazer offers no evidence to support his allegation. However, a later attempt by a second observer in New York City yielded the following evidence:

> No one who rides the subways can fail to see the numerous ads for electrician's helper (about $7,000 per year), subway patrolmen (around $8,000 per year), Office Temporaries, and Kelly Girls. The New York Telephone Company urges people to join them and be trained by them. No one who walks down Madison, Lexington, or Third Avenue will miss the signs for Help. No one who has had the misfortune of staying in a hospital recently, or even visiting one, is untroubled by the shortage of auxiliary and service personnel. . . . and any one who rides taxis with any frequency is aware of the number of taxis in the garage despite the industry's efforts to recruit additional drivers. . . . One of the fascinating statistics about New York City is that fewer persons were employed in domestic service in 1968 than in 1960. This is surely not the result of diminished demand but of a refusal to accept such employment.[12]

Despite this catalogue of apparent opportunities, there seems to be little evidence to support the notion that the poor are turning down abundant job offers. At the time Bernstein related her impressions there were about 5,000 standing job openings for unskilled workers in New York City. Confronting these vacancies were 139,000 unemployed individuals and over 200,000 heads-of-household receiving public assistance. In light of the enormous number of potential and actual job seekers, the number of available jobs for the poor is hardly significant. Even if a poor person desires to secure a dead-end job, his or her chances to do so hardly seem encouraging.

Another study in Washington, DC, compared the job vacancies advertised in the local Sunday paper (the *Washington Post*) with the number and characteristics of the poor people in the metropolitan area. At the time of the study, 36,400 people were officially counted as unemployed, and 28,000 adults were receiving welfare payments. Yet, 3,028 job vacancies were listed in the paper, suggesting that many of the jobless could have found work if they really wanted to. Closer examination of the ads revealed a very different story, however. Most of the jobs required educational attainments or

---

[11]Nathan Glazer, "Beyond Income Maintenance," *The Public Interest* (Summer 1969), p. 120.
[12]Blanche Bernstein, "Welfare in New York City," *City Almanac* (February 1970), p. 6.

experience that poor people simply do not have. In all, only 354 of the job vacancies (12 percent) were jobs that poor people might get. Phone calls to the employers listing these jobs confirmed that nearly all of the job vacancies were filled, usually in a day or two.[13]

Despite evidence to the contrary, the conviction that the poor are shunning job vacancies persists. This conviction is particularly strong regarding welfare mothers, whose families account for an increasing proportion of the poverty population. Not only is their reported search for employment regarded with skepticism, but their claim of overriding child-care responsibility is also questioned. Single mothers not in poverty have the same child-care responsibilities but somehow manage to work. In addition, critics wonder whether the daily example of a nonworking household head might not set undesired expectations and standards for the children of single mothers.[14] Conservatives also stress the role of government welfare programs in encouraging the low level of employment among poor women.[15]

Macroeconomic Forces

Although there is ample scope for arguments about the efforts of the poor to work, no one denies completely the importance of macroeconomic forces. The U.S. economy is subject to periodic bouts of sluggishness—years in which the volume of output declines. In those years workers have a hard time holding onto jobs and people looking for work discover that job vacancies are scarce. In other years the economy is strong and both output and employment increase. This pattern of ups and downs in the business cycle is the central concern of *macroeconomics*.

Policy makers seek to create the conditions that will assure jobs for all individuals who seek them. But our historical record is testimony to the failure of macroeconomics to assure *full employment*. The worst failure was the Great Depression of the 1930s. Total output declined so much in the early 1930s that as many as one out of every four labor force participants was unable to find work. There was no argument about what caused the sudden and widespread poverty—jobs had simply vanished.

In more recent times the U.S. economy has not suffered from such a deep and prolonged period of macroeconomic failure. But there have been 12 recessions since World War II—two of them in the early 1980s, and another in 1990–91. The recession of 1981–82 pushed the national unemployment rate to 10.8 percent, the highest level since the 1930s. These macroeconomic downturns played a direct role in increasing the number of people in poverty and in limiting the employment opportunities of the poor.

To visualize the potential impact of labor-market demand on unemployment and poverty rates, imagine that all potential workers could be ranked on the basis of their employability. That is, suppose that we could somehow assign everyone a relative position based on the amount of human capital they bring to the labor market. The most productive workers will be at the front of the line, the least productive at the back.

---

[13]Bradley R. Schiller, "Want Ads and Jobs for the Poor," *Manpower* (U.S. Department of Labor, January 1974).

[14]Kevin R. Hopkins, *Welfare Dependency: Behavior, Culture, and Public Policy* (Alexandria, VA: Hudson Institute, 1987), esp. Chapter 7.

[15]Charles Murray, *Losing Ground: American Social Policy, 1950–1980* (New York: Basic Books, 1984).

It seems reasonable to assume that employers will seek to hire the most productive workers first, and thus will start filling job vacancies from the front of the line. In many cases, of course, an employer will not be able to determine exactly who is the more or less productive job applicant. But he or she will try to approximate that distinction, perhaps with the aid of aptitude tests, school records, even racial and sexual prejudices. All we need to note at this point is that employers will tend to start making their selections at the front of the line and proceed toward the back.

The question that concerns us now is how far back in the line employers will go; that is, how many jobs will be available. Clearly, an individual's chances of getting a job depend not only on his or her position in line (supply characteristics) but also on how many workers employers decide to hire (demand characteristics). What we want to emphasize here is that deficiencies in demand can overwhelm supply characteristics, leaving otherwise qualified people among the ranks of the unemployed and poor.

The potential of demand fluctuations to overwhelm forces on the supply side of the picture is perhaps most apparent when we compare labor-market conditions at different points in time. Consider the years 1989 and 1992, for example. The average unemployment rate in 1989 was 5.3 percent. That relatively low rate of unemployment left 6.5 million people out of work and searching for jobs. In 1992, by contrast, the unemployment rate was 7.4 percent and 9.4 million people were out on the streets at one time. Can anyone reasonably argue that the increased unemployment was due to deteriorating supply characteristics? Had our labor force grown less educated, less experienced, less motivated, less intelligent, or generally less able? Surely not. In fact, we would expect that the supply characteristics of the labor force improve with the passage of time. Seen in this context, fluctuations in the *demand* for labor emerge as a primary cause of unemployment and, by implication, the level of poverty.

Deficient Demand

The relationship between fluctuations in demand and the extent of unemployment is illustrated in Figure 3.5. Note that we have arrayed all labor force participants according to their skills (human capital), with the most skilled at the top. As we suggested earlier, the distinction between those who are employed and those who are unemployed depends not on any absolute level of skill development, but on just how far down the line employers choose to go. In 1992 employers stopped far short of where they went in 1989, leaving millions of previously employable (and employed) workers on the jobless side of the line. Hence, we may conclude that the additional unemployment represented by the shaded area in the figure was due to a deficiency of demand in 1992.

Although deficiencies of demand clearly emerge as a major cause of unemployment and poverty, we cannot attribute all unemployment to demand forces. Instead, economists distinguish between four types of unemployment: frictional, seasonal, cyclical, and structural. Frictional unemployment arises when people move from one job to another with only a slight interval of time in between. People who are frictionally unemployed normally have visible job prospects and are simply in geographic or occupational transition. Likewise, people who are seasonally unemployed often face the sure prospect of renewed employment as the weather or season changes. This is not to say that their unemployment is not serious; we merely distinguish its sources from other types of unemployment.

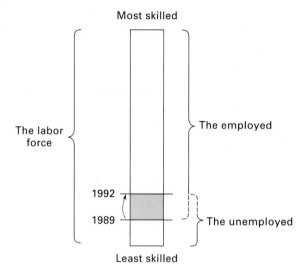

Most skilled

The labor force

The employed

1992

1989

The unemployed

Least skilled

FIGURE 3.5 The Impact of Deficient Demand

Aggregate or cyclical unemployment is markedly different from the first two types of unemployment. Not only is the nature of later job prospects uncertain, but the causes of this type of unemployment are also distinct. Cyclical unemployment exists when there is less demand for labor in the economy than there is labor willingly available. In this situation, neither a change in the weather nor a change of residence is likely to create employment for the jobless. For this reason the jobless have no certain prospect of later employment. Instead, they must wait for an expansion of the demand for labor. This is the kind of unemployment depicted in Figure 3.5.

Structural unemployment is, in many respects, similar to cyclical unemployment. Here, however, the shortage of demand appears to be confined to only a few occupations or areas. While most people seem able to locate jobs, there may be a large number of pipe fitters, coal miners, or flight engineers seeking employment. There may be a large number of people out of work in the Texas Panhandle or downtown Detroit but relatively few in other areas of the country. Thus, it appears that localized or structural deficiencies in demand are more at fault than general demand shortages. The *dislocated worker* has become a popular symbol of such unemployment. Changing technology, trade patterns, and consumer demands have eliminated thousands of jobs in the steel, auto, and textile industries. As a result, many experienced workers have been forced to seek new jobs in other industries, occupations, or locations. In principle, this kind of structural unemployment looks less damaging than cyclical unemployment since an occupational or geographical move appears to hold promise of improved employment opportunities.

The purely structural character of structural unemployment can, however, be easily exaggerated. Can we maintain that the jobless situation of steel workers and flight engineers is impervious to the state of demand in other occupations or areas? While it is reasonable to expect some hesitancy in moving across geographical or occupational boundaries, it is unrealistic to imagine that the speed and extent of such moves are not conditioned by employment opportunities. When good jobs exist in plentiful supply elsewhere, the structural character of structural unemployment is bound to erode. People will move and change occupations as alternative prospects merit. Even in Appalachia, an area often presumed to exist in economic isolation, unemployment rates follow national patterns. Accordingly, the apparent dimensions of structural unemployment are shaped in part by the state of aggregate demand and are subject to the social decisions which we have mentioned. As Paul Samuelson has noted, "the alleged hard core of the structurally unemployed is in fact a core made of ice and not of iron. The core of ice can be melted over a period of time by adequate effective demand, or it can be solidified from inadequate overall demand."[16]

Poverty Impact

The impact of the macroeconomic business cycle on poverty has been documented extensively. Figure 3.6 shows how strong the relationship is, especially for male-headed families with children. This figure uses changes in unemployment rates and the median earnings of full-time workers to predict changes in poverty from year to year. Hence, the *expected* (predicted) poverty rate is based solely on macroeconomic forces. Also shown in Figure 3.6 is the *actual* poverty rate for those same years (1959–1984). As is apparent, the trends in actual versus expected poverty rates are remarkably similar. This suggests that macroeconomic forces are a powerful explanation for changes in the size of the poverty population. According to a study by Rebecca Blank and Alan Blinder, sluggish macro conditions alone raised the national poverty rate by 4.5 percentage points in the ten years from 1973 to 1983.[17]

FIGURE 3.6 Actual and Expected Poverty Rates for Children in Male-Headed Families

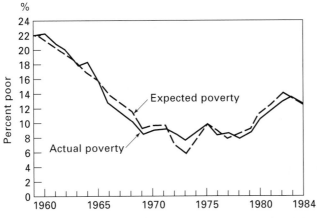

Expected poverty is based solely on the median earnings of full-year, full-time male workers, and the unemployment rate.

Source: David Ellwood, *Divide and Conquer* (New York: Ford Foundation, 1987), p. 16.

---

[16]Paul A. Samuelson, *Economics,* 8th ed. (New York: McGraw-Hill Book Company, 1967), p. 802.

[17]Rebecca M. Blank and Alan S. Blinder, "Macroeconomics, Income Distribution, and Poverty," in *Fighting Poverty,* eds. Sheldon H. Danziger and Daniel H. Weinberg (Cambridge, MA: Harvard University Press, 1986), p. 207.

The relationship between the macroeconomy and poverty is less strong for female-headed families. The number of single mothers in poverty responds much less to the ups and downs of the business cycle. In the period from 1982 to 1988, for example, the economy grew very sharply, but the number of single women (and their children) in poverty declined only slightly. This is consistent with our earlier observation that nearly half of these women report that they are not even looking for work.[18]

SUMMARY

Labor earnings are by far the most important source of income for American families. Distinguishing poor families from nonpoor families most clearly are differences in labor-market earnings.

The earnings gap between poor and nonpoor families is largely explained by differences in labor force participation. Whether in two-parent or single-parent (female-headed) families, poor householders are much less likely to participate in the labor market. The disparity is particularly striking for female-headed households; less than half of single mothers who are poor are active in the job market. By contrast, almost all *nonpoor* mothers either work or actively seek employment.

Poor families rely heavily on income transfers. Food stamps, cash welfare benefits, and housing subsidies provide one-fourth of the total income of two-parent poor families. For female-headed poor families such welfare benefits account for more than half of total income. Lots of single mothers receive child support and alimony as well, but the amount of such income is small.

Labor force participants are assured neither a job nor high income. Many participants remain unemployed, that is, unable to find work. Others are working part-time, part-year, or at skill levels below their capability. Many of these underemployed participants are poor. Finally, we note that the frustrations associated with unsuccessful job search may so discourage job seekers that they cease looking for work. The combination of these forces—subemployment—keeps millions of people in poverty.

The core controversy about poverty focuses on the causes of subemployment. Liberals emphasize the lack of available jobs and other barriers (e.g., child care) that preclude poor people from working more. Conservatives point out that there are always some jobs available and that nonpoor families in similar circumstances do manage to work. The most heated debates focus on poor families headed by single (never married, separated, or divorced) mothers.

However willing or unwilling poor people might be to work, the number of job opportunities is constrained by macroeconomic forces. Strong economic expansion creates more jobs and income; business downturns increase unemployment and poverty. The cyclical component of poverty is particularly important for two-parent families, but less significant for female-headed families.

---

[18]In the economic expansion of the 1980s, poverty among female-headed families with children increased much more than predicted by labor-market changes; see Rebecca Blank and David Card, "Poverty, Income Distribution, and Growth: Are They Still Connected?" *Brookings Papers on Economic Activity,* 1993 (2), pp. 285–325.

FURTHER READING

Blank, Rebecca M., "Why Were Poverty Rates So High in the 1980s?" in *Poverty and Prosperity in the USA in the Late Twentieth Century,* eds. Dimitri B. Papadimitriou and Edward N. Wolff. New York: St. Martins, 1993, pp. 21–55.

Meade, Lawrence M., *The New Politics of Poverty: The Nonworking Poor in America.* New York: Basic Books, 1992.

Newman, Katherine S., *Declining Fortunes: The Withering of the American Dream.* New York: Basic Books, 1993.

Riemer, David R., *The Prisoners of Welfare.* New York: Praeger, 1988; esp. Chapters 2–5.

Schiller, Bradley R., "Who Are the Working Poor?" *The Public Interest* (Spring 1994), pp. 61–71.

Tienda, Marta, and Haya Stier, "Joblessness and Shiftlessness: Labor Force Activity in Chicago's Inner City," in *The Urban Underclass,* eds. Christopher Jencks and Paul E. Peterson. Washington, DC: Brookings, 1991.

Tobin, James, "Poverty in Relation to Macroeconomic Trends, Cycles, and Policies," in *Confronting Poverty,* eds. S. Danziger, Gary Sandefur, and D. Weinberg. Cambridge, MA: Harvard University Press, 1994, pp. 147–167.

U.S. Bureau of Labor Statistics, *A Profile of the Working Poor.* Washington, DC: U.S. Government Printing Office, annual.

APPENDIX

THE PHILLIPS CURVE DILEMMA

The deficiencies of aggregate demand that cause unemployment and poverty are not solely the consequence of unbridled market forces. Nor will the required expansion of demand necessarily emerge as the work of an invisible hand of the kind that Adam Smith described. On the contrary, the level of demand, and hence the level of aggregate unemployment is in part a result of government policy. The government has enormous influence on the economy because of its vast expenditures and related tax revenues. The federal government (via the Federal Reserve Board) also controls the amount of money available. By using its fiscal and monetary powers, the federal government can alter the level and content of aggregate demand.[19]

Given the power to increase aggregate demand, why doesn't the government simply create enough demand to assure everyone a job? The answer is that our employment goals may conflict with our other economic goals.

The goal most often deemed in direct competition with full employment is that of price stability. It is widely believed that we cannot have both price stability and full employment at the same time. This implies that the pursuit of one objective necessarily means the abandonment of the other. As a consequence, some unemployment is tolerated as part of the cost of maintaining existing price levels.

The seriousness with which this trade-off is regarded by policy makers is evident in their actions. Upon taking office, President Carter initiated policies to reduce the

---

[19]For an introduction to the fiscal and monetary policies appropriate to the goal of full employment, see Bradley R. Schiller, *The Economy Today,* 7th ed. (New York: McGraw-Hill, Inc., 1997).

rate of unemployment. As the unemployment rate dropped, however, prices began to rise more quickly. Carter responded by designating inflation "our top economic priority" and slowing the progress toward full employment. President Reagan started out by promising both lower unemployment and less inflation, but quickly abandoned that course. Higher unemployment came to be accepted as the "necessary cost" of achieving less inflation.[20] President Clinton, too, was willing to abandon job-creating expenditure programs when the risk of accelerating inflation became apparent.

The Phillips Curve Problem

The willingness to tolerate high levels of unemployment is based on the historical relationship between inflation and unemployment. As Figure 3.7 suggests, lower rates of unemployment have generally been accompanied by higher rates of inflation. This tendency, first observed in England by A. W. Phillips, has been found to prevail in scores of countries. Accordingly, the Phillips curve not only summarizes a historical relationship between unemployment rates and inflation rates but appears to offer policy makers a finite set of choices. As long as the curve is an accurate description of economic performance, then full employment and price stability are not attainable at the same time. Instead, some point on the curve, a distinct compromise between the two goals, must be selected as a policy target. And so it happens that some policy makers choose to sacrifice full employment in the hopes of achieving lower rates of inflation.

Although the Phillips curve appears to present policy makers with a finite set of trade-offs, we must not be too quick in rejecting the goal of full employment. At best, the Phillips curve is a generalization of historical experience; in fact, we have experienced scores of inflation-unemployment combinations that lie both above and below the curve depicted in Figure 3.7. Thus, it is certainly possible to achieve more desirable combinations of unemployment and inflation than the Phillips curve suggests.

The reasoning behind the Phillips curve is also suspect, resembling as it does certain structural unemployment arguments. Nearly everyone agrees that an expansion of aggregate demand is necessary to reduce high levels of unemployment. The propo-

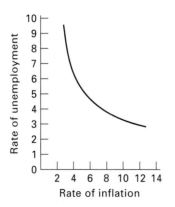

FIGURE 3.7 The Phillips Curve

[20]Council of Economic Advisors, *Economic Report to the President* (Washington, DC: U.S. Government Printing Office, 1979).

nents of the Phillips curve theory argue that comparatively few benefits of increased spending actually reach the unemployed because they have the wrong skills, are too young or old, live in the wrong places, or are simply unaware of new opportunities. Accordingly, demands for new output are met by overworking existing employees rather than by hiring new workers. Wage rates, and then prices, go up while unemployment rates change little. The greater the effort to reduce unemployment, the faster the rate of inflation.

The argument for a trade-off between fuller employment and greater price stability has a solid empirical basis. However, the terms of the trade-off are not immutable. On the contrary, the Phillips curve shifted (moved) to the right many times in the 1970s, leading to both higher unemployment and higher inflation. It should be possible, then, to shift it to the left as well, permitting both less unemployment and less inflation. This actually occurred in the mid-1980s and again in the early 1990s.

Even a fixed (unmovable) Phillips curve need not necessitate a permanent sacrifice. The element of time is important. Suppose, for example, that an increase in the demand for goods and services occurred. To satisfy this demand, producers will have to hire additional workers or employ their existing labor forces more fully. Other workers may not be immediately available, however, and they are likely to require training or orientation before they can contribute to output. As a result, producers probably will have to rely primarily on their existing workers for an initial expansion of output. Such reliance is expensive, however, as overtime wage rates are high; productivity is likely to decline with longer hours; and workers will feel in a better position to demand higher base wages. Producers will have a large and increasing incentive to locate and train new workers as expanded output continues. As time passes, producers will substitute new labor for overtime labor, thus reducing costs.

The labor-market adjustment process described here implies that expansion of demand will, indeed, lead to higher prices but that the increased rate of inflation may be a temporary phenomenon. As new workers are absorbed into the production process, the pressure on prices may abate. What the Phillips curve may portray on an aggregate level is the rate of inflation necessary to evoke the required labor force adjustment. The curve should not necessarily be understood to mean that the same high rate of inflation will continue once the adjustment is made. Not only may the price increase be temporary, but it is an integral feature of the adjustment mechanism. Hence, we might be able to say that an 8 percent rate of inflation is necessary to reduce the unemployment rate from 6.0 to 5.5 percent, but we have no firm reason for anticipating continued high rates of inflation once the lower level of unemployment is reached. High rates of inflation could continue, of course, but they would be the consequence of actions other than the initial effort to reduce employment.

Inflationary expectations are often the source of continued wage-price escalation. When people see prices rising, they may come to expect inflation to continue. Prodded by such expectations, they may themselves demand higher wages and prices, thereby making inflation more permanent. To the extent that structural factors or expectations create a trade-off between unemployment and inflation, attaining full employment is obviously more difficult. This does not mean, however, that we are stuck with any particular trade-off. Policies that reduce structural bottlenecks or restrain inflationary expectations can shift the Phillips curve to the left. In so doing, they make it less costly (in terms of inflation) to reach the goal of full employment. If, for example, the move toward full employment is slowed by the fact that unemployed workers possess skills in small demand or live in the wrong areas, further expansion of demand might be channeled more specifically in their direction. The pattern of demand, both occupationally and geographically, will affect the speed of adjustment and, thus, the dynamic trade-off. Accordingly, there is no unchangeable relationship of inflation to unemployment. The relationship depends on the capability and determination of policy makers to alter the pattern of demand as they expand it.

CHAPTER

The Working Poor

4

If nonemployment is a major cause of poverty, we should be able to eliminate most poverty by providing everyone with a job. According to this reasoning, employment emerges as a sure route to economic security. This route, however, is not so certain. We know, for example, that many poor people whom we think of as unemployed do work a great deal. In fact, a salient characteristic of the subemployed poor is that they are repeatedly engaged in part-time or part-year work. Hence, we can quickly reject the naive assumption that employment automatically lifts a person out of poverty.

A slightly more sophisticated view of the relationship between employment and poverty would suggest that the attainment of economic security depends not just on whether one works but also on how much one works. By and large, economic security is reserved for those individuals and their families who work full-time throughout the year. In this chapter, we examine this expectation in greater detail. In so doing, we focus on those individuals who fail to meet our expectations—the working poor.

WORK EXPERIENCE AND POVERTY

The expectation that increased employment improves one's chances of escaping poverty is fully supported by available data. As Figure 4.1 shows, the more one works, the lower the poverty rate.

Weeks of Work and Hours

The amount of time a person works is typically measured in two distinct ways: (1) the number of employed weeks in a year, and (2) the number of employed hours per week. In principle, these two measures could be combined so that people could be classified on the basis of how many hours they work during the year. The Census survey procedures used to collect work experience data preclude such simple multiplication, however. The Census survey asks how many hours a person "usually" works when employed. Since an individual may depart frequently from his or her "usual" hours, the implied annual hours of work are likely to be in error.[1] As a result, annual hours of work

---

[1]See Bradley R. Schiller, "Who Are the Working Poor?" *The Public Interest* (Spring 1994), pp. 61–71.

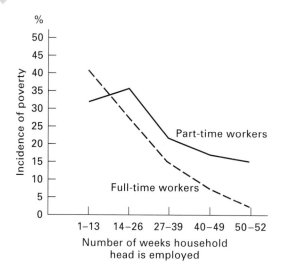

Source: U.S. Bureau of the Census (1995 data).

FIGURE 4.1 Poverty and Work Experience

can only be approximated. In any case, there is some interest in the separate measures of employment activity since they distinguish year-round workers from people who work sporadically.

Figure 4.1 clearly shows that poverty rates fall when householders work more weeks in the year. Among household heads who typically work full-time (35 hours per week), those who are employed less than half the year have a one out of three chance of being poor. By contrast, household heads who work full-time all year round have a one in thirty chance of being poor. The same relationship between the duration of employment and poverty is true for part-time workers, as Figure 4.1 also indicates.

The Working Poor

The relationships depicted in Figure 4.1 are likely to instill the comfortable feeling that there are few full-time, year-round workers among the poor. But this impression is dispelled quickly when the numbers are examined more closely. Because year-round workers in the economy vastly outnumber part-year workers, the incidence rates do not adequately reflect the work experience of the poor. Once again, numbers and proportions convey very different impressions.

Table 4.1 summarizes the work experiences of the poor in absolute numbers. This table includes all poor adults aged 16 and over. As noted in Chapter 3, less than half of all poor adults have any work experience during the year. What is new about Table 4.1 is the amount of work experience by those poor people who do participate in the labor market. Among those who work, the largest subgroup is clearly the 2 million-plus adults who work year-round (50–52 weeks) and full-time. More than 1 million other adults in poverty appear to work year-round at part-time jobs.

While Figure 4.1 seems consistent with the notion that hard work pays off, Table 4.1 appears to contradict that same expectation. Indeed, statistics like those in Table 4.1 have led many observers to conclude that the working poor are a contradiction of

TABLE 4.1   Work Experience of the Poor

Work Experience During Year	Number of Poor Adults	
	Part-Time	*Full-Time*
Worked		
1–26 weeks	1,918,000	2,062,000
27–49 weeks	763,000	1,166,000
50–52 weeks	<u>1,157,000</u>	<u>2,418,000</u>
Subtotal	3,838,000	5,646,000
Did not work	13,593,000	
Total, poor adults age 16 and over	23,077,000	

Source: U.S. Bureau of the Census (1995 data).

the American ethos. This in turn has spawned calls for more education and training, higher minimum wages, and tougher policies that will increase the rewards gained from working.[2]

How Much Work?

The increased attention given to the working poor has sparked some measurement questions. The most obvious question is who should be included in this new category. The U.S. Department of Labor defines the *working poor* as all "persons who have devoted 27 weeks or more to working or looking for work and who lived in families with incomes below the official poverty threshold."[3] That is a broad definition, however, since it encompasses all individuals who participate in the labor market at least six months of the year, rather than just those who actually *work.*

Another definition includes among the working poor all workers whose annualized earnings are too low to lift a family of four out of poverty.[4] There are two problems with this definition. Earnings are annualized by extrapolating actual earnings into a full-time, year-round equivalent. Full-time jobs seldom offer the same pay or conditions as part-time or occasional jobs, however. Furthermore, the decision to work only part-time or part-year may entail individual choices (e.g., attending school, raising a family) that preclude better job opportunities.

Even if this second notion of working poor is restricted to full-time, year-round workers, its validity is questionable. The presumption is that every full-time worker must be able to support a family of four. Most low-wage workers are not even household heads, however, much less responsible for four-person families. They are more likely to be spouses, teen-aged children, or unrelated individuals.[5]

---

[2]See, for example, Lucy Gorham and Bennett Harrison, *Working Below the Poverty Line* (Washington, DC: Aspen Institute, 1990).

[3]Earl Mellor, "A Profile of the Working Poor" (Washington, DC: U.S. Bureau of Labor Statistics, March 1994), p. 1.

[4]Gorham and Harrison, *Working Below the Poverty Line,* are among those who use this definition.

[5]U.S. Bureau of the Census, *Workers with Low Earnings: 1964 to 1990,* Series P-60, No. 178 (revised May 1994).

In view of these considerations, the definition of the working poor should focus on the key dimensions of *work* (not just labor force participation) and poverty (income in relation to actual family size). Were year-round, full-time employment used as the index of working, then just over 2 million adults would be counted as working poor according to Table 4.1. That would account for one out of ten poor persons in the 16–64 age group.

More Measurement Problems

Conceptually, the designation of poor adults working year-round, full-time as working poor is unobjectionable. There are problems, however, with the empirical identification of individuals who fit this classification.

As noted earlier, the Census Bureau does not measure actual hours worked in a year. The Census survey instead asks how many hours an individual "usually" worked when employed. A person might usually work full-time, but experience occasional "short weeks" as well. In reality, one out of ten individuals classified as a year-round, full-time worker was actually employed part-time at least six weeks of the year.[6] Accordingly, the official Census data in Table 4.1 exaggerate the number of working poor.

The Census count of the working poor is also exaggerated by the incomplete accounting of income. The annual Census survey inquires about regular wages but neglects tips, commissions, and bonuses. These irregular forms of compensation may be particularly important for workers with low hourly pay (e.g., salespeople and food servers).

Finally, the concept of the working poor is often thought to apply to people who work for low wages. However, the official statistics on working poverty do not distinguish paid workers from individuals who are self-employed. Closer examination of Census data reveals that of the 2.4 million individuals identified as year-round, full-time workers in Table 4.1, nearly 600,000 are *self-employed*. Although these self-employed individuals may have had similarly low incomes in a given year, their circumstances are not the same as the working poor who are paid by the hour. Self-employed persons may own farms or business assets of considerable value. Self-employed persons also have some discretion in calculating their incomes and are prone to underreporting it. This does not mean that all self-employed persons are well-off, but rather that the perceived poverty of the self-employed working poor is exaggerated.

These measurement issues substantially change the portrait of the working poor painted by official Census data. Clearly, the number of year-round, full-time workers with incomes below the poverty index is much lower than Table 4.1 suggests. That still leaves a lot of hard-working poor, but they are a very small portion of the poverty population.

The Significance of Secondary Workers

So far, we have examined the extent of poverty among *individuals* of varying work experience. Most individuals live in *families,* however, and families may supply more than one worker to the labor market. In fact, in more than half of America's families at least two people work for pay during the year. Accordingly, a family's participation in the

[6]Ralph E. Smith and Bruce Vavrichek, "The Minimum Wage: Its Relation to Incomes and Poverty," *Monthly Labor Review* (June 1987), p. 29.

labor market should be gauged not solely by the work activity of the householder (household head) but also by the work experience of other family members (secondary workers).

Secondary workers are in fact often decisive in keeping a family out of poverty, among two-parent families with children:

> 7 out of 10 *non*poor families have the equivalent of at least 1.5 full-time workers at work all year round;
>
> Only 2 out of 10 poor families have at least 1.5 "full-time worker equivalents."[7]

Such statistics suggest that the difference between poverty and a more comfortable living standard for the typical family may depend on the paychecks of secondary workers. Indeed, Professor Sar Levitan figured that 50 to 70 percent *more* two-earner families would be in poverty without the earnings of a secondary worker.[8] As it is, over 3 million families who *are* in poverty have at least two members in the work force. A broader concept of the working poor might well encompass the combined employment activity of an entire family. If this were done, working poverty would appear more widespread than earlier suggested.

SEARCHING FOR EXPLANATIONS

Although the actual number of working poor is undoubtedly less than official estimates, *any* overlap between full-time, year-round work and poverty seems incongruous. Why, we may ask, are so many people poor if their families work so much? Doesn't the existence of this paradox violate the very same principles that comprise our capitalist ideology? If we cannot guarantee economic security to those individuals who contribute their maximum work effort, what sort of admonitions or incentives can be directed to those who work less?

Setting aside the conceptual and statistical problems of identifying the working poor, we may proceed to potential explanations for the overlap between work and poverty. Two general explanations for the status of the hard-working poor come to mind.

The most obvious suggestion is that their wages are unusually low. At poverty wages, very few people can work hard enough or long enough to attain economic security. But low wages are not the only possible explanation for the plight of the working poor. Poverty refers to the relationship between a family's income and its needs. Thus, it might also be the case that the poor simply have above-average needs, due to either larger families or special expenses, for example, medical bills. In this situation, even standard wages would tend to leave the family financially destitute. The distinction between income and needs is vital for policy concerns. The one situation implies the need for labor-market intervention of some kind, while the second implies the need to address nonmarket phenomena, such as family planning or health insurance.

[7]U.S. Congress, Committee on Ways and Means, *1992 Green Book* (Washington, DC: U.S. Government Printing Office, 1992), pp. 1280–81. For more detail on recent employment activity by married mothers, see Howard V. Hayghe and Suzanne M. Blanchi, "Married Mothers' Work Patterns: The Job-Family Compromise," *Monthly Labor Review* (June 1994), pp. 24–30.

[8]Sar Levitan, "Part-Timers: Living on Half-Rations," *Challenge* (May–June 1988); see also Jennifer M. Gardner and Diane E. Herz, "Working and Poor in 1992," *Monthly Labor Review* (December 1992), pp. 20–28.

MINIMUM-WAGE JOBS

The federal minimum wage is an obvious candidate for explaining the coexistence of work and poverty. Congress first set the minimum wage at 25 cents per hour in 1938 (Fair Labor Standards Act). Since that time the wage floor has been increased numerous times (see Table 4.2) and reached $5.15 in 1997. Accordingly, a person who worked year-round, full-time (roughly 2,000 hours) in 1998 at the minimum wage would have earned only $10,300. That was barely enough income to keep one individual out of poverty, much less a family (see Table 2.4).

In 1981, a minimum-wage job was more effective in helping people out of poverty. In 1981, the minimum wage was only $3.35 an hour. But prices were much lower, too. Accordingly, the income from a year-round, minimum-wage job could have almost kept a three-person family out of poverty. Between 1981 and 1990, however, the federal minimum wage was not increased, even though prices of goods and services kept rising. As the *real* (inflation-adjusted) value of the minimum wage declined, it became more difficult for the working poor to escape poverty.

Although the declining real value of the minimum wage contributes to working poverty, it is not as complete an explanation as it first appears. Most of the people who hold minimum-wage jobs are *not* poor. They are more likely to be teenagers or other secondary workers from families with above-poverty incomes. Only one out of five minimum-wage workers lives in a poor family.[9]

It is also important to recognize that workers don't *stay* in minimum-wage jobs. By and large, minimum-wage jobs are simply stepping stones for workers who are moving on to better-paying employment.[10] Minimum-wage jobs give labor-market entrants the opportunity to acquire experience, job information, and the employment references that are critical for career advancement. Accordingly, many individuals who

TABLE 4.2   Minimum-Wage History

Date	Minimum Wage	Date	Minimum Wage
October 1938	$0.25	January 1975	$2.10
October 1939	0.30	January 1976	2.30
October 1945	0.40	January 1978	2.65
January 1950	0.75	January 1979	2.90
March 1956	1.00	January 1980	3.10
September 1961	1.15	January 1981	3.35
September 1963	1.25	April 1990	3.80
February 1967	1.40	April 1991	4.25
February 1968	1.60	October 1996	4.75
May 1974	2.00	September 1997	5.15

[9]See Ralph E. Smith and Bruce Vavrichek, "The Minimum Wage: Its Relation to Incomes and Poverty," *op. cit.*
[10]See Bradley R. Schiller, "Moving Up: The Training and Wage Gains of Minimum-Wage Entrants," *Social Science Quarterly* (Summer 1994), pp. 622–636.

are presently working for minimum wages and in poverty may be earning higher wages and out of poverty quickly.

Were the minimum wage increased, relatively few poor people would be lifted out of poverty.[11] There is also a risk that a higher minimum wage might reduce job opportunities for new labor-market entrants. If that were the case, some people would be worse off and poverty might spread. Although the exact dimensions of such *disemployment* are hotly debated, the risk of job losses is universally recognized.[12]

LOW WAGES

Even though the federal minimum wage may not play a major role in explaining working poverty, wage rates are still relevant. The issue, however, is *low* wages, not necessarily the *minimum* wage set by Congress. The hourly wage needed to escape poverty via the route of year-round, full-time employment started at $7 in 1992 for a family of four and ratchets upward with increasing family size. In 1998 the threshold wage was over $8 an hour. Accordingly, there is a long gap between the federal minimum wage and the wage needed to escape poverty. Any household head earning wages in that gap is likely to be among the working poor.

Table 4.3 provides some evidence on the actual earnings of individuals who head poverty families. Those who worked year-round, full-time (the prototypical "working poor") are distinguished from those who worked less than that or not at all. If it is assumed that "year-round, full-time" work entails at least 1,820 hours of work per year, a minimum-wage worker would have earned close to $8,000 in 1995. According to Table 4.3, at least 6 out of 10 working poor heads earned wages in excess of that threshold. But only 15 percent of these year-round, full-time workers earned enough to keep a four-person family out of poverty, i.e., at least $14,000 a year. The median wage of the working poor was around $5 per hour.

The working poor are not the only workers paid low wages. Table 4.4 shows the distribution of wages for all workers paid on an hourly basis.[13] Nearly 6 million workers were paid less than $5 an hour in 1996. At those wages they could not have kept a three-person family out of poverty. Nearly 30 million workers were paid less than the $8 an hour needed to keep a four-person family out of poverty. What keeps most of

---

[11]Most of the benefit of a higher minimum wage would go to families that depend on it the least; see Michael W. Horrigan and Ronald B. Mincy, "The Minimum Wage and Earnings and Income Inequalities," in *Uneven Tides: Rising Inequality in America,* eds. Sheldon Danziger and Peter Gottschalk (New York: Russell Sage, 1993), pp. 251–275.

[12]For an early review, see Charles Brown, Curtis Gilroy, and Andrew Kohen, "The Effect of the Minimum Wage on Employment and Unemployment," *Journal of Economic Literature* (June 1982), pp. 487–528; for updates, see Allison J. Wellington, "Effects of the Minimum Wage on the Employment Status of Youths," *Journal of Human Resources* (Winter 1991), pp. 27–46.

The nature and impacts of state minimum-wage laws are examined in Bradley R. Schiller, "State Minimum Wage Laws: Youth Coverage and Impact," *Journal of Labor Research* (Fall 1994), pp. 317–329; David Neumark and William Wascher, "Employment Effects of Minimum and Subminimum Wages: Panel Data on State Minimum Wage Laws," *Industrial and Labor Relations Review* (October 1992), pp. 55–81; David Card, "Do Minimum Wages Reduce Employment? A Case Study of California, 1987–89," *Industrial and Labor Relations Review* (October 1992), pp. 38–54.

[13]Recall that the Census Bureau tends to underestimate wage rates by overestimating hours worked and omitting tips, commissions, and bonuses.

TABLE 4.3   Annual Earnings of Household Heads of Poor Families

| | *Worked During Year* | |
| | Full-Time | Less Than |
Earnings	Year-Round	Full-Time
Less than $2,000	8.5%	36.0%
$2,000–$3,999	3.6	20.3
$4,000–$5,999	8.1	14.6
$6,000–$7,999	12.5	14.2
$8,000–$9,999	17.7	9.8
$10,000–$11,999	20.8	6.0
$12,000–$13,999	13.4	2.0
$14,000–$19,999	14.5	1.9
Over $20,000	0.9	0.3
	100.0	100.0
Number who worked	1,337,000	2,426,000
Number without earnings	3,674,000	

Source: U.S. Bureau of the Census (1995 data).

these low-wage workers out of poverty is the absence of family responsibilities or the work efforts of other family members.

Danziger and Gottschalk looked specifically at household heads, rather than all workers. They discovered that one-fourth of all household heads who are neither aged, disabled, nor single parents of preschool children earn less than the average poverty

TABLE 4.4   Hourly Wage Rates, by Age, 1996

| | *Number of Workers (in thousands)* | | | |
Hourly Wage	*Age 16–19*	*Age 20–24*	*Age 25 +*	*Total*
Under $4.00	240	244	562	1,044
$4.00–4.99	1,706	991	2,122	4,820
$5.00–5.99	2,159	1,960	4,736	8,854
$6.00–6.99	977	1,756	5,420	8,153
$7.00–7.99	442	1,459	5,420	7,321
$8.00–8.99	228	1,134	5,328	6,690
$9.00–9.99	74	604	4,216	4,894
$10.00 or more	125	1,343	26,010	27,428
Median Wage	$5.17	$6.69	$ 9.62	$ 8.40
Mean Wage	$5.50	$7.23	$11.02	$10.03

Source: U.S. Bureau of Labor Statistics. Table includes only those workers normally paid on an hourly basis (U.S. total = 69.3 million).

threshold. Surprisingly, two-thirds of these low earners were able to escape poverty. Table 4.5 shows how they escaped. Smaller family size was the most frequent explanation for escaping poverty, followed by the presence of an additional worker in the family.

The low-wage workers who escaped poverty in Table 4.5 may not stay out of poverty long. Although nonpoor, these families are not far removed from poverty. A downturn in the economy, illness, or a new birth can push these low-earning households back into poverty quickly. This is, in fact, a frequent sequence.[14] In view of the fact that over *6 million* year-round, full-time workers were still earning less than $10,000 per year in 1996, the potential for sudden surges in poverty is apparent. In the best of circumstances, they are referred to as the near-poor. In less favorable times these workers and their families become part of the poverty population.

Poor Jobs

If there is any moral to be gleaned from the foregoing figures, perhaps it is this: A poor janitor who works hard stands a very good chance of becoming a hard-working poor janitor. Low wages can be a barrier to escaping poverty. They can also deter people from taking jobs that are available. Elliot Liebow summarized the dismal prospects of many low-wage workers in this way:

> . . . the man does not have any reasonable expectation that, however bad it is, his job will lead to better things. Menial jobs are not, by and large, the starting point of a track

TABLE 4.5   Escape Routes from Low-Income Earnings (percent distributions)

Number of low-earning households*	17.03 million
In poverty	36%
Not in poverty	64%
Escape routes from poverty	
Small family size	43.5%
Other workers in family	27.1%
Nonearnings income	13.1%
Welfare benefits	11.6%
Combinations of above	4.3%

Notes: Households include only those "expected to work," i.e., heads under age 65, nondisabled, not in school, and not sole parent of child under six. Low earnings are defined as wages below $204 per week, the amount needed in 1984 to reach the poverty threshold for a family of four.

Source: Adapted from Sheldon Danziger and Peter Gottschalk, "Work, Poverty, and the Working Poor: A Multifaceted Problem," *Monthly Labor Review* (September 1986), p. 19.

---

[14]See Duncan Greg et al., *Years of Poverty, Years of Plenty* (Ann Arbor, MI: Institute for Social Research, 1984); also Peter Gottschalk, Sara McLanahan, and Gary D. Sandefur, "The Dynamics and Intergenerational Transmission of Poverty," in *Confronting Poverty,* eds. S. Danziger, G. Sandefur, and D. Weinberg (Cambridge, MA: Harvard University Press, 1994), pp. 85–108. Transitions in and out of jobs and poverty look even more frequent when viewed in monthly (versus annual) periods; see Kathleen Mullan Harris, "Work and Welfare Among Single Mothers in Poverty," *American Journal of Sociology* (September 1993), pp. 317–352.

system which leads to even better jobs for those who are able and willing to do them. The busboy or dishwasher in a restaurant is not on a job track which, if negotiated skillfully, leads to chef or manager of the restaurant. The busboy or dishwasher who works hard becomes, simply, a hard-working busboy or dishwasher. Neither hard work nor perseverance can conceivably carry the janitor to a sit-down job in the office building he cleans up.[15]

Not all the poor, of course, are janitors. Most middle-class persons, in fact, probably think of janitors as low-income workers, but not poor. More likely to come to mind—if we admit the poor work at all—are bellboys, busboys, and nonunionized street cleaners, plus a small army of aged farmers and migrant farm workers. Once again, however, the preconception departs considerably from the reality of everyday poverty. The working poor are likely to be found in all broad occupational categories. Table 4.6 depicts the actual occupational distribution of the poor. While it is true that nearly 30 percent of all farmers and farm workers are poor, these two occupations account for less than one-seventh of the jobs held by the poor; just as many poor people work as craft or production workers. Even white-collar jobs do not guarantee financial security, as more than 500,000 people depicted in the table testify.

It is just as easy to overstate the occupational status of the poor as it is to understate it. The occupational profile of Table 4.6 includes very broad employment categories and may lead to erroneous impressions. While there are 272,000 poor professional and managerial workers, there are very few poor scientists, dentists, or even college professors among them. More likely to be poor within that occupational classification are hospital technicians, recreation and social workers, and evangelist healers. Similarly, in other occupational categories, the poor tend to hold the least desirable, most marginal kinds of jobs. They are dishwashers, loggers, food processors, porters, tai-

TABLE 4.6 Occupations of the Poor Heads-of-Household

Occupation	Number of Persons
Managerial and professional	272,000
Technicians and support	14,000
Clerical workers	225,000
Sales workers	346,000
Craftspeople and precision production	418,000
Protective service	50,000
Private household workers	93,000
Other service workers	835,000
Operators and unskilled laborers	725,000
Farmers and farm managers	130,000
Armed forces	4,000
Total	3,311,000

Source: U.S. Bureau of the Census (1987 data).

[15]Elliot Liebow, *Tally's Corner: A Study of Negro Streetcorner Men* (Boston: Little, Brown and Company, 1967), p. 63.

lors, office cleaners, and laundry workers. Accordingly, while it is true that the working poor are distributed throughout the labor market and in all industries, they will always be found in the lowest-ranking, least noticeable jobs. They constitute what might be called a phantom labor force. John Schwartz calls them the "forgotten Americans": As they continue working hard for poverty wages, the problems of other poor people (e.g., displaced workers, teenage mothers) capture the public's attention.

WHY WAGES ARE SO LOW

While poverty and employment might seem incompatible, there is no shortage of available explanations for the low wages of the working poor. The poor are undereducated, inexperienced, underskilled, geographically handicapped, and trained in the wrong occupations. Abundant evidence exists to support each of these explanations. We must also recognize, however, that these explanations focus almost exclusively on the *supply* side of the labor market. They tell us what qualities an individual brings to the labor market but do not provide a complete explanation of why the worker is paid so little for them. To understand the process by which wages are determined, we must also ask what the *demand* side of the labor market looks like.

In the most general terms, we say that a worker's wages are determined by the contribution he or she makes to output, that is, by his or her marginal product. But what is it that makes the output of a pipe fitter less valuable than the output of an advertising executive? What differentiates the incomes of these two people is not the physical output that each produces, but rather the value that society attaches to their products. If society suddenly became disenchanted with the wares of advertising executives and found increased value in fitted pipes, the incomes of pipe fitters would exceed those of advertising executives, regardless of their respective physical outputs. By the same reasoning, if society were to attach more value to the kinds of output that the poor can and do produce, we could expect the incomes of the working poor to rise.

The notion that the extent and structure of demand are significant determinants of the wages of the poor does not constitute a revolution in economic thinking. Economists have long taken credit for the discovery that prices, and thus wages, are determined by the interaction of supply and demand. In antipoverty discussions, however, the impact of the demand side of the market on the economic position of the poor is easily neglected. Doing so ignores tremendous potential for eliminating poverty.

During the 1940s, there was a tendency for wage rates and incomes at the bottom of the occupational ladder to rise faster than those at the top. This was due to an upsurge in demand for unskilled, semiskilled, and operative kinds of labor needed for war production. The structure of demand since the 1940s, however, has primarily benefited workers with higher education and more technical expertise. This trend has been particularly strong since 1979.[16] Accordingly, we find the unskilled, semiskilled, and operative workers heavily represented among the poor. The distribution of wages and incomes is partly a reflection of collective social decisions regarding the merits of particular kinds of output. Sociopolitical decisions to expand the educational system, to arm for peace, to build an information highway, to explore space, and to expand international trade have

---

[16]See the symposium on wage inequality in the *Journal of Economic Perspectives* (Spring 1997).

all had a profound impact on the structure of demand for labor. Had we decided instead to dredge more rivers, to build more houses, or to clean up our cities, the extent and nature of poverty might now be markedly different. Without attempting to predict those changes here, we may at least take note of the fact that the poor now suffer from some of society's past and current labor utilization decisions and stand to benefit if and when society decides to place higher value on the available services of the poor. In later chapters we will examine policies that affect both the supply and demand for workers from low-income backgrounds.

SUMMARY

Labor force participation is a necessary but not sufficient prerequisite for escaping poverty. Millions of people live in poor families despite extensive labor force activity by family members.

There are several definitions of the working poor. Of these, the focus on individuals who live in poverty despite working year-round at a full-time job is the most compelling. These full-time workers are only a small fraction of the poverty population. Nevertheless, their plight is incompatible with the notion that work is a sure route out of poverty.

While it is true that the federal minimum wage is not high enough to keep a family out of poverty, most minimum-wage workers are not poor. They are more likely to be teenagers or secondary workers from middle-class families. The broader phenomenon of low (not necessarily minimum) wages is a better explanation for working poverty.

The structure of wages reflects both supply characteristics of workers and the pattern of demand for labor. The low end of the wage structure does not itself necessitate poverty, as millions of low-wage but nonpoor workers attest. However, low wages in combination with greater family needs do leave millions of individuals in poverty and others near-poor.

FURTHER READING

Bound, John, and George Johnson, "Changes in the Structure of Wages in the 1980s: An Evaluation of Alternative Explanations," *American Economic Review* (June 1992), pp. 371–392.

Card, David, and Alan Krueger, *Myth and Measurement: The New Economics of the Minimum Wage.* Princeton, NJ: Princeton University Press, 1995.

Danziger, Sheldon, and Peter Gottschalk, eds., *Uneven Tides: Rising Inequality in America.* New York: Russell Sage, 1993.

Haveman, Robert, and Demetra Nightingale, eds., *The Work Alternative.* Washington, DC: Urban Institute, 1994.

Katz, Lawrence F., and Kevin Murphy, "Changes in Relative Wages, 1963–1987: Supply and Demand Factors," *Quarterly Journal of Economics* (February 1992), pp. 35–79.

Levy, Frank, and Richard J. Murnane, "Earnings Levels and Earnings Inequality: A Review of Recent Trends and Proposed Explanations," *Journal of Economic Literature* (September 1992), pp. 1333–1381.

Riemer, David R., *The Prisoners of Welfare.* New York: Praeger, 1988; esp. Chapters 2–5.

Schiller, Bradley R., "Who Are the Working Poor?" *The Public Interest* (Spring 1994), pp. 61–71.

Schwartz, John E., and Thomas J. Volgy, *The Forgotten Americans.* New York: Norton, 1992.

U.S. Bureau of the Census, *Workers with Low Earnings: 1964 to 1990.* Washington, DC: U.S. Government Printing Office, May 1994.

U.S. Bureau of Labor Statistics, *A Profile of the Working Poor.* Washington, DC: U.S. Government Printing Office, annual.

APPENDIX

DOES PROSPERITY TRICKLE DOWN?

This and the previous chapter have documented the labor-market problems of poor people. Poor people don't participate enough in the labor market. When they do, however, a combination of unemployment and low wages keeps them in poverty.

While the poverty population has remained at a high level since 1980, the U.S. economy has grown substantially. This has led many people to question whether and how Main Street's prosperity is shared with the poor. Do the poor benefit from general economic growth or do they live in an isolated subeconomy?

The Trickle-Down Perspective

The *trickle-down theory* asserts that people at the bottom of the economic hierarchy benefit from any increased prosperity at higher income levels.[17] If this is true, then public policy need not focus on the poor but can instead pursue more general growth and income strategies.

The reasoning behind the trickle-down theory is straightforward. Suppose that the federal government decides to build a moon shuttle capable of taxiing busloads of scientists and tourists back and forth to the moon. Such an undertaking would require the expenditure of tens of billions of dollars and the employment of highly skilled labor and capital equipment. The question is whether and how the poor folks back in the ghetto would benefit from this excursion into space.

It is possible, of course, that some of the poor would be employed directly in the moon shuttle program, say as grounds sweepers, gate attendants, or other low-skilled jobs. But the potential for such direct job creation is apt to be small. A far likelier source of jobs are the multiplier effects that will take place once the program gets under way. The aerospace workers will want to spend their increased incomes, and in so

---

[17]The expression *trickle down* was coined by W.H. Locke Anderson in "Trickling Down: The Relationship between Economic Growth and the Extent of Poverty among American Families," *Quarterly Journal of Economics* (November 1964) and has earlier origins in William Jennings Bryan's 1896 "Cross of Gold" speech in which he declared, "There are those who believe that, if you will only legislate to make the well-to-do prosperous, their prosperity will leak through on those below."

doing will add to the demand for more conventional goods and services, such as houses, hot dogs, beer, gardeners, and maids. As the production of these goods and services expands, more jobs and incomes will be created, thereby increasing the chances that some needy souls from the ranks of the poor will obtain better jobs and wages. Such multiplier effects will continue to reverberate through the economy as the income spent by the aerospace workers is passed from hand to hand.

Although multiplier effects provide the best hope of jobs and income for the folks in the ghetto, there are other ways in which the poor might benefit from the moon shuttle program. The people who obtain jobs directly in the moon shuttle program will probably vacate positions that offered lower wages or benefits, jobs which then are available to others, including the poor. Such substitution effects may continue all the way down the occupational ladder, ultimately resulting in job vacancies for the poor. In addition, employers faced with a sudden shortage of labor will have an economic incentive to train the poor and unskilled, thereby further enlarging the size of the trickle.

The Dual Labor-Market Perspective

Although the trickle-down hypothesis seems plausible enough, not everyone shares the expectations it generates. In particular, it is argued that the poor do not really participate in the mainstream economy, and are excluded from the jobs and income that a moon shuttle program would create. In effect, it is argued, the poor participate in a separate and distinct labor market, a *secondary labor market,* which is distinguished from the mainstream or *primary labor market.*[18] From the perspective of the dual labor-market hypothesis, an expansion of demand that occurs in the primary market such as in a moon shuttle program will not benefit workers in the secondary market. A variety of barriers allegedly exclude the poor from the primary labor market, in effect creating the secondary market. Outright discrimination against minority groups or the poor, for example, would exclude the poor from the trickle. So, too, would recruiting practices that emphasized skill, experience, and stable work histories, prerequisites that the poor job seeker can rarely satisfy. Institutional barriers like strong labor unions could have the same effect, especially if unions opted to maximize the earnings of their current members rather than to expand employment and union membership.

It is unlikely, of course, that these barriers would be so great as to exclude all poor job seekers from the benefits created by a moon shuttle program (or any other form of demand expansion). It is much more reasonable to expect that some additional jobs and income will in fact trickle down, thereby reducing the number of people we count as poor. This expectation still appears valid.[19] However, recent changes in the structure

---

[18]Peter Doerringer and Michael Piore popularized these concepts in "Unemployment and the Dual Labor Market," *The Public Interest* (Winter 1975). Also see Glen G. Cain, "The Challenge of Segmented Labor Market Theories to Orthodox Theory: A Survey," *Journal of Economic Literature* (December 1976).

[19]For case studies of trickle down, se Paul Osterman, "Gains from Growth? The Impact of Full Employment of Poverty in Boston," and Richard B. Freeman, "Employment and Earning of Disadvantaged Young Men in a Labor Shortage Economy," both in C. Jencks and P. Peterson, eds., *The Urban Underclass* (Washington, DC: Urban Institute, 1991).

For more aggregated results, see N. S. Balke and D. J. Slottje, "Poverty and Change in the Macroeconomy: A Dynamic Macroeconomic Model," *Review of Economics and Statistics* (February 1993); Rebecca Blank and David Card, "Poverty, Income Distribution, and Growth: Are They Still Connected?" *Brookings Papers*

of labor markets may have slowed the trickle. What the dual labor-market hypothesis tells us is that the really critical issue is *how* much actually trickles down. And it also suggests that public policy can be used to increase the size of that trickle by reducing the barriers that separate the poor from the jobs and incomes we create.

on Economic Activity (1993:2); James Tobin, "Poverty in Relation to Macroeconomic Trends, Cycles, and Policies," in *Confronting Poverty,* eds. S. Danziger, G. Sandfur, and D. Weinberg (Cambridge, MA: Harvard University Press, 1994).

CHAPTER

Age and Health

5

L ack of employment is the principal cause of poverty for able-bodied adults of working age. But what about people who are past traditional working ages and people with illness or disabilities that preclude employment? What special problems do they have? Why are some older individuals poor while others live comfortably? How completely do illness or disability explain the poverty of people with such problems? These are the questions pursued in this chapter.

AGE

We observed in Chapter 2 that over 3 million individuals over age 65 were officially counted as poor in 1995. We also noted that the official poverty count omits institutionalized persons and older individuals who live with nonpoor relatives because they cannot afford to maintain households of their own. Accordingly, the official count understates the number of older individuals with incomes below the poverty index. Yet even the official count suggests that one out of ten Americans in poverty is over the age of 65.

Declining Poverty Rate

Although a sizable fraction of the poverty population, the aged actually have a lesser probability of being poor. While popular images of poverty often feature older people, persons over age 65 are less likely to be poor than are younger adults. Older individuals are also much less likely to be poor than are children.

The lower incidence of poverty among the aged is a relatively new phenomenon. When the war on poverty began in the mid-1960s, poverty rates among the aged were triple those of younger adults and far above those of children. As Figure 5.1 illustrates, that disparity has been reversed. The incidence of poverty among the aged has declined dramatically, while poverty rates for younger groups have crept upward.

The dramatic decline in poverty among the aged is cause for celebration. Despite these favorable trends, however, poverty among the aged remains a serious concern. As people age they become more vulnerable to changing health, economic con-

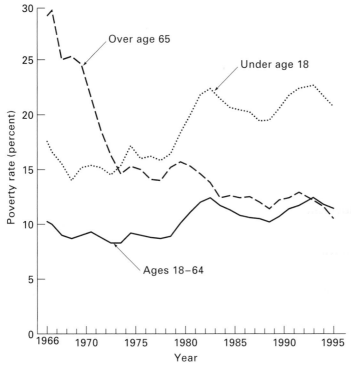

Source: U.S. Bureau of the Census.

FIGURE 5.1 Poverty Rates, by Age, 1966–1995

ditions, and public policy. Most of the decline in aged poverty since the mid-1960s is due to rising income transfers like Social Security, Medicare, and Medicaid. Without these financial props, poverty among the aged would be far more common. We might wonder, therefore, why so many older people *would* be poor without such public support.

We should also note that the economic problems of the aged will become increasingly important as the number of people living past the age of 65 continues to grow. Since 1900, the number of people living until age 65 has increased dramatically. In addition, the life expectancy of people at age 65 has also increased. Life expectancy for people reaching 65 was about 11 years in 1900; now it is more than 17 years. Hence, there are far more aged people today and they are living longer. This is partly reflected in the overall increase in life expectancies. In 1900, life expectancy at birth was 49 years; today it is over 76 years.

This increase in the size of the older population is continuing. In fact, the post–World War II "baby boom" will become a "seniors' boom" in the early part of the twenty-first century. In the process, the number of aged persons will jump from 30 million in 1990 to 51 million in the year 2020. By 2030, over one-fifth of the total U.S. population will be over age 65. Continuing discoveries in medical science may expand the aged population still further. Just to hold the line on the *number* of aged poor, we will have to reduce their *rate* even more.

These considerations led Michael Harrington to observe that "the poverty of old age in America is rooted in a biological revolution."[1] We must take care, however, not to attribute to biology the economic ills of the aged. Changing fertility patterns and medical advances are responsible only for the fact that so many more people live to old age. They do not explain why so many of these people live in poverty.

Diversity Among the Aged

Before looking closer at the economic situation of the aged, it is important to recognize the diversity among the aged. Young people tend to regard all people over 65 as "old." But people in their sixties often feel quite youthful and look at their *parents* or similarly aged individuals when asked about the "old people." With so many Americans living long past age 65, it has become increasingly necessary to distinguish the old old from those who are merely old. Traditionally, age 65 has been the threshold for defining *old,* while ages 75, 80, or even 85 have been used to identify the *old old.*

The distinction between the old and the old old is not simply a matter of age. The old old tend to have more health problems, to live alone, and to be poor. The young old, by contrast, often still work, are generally healthy, and typically live with a spouse. Because men die at earlier ages than women, the old old are predominantly widows: Three out of four poor individuals over age 75 are women.

These demographic changes that occur past age 65 are summarized in Table 5.1. The largest subgroup of people over age 85 are widows living alone. For people aged

TABLE 5.1 Age, Sex, and Marital Status of Individuals Over Age 65

Characteristic of Person	Age of Person			
	85 or Older	*80 or Older*	*65–69*	*65 or Older*
Total (percent)	100	100	100	100
Female	67	65	55	58
Married	6	11	32	24
Widowed	55	48	15	28
Living alone	35	33	10	20
Living with others	20	15	5	8
Other	5	6	7	7
Male	33	35	45	42
Married	17	22	37	31
Widowed	15	11	3	6
Living alone	8	7	2	4
Living with others	7	4	1	2
Other	1	2	5	4
Number of persons (in millions)	2.4	6.0	10.1	30.1

Source: Daniel B. Radner, "Economic Well-Being of the Old Old," *Social Security Bulletin* (Spring 1993).

[1]Michael Harrington, *The Other America* (New York: Macmillan Company, 1962), p. 102.

65–69 married couples are the most frequent living situation. Whereas only 4 percent of the married couples aged 65–69 are poor, one out of four widows over age 85 is poor. What makes the latter statistic particularly frightening is that the fastest growing subgroup among the aged are the widows over 85.

Racial patterns also change at older ages. As is true for younger people, poverty rates among the old are much higher for blacks (25 percent) and Hispanics (24 percent) than whites (10 percent). However, whites far outnumber minorities among the aged poor, accounting for eight out of ten of the old old poor. In part, this discrepancy reflects the fact that low-income blacks and Hispanics die at earlier ages than whites (Anglos).[2]

Sources of Economic Support

Earnings   The most obvious constraint on the incomes of the aged is the fact that so few older individuals remain in the labor force. Only about one out of ten older persons participates in the labor market. Moreover, participation and actual employment decline rapidly with increasing age. The poor among the aged are even less likely to work and this absence of employment income is a major determinant of their economic status.

Low labor force participation among the aged reflects a continuing trend in American society. At the beginning of the century, more than two-thirds of all men over the age of 65 were in the labor force; today, only one out of six older men works. The reasons for this decline in labor force participation are many, but surely they do not include the increased physical requirements of labor or diminished health status of the aged. An increased desire for leisure, an abatement of the economic necessity to work, and a reduced demand for the skills of the aged are more likely to have contributed to the decline in labor force participation.

There is evidence that many of the aged are involuntarily removed from the labor force because of forced retirement and prolonged unemployment. If older workers are laid off for any reason (for example, plant shutdowns, production slowdowns, or forced retirement), they face little chance of finding another job. They probably have developed highly specialized skills in a declining occupation. Moreover, because of their advanced age, other employers see little benefit in retraining them or redirecting their skills. Other employers also anticipate the increased costs of higher disability rates and imminent retirement. Simple economics weigh against the older job seeker. Because employment prospects are so unpromising, the older job seeker is likely to drop out of the labor force earlier than desired, eliminating a prospective income source.[3] Of those older persons already retired, over one-third report they were forced out of their jobs. Nearly half of those older persons in poverty report forced retirements.[4]

---

[2]Race differences in mortality and morbidity rates are discussed in J. Paul Leigh, "Distribution of Lifetime Income Allowing for Varying Mortality Rates, Among Women, Men, Blacks and Whites," *Journal of Economic Issues* (December 1992), pp. 1191–1220, and Gregory Pappas et al., "The Increasing Disparity in Mortality Between Socioeconomic Groups in the United States, 1960 and 1986," *New England Journal of Medicine* (July 1993), pp. 103–109.

[3]The influence of age on postdisplacement labor force status is discussed in Congressional Budget Office, *Displaced Workers: Trends in the 1980s and Implications for the Future* (Washington, DC: U.S. Government Printing Office, 1993).

[4]National Council on Aging, *The Myth and Reality of Aging in America* (Washington, DC: National Council on Aging, 1977), p. 87.

Assets   There are alternatives to employment income, of course. Some of the most common substitutes are income from savings, assets, and various retirement plans. The income flow from such assets can help reduce the impact of lost employment income. Indeed, the availability of alternative sources of income could actually encourage retirement, with no implied loss of individual welfare. The question is: Are the aged adequately provided with nonemployment retirement income?

A potentially important source of income for the aged is the savings they accumulated during their working years. Unfortunately, such savings are typically inadequate. Because the aged live longer and retire earlier today, they must accumulate greater savings than they once did. The unfortunate but simple economic fact is that the longer one lives, the greater are the chances of destitution. A person's employment capabilities and opportunities disappear at the same time that their savings are depleted. Today's aged must command considerable assets and savings if they are to experience a comfortable retirement.

In reality, most Americans save relatively little during their working years. As a result, their wealth in the "golden years" is typically modest. The *median* household wealth of persons over age 65 is around $90,000. That in itself is not a large number, particularly in view of the long life expectancies of people at age 65. To make matters worse, most of that wealth is held in the form of home equity, which cannot easily be converted to cash unless the house is sold or mortgaged. *Financial* assets like stocks and bonds, which are more readily convertible to cash, account for less than a third of all assets held by the aged.

As might be expected, there is a high correlation between wealth and income. In fact, the value of accumulated wealth rises disproportionately with income. Older people in the highest income quintile have 25 times more wealth than those in the lowest quintile.[5] Low-income persons *approaching* retirement age (ages 55–64) have median nonhousing wealth of less than $30,000. These people certainly won't be able to live off their wealth when they retire.

Income Sources   Table 5.2 and Figure 5.2 illustrate the consequences of these low savings accumulations. Notice in Table 5.2 that nearly 80 percent of the aged nonpoor receive dividends and interests, while only 33 percent of the aged poor get any income from stocks, savings accounts, and bonds. Moreover, the amount of such income is pitifully small, averaging less than $200 a year for poor households. By contrast, aged nonpoor households get over $4,000 a year—nearly a sixth of their income—in dividends and interest. If the poor had comparable portfolios of accumulated stocks, bonds, and savings, they would not be poor.

Squandered Income?   Two more questions arise with regard to the savings of the aged: First, did the aged poor ever possess enough resources to save for old age? And second, did they save what resources they had? The distinction is important for policy purposes because many observers still believe it is necessary to distinguish the deserving poor from the undeserving poor, even among the aged. From this perspective, an

---

[5]U.S. Bureau of the Census, *65+ in the United States* (Washington, DC: U.S. Government Printing Office, 1996), Table 4-6; also see Congressional Budget Office, *Baby Boomers in Retirement: An Early Perspective* (Washington, DC: U.S. Government Printing Office, 1993).

TABLE 5.2 Income Sources of Aged Households

	Percent of Households Receiving Income	
Income Source	*Poor*	*Nonpoor*
Earnings	8.9	36.4
Interest, dividends	33.2	76.0
Alimony	3.4	5.4
Pensions	8.2	49.4
Social security	80.9	94.0
Unemployment, disability, or veterans benefits	5.1	8.9
Welfare		
Cash welfare benefits	23.5	4.8
Food stamps	24.1	2.8
Housing assistance	18.0	4.3

Note: The term *household* refers here to individuals living alone or multiperson households in which any member is 65 or over; 1994 data.

Source: U.S. House of Representatives, Committee on Ways and Means, *1996 Green Book* (Washington, DC: U.S. Government Printing Office, 1996).

impoverished older individual may simply be suffering the consequences of an earlier Flawed Character, one which chose to make merry while the sun was shining rather than save for a rainy day.

There is no evidence that the aged poor enjoyed especially lascivious or spendthrift lives. A University of Michigan study suggests that the aged poor had never earned enough income to provide for a comfortable living either before or after retirement. A Congressional review of poverty among older women concluded that:

> Many have been poor or low income for a large part of their lives. If they spent time in the labor force, it was at low paying and often intermittent jobs; many were married to someone who was a low-wage worker. The low-income and poor elderly did not, in their younger years, have the kind of work and income history that would permit accumulation of savings, pensions, and large social security benefits. A recent study on the causes of poverty among widows found that these women were likely to have had husbands whose health was poor, with the concomitant problems of lower earnings, less savings (or perhaps depleted savings), early labor force withdrawal due to health factors and early death. About half of poor widows had been poor before widowhood, and half became poor upon widowhood either through lack of accrual of retirement income or because of medical or death expenses.[6]

One observer of these statistics concluded that "the misery of their old age is simply the conclusion to a life of misery. They are the ones who have grown up, lived, and will die under conditions of poverty."[7] Many, probably most, of the aged poor were always in or on the margin of poverty.

---

[6]Congressional Research Service, *Retirement Income for an Aging Population* (Washington, DC: U.S. Government Printing Office, 1987), p. 45.

[7]Harrington, *The Other America,* p. 105.

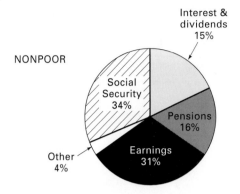

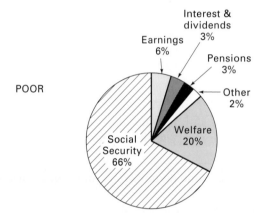

Source: U.S. House of Representatives, Committee on Ways and Means, *1996 Green Book,* p. 962.

FIGURE 5.2 Relative Income Sources of Poor and Nonpoor Aged Households

Some individuals do experience impoverishment for the first time, however, as they grow old. Just as few people think about dying, few ever plan to grow old and retire. Only a small number of people make provisions for old age in spite of statistical evidence showing the diminished income during retirement. People's essential optimism is revealed in consumer surveys such as one disclosing that families who have not had as much as $500 in the bank during the last five years confidently anticipate a comfortable retirement. Confidence fades with age, however; among younger families, only 9 percent foresee hard times after retirement; among middle-aged families, 16 percent sense trouble ahead. But when they reach old age, at least 25 percent of these individuals end up in poverty.[8] Projections for *future* poverty of today's workers are, therefore, discouraging.[9]

---

[8]The substantial discrepancy between actual saving rates and those required to support postretirement living standards is illustrated in James A. Schulz and Guy Carrin, "The Role of Savings and Pension Systems in Maintaining Living Standards in Retirement," *Journal of Human Resources* (Summer 1972).

[9]The slowdown in wage growth during the 1970s and 1980s will be reflected in diminished retirement incomes; see Frank Levy and Richard C. Michel, *The Economic Future of American Families* (Washington, DC: Urban Institute, 1991).

Pensions   Aside from their own savings, aged persons may draw income either from private pension plans or Social Security. In fact, a 1981 poll sponsored by the President's Commission on Pension Policy disclosed that most workers expect Social Security and private pensions to provide most of their retirement income. Unfortunately, pension plans are often great disillusionments. Many workers confidently subscribe to company pension plans only to find that they have no pension rights upon retirement. If a worker is laid off or disabled before working, say, nine years with the same firm, he or she may not be eligible for any pension payments.

Many workers fail to acquire pension rights because they work for companies without pension plans (most small firms), or because they don't work long enough for a company with pensions. At present, less than 50 percent of all aged people receive private pensions. Moreover, these pensions are generally reserved for the *nonpoor* aged, that is, for those with higher preretirement earnings and savings. Only 8 percent of all aged poor households receive a private pension and those pension benefits account for only 3 percent of their total income (see Table 5.2 and Figure 5.2). Furthermore, even those receiving private pension benefits are often disappointed to learn that private pensions are typically not adjusted for inflation. As a result, the real value of private pensions diminishes with age.

Social Security   Social Security payments reach far more of the aged—90 percent presently—and constitute the single most important source of income for the elderly. Social Security benefits account for one-third of the total income of aged nonpoor families and a whopping two-thirds of the income of the aged poor. Moreover, Social Security retirement benefits are adjusted for inflation, thereby retaining their real value. Nevertheless, Social Security benefits alone do not assure an adequate income. Because the amount of monthly benefits depends in large part on the amount of prior earnings, individuals who are poor while working are likely to be poor after retirement as well.

Families   Another source of potential support for the aged may be found in their own families. The extended family unit has in the past represented the most dependable source of social and economic security for many people. However, industrialization and urbanization have tended to disintegrate the extended family, leaving each core family unit to fend for itself. Despite the material and social benefits this development yields for others, it deprives the aged of a source of support, immediate companionship, and in many cases a roof over their heads. Today, less than a third of the aged live with relatives, and of those who do not, less than 3 percent receive any income support from their offspring. Accordingly, relatives rarely constitute a source of economic security for the aged and cannot be expected to provide an escape from poverty.

Even when the aged are supported by their families, such support may be regarded as a mixed blessing. Many aged people live with relatives simply because they cannot afford to live by themselves. Moreover, they may not be counted as poor because the income of the household in which they live exceeds poverty standards. Yet, these older people are truly dependent if their living arrangements are dictated solely by economic necessity. The basic issue is not whether the aged live with their relatives or not, but whether the aged command enough economic resources to make a free choice of their own.

Welfare   Table 5.2 and Figure 5.2 show how the aged poor have come to depend on welfare for basic support. Over one out of three aged poor individuals receives cash welfare benefits, food stamps, or a housing subsidy. Taken together, this welfare assistance accounts for one-fifth of their total income. Clearly, the aged poor would be much poorer without welfare—and destitute without Social Security.

Rising Health Costs

The serious decline in the sources and amounts of income that the aged command creates enough momentum to impoverish a high proportion of these individuals. But dwindling incomes are not their only burden; the aged also confront large, and often rising, expenses. The interaction of these two forces is a virtual guarantee that a still higher proportion of the aged will experience material want before they die.

Everyone realizes that the aged are likely to experience high rates of sickness and disability. Over half of the people over age 65 have arthritis. Aged individuals also have a high incidence of high blood pressure, hearing impairments, heart disease, cataracts, and bone deterioration. As a result of these and other ailments, only one out of six older persons rates their own health as "excellent." The elderly poor are more likely to rate their health "poor" or "fair" than "excellent" or "very good."

As people age, they not only incur more illness, but also lose the ability to perform everyday tasks. The Activities of Daily Living (ADLs) include eating, bathing, dressing, toileting, and simply getting in and out of a bed or a chair. As people age, they need more and more assistance with these activities. As Figure 5.3 shows, the "old old" are particularly dependent on ADL assistance.

The declining health and functional capacity of older persons not only increases their physical dependence on others, but also adds to their financial burden. The average health bill per year for a person 65 or older is over $6,000 including the expenses of hospital care, physician's services, and all drugs. This is a bill the average aged person cannot afford to pay. These health costs are equal to one-third of an aged individual's annual income and over 50 percent of yearly income if he or she is old and poor.

Even these average expenses understate the burden of illness for those most sick. Hospitalization expenditures, for example, are incurred by only a portion of the poor, and these individuals pay all the costs, not just the "average" cost. Furthermore, those who have endured impoverishment and hard labor the longest are most likely to be sick and least able to afford the costs of sickness. Accordingly, many individuals who manage to fend off poverty during their working years succumb to financial impoverishment when illness strikes. For those who have always been poor, illness in old age represents one more burden and indignity.

Medicare and Medicaid have done a great deal to reduce the threat of impoverishment among the aged due to illness. By providing subsidized medical insurance (Medicare) and the purchasing power required to buy needed medical services (Medicaid), the government has greatly diminished a major financial burden of the aged. However, the financial protection provided by Medicare and Medicaid is not complete. Like most private health insurance plans, Medicare does not pay all medical costs and there are limits on the type and extent of coverage. As a consequence, the elderly

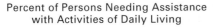

Percent of Persons Needing Assistance
with Activities of Daily Living

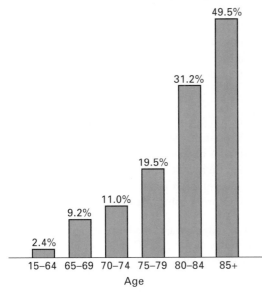

Source: U.S. Bureau of the Census, *65+ in the United States* (Washington, DC: U.S. Government Printing Office, 1996), Figure 3–13.

FIGURE 5.3 Functional Disability of the Aged

spend nearly 12 percent of their incomes on health care, more than triple the percentage spent by nonelderly households.

Medicaid pays a larger share of the medical expenses of aged recipients. However, an individual must be poor to receive Medicaid benefits. Typically, this means that an aged individual must exhaust most personal income and assets before becoming eligible for Medicaid assistance. Moreover, neither Medicaid nor Medicare provides preventive health care. As a consequence, all too many older poor people are burdened with both discomfort and poverty, sometimes even relegated to unsympathetic and inadequate institutions to wait idly for death.

Tax Burdens

In many areas of the country, the aged are also burdened by taxes, particularly property taxes. For most of the aged, their homes represent the only significant asset they possess and embody a lifetime of savings. But because local property taxes continue to rise, many of the aged find themselves unable to maintain their investment. Property taxes alone may consume as much as 30 percent of the incomes of aged persons living just above the poverty line. As a result, the U.S. Senate Special Committee on Aging reports that hundreds of thousands of aged persons are driven from their homes by mounting property taxes. Still more are forced to liquidate other assets to pay their taxes. Thus, the only visible economic security of many of the aged may itself contribute to their impoverishment.

Home ownership often imposes another unforeseen cost. Many of the aged purchased their homes in central cities at a time when inner city locations seemed most attractive. As the years have passed, however, inner city neighborhoods have deteriorated. Younger families have sought the freshness and space of the suburbs, while racial segregation and hostility have contributed to a general depreciation of inner city property values. As a consequence, the aged often find themselves socially and racially isolated in neighborhoods they once thought attractive. They cannot afford to move because the value of their homes has fallen while suburban values have skyrocketed. Hence, they can only hold on until the burden of property taxes leads them to rented quarters or nursing homes.

Making Do

An aged person with diminishing income and mounting expenses has little hope for economic security. An aged person's chances have simply run out; past labors and thrift are able only to postpone impoverishment in most cases. The question arises, then, as to how the aged actually manage in the face of such imposing circumstances. The most succinct answer came forth in hearings before a committee of the U.S. Senate:

> "How do you manage?" I asked. A lady replied, "It's hard, Pat, oh, it's hard." "Well, What do you do?" "We don't do," someone replied, "That's how we manage!"
>
> "I don't" is a most accurate description of the older adult living in retirement. I don't entertain. I don't go out with friends. I don't eat in restaurants. I don't go to movies. I don't buy new clothes. I don't ride subways and buses. I don't buy cake. I don't eat a lot. I don't take care of my health like I should. I don't, I don't, I don't.[10]

For the aged, then, growing older means giving up one thing after another until there is nothing left. When that time comes, they can only wait for death; sometime before that, they are unquestionably poor.

Assessing Causation

Poverty among the aged is not a natural product of biological development. Rather, it emerges from a diminution of income sources, a lack of accumulated resources, and frequently rising expenses. Maintaining income sources or providing financial relief from taxation and illness will effectively prevent many aged individuals from falling into poverty. For others, however, poverty does not emerge in old age but is, instead, a continuing condition.[11] The causes of poverty for these people must be sought elsewhere and earlier. Identifying and eliminating the causes of poverty for the nonaged will help to prevent later poverty among the aged.

HEALTH

One way to assure individuals greater prosperity and security in old age is to maintain their good health in younger years. Better health contributes to economic security in two important ways: by permitting persons to earn more income and by reducing fi-

---

[10]Special Committee on Aging, *Economics of Aging: Toward a Full Share in Abundance,* U.S. Senate, 91st Cong., 2d session, 1970 (Washington, DC: U.S. Government Printing Office, 1970), p. 34.

[11]This is particularly true in nonmetropolitan areas; see Diane McLaughlin and Karen C. Holden, "Nonmetropolitan Elderly Women: A Portrait of Economic Vulnerability," *Journal of Applied Gerontology* (September 1993), pp. 320–334.

nancial expenditures arising from health needs. All other things being equal, a person with good health is likely to accumulate greater financial reserves when young and to need them less when old.

Health Costs

It is not difficult to surmise the potential that poor health has for undermining a family's economic security. A sick or disabled parent not only fails to earn a full income; he also increases household expenses. A sick or disabled child may limit a parent's ability to work and also add to household expenses.

Figure 5.4 illustrates the income dimension of the health problem. The probability of having a low income is highly correlated with physical and mental disability. A nondisabled person has only a 13 percent probability of low-income status. Any disability more than doubles the odds of low-income status. A severe disability raises the risk of poverty even further.

Ill health and disability not only reduce incomes, but also increase household expenses. In 1997 Americans spent roughly $1 trillion on health maintenance and care. This works out to nearly $4,000 per person per year. While the lion's share of these expenses fall on the aged population, even the average worker is at financial risk when illness or disability occurs.

Causality

The relationship between health and income status is not simple enough, however, to permit the use of averages in ascertaining the cost of illness to the poor. Just as illness may tend to deplete a family's resources and leave it poor, so may poverty itself increase the likelihood of getting sick. Poor families suffer notoriously from chronic malnutrition and unsanitary environments, both of which nurture ill health. As a consequence, they are apt to be ill or disabled more often than the nonpoor. Poor families have higher disease and mortality rates and miss more than twice as many days of work due to illness than do the nonpoor.

Poverty and illness, then, interact in a reciprocal relationship. As shown in Figure 5.5, illness leads to poverty and poverty leads to poor health. However, the relationship is not equally strong in both directions. We may still ask how many families or persons actually fall into poverty as a result of illness or disability, that is, ask to what extent poverty is actually caused by ill health. Many persons were poor before they were sick, so we cannot claim that illness caused their poverty. At most, we may say that illness maintains their poverty or that it makes poverty more miserable.

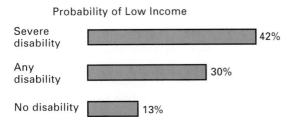

Probability of Low Income

Severe disability — 42%

Any disability — 30%

No disability — 13%

Source: 1994–1995 data for persons aged 22 to 64 years old from U.S. Bureau of the Census, *Americans with Disabilities, 1994–1995* (Washington, DC: U.S. Government Printing Office, 1997).

FIGURE 5.4   Disability and Poverty

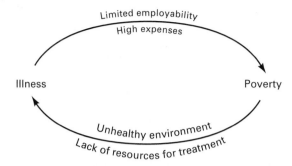

FIGURE 5.5   Illness and Poverty

The search for causal significance thus centers on the question of how many non-poor persons sink into poverty as a result of illness or disability. The answer, of course, depends on how far above the poverty line families begin and how much illness they contract. Also important is the extent to which families are protected by insurance from the impositions of work loss and medical expenses.

A family need not be far above the poverty line to have an adequate margin against the burdens of ill health. Our 1995 poverty line for a family of four was just under $16,000. Average yearly medical expenses for a family this size are around $3,000 per year. Hence, for the typical family, an income of over $19,000 would easily prevent slippage into poverty as a result of illness. Moreover, as we have already suggested, the incidence of illness falls as income rises, further immunizing the nonpoor against poverty.

Health Insurance

Health insurance is another important component of economic security. In the event of severe illness or disability, health insurance can protect a family's finances from an on-slaught of medical expenses. Even the more routine medical problems that can upset household budgets are typically alleviated by insurance.

The problem with health insurance is that not everyone has it. In 1996, the Congressional Budget Office estimated that 41 million Americans had no health insurance. Although many of these uninsured individuals had enough income to purchase insurance, people in poverty are the most likely to be uninsured. As Table 5.3 shows, only 22 percent of the poor have private health insurance as compared to 70 percent coverage among the nonpoor. In large part, the difference in coverage is explained by the lower labor force participation of the poor. Because most private health insurance is employer-based, people without jobs are less likely to be covered. Even when health insurance is available, poor people often choose not to take it. For them, the health insurance may be viewed as a lower priority than rent, food, or other essentials.

The lack of private health insurance does not mean that poor people get no health care. About half of the poverty population is eligible for the government's Medicaid program, which pays hospital and doctor bills. To become eligible for Medicaid, however, a family must first deplete its own savings. In addition, many doctors and hos-

TABLE 5.3   Health Insurance Coverage

	Percent with Coverage	
Insurance Coverage	*Poor*	*Nonpoor*
Private insurance	22	70
Medicare	12	13
Medicaid	46	12
Military	2	3
No coverage	31	16

Source: U.S. Bureau of the Census, Current Population Survey, March 1997.

pitals try to avoid treating Medicaid patients because of the paperwork and cost limits the program imposes.

Another option for poor people is to use emergency rooms as their basic source of health services. Emergency room services are not oriented toward *preventive* health care, however. As a result, poor people may wait too long before diagnosing or treating health problems. Emergency rooms may also refuse to treat patients without the ability to pay.[12]

Although the lack of private health insurance reduces the quality and quantity of health care received by the poor, it may not be a major cause of poverty. Health problems will push a family into poverty only if the related costs are substantial and uninsured. Even then, the poverty experience may be only temporary. Nevertheless, the economic security of families with incomes just above the poverty line is always threatened by illness or injury even if relatively few fall into poverty for those reasons.

Intergenerational Links

The intergenerational links between health and poverty are more discouraging. Until now, we have considered only the impact of health on an existing family's economic status. But the illness bred by poverty may leave scars that last for generations. A child born to a poverty-stricken mother is likely to be undernourished both before and after birth. Furthermore, the child is less likely to receive proper postnatal care, to be immunized against disease, or even to have his or her eyes and teeth examined. As a result, the child is likely to grow up prone to illness and poverty, and, in the most insidious of cases, be impaired by organic brain damage. A study by the U.S. Department of Health, Education, and Welfare reported that poor children

Suffer 23 percent more hearing impairment.

Do not grow as tall as other children.

Are more likely to have low hemoglobin values during their years of growth.

---

[12]Thirteen percent of uninsured families fail to get all the medical care they feel they need; see Paul Starr, "Health Care for the Poor: The Past Twenty Years," in *Fighting Poverty,* eds. S. Danziger and D. Weinberg (Cambridge, MA: Harvard University Press, 1986), p. 118.

Suffer a higher incidence of impetigo, gastrointestinal diseases, parasitic diseases, and urinary-tract infections.

In urban areas, are more often the victims of lead-paint poisoning and insect and rodent bites.[13]

To what extent do these childhood health impairments affect later education, job skills, or income? No one knows for sure. However, there is a strong suspicion that poverty in one generation may result in illnesses and disabilities that become a significant cause of poverty in the next generation.[14]

Mental Health

Mental health, as well as physical health, is an important dimension of poverty. The issue here is the same as before: Does mental disability lead downward to the slums, or does slum life accentuate tendencies toward mental illness? The former question embodies a popular "drift" hypothesis. According to this thesis, failures from all walks of life drift into the slums, creating our present poor population. The available evidence, however, once again shatters the popular myth. One of the few detailed studies undertaken on this subject traced the socioeconomic histories of schizophrenic individuals. The results were unambiguous: 91 percent of such patients were in the same socioeconomic class as their parents.[15] There was no evidence of substantial drift. Instead, the results suggest that poverty is more likely to lead to ill health than to result from it.

SUMMARY

Age and illness are highly visible correlates of poverty and, because of this, are often assumed to bear a causal relationship to economic impoverishment. The reasoning behind such an assumption is simple and appears eminently plausible. As logical as such a conclusion is, however, there are several reasons for attaching only limited causal importance to the impact of age and illness. Many of the aged poor, for example, were always poor, so that aging itself causes little change in their economic status. Similarly, poor persons are more prone to illness, and illness for them represents no sudden loss of economic well-being. Even for those who are driven to poverty for the first time by age or illness, the loss of economic status is occasioned by a variety of forces, none of which is inseparable from the natural processes of aging and illness.

Even though age and illness do not explain a high proportion of poverty, there are identifiable subgroups for whom the causal link is particularly threatening. Among

---

[13]U.S. Department of Health, Education and Welfare, Office of Child Health Affairs, *A Proposal for New Federal Leadership in Maternal and Child Health Care in the United States* (Washington, DC: U.S. Government Printing Office, 1976), pp. 9–10, 15.

[14]Poverty is shown to have a greater effect on children's health than family structure or race in L. Montgomery, J. Kiely, and G. Pappas, "The Effects of Poverty, Race, and Family Structure on U.S. Children's Health," *American Journal of Public Health* (October 1996), pp. 1401–1405. See also Roger L. Hurley, *Poverty and Mental Retardation: A Causal Relationship* (Trenton, NJ: New Jersey Department of Institutions and Agencies, April 1968).

[15]The effects of socioeconomic background on IQ are discussed in Chapter 8. Also see R. J. Karp, ed., *Malnourished Children in the United States* (New York: Springer, 1993).

the aged, the most vulnerable to poverty are the old old who are at risk of exhausting their financial reserves and confront increasing health problems. Illness and disability are also especially costly for younger families without health insurance who are already perilously close to the poverty threshold.

FURTHER READING

Age

Borus, Michael E., et al., eds., *The Older Worker.* Madison, WI: Industrial Relations Research Association, 1988.

Congressional Budget Office, *Baby Boomers in Retirement: An Early Perspective.* Washington, DC: U.S. Government Printing Office, 1993.

President's Commission on Pension Policy, *Coming of Age: Toward a National Retirement Income Policy.* Washington, DC: U.S. Government Printing Office, 1981.

Schace, K. W., and W. A. Achenbaum, eds., *Social Impact on Aging.* New York: Springer, 1993.

Schulz, James, *The Economics of Aging,* 5th ed. Westport, CN: Greenwood, 1992.

U.S. Bureau of the Census, *65+ in the United States.* Washington, DC: U.S. Government Printing Office, 1996.

U.S. Senate, Special Committee on Aging, *Developments in Aging.* Washington, DC: U.S. Government Printing Office, annual.

Wise, David A., ed., *Topics in the Economics of Aging.* Chicago: University of Chicago Press, 1992.

Health

Davis, Karen, "Access to Health Care in a Cost-Conscious Society," *Access to Social Care: Who Shall Decide What?* ed. Helen Rehr. Lexington, MA: Ginn Press, 1986.

Ferrara, Peter, and Kevin Hopkins, "Health Status of the Poor," *Welfare Dependency,* ed. Hopkins. Alexandria, VA: Hudson Institute, 1987.

Karp, Robert J., ed., *Malnourished Children in the United States.* New York: Springer, 1993.

Montgomery, Laura E., John L. Kiely, and Gregory Pappas, "The Effects of Poverty, Race, and Family Structure on U.S. Children's Health," *American Journal of Public Health* (October 1996).

Starr, Paul, "Health Care for the Poor: The Past Twenty Years," in *Fighting Poverty,* eds. S. Danziger and D. Weinberg. Cambridge, MA: Harvard University Press, 1986.

U.S. Bipartisan Commission on Comprehensive Health Care, *Fewer Resources, Greater Burdens: Medical Care Coverage for Low Income Elderly People.* Washington, DC: U.S. Government Printing Office, 1990.

Wolfe, Barbara L., "Reform of Health Care for the Nonelderly Poor," in *Confronting Poverty,* eds. S. Danziger, G. Sandefur, and D. Weinberg. Cambridge, MA: Harvard University Press, 1994.

CHAPTER

Family Size and Structure

6

There are two persistent accusations leveled against the poor. One is that the poor have too many babies; the other is that they do not maintain stable families. The implication in both cases is that the poor have flawed characters: They exhibit too little self-control and are thus responsible for much of their own plight. These accusations are examined in this chapter. As in Chapter 5, the focus of the analysis is on probable causation, highlighting the temporal relationship between poverty and family size or status. Did either large family size or family instability precede economic impoverishment? If so, then there may be some validity to the claim that the poor caused their own poverty by creating conditions that make it difficult or impossible to hold a job that pays an adequate income.

Although the sequence of events is important in establishing causality, it does not resolve the issue of culpability. Even in cases where family instability precedes a decline into poverty, flawed characters may not be the only explanation. Restricted opportunities may have contributed to family breakup or limited the attractiveness of marriage. The welfare system (Big Brother) may also create perverse incentives for family breakup and more children.

In cases where poverty precedes family breakup or additional childbearing, the causal analysis is simpler. Here there is no reason to single out family size or status as a cause of poverty. At the most, such conditions may perpetuate or worsen poverty that already existed.

FAMILY SIZE

Children are a distinct threat to the financial security of a family. Additional children not only increase the need for more income but also limit the ability of parents to earn it. More children imply a greater demand for homemaker services, including child care, meal preparation, transportation, and other household activities. As that burden grows, it becomes more difficult to supply labor in the outside job market. If the parents choose to pay someone else to provide child-care services, they may find that the net income from outside employment is too small. These considerations make paid employment increasingly difficult or financially unrewarding as family size increases. For single parents, the arithmetic of outside (paid) employment is even worse.

Poverty Rates

The combination of increased financial need and more limited employability implies that larger families will be more prone to poverty. Figure 6.1 confirms this expectation. In both two-parent and one-parent families there is a dramatic increase in the incidence of poverty as family size increases. Among two-parent families, the poverty rate starts at less than 5 percent if there is only one child and jumps to 30 percent if there are five or more children. One-parent families have much higher poverty rates at all family sizes. Even here, however, the poverty rate nearly triples as the number of children increases from one to five or more. Over 80 percent of female-headed families with at least five children are poor.

The Potential Impact

To grasp the implications of larger family sizes among the poor, we may ask how many larger poor families would move out of poverty if they had fewer family members. For example, we know that five-member families were considered poor if their 1995 incomes were under $18,408 but the same poverty standard for a family of four was $15,569. Hence, any family of five whose income was less than $18,408 but more than $15,569 would no longer be counted as poor if it could somehow eliminate one family member. Or, to put it slightly differently, we may say that such a family would not have fallen into poverty if it had bred one less child. By counting the total number of such families, we may estimate the potential of family planning as a means for reducing poverty.

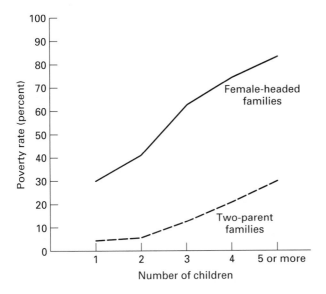

Source: U.S. Bureau of the Census (1995 data).

FIGURE 6.1 Poverty Rates, by Family Size

The statistical exercise required to make such an estimate is carried out on two levels. The first calculation tells how many larger poor families (of five or more persons) would move out of poverty if they had one less member. Among poor five-person families, we look for all those whose current income could support four persons; among six-person families, incomes that will support five people, and so on. Based on these calculations, we observe that 330,000 poor families, a total of nearly 2 million individuals, would no longer be counted as poor if each family had one person less.

The second calculation imposes an even stricter constraint on family size. Rather than trim all larger poor families by one person, it reduces all such families to the standard four persons. Hence, six-person families statistically lose two members, and their poverty line falls from $20,804 to $15,569. This kind of standardization creates an astounding reduction in the size of the poverty population. On these assumptions, over 500,000 families (3.3 million individuals)—nearly one-eighth of all the nonaged poor—would no longer be counted as poor.

This kind of statistical exercise leads us to the conclusion that mild restraints on family size (one person less) would reduce the nonaged poverty population by 6 percent, while severe limits on family size (maximum of four) would effect a 12 percent reduction in the number of poor. Such results underscore the potential importance of the causal link between family size and poverty. Before turning to a discussion of causality, however, we need to consider the assumptions underlying this statistical exercise.

First, our statistical exercise tacitly assumes that there is no positive relationship between family size and family income. The statistical elimination of one family member is presumed to have no effect on family income. But this is not a realistic assumption. The amount of welfare, food stamps, or other assistance a family gets depends on its size. More children, then, implies more welfare. If we were to eliminate one family member, we would also have to reduce the family's income. As a result, far fewer families would escape poverty than the foregoing arithmetic implies. Since over half of all poor families receive some form of welfare benefit, this is a serious qualification to our calculations.

Family income may also rise with family size for other reasons. The father of the family may be impelled to work overtime or at a second job as his family responsibilities expand; hence, larger families may constitute a special kind of incentive to work. Larger families may also enable other family members to work; they may have older children who can contribute directly to family income by working part-time or who enable the mother to work by assuming child-care responsibilities.[1] Hence, the statistical reduction previously carried out may diminish family income more than it reduces family needs.

Further consideration must also be given to those families and persons whom we suppose statistically to escape poverty by our calculations. Some family members are constrained by our arithmetic to disappear, and we can ignore them for the moment. Surviving family members, however, improve their economic status only marginally. Their statistical "escape" is, therefore, not very impressive. Almost all such families remain within a few hundred dollars of our poverty standards, even after they manage to leave the poverty population.

---

[1]The impact of household size and composition on a single mother's supply of labor is examined in Janis Barry-Figueroa and Edwin Melendez, "The Importance of Family Members in Determining the Labor Supply of Puerto Rican, Black, and White Single Mothers," *Social Science Quarterly* (December 1993), pp. 867–883.

Declining Family Size

The foregoing purely statistical exercise has an historical parallel. More women are electing not to have children and those that do become mothers are bearing fewer children. This downward trend in childbearing has been visible for over 30 years. In the 1960s, roughly one-third of all children were in families with at least four children. In 1990 only 15 percent of all children had so many siblings. According to estimates by Peter Gottschalk and Sheldon Danziger, this reduction in family size has had a dramatic impact on poverty, cutting the poverty rate by roughly a fifth below the trend based on the larger family sizes that prevailed in the 1960s.[2]

The Causal Relation

Theory and historical experience thus both confirm the importance of family size in shaping poverty trends. These statistics do not settle the question of causation, however. There is no evidence yet that larger families now in poverty enjoyed a higher standard of living when they were smaller. It could be that more children simply lengthen a family's stay in the poverty population rather than cause it to fall from non-poverty to poverty. Large family size thus retards the flow of people moving out of poverty and contributes over time to an expansion of the poverty population. By itself, however, it creates very little new poverty.

Against this background, we must also ponder the accumulation of evidence suggesting that the poor continue to have less access to birth control information. Public schools, especially in low-income areas, are still reluctant to provide birth control information, while public welfare authorities are, in most cases, prohibited from providing it.[3] Low-income families are also less able to afford abortions, even if they are desired. Even in quasi-public clinics, abortions cost several hundred dollars. Moreover, Congress has greatly limited the availability of Medicaid or other income transfers to pay for abortions.

Because of these constraints, poor families often end up with more children than other families, not because they want them, but because they are unable to prevent them. One study by the National Academy of Sciences indicated that over one-third of the least educated families had unwanted children, and a survey of welfare mothers in New York yielded similar findings. Even more revealing are studies that indicate the extent to which unwanted births increase at lower income levels; 17 percent of all nonpoor families report unwanted births, compared to 26 percent for near-poor families, and a whopping 42 percent for poor families.[4] This has become an urgent concern in recent years as unmarried teenage mothers have become the fastest growing subgroup in the poverty population. This is not so much a question of family *size*, however, as a problem of family *formation*.

---

[2]Peter Gottschalk and Sheldon Danziger, "Family Structure, Family Size and Family Income," in *Uneven Tides*, eds. Danziger and Gottschalk (New York: Russell Sage, 1993), pp. 167–193.

[3]However, a universal sex-education program in New Jersey revealed that sex education alone is no panacea; see Barbara Defoe Whitehead, "The Failure of Sex Education," *Atlantic Monthly* (October 1994).

[4]"Why the Poor Get Children: Findings of Two Major Studies," *Newsweek*, June 19, 1972. See also James Cramer, "Births, Expected Family Size, and Poverty," in *Five Thousand Families: Patterns of Economic Progress*, ed. James N. Morgan (Ann Arbor, MI: Institute for Social Research, 1974); Sylvia B. Perlman, Lorraine Klerman, and E. Milling Kinard, "The Use of Socioeconomic Data to Predict Teenage Birth Rates," *Public Health Reports* (July–August 1981); and Joy G. Dryfoos, "Contraceptive Use, Pregnancy Intentions and Pregnancy Outcomes Among U.S. Women," *Family Planning Perspectives* (March/April 1982).

FAMILY STRUCTURE

The phenomenon of family formation raises one of the most contentious issues in poverty debates: the single-parent family. Single parenthood has transformed the demographic profile of America and feminized poverty. In the process it has spawned intense debates about why the traditional two-parent family has broken down and whether poverty can be eliminated in its absence.

Changing Family Patterns

Recent changes in family structure have been nothing short of dramatic. In 1960, nearly nine out of ten children lived with both parents. Today, only about seven out of ten children do so. As Table 6.1 shows, the percentage of children living with only one parent has nearly tripled. In most cases the single parent is the mother, but single fathers are also becoming more common.

 Although the image of female-headed families is popularly associated with race, the upsurge in single parenthood cuts across racial boundaries. Since at least 1950, black children have been much more likely than white children to live in female-headed families. Today, over half of all black children do so. White families are following the same trend, however. The percent of white children living in female-headed families has more than tripled since 1970 and is now around 20 percent. This has led Charles Murray to predict the emergence of a "white ghetto" dominated by the same fatherless families that have characterized urban black ghettos.[5]

 The spectacular growth of single-parent families reflects two distinct phenomena. The first is the increase in divorce rates. Since 1960, the divorce rate has more than doubled. This has led to a surge in "broken" families with the mother often maintaining an independent household for many years.

 The second source of growth in single parenthood has been a surge in births to unmarried women. These are not cases of family breakup but rather a failure of family formation. As Figure 6.2 illustrates, two-thirds of all black births and one-fifth of all white births are now to unmarried mothers. The problem is particularly evident among

TABLE 6.1 Living Arrangements of Children

Family Structure	Percent Distribution	
	1960	*1995*
Two-parent family	87.7%	68.7%
One-parent family		
Mother only	8.0	23.5
Father only	1.1	3.5
Other custodian	3.2	4.3
	100%	100%

Source: U.S. Congress, Ways and Means Committee, *1996 Green Book,* p. 1181.

---

[5]Charles Murray, "The Coming White Underclass," *Wall Street Journal* (October 29, 1993), p. A14.

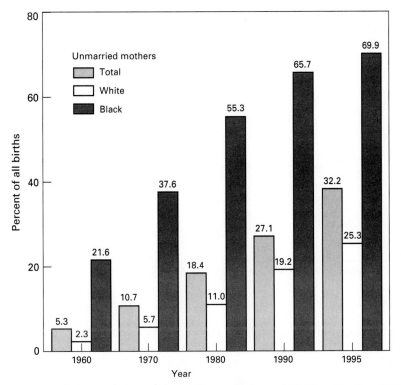

Source: U.S. Congress, Committee on Ways and Means, *1992 Green Book,* p. 1074; and National Center for Health Statistics, *Monthly Vital Statistics Report,* June 1997.

FIGURE 6.2   Percentage of Births to Unmarried Mothers, by Race for Selected Years

teenagers: Over 90 percent of births to black teenagers and more than half of births to white teenagers occur among unmarried mothers.

Table 6.2 illustrates how these demographic changes have altered the living arrangements of children. A generation ago very few children lived with a never-married parent. Widowed mothers were far more common than never-married mothers, both among whites and blacks. By 1995, however, never-married mothers were the most common single parent among blacks and had become a substantial presence among whites as well.

Economic Implications

The economic implications of these demographic trends are profound. A one-parent family is severely handicapped in the effort to attain economic security. The absence of one potential breadwinner is a large and obvious constraint on economic stability. Potential family income is reduced by *more than half* with the departure of one parent. Where two parents exist in the family, one parent can devote full-time to labor-market activity while the other is free to combine household and labor-market activity. When only one parent resides in the family, such flexibility is diminished. The single parent is unable to devote all time to labor-market activity, at least not without paying someone

TABLE 6.2   Distribution of Children by Marital Status of Single Parents

PERCENT OF CHILDREN

Marital Status of Parent	White		Black		Hispanic	
	1960	*1995*	*1960*	*1995*	*1960*	*1995*
Never married	1.6	23.6	9.6	54.7	19.8	37.3
Married, spouse absent (including separated)	41.1	23.9	57.2	20.9	40.6	30.1
Divorced	28.4	48.1	11.9	20.5	30.6	28.0
Widowed	29.0	4.5	21.3	3.9	8.9	4.5
Total	100.0	100.0	100.0	100.0	100.0	100.0
Number of children (in millions)	3.9	11.7	1.9	6.4	1.2	3.2

Source: U.S. Congress, Committee on Ways and Means, *1996 Green Book,* Tables G-7 to G-9.

else to assume household responsibilities. Hence, the potential net income of a one-parent family is often closer to one-third rather than to one-half of a two-parent family's income. If women's employment opportunities in the labor market are further constricted by conventional sexual stereotypes, their potential income will be lower still. Accordingly, one-parent families bear an extraordinarily high risk of economic impoverishment.[6]

The origin of single parenthood will also affect economic prospects. A divorced mother may have a home, a car, or other household property accumulated during her marriage. She may also be entitled to alimony or child-support payments. By contrast, a never-married mother will tend to have fewer assets, has no claim to alimony, and may face greater obstacles in securing child support from the father of her children.

The young age of most never-married mothers also handicaps their income potential. Teenage mothers, in particular, are likely to drop out of school. They have little or no work experience. By starting families before they accumulate human capital, they run the highest risk of living in poverty.[7]

Finally, society tends to be more sympathetic to widows and divorced mothers than to never-married mothers. Even though out-of-wedlock births have become more common, there is still a social stigma attached to them. This stigma may constrain the kinds of assistance society offers to never-married mothers.

---

[6]Single mothers also have more health problems and a greater likelihood of having disabled children, further limiting their earnings capacity; see Barbara L. Wolfe and Steven Hill, "The Health, Earnings Capacity, and Poverty of Single-Mother Families," in *Poverty and Prosperity in the Late Twentieth Century,* eds. D. Papadimitriou and E. Wolff (New York: St. Martins, 1993).

[7]For more discussion, see David Ellwood and Mary Jo Bane, *The Impact of AFDC on Family Structure and Living Arrangements* (Cambridge, MA: Harvard University Press, 1984); *Welfare Dependency,* ed. Hopkins, esp. Chapters 2, 4, 5, 6; and Douglas Besharov and Alison Quin, "Not All Families Are Created Equal," *The Public Interest* (Fall 1987).

Poverty Impact

The greater economic insecurity of single-parent families is apparent in poverty statistics. Table 6.3 summarizes the consequences. Notice first which family-race group has the most people in poverty—*white* families with only a mother present. The second largest group of families consists of white *two*-parent families.

Despite the large number of two-parent families in poverty, their poverty *rate* is very low, at only 7 percent. By contrast, one out of three white mother-only families is poor and one out of two minority mother-only families is poor. Hence, the *risk* of poverty escalates dramatically when mothers try to raise children on their own.

Families headed by women are not only more likely to be poor but are also more likely to *stay* in poverty longer. Never-married mothers are particularly prone to chronic poverty and welfare dependency.[8]

Table 6.3 also confirms that the economic handicaps of single parenthood are not confined to mothers. Fathers who attempt to raise children on their own also bear higher risks of poverty. Although poverty rates of father-only families are way below those of mother-only families, they are substantially above those of two-parent households.

These varied poverty rates underscore the importance of family structure as a potential cause of poverty. Table 6.3 implies that there would be a lot less poverty in America if two-parent families were more prevalent. This proposition was put to an interesting test by Professors Peter Gottschalk and Sheldon Danziger. They asked what today's poverty population would look like if family patterns had not changed so much. To answer this question, they used the poverty rates for different family types, like those depicted in Table 6.3. They then applied these to the patterns of family types

TABLE 6.3   Poverty by Family Structure and Race

Family Type and Race	Number in Poverty (thousands)	Poverty Rate (percent)
White		
Two parents	1,583	7.0
Mother only	1,980	35.6
Father only	276	18.4
Black		
Two parents	209	9.9
Mother only	1,533	53.2
Father only	79	23.4
Hispanic		
Two parents	657	22.6
Mother only	735	57.3
Father only	78	32.9

Source: U.S. Bureau of the Census (1995 data for families with children).

[8]See Mary Jo Bane and David J. Ellwood, *Welfare Realities* (Cambridge, MA: Harvard University Press, 1994), Chapter 2.

that existed in 1968. The resultant computations showed how much poverty would exist today if family types had not changed since 1968.[9]

The Gottschalk-Danziger computations pointed to single parenthood as a major cause of poverty. Had the pattern of family structure not changed since 1968, the poverty rate among blacks would be a third less and among whites a fifth less. Similar analyses by Robert Lerman and James Smith concluded that the surge in female-headed families completely explains the increase in childhood poverty since 1968.[10]

Causation

While the potential of family breakup (or nonformation) for impoverishment is clear, the direction of causation is once again not apparent. Indeed, the surge in female head-ship has ignited a raging controversy about cause and effect. While some observers point their fingers at Flawed Characters, others argue that family instability is a *symptom* of poverty, not an independent cause. They point to diminished economic opportunities for men, increased economic insecurity for families, and the lack of access to birth control as Restricted Opportunities that spawn single-parent families.[11]

Historically, there has seldom been any reluctance to "explain" the existence of one-parent families among blacks. As late as the 1920s, allegations of "animalism," "moral putridity," and "primitive sexualism" were often advanced as explanations for the great incidence of broken families among American blacks. The latent implication was always that blacks were responsible for their own destitution because they were morally, physically, or culturally unable to stabilize family relationships. Recent proponents of socioeconomic forces emphasize that family instability has worsened even when economic opportunities have been increasing. And they point out that instability among black families is substantially higher than among white families of similar income, education, and housing arrangements.[12]

Other observers place more blame on institutional barriers, particularly the welfare system. The nation's largest welfare program provides automatic income support for female-headed families but less certain support for intact families. This gives families a perverse incentive to split up. It also enables young unwed mothers to establish households on their own rather than with their own families. The result is a "blight of dependency" that undermines family stability.[13]

Still another explanation for the increasing feminization of poverty emphasizes the economic status of *males*. This perspective was first highlighted in the mid-1960s. Daniel Moynihan, then assistant U.S. Secretary of Labor (and later a U.S. Senator), focused on the relationship between unemployment rates and family structure. Looking

---

[9]Gottschalk and Danziger, "Family Structure, Family Size and Family Income."

[10]Robert Lerman, "The Impact of the Changing U.S. Family Structure on Child Poverty and Income Inequality," *Economics* (May 1996), pp. 119–139; James Smith, "Children Among the Poor," *Demography* (May 1989), pp. 235–248.

[11]For a forceful statement of this position, see Katha Pollit, "Subject to Debate," *Nation,* May 30, 1994. A critique is offered in Midge Decter, "Welfare Feminism," *Commentary,* July 1994.

[12]Kevin Hopkins, "Marriage, Marital Dissolution, and Remarriage" in *Welfare Dependency,* ed. Hopkins.

[13]For elaboration of this argument, see Charles Murray, "Does Welfare Bring More Babies?" *Public Interest* (Spring 1994), and *Losing Ground: American Social Policy, 1950–1980* (New York: Basic Books, 1984). Lowell Gallaway and Richard Wedder present a similar argument in *Poverty, Income, the Family and Public Policy,* study for Joint Economic Committee, U.S. Congress (Washington, DC: U.S. Government Printing Office, 1986).

at the trend of unemployment rates and family structures, Moynihan found that the rates of separation and divorce followed economic events very closely. Thus, the rate of separations among black women shot up shortly after the economy faltered, while it sank when the economy prospered (see Figure 6.3). Family stability was apparently the result, not the cause, of economic events. As a family faced increased unemployment and deprivation, the father's position as breadwinner and family head became untenable; divorce, separation, or desertion often followed.

Further support for this position was found in illegitimacy statistics: In poor black neighborhoods rates of illegitimacy were more than triple those of black neighborhoods with middle-class incomes. Again it appeared that family formation itself was significantly affected by economic circumstances. Those parents with little prospect for economic security foresaw little hope for family stability; they decided not to marry.

A. Philip Randolph, long a leader in labor and civil rights movements, found evidence similar to Moynihan's in World War II experience. During the exceptionally low unemployment years of the war, rates of divorce and illegitimacy among blacks took a sharp drop. Greater economic security thus manifested itself in greater family stability.

A variant on this economic perspective has been advanced by William Darity, Jr., and Samuel Myers, Jr. In 1981, there were only 86 black men for every 100 black women in the age group 25 to 44. Among whites the ratio was 100 to 100. Hence, a *shortage* of black men precludes many black women from forming two-parent families.[14] William Wilson and Kathryn Neckerman have emphasized that the pool of *marriageable* men has declined even more, especially for blacks. Specifically the ratio of *employed* men to women of similar age has declined sharply in the last decade for blacks. This gives young black women very few eligible prospects. Among whites, there has also been a decline in the ratio of marriageable young men, but it has been a less severe drop.[15]

Undoubtedly, social, cultural, institutional, and economic forces all influence family structure. It is difficult, however, to sort out these many forces and assign a

FIGURE 6.3 Black Unemployment and Separation Rates

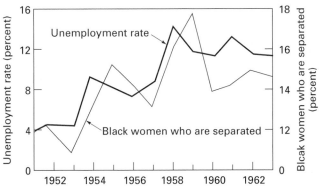

Source: U.S. Department of Labor, *The Negro Family: The Case for National Action* (March 1965), p. 22.

[14]William Darity, Jr., and Samuel L. Myers, Jr., "Changes in Black Family Structure: Implications for Welfare Dependency," *American Economic Review* (May 1983).

[15]William Julius Wilson and Kathryn M. Neckerman, "Poverty and Family Structure," in *Fighting Poverty,* eds. Danziger and Weinberg (Cambridge, MA: Harvard University Press, 1986).

quantitative weight to each. Nevertheless, there are ways of narrowing the range of uncertainty about whether marital instability causes poverty. The simplest way is to observe families over time. By observing whether marital instability precedes poverty, or vice versa, one can surmise the direction of causation.

This longitudinal approach was used by Mary Jo Bane. She discovered that a majority of poor female-headed *white* families were not poor prior to marital breakup. Among blacks, however, the ratios are reversed. Nearly two-thirds of black female-headed families were also poor prior to the split.[16]

Other data on family and income patterns seem to confirm these observations. Table 6.4 shows the income status of families in which no wife is present. These single-parent *male* families are also disproportionately poor. Such a family structure is nearly twice as likely in low-income circumstances (7.2 percent) as in higher-income circumstances (3.8 percent). Similar correlations exist between income and the probability of married men living without their wives. This suggests that the men who are missing from the single-parent *female* households in poverty are likely to be poor as well. Under these circumstances, the presumption that family breakup *caused* poverty is difficult to accept.

The impact of economic insecurity on marital instability was also noted in a seven-year study of 5,000 families. The families were first interviewed in 1967, then reinterviewed in each of the following years, until 1973. These observations, by the University of Michigan Survey Research Center, show how divorce and separation are often linked to economic status. In general, average family income turned out to be the best predictor of family stability for both whites and blacks. In addition, families that owned their own homes in 1967 or had significant savings were much more likely to be still intact in 1973. By contrast, families in which the husband was encountering employment problems in 1967 were more likely to have broken up by 1973.[17]

The relationship between family status and poverty, then, is best described as dynamic. Continued economic deprivation is likely to undermine a family's stability. At

TABLE 6.4   Single-Parent Male Families, by Income

Income Group	Percent of Families Headed by Male with No Wife Present
Under $10,000	7.2
$10,000–14,999	7.2
$15,000–24,999	7.1
$25,000–34,999	6.1
Over $35,000	<u>3.8</u>
All families	5.0

Source: U.S. Census Bureau (1995 data).

---

[16]Mary Jo Bane, "Household Composition and Poverty," in *Fighting Poverty,* eds. Danziger and Weinberg.

[17]Greg J. Duncan and James N. Morgan, eds., *Five Thousand American Families: Patterns of Economic Progress,* Vol. IV (Ann Arbor, MI: Institute for Social Research, 1976). A parallel study of low-income and welfare families in Camden, New Jersey, found that the husband's economic performance was important for family attitudes and stability; see Samuel Klausner, "Six Years in the Lives of the Impoverished: An Examination of the WIN Thesis" (Philadelphia: Center for Research on the Acts of Man, 1978).

some point, the family unit is ruptured, and the female-headed family is left to fend for itself. No loss of economic status is necessarily implied by the departure of the father, especially where he was unemployed and/or the female-headed unit turned to public assistance. In the University of Michigan study noted earlier, 20 percent of the families that broke up during the seven-year observation period did fall into poverty, and most of these turned to welfare. However, the average loss of income status amounted to only 6 percent of prior income status.[18]

While at any point in time a high proportion of poor families will be female-headed, family breakup cannot be identified as a major cause of poverty. Family disunity may help sustain poverty, but in most cases it appears that poverty preceded, and itself helped to cause, family dissolution.

This conclusion does not necessitate a purely economic deterministic view of family relations. Clearly, not all divorces and separations are occasioned by financial stress. Family dissolutions will continue to take place even after all families are assured of economic security. The point is that a disproportionately high percentage of family breakups occurs among the poor due to economic stress and that relatively few broken poor families were decidedly nonpoor before family dissolution occurred.

The causal sequence for never-married mothers is different. In these cases, childbirth itself may be the decisive factor in establishing another poor household. Even here, however, economic circumstances may have influenced both the decision to have a child and the decision not to marry. The Wilson thesis about a scarcity of marriageable men may be particularly relevant here, especially in view of the youthfulness of both the mother and father. The lack of visible career prospects may also convince young women that they have "nothing to lose" by having a baby.

Intriguing evidence on the "nothing-to-lose" syndrome comes from observing the *sisters* of teen mothers. While teen mothers are likely to be poor and welfare dependent, their sisters don't fare much better. Indeed, by the time they are in their mid-twenties, teen mothers and their sisters are economically indistinguishable.[19] This suggests that factors other than early childbirth are the primary cause of high poverty rates.

Although economic forces have played a significant role in shaping marital patterns, they are far from a complete explanation.[20] Single parenthood has spread beyond low-income neighborhoods and across national boundaries.[21] Moreover, single parenthood has continued to spread even when economic conditions have improved. Some even fear that single parenthood has taken on a life of its own.[22] As single parenthood

---

[18]Larger income losses are reported for nonpoor families; see Duncan and Morgan, *Five Thousand American Families*, Vol. IX.

[19]See Arline T. Geronimus and Sanders Korenman, "The Socioeconomic Costs of Teenage Childbearing: Evidence and Interpretation," *Demography* (May 1993), pp. 281–296; Jospeh J. Hotz, Susan W. McElroy, and Seth G. Sanders, "The Costs and Consequences of Teenage Childbearing for Mothers."

[20]Labor-market problems may explain no more than 20 percent of the increase in female headship, according to Robert D. Mare and Christopher Winship, "Socioeconomic Change and the Decline of Marriage for Blacks and Whites," in *The Urban Underclass*, eds. C. Jencks and P. Peterson. Also see Robert I. Lerman, "Employment Opportunities of Young Men and Family Formation," *American Economic Review* (May 1989), pp. 62–66.

[21]U.S. Congress, Ways and Means Committee, *1992 Green Book*, p. 1077.

[22]Rather than fearing the spread of single parenthood, Shere Hite views it as a positive development in the evolution of adult relationships and child development; see *Women as Revolutionary Agents of Change: The Hite Report and Beyond* (Madison, WI: University of Wisconsin Press, 1994).

has spread, it has altered expectations for family life. The disruptions accompanying family dissolutions may have also contributed to higher premarital birth rates of affected children.[23]

SUMMARY

Large families and broken families are among the most salient characteristics of the poor. Nearly 30 percent of all the poor are in families with at least five members; while 40 percent of the poor are in one-parent families, many of the latter are also from large families. Accordingly, there exists a strong presumption that family size and structure are important causes of poverty.

As is often the case, the lines of causality are not unambiguous. Poverty often precedes and even contributes to larger family size, family breakup, and premarital childbearing. By increasing stress or reducing opportunities, unfavorable economic circumstances can create demographic problems that perpetuate poverty. Available evidence suggests that most large and single-parent poor families were in or near poverty prior to a change in family size or structure. In these cases, family size and structure do more to deepen and prolong poverty than create it.

Although family size and structure do not account for as much poverty as might be expected, they are still significant causes of poverty. This is particularly true for unwed teenagers who are producing an increasing percentage of all teenage births and are most likely to become permanently poor and dependent.

FURTHER READING

On Family Size

Bogue, Donald J., "A Long Term Solution to the AFDC Problem: Prevention of Unwanted Pregnancy," *Social Science Review* (December 1975).

Gottschalk, Peter, and Sheldon Danziger, "Family Structure, Family Size, and Family Income," in *Uneven Tides,* eds. S. Danziger and P. Gottschalk. New York: Russell Sage, 1993.

Sheppard, Harold L. *The Effects of Family Planning on Poverty in the United States.* Kalamazoo, MI: Upjohn Institute, 1967.

Shostak, Arthur, "Birth Control and Poverty," in *New Perspectives on Poverty,* eds. Arthur Shostak and William Gomberg. Englewood Cliffs, NJ: Prentice-Hall, Inc., 1965.

Smith, James P., "Children Among the Poor," *Demography* (May 1989), pp. 235–248.

On Family Structure

Bane, Mary Jo, "Household Composition and Poverty," in *Fighting Poverty,* eds. Danziger and Weinberg. Cambridge, MA: Harvard University Press, 1986.

Ellwood, David T., *Poor Support.* New York: Basic Books, 1988, Chapter 5.

---

[23]The nature of the intergenerational link between single parenthood and second-generation premarital births is examined in Lawrence L. Wu and Brian Martinson, "Family Structure and the Risk of a Premarital Birth," *American Sociological Review* (April 1993), pp. 210–232. Also see James Q. Wilson, "On Gender," *The Public Interest* (Spring 1993), pp. 3–26, for a discussion of male childrearing in female-headed families.

Lerman, Robert, and Theodora Ooms, eds., *Young Unwed Fathers: Prospects and Policies.* Philadelphia, PA: Temple University Press, 1993.

Mare, Robert D., and Christopher Winship, "Socioeconomic Change and the Decline of Marriage for Blacks and Whites," in *The Urban Underclass,* eds. C. Jencks and P. Peterson. Washington, DC: Brookings, 1991, pp. 175–202.

McLanahan, Sara, and Gary Sandefur, *Growing Up with a Single Parent: What Hurts and What Helps.* Cambridge, MA: Harvard University Press, 1994.

Rodgers, Harrell, Jr., *Poor Women, Poor Families.* Armonk, NY: M.E. Sharpe, 1990.

Wu, Lawrence L., and Brian C. Martinson, "Family Structure and the Risk of a Premarital Birth," *American Sociological Review* (April 1993), pp. 210–232.

CHAPTER

The Underclass:
Culture and Race

When Lyndon Johnson initiated the War on Poverty in the mid-1960s, there were great expectations that the combination of a growing economy and targeted assistance would eliminate poverty in America. Since then, the U.S. economy has nearly tripled in size, the average household income has increased by 40 percent, and the employed labor force has grown by 60 million persons. In the same 30-year period the government has spent hundreds of billions of dollars on programs to aid the poor. But poverty hasn't disappeared. As we observed in Chapter 2, the number of poor people in America today is little changed from the number in 1965. Even during the strong economic expansion of the 1980s, the poverty population shrank only modestly.

This paradox of persistent poverty in an otherwise affluent America has reignited debates about the true origins of poverty. The most recent debate is largely focused on the proposition that an *underclass* exists that is so poor and socially isolated that it does not respond to mainstream prosperity, incentives, or values. The culture of the underclass spawns single-parent households (Chapter 6), discourages labor force participation (Chapters 3 and 4), and perpetuates poverty.

There are two distinct issues bound up in the underclass debate. The first focuses on the *existence* of such an economically and socially isolated subgroup. The second one focuses on *explanations.* Do members of the underclass have only themselves to blame (Flawed Characters) for their plight, or have economic obstacles (Restricted Opportunity) or perverse government incentives (Big Brother) fostered a separate and self-defeating way of life?

THE CULTURE OF POVERTY

In colonial America poverty was regarded as the manifestation of vice and sin. Because everyone except Negro slaves was thought to enjoy the opportunity to acquire economic security by his or her own labor, those who did not attain such security were deemed to be morally flawed. Poverty thus became proof of moral bankruptcy, and the poor were treated accordingly. In Pennsylvania, paupers had the shoulders of their right sleeves adorned with the letter P to warn unsuspecting strangers. In other jurisdictions the poor were sent packing, sometimes after a public whipping. As the puritanical Humane Society summarized the situation in 1809, ". . . by a just and inflexible law of Providence, misery is ordained to be the companion and punishment of vice."[1]

In more modern times the theoretical link of poverty to sin has not fared well. There now exists a general reluctance to ascribe the misery of the poor to the laws of Providence. Nevertheless, belief in the universality of economic opportunity remains firmly embedded in the American consciousness. Accordingly, we need a substitute explanation for the persistence of poverty in a land of abundance and opportunity. This, in part, explains the popularity of cultural theories of poverty. Most cultural theories of poverty assert that the poor lack sufficient desire and motivation to escape poverty. They allege that the goal of economic security is of lesser importance in the value matrix of the poor. Welfare mothers would rather have kids than jobs. Young men would rather "hustle" on street corners than accept a regular job. An overriding focus on immediate gratification discourages family planning, the pursuit of education, or the accumulation of savings. Because they are trapped by this culture, the members of the underclass don't behave in ways that would help them escape from poverty.

Norms versus Traits

To assess the extent to which an underclass culture perpetuates poverty, the nature of such a culture must be examined. *Culture* is not just about *behavior,* but rather the norms, values, and aspirations that underlie behavioral patterns. In other words, the key elements of a culture are not directly observable but must instead be *inferred* from observed behavior.

The potential gap between unseen norms and observable traits largely explains why the underclass controversy is so intense. Very different interpretations can easily be grafted onto commonly observed behavior. Consider the case of a welfare recipient who declines what appears to be a reasonable job offer. For many middle-class observers, such a rejection constitutes incontrovertible proof that the recipient lacks normal initiative, aspirations, and goals—clear evidence of a culture of poverty. Middle-class individuals, it is argued, would never reject an offer to improve their economic status, especially in the dire financial straits of the welfare recipient. A different set of values—flawed ones—must be shaping the welfare recipient's response.

The job rejection isn't necessarily the symptom of a flawed character, however. The rejection of employment opportunities may reflect other circumstances not readily apparent to the nonpoor observer. The job itself may, of course, be inherently unattractive and provide no economic advancement. Or the job may pose transportation or child-care problems that can't be readily resolved. In that case restricted opportunities would be a better explanation of the job rejection.

The Big Brother argument may also be relevant. Welfare rules sharply limit the economic gain associated with employment. A loss of welfare benefits, as well as Medicaid, food stamps, and economic assistance, could actually *lower* a family's income when the mother leaves welfare for work.[2] Even where a job pays more than welfare,

---

[1]Cited by Paul Jacobs in Jeremy Larner and Irving Howe, eds., *Poverty: Views from the Left* (New York: William Morrow & Company, Inc., 1968), p. 40.

[2]The structure of welfare benefits and incentives is discussed in Chapter 11.

there is a distinct risk of ending up worse off. It is easy to get off welfare but time-consuming to get back on. If the job proves to be unsatisfactory or temporary, then she and her family are left without any financial support while she awaits a new job or more welfare. For families at the margin of impoverishment and confronting largely transitory kinds of jobs, such a risk may be unwarranted. Thus, the job rejection may proceed not from different values and aspirations but from tangible behavioral constraints. Middle-class job seekers, with savings accounts and better job prospects, are not subject to these same constraints.

The culture of poverty hypothesis requires rather stringent evidence. It must be shown that the norms and aspirations—not just the behavior—of the poor are different and that these differences impede escape from poverty. It should also be shown whether and to what degree such differences would disappear under changing socioeconomic circumstances.

Anthropological Studies   Oscar Lewis was one of the most forceful proponents of the culture of poverty thesis. His anthropological observations of lifestyles among the poor convinced him that the behavior patterns of the poor are different and that these differences reflect distinct values. Although his empirical research was confined largely to Mexico and Puerto Rico, he believed that these differences transcend national boundaries. He offered the following explanation for the perpetuation of poverty:

> Once [the culture of poverty] comes into existence it tends to perpetuate itself from generation to generation because of its effect on the children. By the time slum children are age six or seven they have usually absorbed the basic values and attitudes of their subculture and are not psychologically geared to take full advantage of changing conditions or increased opportunities which may occur in their lifetime.[3]

From Lewis's perspective, the poor are clearly prolonging their own impoverishment. As evidence, he identified no less than 70 behavioral traits that distinguish the poor, including little use of banks or museums and nonparticipation in labor unions. Although he acknowledged that the poor may be aware of, or even profess, middle-class values, he regards their aberrant behavior as proof that they do not share those values.

Other sociologists and anthropologists have followed Lewis's lead. Another popular diagnosis of the poor, for example, focuses on their alleged self-indulgence. Out of Lewis's more general depiction of lower-class culture, other observers claim to perceive a pattern of nondeferred gratification: Whereas the middle-class person supposedly feels the need and desire to save, postpone, and renounce certain immediate pleasures, the poor person is alleged to experience no such motivations.[4] This alleged impulse following is presumed to be embedded in the personality dynamics of the poor individual, thus obstructing his or her self-improvement.

This pattern of self-indulgence is additionally presumed to have strong intergenerational effects. Self-indulgent parents have little interest in their children's futures, thus contributing to further poverty. As one observer has asserted:

---

[3]Oscar Lewis, *La Vida* (New York: Random House, Inc., 1966), p. xiv.

[4]Variations in time preferences by socioeconomic status are examined in J. Paul Leigh, "Accounting for Tastes: Correlates of Risk and Time Preference," *Journal of Post-Keynesian Economics* (Fall 1986), pp. 17–31.

Where middle and upper class parents think in terms of a college education for their offspring, lower class parents' aspirations usually stop at a high school diploma, at the very best. Poor parents, with little education, are more likely to believe in luck than in education and to be contemptuous of "book learning" . . . Indeed, among low-income families, both the low educational attainment of the head of the household and the quality of family life create a social environment that leads the poor to believe that "education is not for them."[5]

A Question of Opportunities

Not all observers share these views of lower-class culture. On the contrary, much recent sociological discussion has focused on some of the basic weaknesses in the culture of poverty thesis. It has been pointed out, for example, that the attribution of cultural differences based on observed behavioral differences incorporates many assumptions of questionable validity. Consider again the phenomenon of deferred gratification. Do the poor act differently because of circumstances or values? To conclude that differential values cause the poor to seek more immediate gratification, the following conditions must be met:

1. The satisfaction being deferred must be equally important to the poor and nonpoor.
2. There must exist equal opportunity to defer the satisfaction.
3. The poor and nonpoor must equally suffer from deferment.
4. The probability of obtaining gratification at the end of the deferment period must be equal for both groups.

If any or all of these conditions are violated, then behavioral differences may be explained by situational differences, by differences in opportunity; no reference to alleged cultural phenomena is necessary.

The case of educational attainment illustrates some of the foregoing conditions. The children of the poor undeniably drop out of school earlier than other children. But does this behavioral difference reflect cultural orientations? Schools in lower-income areas are notoriously ill equipped to transmit interest, enjoyment, or ability. The third and fourth conditions in our list are violated: Middle-class school experience is both more pleasant and more profitable. Furthermore, the low-income family cannot afford to support a child's education for as long as a middle-class family; thus, the second condition is also violated. Given these inequalities in opportunity, it might be equally valid to conclude that the poor value education more highly than the nonpoor because of the greater sacrifices they make to get as far as they do.

A similar array of qualifications to the "impulse following" hypothesis is encountered when saving behavior is considered. The poor save less money less often than the nonpoor. Does this reflect a present-time orientation (as contrasted with a future-time orientation)? Perhaps not. The poor have very little to save in the first place. Whatever they do manage to put aside represents a real sacrifice in terms of present consumption.

[5]Oscar Ornati, *Poverty Amid Affluence* (New York: Twentieth Century Fund, 1966), p. 66. This argument has been used to explain why poor families do not undertake as much preventive health care as nonpoor families; see Peter Ferrara and Kevin Hopkins, "Health Status of the Poor," in *Welfare Dependency,* ed. Hopkins (Alexandria, VA: Hudson Institute, 1987).

Hence, there is no foundation for inferring cultural inadequacies on the basis of observed differences in saving.

The central weakness of the culture of poverty proposition is the assumption that behavioral differences between the poor and nonpoor reflect differences in goals and aspirations. In reality, the poor do not have an equal opportunity to fulfill, or even to pursue, their goals. Hence, there may be a sharp divergence between the aspirations and the behavior of the poor that does not exist among middle-class groups.

WILSON'S UNDERCLASS THEORY

Sociologist William Julius Wilson offered a different explanation for the apparent culture of poverty. Like earlier observers, he confirmed that people who lived in areas of concentrated poverty (ghettos) behave differently than people on Main Street. He also noted that their behavior was consistent with a unique set of values that might be characterized as a culture of poverty. Rather than ascribing underclass behavior to a distinct culture, however, he emphasized its *external* causes. The restructuring of the American economy had reduced job opportunities available to inner-city residents and made high-wage jobs particularly remote. The exodus of middle-class blacks from inner-city neighborhoods had also increased the social isolation of increasingly impoverished core poverty areas. In Wilson's view, a reduction in the economic and social isolation of the underclass would alter its behavior.[6]

Testing the Theory

Wilson's underclass hypothesis inspired a resurgence of research on the alleged culture of poverty. The research has pursued two distinct questions:

1. How large is the underclass?
2. What explains its unique behavior?

Size   There was a certain vagueness in Wilson's original formulation about who was a member of the underclass. Was everyone in the underclass poor? Was the underclass defined by geographic boundaries or by the socially deviant behavior of individuals? Did a person have to live in a particular neighborhood to belong to the underclass? If so, how was that neighborhood to be defined? Was everyone in that neighborhood a member of the underclass, even those who didn't exhibit deviant behavior? Was there a racial exclusiveness to the underclass, or was membership color-blind?

A dozen or so studies pursued these measurement questions and produced just as many different answers. The size of the resultant underclass was estimated as low as 800,000 individuals (persistently poor people who exhibit deviant behavior) to as many

[6]See William Julius Wilson, *The Truly Disadvantaged* (Chicago: The University of Chicago Press, 1987) and his further elaboration in "Public Policy Research and the Truly Disadvantaged," in *The Urban Underclass,* eds. C. Jencks and P. Peterson (Washington, DC: Brookings, 1991), pp. 460–481. For an international view, see Godfried Engberson et al., *Cultures of Unemployment* (Boulder, CO: Westview, 1993), which describes the "fatalistic street culture" of long-term unemployed individuals in three Dutch cities.

as 41 million (all persons living in census tracts with poverty rates of at least 20 percent).[7]

Wilson tried to facilitate more precise measurements by later stipulating that an underclass neighborhood would have a poverty concentration of at least 40 percent.[8] He even suggested that the term *ghetto poverty* might be a more accurate label than the *underclass* concept. By these standards, the underclass would include only 1 percent of the U.S. population and less than 10 percent of the poverty population.

Causation   Regardless of how large or small the underclass might be, there is still the underlying question of causation. Are the deviant behaviors associated with the underclass a product of a dysfunctional culture or external forces?

Two approaches are used to disentangle cause and effect. One approach entails direct tests of cultural components like aspirations and goals. The other approach tests the *predictions* of the model by seeing how behavior changes when external circumstances change. If the underclass responds positively to improved job opportunities or housing alternatives, then the cultural explanation loses validity.

Direct Tests of Aspirations

If testimony of the poor themselves is valid, there is little reason to believe that their behavior patterns will remain the same under improved socioeconomic conditions. Welfare mothers, for example, express a strong desire to see their children attain better social and economic positions. Moreover, they perceive clearly—more so than many academic observers—the great divergence between their aspirations and their actual opportunities. One survey, for example, questioned welfare mothers about their desires and expectations for their children's employment. The responses, portrayed in Table 7.1, are illuminating. Seventy percent of the mothers had white-collar aspirations for their eldest child, yet only 46 percent had any expectation that their children would

TABLE 7.1   Welfare Mothers' Desires and Expectations for Eldest Child's Occupational Status (percent)

Occupation	Desire	Expectation
Professional and managerial	48	27
Clerical	22	19
Craft	8	8
Police, army	2	6
Other paid work	6	14
Homemaker	1	4
Undecided	13	23

Source of data: Lawrence Podell, *Families on Welfare in New York City* (New York: City University of New York Press, 1968), Tables 7-C and 7-D.

---

[7]A summary of alternative definitions and size estimates is contained in Ronald B. Mincy, "The Underclass: Concept, Controversy, and Evidence," in *Confronting Poverty,* eds. S. Danziger, G. Sandefur, and D. Weinberg (Cambridge, MA: Harvard University Press, 1994), pp. 109–146.

[8]Wilson, "Public Policy Research and the Truly Disadvantaged," p. 461.

attain this status. (Even fewer actually do.) The lower occupational status of poor children apparently does not reflect their parents' aspirations as much as it reflects the opportunities of the poor.

Other studies have come to similar conclusions regarding work orientations and other dimensions of culture. When poor families are compared to nonpoor families of the same ethnic background (for example, white, black, Hispanic), no significant cultural differences appear.[9] This conclusion also applies to welfare recipients. After reviewing available studies of work attitudes and behavior of welfare mothers, Leonard Goodwin concluded that "welfare recipients do not differ markedly from other Americans with respect to general personality characteristics or with respect to the work ethic and basic life goals."[10]

Other case studies have shown that teenage welfare mothers—included in almost every definition of the underclass—have mainstream aspirations for family, education, and careers. They are less certain, however, about how to attain them and less hopeful that they will.[11] Their lowered expectations could easily be a realistic response to their childrearing responsibilities rather than a source of their predicament.

The *children* in poor families also offer relevant testimony. A 1992–1993 national survey asked students in grades 6 through 12 whether they expected (1) to attend college and (2) to graduate from college. Children from poor and single-parent families had expectations resembling those of nonpoor children. Another survey revealed the chances of realizing those expectations. As Figure 7.1 reveals, poor children are much less likely than nonpoor children to achieve their educational goals.

Indirect Tests of Predicted Behavior

If their aspirations and values were really as different as some observers claim, then the poor would be satisfied with their standard of living and resistant to new opportunity. Many modern cultural theorists argue, in fact, that the poor are content and unable to progress. (Similar arguments were once employed in defense of slavery.) Such views are not consistent with reality. Not only have organized groups of the poor repeatedly expressed their discontent, but the poor have demonstrated a marked ability to move out of poverty when economic opportunities have improved.

Specific tests of the underclass theory have focused on these responses of the poor to changed economic opportunities. Aggregate studies have shown that both poverty rates and welfare rolls are sensitive to economic downturns and upswings. This implies that opportunities are seized when they arise. More convincing results emerge,

---

[9]See, for example, Marta Tienda and Haya Stier, "Joblessness and Shiftlessness: Labor Force Activity in Chicago's Inner City," in *The Urban Underclass,* eds. C. Jencks and P. Peterson, pp. 135–154; Barbara Coward, Joe Feagim, and J. Allen Williams, Jr., "The Culture of Poverty Debate: Some Additional Data," *Social Problems* (June 1974); Chandler Davidson and Charles Faitz, "Are the Poor Different?: A Comparison of Work Behavior and Attitudes Among the Urban Poor and Nonpoor," *Social Problems* (December 1974); also Roberta H. Jackson, "Some Aspirations of Lower Class Black Mothers," *Journal of Comparative Family Studies* (Autumn 1975).

[10]Leonard Goodwin, "What Has Been Learned from the Work Incentive Program and Related Experiences: A Review of Research with Policy Implications" (Worcester, MA: Worcester Polytechnic Institute, 1977), p. 31; see also Goodwin's *Causes and Cures for Welfare* (Lexington, MA: Lexington Books, 1983).

[11]See Naomi B. Farber, "The Significance of Aspirations Among Unmarried Adolescent Mothers," *Social Service Review* (December 1989), pp. 518–532; Elizabeth T. Oritz and Betty Z. Bassoff, "Adolescent Welfare Mothers: Lost Optimism and Lowered Expectations," *Social Casework* (September 1987), pp. 400–405.

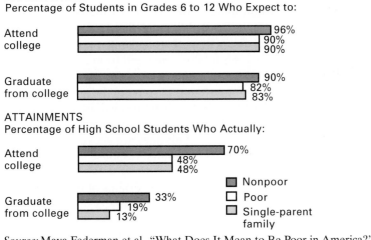

EXPECTATIONS
Percentage of Students in Grades 6 to 12 Who Expect to:

Attend college
96%
90%
90%

Graduate from college
90%
82%
83%

ATTAINMENTS
Percentage of High School Students Who Actually:

Attend college
70%
48%
48%

Graduate from college
33%
19%
13%

■ Nonpoor
□ Poor
□ Single-parent family

Source: Maya Federman et al., "What Does It Mean to Be Poor in America?" *Monthly Labor Review* (May 1996), Table 7.

FIGURE 7.1 Expectations versus Reality

however, from studies that focus on specific subgroups of the underclass. One study found that young black men benefited disproportionately in terms of higher wages and lower unemployment when the local labor market tightened.[12] Another found that such gains were not limited to black males but in fact were shared by all poor persons (including single-parent families).[13] Such evidence is consistent with the notion that structural forces rather than cultural value systems are the decisive factors in shaping underclass behavioral patterns.

Assessment

Even the most adamant exponents of the culture of poverty thesis do not argue that all persons in poverty are psychodynamically attached to impoverishment. Oscar Lewis himself estimated that only 20 percent of the poor in America are culturally bound to poverty. Walter Miller, another advocate of the culture of poverty theory, does not specify what proportion of the poor are so afflicted but warns that the proportion is rising. Others, like Charles Murray and Lawrence Mead, focus on the long-term dependent, that is, those female-headed families who are poor and on welfare year after year. This group has a high degree of intergenerational welfare dependency, is least responsive to improved economic opportunity, and often becomes dependent on welfare at an early age. In that context, they survive with little self-esteem, low expectations, and minimal aspirations.

---

[12]Richard S. Freeman, "Employment and Earnings of Disadvantaged Young Men in a Labor Shortage Economy," in *The Urban Underclass,* eds. C. Jencks and P. Peterson, pp. 103–121.

[13]Paul Osterman, "Gains From Growth? The Impact of Full Employment on Poverty in Boston," in *The Urban Underclass,* pp. 122–134.

Among the 36 million people who were officially poor in 1995, there were, no doubt, some individuals with extraordinarily low aspirations. Many (for example, discouraged workers) may even have succumbed to a fatalistic attitude regarding their condition and future prospects, thus diminishing their ability to exploit new opportunities. We cannot assume, however, that this fatalism emerged from a cultural orientation or that it is totally impervious to changing circumstances. Yet the culture of poverty theory rests on these assumptions. To the extent that some of the poor do believe their chances for advancement are negligible, new opportunities will be grasped hesitantly. The more the poor experience repeated failure and disappointment, the more skeptically they will respond to new policy initiatives. This does not necessarily imply cultural dissonance; their skepticism may very well be a rational response based on prior experience.

The controversy over the nature, the size, and the origins of the so-called underclass continues. Although accumulating evidence suggests that a separate and isolated set of cultural norms may not drive underclass behavior, there is ample evidence of overlapping social and economic problems—what Kenneth Clark called a "tangle of pathologies." This suggests that the response to any particular policy initiative will be slow. Christopher Jencks asserts that it is more productive to focus on specific pathologies and opportunities, however, than to continue the search for an underlying cultural nexus that awaits a "metasolution."[14]

THE RACIAL INFERIORITY THEORY

The theory of a poverty-trapped underclass has distinct racial overtones. Indeed, Wilson's formulation of underclass dynamics stressed the spatial isolation of the black community and the declining pool of marriageable black men. Subsequent research largely focused on the experiences of urban blacks, leading some observers to conclude that the whole underclass concept was just a new way of referring to longstanding racial problems.[15] To blacks, the problems of the underclass originated in and are still aggravated by structural, institutional, and personal discrimination. To many whites, ghetto poverty is just another symptom of aberrant cultural values and inherent racial deficiencies. These divergent explanations are readily applied not only to the black community but to Hispanics as well.

In 1995 median family income among black and Hispanic Americans was around $26,000 while among white Americans it was nearly $43,000. As we have already seen, nearly one out of every three blacks and Hispanics is poor, compared with only one out of nine whites. There is no question about whether a link exists between race and poverty; instead, we are concerned with the causal nature of the established link. Fur-

---

[14]Christopher Jencks, "Is the American Underclass Growing?" in *The Urban Underclass,* pp. 28–100.

[15]Mickey Kaus went so far as to assert that "it is simply stupid to pretend that the culture of poverty isn't largely a black culture" in "The Work Ethic State," *The New Republic,* July 7, 1986, p. 22. Darity et al. appear to come to a similar conclusion in *The Black Underclass* (New York: Garland, 1994). Douglas Massey emphasizes racial segregation as the wellspring of the underclass in "American Apartheid: Segregation and the Making of the Underclass," *American Journal of Sociology* (September 1990), pp. 329–357. However, Hispanic communities often exhibit underclass behavior and confront similar barriers to unemployment and education.

thermore, in discussing the causal association between race and poverty, we need not worry about the circular relationships that attracted our attention earlier. Poverty may lead to ill health, broken families, or more children, but there is no prospect of poverty's changing people's skin color. Accordingly, both the existence of a link and the direction of causality are known: Being black or Hispanic does lead to poverty.

The causal path leading from race to poverty may be explained in two ways. Inherent racial disabilities may limit income-earning abilities. This, of course, is the racial argument that has arisen before. Another possible explanation for the established path emanates from the alleged existence of discrimination. By this argument, minorities are more apt to be poor, not because of different physical, mental, or cultural capacities, but because they are treated differently by society. Whites have no difficulty in choosing between the alternative explanations of black status: The President's National Advisory Commission on Civil Disorders discovered that white Americans favor the racial explanation three to one. As recently as 1978, one out of two white Americans asserted that blacks have less ambition than whites. Fewer than one out of six whites saw racial discrimination as a serious problem.[16] We postpone a discussion of the discrimination argument until Chapters 9 and 10 and focus here on the racial inferiority theory.

The thesis of racial inferiority is not new. Aristotle, for example, used it to explain Greek superiority over the European barbarians. Still later, the barbarians, who by then had produced Shakespeare, Kant, and Newton, used this argument to explain their superiority over the Greeks. Later still, English intellectuals were predicting that America would never achieve greatness because its colonies were heavily populated by the rejected and inferior classes of Europe.

Despite the somewhat dismal record of racial theories, they remain popular. Among the most quoted proponents of a racial explanation of black socioeconomic status in America is Dr. William Shockley. Shockley was an inventor of the transistor and a recipient of the Nobel Prize in Physics. As he explained to the National Academy of Sciences in 1969: "The major deficit in Negro intellectual performance must be primarily of hereditary origin and thus relatively irremediable by practical improvements in the environment." In other words, blacks are poor because they are not smart, and they are not smart because they are black.

Shockley's position is extreme, but he is not alone in his beliefs about innate racial differences. Such beliefs are a common component of racial prejudice and linger on in the minds of many. They even acquire a certain plausibility for most white people because of the demonstrated link between genetic characteristics and achievement: Nearly everyone accepts the notion that smarter people do better and get further. Such a notion leads easily to the position that blacks fare poorly because they are not as smart as whites. The argument is readily extended to Puerto Ricans, Mexican Americans, American Indians, and other poor minorities.

Intelligence and Status

What keeps the racial inferiority debate going (aside from ingrained prejudices) is the fact that intelligence is an unobservable dimension of an individual's genetic endowment. Although we all give nodding agreement to the notion that mental capacities,

---

[16]Louis Harris and Associates, *A Study of Attitudes Toward Racial and Religious Minorities and Toward Women* (New York: National Conference of Christians and Jews, 1978).

like physical capacities, are inherited, we have no direct way of weighing or measuring that inheritance. Accordingly, we depend largely on inferential reasoning to provide clues about the relationship of intelligence to economic status. Unfortunately, such reasoning often turns out to be circular. We have all heard statements like "Wow! John made a fortune in the dry cleaning business; I never realized he was so smart." From this perspective, the true test of intelligence is a person's tax return. According to this test, poverty *must* be explained by a lack of intelligence. If blacks and Hispanics tend to be poorer than whites, their plight must be explained in the same way.

Fortunately, our knowledge of the relationship between intelligence and economic status does not depend exclusively on such superficial reasoning. We know, for example, that identical twins inherit identical genes, and thus identical intelligence (even if we cannot measure that intelligence). Accordingly, if genetic endowments are important for economic status, identical twins should end up with the same status. And they tend to. A study by English sociologists determined that even when they are separated and reared in different environments, identical twins attain very similar socioeconomic statuses. Such observations confirm the significance of inherited abilities, at least for differences among *individuals*.

Demonstrating that genetic abilities are important for economic status does not deny the existence of environmental influences. In the studies of English twins, varying environments were shown to have *some* effect on achievement. Those effects would be still stronger where environmental differences were greater. The Osage Indians in America provide a dramatic illustration: Not only achievements but even measured IQ increased substantially after the tribe discovered oil!

A broader understanding of human achievement recognizes that both genetic and environmental factors influence the attainments of individuals and puts the issue of racial differences in an entirely different setting. Because black and white Americans live in distinct areas and under different conditions, racial abilities alone cannot explain disparities in economic status. To the extent that differences in racial abilities exist at all, we are led to inquire what *proportion* of observed status disparities can be attributed to them. In logical order, then, we must focus on three separate questions:

1. Do genetic differences exist between whites and blacks?
2. If so, how large are any such differences?
3. What is the relative significance of any such differences for observed socioeconomic status?

Very little interest attaches to the question of physical differences between whites and blacks, at least as far as socioeconomic status is involved. Instead, the issue of genetic differences focuses on the relative mental abilities of the two races. The first question, then, really asks whether whites are innately more intelligent than blacks.

IQ Scores

Because we have no way of directly measuring intelligence, we cannot answer the foregoing questions directly. Instead, we must first find some independent indicator of intelligence, then test for differences among people on this basis. This is where IQ tests come in: An IQ score indicates how well an individual has performed on a standardized test relative to others of the same age. An IQ score of 100 indicates that one has performed up to average, while higher or lower scores indicate above- or below-average performance. There is a variety of such tests available, but all incorporate exercises of perceptual, verbal, arithmetical, and reasoning abilities.

Since the nineteenth century there have been literally hundreds of research studies directed toward measuring the relative IQ of blacks and whites. All of them have demonstrated that blacks, on average, score lower on intelligence tests than whites. The average difference between whites and blacks amounts to 15 to 20 IQ points, indicating that the typical black has an IQ of 80 to 85. These figures are now widely accepted; what is still debated is how they should be interpreted.

Basically, an IQ test measures various kinds of performance abilities, such as perception, memory, and verbal knowledge. Accordingly, it is subject to the influences of both genetic intelligence and environmental experience. A child who has never seen a giraffe or a waterfall, for example, has difficulty identifying them in an IQ examination, whatever his native intelligence may be. Because IQ scores incorporate both environmental and genetic experiences, there is no easy method for isolating genetic factors. All we can say with assurance is that IQ differences reflect genetic differences when administered to children who have shared very similar environmental experiences. Clearly, black and white children do not satisfy this condition.

The nature of IQ-score determinants suggests that black and white IQ scores could be brought into harmony by appropriate environmental changes. In fact, studies that have attempted to control for such differences by testing black and white children from similar backgrounds have narrowed the average IQ score difference to as little as five points. Black children adopted by white parents have also scored higher on IQ tests. Other research has demonstrated that the IQ test performances of blacks and whites move further apart the longer they are maintained in unequal situations— ghetto schools, for example. Accordingly, it appears that there is nothing natural or unchangeable in any observed racial pattern of IQ scores.

Further evidence of environmental impact on IQ scores is provided by the variation in these scores for individuals and groups. We have already noted the effect of oil discoveries for the Osage Indians. For the country as a whole, IQ scores have been rising consistently over the last 50 years.[17] This suggests either that we are breeding selectively or that IQ scores are subject to environmental improvement (and perhaps even familiarity with testing procedures). More to our point, it has also been observed that black children moving from rural to urban areas raise their IQ scores significantly, reflecting an improved environment. Still other studies have shown that intensive teaching and supportive environments can materially improve the IQ scores of any group, even mentally retarded children. And finally, it has been demonstrated that improving the diets of poor expectant mothers results in higher IQ scores for their children.

Resolving the Issues

The relationship between intelligence, IQ scores, and economic status is summarized in Figure 7.2. Notice that IQ scores and economic status are directly affected by intelligence. But notice also that both IQ scores and economic status are influenced by environmental factors as well. Accordingly, any demonstrated link between IQ and status

---

[17]The same rise in IQ scores has been observed in 14 European countries; see J. R. Flynn, "Massive IQ Gains in 14 Nations: What IQ Tests Really Measure," *Psychological Bulletin* (1987), pp. 171–191.

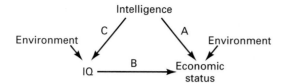

FIGURE 7.2 Intelligence, IQ, and Economic Status

may be explained by environmental forces alone. At least we may be certain that differences in IQ scores and status are less likely to reflect intelligence differences the greater are the environmental differences between the two individuals or groups in question. And this turns out to be an important qualification when comparing blacks and whites in America.

Guided by Figure 7.2 and our previous discussion, we can answer the three questions posed before. First, we must note that there is no basis for concluding that genetic differences in intelligence exist between blacks and whites. This conclusion emerges from the fact that we do not really know what intelligence is and from the observation that the test scores we use to measure intelligence are themselves subject to environmental influence. We could just as easily assert that blacks are *more* intelligent than whites as the reverse. Indeed, many people argue that the entire search for an *explanation* of IQ differences is misplaced and racist. If IQ scores don't measure intelligence, then there is no white-black gap to explain.[18]

Even if there are no genetic differences in *intelligence* between blacks and whites there are differences in *measured IQ* and these differences may be important in their own right. Measured IQ is a manifestation of cognitive ability (however acquired) that is likely to affect one's ability to succeed in the marketplace. The controlled IQ difference between blacks and whites, however, is only 5-10 points. To suggest that this relatively small difference could account for an existing income disparity of over $17,000 a year would be extremely tenuous. One would then be arguing that a 5 or 10 percent difference in intelligence could account for a 40 percent disparity in income, and that status differences were not at all affected by differences in opportunities. Even if genetic differences do exist between blacks and whites, such differences are of relatively minor significance for observed socioeconomic status.[19]

Other Complications

The foregoing observations demonstrate the essential weaknesses in the racial inferiority doctrine. The evidence presented has been rather technical, but there are even simpler inconsistencies that discredit racial theories of black poverty. To begin with, blacks do not fare equally well or poorly in all regions of the country. For the nation as a whole,

---

[18]See James Cronin et al., "Race, Class, and Intelligence: A Critical Look at the IQ Controversy," *International Journal of Mental Health* (Winter 1975); also Cedric X. Clark, "The Shockley-Jensen Thesis: A Contextual Appraisal," *The Black Scholar* (July 1975).

[19]A very different view is propounded by Richard Herrnstein and Charles Murray, who argue that IQ differences are the pre-eminent determinants of inequality; see their *The Bell Curve: Intelligence and Class Structure in American Life* (New York: Free Press, 1994). See also the critiques of their argument in Claude S. Fischer et al., *Inequality by Design: Cracking the Bell Curve Myth* (Princeton, N.J.: Princeton University Press, 1996).

median black family incomes are 54 percent as large as white incomes. In the Midwest, however, they were only 52 percent as large, while in the West, 63 percent. Hence, to argue that genetic disabilities account for status disparities would require one to argue that western blacks are genetically better equipped than midwestern blacks.

A similar problem arises with the rise in black status over time. In the last twenty years, black incomes have risen considerably relative to white incomes. A theory of racial determination would be compelled to explain this development on the basis of improving genetic abilities among blacks or declining genetic potential among whites.

Finally, and most damaging to the doctrine of racial superiority, is the concept of race itself. There is not, and never has been, a clear understanding of what the term *race* means, or for that matter, of how many races exist. As an English zoologist has noted, "geneticists believe anthropologists know what a race is, ethnologists assume their racial classifications are backed up by genetics, and politicians believe that their prejudices have the sanction of both genetics and anthropology."[20] In the resultant confusion, anywhere from three to thirty separate races have been identified at various times. In the American context, the term is used interchangeably to refer to religious, national, or ethnic groups. In the context of the immediate discussion, the term refers basically to skin color. Given the history of miscegenation in America, no one could conceivably argue that distinctive pure white and black genetic characteristics exist: It is estimated that over 90 percent of American blacks have some white ancestry. Hence, American blacks hardly comprise a suitable test for racial theories in inherent differences.

Interestingly enough, adherents to the racial doctrine have attempted to employ this phenomenon of miscegenation to their advantage. They argue that the success of mulattos is due to the presence of "white" genes, which improve their intellectual endowments, proving the thesis of racial superiority. The argument is also used to explain rising black status over time. The evidence presented, however, is exceedingly weak. Mulattos apparently did fare relatively better than "pure" blacks during and shortly after the slave era, but children of mixed parentage were often favored by their white father-masters. Thus, they received greater opportunity and support. Other research has shown that more successful blacks today do not differ in patterns of white ancestry. Moreover, the highest black IQ score yet reported—200—was attained by a child who had no traceable white heritage whatsoever. Hence, whatever the other virtues and liabilities of miscegenation may be, its effects on genetic abilities appear to be negligible.

SUMMARY

Theories of poverty causation based on cultural or racial phenomena have long commanded a certain popularity. In part, they are based on prejudices of the nonpoor against the poor and, in part, on the confidence with which the nonpoor perceive economic opportunity to exist for all. Since the earliest days of colonization, it has been asserted that anyone with enough stamina and initiative could succeed in America. Accordingly, those who did not succeed have been regarded variously as immoral, culturally apart, or racially inferior.

---

[20]Anthony Smith, *The Body* (New York: Walker and Company, 1968), p. 14.

The culture of poverty theory posits that a subculture of fatalistic aspirations, goals, and values generates deviant behavior that perpetuates poverty. The underclass concept focuses on that same self-defeating behavior that occurs in areas of concentrated poverty (ghettos) but can accommodate both cultural and structural explanations.

Because the components of culture are not directly observable, the debate over the origins of underclass behavior hinges on (1) surveys of aspirations and goals, and (2) observed responses to changed circumstances. The inferences drawn from such studies suggest that the underclass is a small fraction of the poverty population and that its behavior is shaped more by external forces than inbred cultural dissonance.

Allegations about racial disabilities suffer equally from misconception and prejudice. There is no basis for concluding that differences in intelligence exist between whites and blacks. Not only do we not yet know what intelligence is, but the instruments we assume to measure it yield ambiguous results. Moreover, even the most extreme assumptions about the meaning and reliability of observed IQ scores would still lead to the conclusion that genetic factors are of negligible significance in explaining the existing economic disparities between whites and blacks.

FURTHER READING

On Culture and the Underclass

Burton, C. Emory, *The Poverty Debate.* Westport, CN: Praeger, 1992, Chapters 2–3.

Crane, Jonathan, "The Epidemic Theory of Ghettos and Neighborhood Effects on Dropping Out and Teenage Childbearing," *American Journal of Sociology* (March 1991), pp. 1226–1259.

Darity, W., S. Myers, E. Carson, and W. Sabol, *The Black Underclass.* New York: Garland, 1994.

DeVine, Joel A., and James D. Wright, *The Greatest of Evils: Urban Poverty and the American Underclass.* New York: Aldine de Gruyter, 1993.

Gans, Herbert, *The War Against the Poor: The Underclass and Antipoverty Policy.* New York: Basic Books, 1995.

Jargowsky, Paul A., "Ghetto Poverty Among Blacks in the 1980s," *Journal of Policy Analysis and Management* (April 1994), pp. 288–310.

Jencks, C., and P. Peterson, eds., *The Urban Underclass.* Washington, DC: Brookings, 1991.

Lewis, Oscar, *La Vida.* New York: Random House, Inc., 1966.

Liebow, Elliot, *Tally's Corner: A Study of Negro Streetcorner Men.* Boston: Little, Brown and Company, 1967.

Mayer, Susan, *What Money Can't Buy.* Cambridge, MA: Harvard University Press, 1997.

Mincy, Ronald B., "The Underclass: Concept, Controversy and Evidence," in *Confronting Poverty,* eds. S. Danziger, G. Sandefur, and D. Weinberg. Cambridge, MA: Harvard University Press, 1994.

Wilson, William Julius, *The Truly Disadvantaged.* Chicago: The University of Chicago Press, 1987.

On Race and IQ

Cartwright, Walter J., and Thomas R. Burtis, "Race and Intelligence: Changing Opinions in Social Science," *Social Science Quarterly* (December 1968), pp. 603–618.

Herrnstein, Richard, and Charles Murray, *The Bell Curve: Intelligence and Class Structure in American Life.* New York: Free Press, 1994.

Jensen, Arthur R., "IQ and Science: The Mysterious Burt Affair," *The Public Interest* (Fall 1991), pp. 93–106.

Shipman, Pat, *The Evolution of Racism.* New York: Simon & Schuster, 1994.

Snyderman, Mark, and Stanley Rothman, "Science, Politics, and the IQ Controversy," *The Public Interest* (Spring 1986).

Vincent, Ken R., "Black/White IQ Differences: Does Age Make a Difference?" *Clinical Psychology* (March 1991), pp. 266–270.

Wolfe, John R., "The Impact of Family Resources on Childhood IQ," *Journal of Human Resources* (Spring 1982).

CHAPTER

Education and Ability

8

The empirical relationship between education and ability on the one hand and economic status on the other are essential components of American folklore. In fact, the observations that "to get ahead, get an education" and "you can't keep a good man down" have acquired the aura of ideological convictions. Everyone has heard of Horatio Alger, and no one doubts that doctors get rich. Conditioned by these examples and mindful of their own security, Americans react accordingly. Middle-class parents begin preparing their children for college soon after birth, and the children themselves learn to regard success as the reward to virtue, ability, and good grades in school. By the same token, those who do not succeed are regarded as less virtuous, less able, or less diligent in the pursuit of education. From this perspective, lack of ability or education emerges as an important cause of poverty. The distribution of poverty even acquires a democratic flavor, as it is also presumed that the development of abilities and education is largely a matter of individual choice.

The conviction that education and ability lead to material success is not easily challenged. Few persons even pause to reflect on the nature and reliability of the underlying associations. With educated people moving ahead all around them, how many individuals can take the time and effort to question the pace of events? Nevertheless, the implied importance of education for the existence of poverty demands that such an inquiry be made. Our discussion focuses on two issues: (1) whether educational achievement determines who is poor; and (2) whether the level of educational achievement determines *how many* people are poor. The same questions are asked of the relationship between ability and poverty.

EDUCATION AND INCOME

The conviction that more education leads to higher income finds extensive support in statistical data. The simple correlation between educational attainment and income is very strong and consistent: More years of education do lead to higher income. In 1995, for example, prime-aged men who never attended high school had average earnings of only $15,720; high school dropouts commanded average earnings of $21,467; high school graduates had incomes of $28,878; and college graduates had average earnings of nearly $50,000 (see Table 8.2). Hence, there is an impressive foundation to the belief that education pays.

Poverty Rates

The relationship between education and income is equally effective in separating the poor from the nonpoor. The typical nonpoor family head has at least a high school diploma, while the head of a poor family is likely not to have even *attended* high school. This disparity in educational attainment is reflected in the incidence of poverty. As Table 8.1 confirms, the likelihood of poverty declines rapidly as a person scales the educational ladder. Less than one out of 30 people who had attended college ended up in poverty in 1995, while one out of four adults who failed to complete high school ended up poor.

Labor-Market Effects

Higher educational attainment contributes to income in several ways. It increases people's productivity (their human capital) by expanding their knowledge and skills. Prospective employers also tend to regard educational degrees as proof of commendable diligence. Diplomas, regardless of their content, are likely to provide access to more jobs. Educational institutions typically offer job placement services, providing employers and students with ready access to each other. The combination of these factors suggests that the person who stays in school longer will be treated and will perform differently in the labor market. Educational attainment affects every facet of labor-market success. A person's participation in the labor force, his or her occupation, the frequency of his or her employment, the number of hours worked, and the wage rate received are all affected by the schooling the person has achieved. In conjunction, these factors determine an individual's income.

People with little education are least likely to get and hold a job. If they do obtain jobs, they are first to be laid off by employers when production schedules change. With fewer skills and credentials, their ability to acquire other jobs will be restricted. Consequently, they are apt to be unemployed far more often and for longer periods than those with greater educational attainments. In 1995, high school dropouts experienced an 8.1 unemployment rate, while high school and college graduates confronted unemployment rates of 4.7 and 2.1, respectively (Table 8.2).

As was noted in Chapter 3, long and repeated spells of unemployment may induce people to leave the labor force altogether. Frustrated by lack of employment

TABLE 8.1   Incidence of Adult Poverty, by Education

Education	Number in Poverty	Incidence of Poverty (percent)
No high school diploma	7,670,000	25.0
High school graduate (no college)	5,416,000	9.6
Some college	2,850,000	7.1
College graduate	1,171,000	3.0

Source: U.S. Bureau of the Census (1995 data for persons 25 years and older).

TABLE 8.2   Education and the Labor Market*

	High School Dropouts	High School Graduates	College Graduates
Unemployment rate (percent)	8.1	4.7	2.1
Labor force participation (percent)	74.9	87.5	93.4
Full-time workers (percent)	49.1	70.0	79.8
Occupational status	Blue collar	Clerical	Professional
Average earnings	$21,467	$28,878	$48,705

*For males aged 25 to 64.

Source: U.S. Department of Labor (1995 data).

opportunities, they may give up the job search, relying instead on public or private financial assistance. Few men can, however, resign themselves to nonparticipation, in part because available social and financial supports are extremely limited. Nevertheless, the impact of educational attainment is discernible in the relevant statistics. Whereas nearly all (93.4 percent) male college graduates participate in the labor force, only 75 percent of male high school dropouts do so. Differences are even more striking among women: The labor force participation rate for female college graduates is nearly 75 percent versus only 30 percent for women who never got a high school diploma.

Getting and holding a job does not guarantee financial success, of course. The nature of the job one obtains, how many hours one works, and what wage one is paid are equally as important. On all these fronts, the less educated individual fares poorly. High school dropouts are disproportionately concentrated in the blue-collar occupations as unskilled laborers, operatives, service workers, and craftspeople. By contrast, high school graduates are most heavily concentrated in the lower white-collar occupations, at the clerical and sales levels, and in the higher blue-collar positions. College graduates crowd the professional and managerial classes and are virtually nonexistent in the lowest job categories.

The cumulative impact of these labor-market phenomena sharply differentiates the incomes of the lesser and greater educated. As we have already noted, the income differences amount to thousands of dollars a year. Over a lifetime, this disparity becomes tremendous. During their careers, high school graduates can anticipate earning $400,000 more than high school dropouts, while college graduates will earn $500,000 more than high school graduates before retiring.[1]

Increasing Skill Premiums

As if high school dropouts were not already sufficiently disadvantaged in the labor market, the earnings gap between better- and lesser-educated workers appears to be widening. In 1973, for example, college graduates earned 46 percent more than high

---

[1]Because these estimates do not account for productivity or price increase, they understate income differences; see U.S. Bureau of the Census, *Lifetime Earnings Estimates for Men and Women in the United States: 1979* (Washington, DC: U.S. Government Printing Office, 1983); updated by author.

school graduates. By 1989, that college premium had risen to 53 percent. Today the college premium is even higher.

While the real earnings of college graduates were rising, the real earnings of workers without any college experience were actually falling. Hence, lower-skilled workers have not only fallen behind in a *relative* sense, but in an *absolute* sense as well. In the process, their odds of falling into poverty have increased.

The increased wage premiums paid to better-educated workers reflect an increased demand for skilled labor. Technological advances, international competition, and changes in the mix of output have all fueled demand for skilled labor. At the same time, a steady flow of immigrants and low-wage goods have helped to hold down the wages of less-skilled workers.[2] The combination of these market forces has made educational attainment an even stronger predictor of income status.

Income Overlaps

The weight of accumulated evidence on the association between income and education reinforces the belief that inadequate education is a major cause of poverty. That the least educated will bring the least amount of human capital to the labor market and therefore receive the least income appears obvious. From this perspective, poverty can be explained by a failure to stay in school, by underinvestment in one's own human capital (by implication, flawed characters). Before fully accepting this interpretation, however, several additional issues must be considered.

Even if, on average, better-educated individuals can earn more money, all persons with more schooling will not necessarily have higher incomes. No one has seriously suggested that education is the *only* determinant of income.

In fact, empirical studies that examine variations in *individual* (as opposed to *group*) wage levels find that educational attainment accounts for a very small proportion of that variation. Indeed, earnings gaps *among* people of equal education have been increasing at least as fast as gaps between individuals of different educational attainments.[3] Inherent ability, inherited wealth, geographical location, motivation, discrimination, economic conditions, and simple luck will all influence a person's income opportunities. As a result, the income distribution of college graduates overlaps that of high school dropouts. Although the *average* high school dropout earns less than the *average* college graduate, some high school dropouts earn more than college graduates. Recall also (Table 8.1) that over a million college graduates are poor.

The overlap in income distributions of individuals with different educational attainments is particularly apparent when race and sex are examined. Indeed, the labor-market rewards the educational attainments of some people much more handsomely than that of others. Consider Figure 8.1, for example: Each step up the educational

---

[2]For a description and analysis of widening wage inequalities, see the symposium in the *Journal of Economic Perspectives* (Spring 1997), pp. 21–91. Further analyses are contained in Gregory Acs and Sheldon Danziger, "Educational Attainment, Industrial Structure, and Male Earnings Through the 1980s," *Journal of Human Resources* (Summer 1993), pp. 618–648; C. Juhn, K. Murphy, and B. Pierce, "Wage Inequality and the Rise in Returns to Skill," *Journal of Political Economy* (January 1993), pp. 410–442.

[3]See Lynn A. Karoly, "The Trend in Inequality Among Families, Individuals, and Workers in the United States: A Twenty-Five Year Perspective," in *Uneven Tides,* eds. S. Danziger and P. Gottschalk (New York: Russell Sage, 1993); Lawrence F. Katz and Kevin Murphy, "Changes in Relative Wages, 1963–1987: Supply and Demand Factors," *Quarterly Journal of Economics* (February 1992), pp. 35–78.

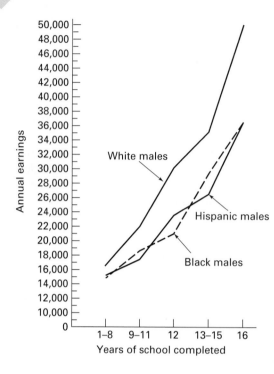

Annual earnings

White males

Hispanic males

Black males

Years of school completed

1–8 9–11 12 13–15 16

Source: U.S. Bureau of the Census (1995 data).

FIGURE 8.1 Mean Earnings of Males 25–64 Years of Age, by Educational Attainment, by Race

ladder clearly improves the incomes of black, white, and Hispanic men. Even more striking, however, is the gross disparity shown on the graphs that exists between white and minority males. The average black college graduate, for example, earns barely more than a white high school graduate; while a white high school dropout earns more than a black high school graduate. Whatever benefits education provides, they are clearly not equally accessible to all. Hence, if lack of education is regarded as an explanation for poverty, it must be recognized at the outset that the explanation is not complete.

The same disparity can be observed between men and women (see Figure 8.2). Women college graduates earn slightly less on average ($28,000) than men who complete only high school ($28,900). Moreover, the average male with one to three years of college commands an income that is higher than all groups of women, including those who have attended graduate school. Again, the rewards for educational achievement, while perhaps large, are not evenly distributed.

Explanations for the income disparities that exist between races and sexes are not difficult to find. Some of these are discussed more thoroughly in Chapters 9 and 10. For present purposes, we confine ourselves to the observation that more education does not guarantee a higher income or escape from poverty. Keeping some poor persons in school longer may not effectively raise their incomes. Even in situations where racial or sexual discrimination is not present, the link between education and income is far from perfect.

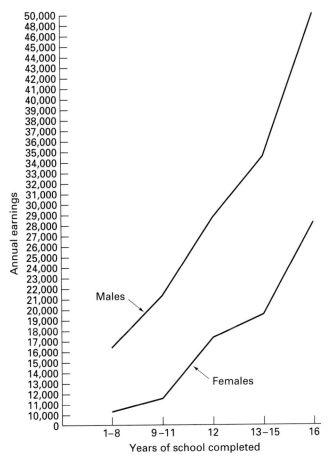

Source: U.S. Bureau of the Census (1995 data for persons age 25 and older).

FIGURE 8.2   Mean Earnings by Educational Attainment, by Sex

Education as a Sorting Device

The full significance of education for the distribution and extent of poverty can be understood only in the framework of the entire labor market. As we have seen, the simple correlation between average incomes and average educational attainments can lead to erroneous impressions about the importance of education. A certain quantity of job vacancies and prospective employees exists in any labor market. When the number of vacancies falls far short of the number of job seekers, the economy is in a depressed state, and unemployment rates are high. This implies that employers will be able to choose among many applicants in filling any job vacancy. How will employers proceed? That is, on what basis should they or will they make their selection?

In Chapter 3, we suggested that employers will tend to select new employees on the basis of their human capital, their potential contribution to output. In some cases, the process of selection is comparatively simple. If the job is highly technical, identifying the most competent applicants on the basis of tests or prior accomplishments may be easy.

But differences in human capital are not always large or easily observed, compelling employers to depend on some guesswork. In these cases—probably the majority—employers come to rely on only a few selection criteria, educational attainment being one of the most important. The employer has several reasons for separating the more educated from the less educated in the application process. First, it is assumed that more schooling results in greater ability. The employer may also feel that perseverance in school signals a certain disposition to achievement. An employer may even feel that school graduates "deserve" better opportunities. Last, but not least, employers may view an educational degree as a cheap, easy, and fairly reliable mechanism for sorting out job applicants. These considerations transform educational credentials (for example, a high school diploma) into admission tickets for job interviews, especially in times of high unemployment.[4] A recession amply illustrates how selective employers can become; consider this help-wanted ad from the Austin, Texas, *American*, which appeared in the midst of the 1971 recession:

> TOPLESS DANCERS. Must have two years college. Prefer English major, languages or humanities.[5]

From the standpoint of this employer, all prospective dancers are in competition for available jobs, and educational attainments separate the finalists from the rejects. Other employers are likely to react similarly when jobs are scarce. For example, even though a high school dropout could easily perform the responsibilities of a sales clerk, he or she is not given the opportunity if high school graduates are also available. As a consequence, the dropout remains unemployed and poor.

The implications of this selection process for the relationship of education to poverty are profound. The distribution of education will have a significant impact on the distribution of poverty. As a rule, those with the least education will end up in poverty. This will be especially true among otherwise similar labor-market, racial, and sexual groups. But what about the extent of poverty? Will education have a similar influence in determining how many persons are poor? Consider again the case of the high school dropout seeking the job of sales clerk. A high school diploma would undoubtedly make his or her competitive position stronger. But would his or her graduation, by itself, increase the number of available jobs? Clearly not. While graduation may enable one to compete successfully for the available job, the applicant's success will leave someone else unemployed. If there is only one job and there are four applicants, no amount of educational improvement or redistribution will succeed in leaving fewer than three persons unemployed. Education may influence who gets the available jobs, but the demand for labor will determine how many jobs there are.

Confusion about the causal significance of education comes from the failure to distinguish between individual and group dynamics. Observing that individual incomes are related to educational attainments easily leads to the supposition that raising the educational attainments of all the poor will eliminate poverty. Yet, bestowing a high

---

[4]The "sheepskin" effects associated with credentialism are examined in D. Belman and J. S. Heywood, "Sheepskin Effects in the Return to Education: An Examination of Women and Minorities," *Review of Economics and Statistics* (November 1991), pp. 720–724.

[5]Cited in *Playboy* (December 1971), p. 26.

school diploma, or even a Ph.D., on all the poor will do little to alter the number or kinds of jobs available. A few more vacancies might be filled, but the greatest impact would be to alter the composition of the poor and to raise their educational attainments. By itself, such an effort would do little to reduce the extent of poverty.

The Content of Education

The foregoing discussion says nothing about the content of education. Instead, the term has been used to refer to schooling in general. Accordingly, some of the most vital and controversial issues relevant to the education-income nexus have been neglected. Among the more salient of those issues are the questions of how much vocational content should be offered in school curricula and who should provide it. Training in specific skills might be especially valuable to those who are not going to pursue higher education. One study suggests that the incomes of black workers are particularly sensitive to the degree of vocational instruction in their high school curriculum.[6] Greater earning potential could be generated by simply restructuring educational curricula rather than by extending them.

Of even greater importance for policy consideration is the question of access to education. Because educational attainments significantly determine who will be poor in any given economic situation, we must also determine who receives the necessary credentials and why. Some consideration of these issues is taken up in Chapters 9 and 10. For the present, we may note that neither the issue of educational content nor that of access materially alters the conclusions previously cited. Regardless of what is taught or who it is taught to, education by itself can do very little to alter the number of jobs available at any given moment.[7]

ABILITY AND INCOME

Ability, like education, is presumed to be an important determinant of income. In fact, it is generally deemed desirable for the distribution of incomes to reflect the distribution of productive abilities. We are accustomed to thinking that greater ability merits richer rewards and, indeed, that material success manifests ability. The idea that income *should* reflect ability can be questioned, however. Why, for example, should a man who inherits the capacity to learn to steer rockets through space command a higher income than the man who is born with the capacity to learn to drive buses? Are justice and equity any better served when rewards are distributed according to inherited genes rather than according to inherited dollars?

Which Ability Matters?

In Chapter 7, we encountered some of the difficulties that engulf discussions of individual ability. The term *ability,* as it is commonly employed, incorporates elements of both innate capacity and developed performance. Accordingly, there is a certain vagueness in

---

[6]Alan C. Kerckhoff and Robert A. Jackson, "Types of Education and the Occupational Attainments of Young Men," *Social Forces* (September 1982).

[7]Over a longer period of time, rising educational attainments may increase national productivity and employment, even if there is little immediate impact on the level of poverty.

the question whether the income distribution reflects the ability distribution. If we refer to innate abilities, then we really have no means for answering the question because we do not know precisely what innate abilities are or how to measure them. However, if we look only at developed performance, we must recognize that we are departing from the pattern of innate abilities because all individuals do not share equal opportunity to develop their capacities. An income distribution based on performance abilities may not meet our standards of equity.

Another problem with the measurement of performance ability is the fact that no single, all-inclusive performance criterion exists. The ability to sing or to run is distributed differently from the ability to solve complex mathematical problems. There are literally hundreds, if not thousands, of varied abilities, all uniquely distributed among the population. Determining whether incomes accurately reflect performance ability is impossible. At most, one could assert that the distribution of incomes reflects the distribution of abilities valued highly in the marketplace. But even that cautious assertion masks a tautology. One could assert that *any* income distribution reflects the same thing. There is no means for determining whether a given income distribution departs from the distribution of abilities. In the face of this impasse, we usually proceed in reverse. That is, we infer the distribution of abilities from the distribution of incomes: People with more money are *assumed* to be more able. In this way the income distribution justifies itself.

In view of these considerations, we apparently have little basis for objectively assessing the fairness or appropriateness of any existing income distribution. At most, we may simply observe how well the distribution reflects certain specific kinds of attainments or characteristics. We must then resort to our own values to determine how appropriate these criteria are and how equitably they are reflected in incomes. The inherent subjectivity of this approach does not render it impracticable, but it does make consensus difficult.

IQ and Schooling

Two kinds of abilities continue to attract the most attention in discussions of income distribution—measured IQ and educational attainment. IQ is of interest both because it gauges highly valued performance abilities, such as perception and problem solving, and because, despite admonitions to the contrary, it is assumed to reflect innate capacities. As we saw in Chapter 7, IQ differences are also the focus of debates about race and class differences in income. Educational attainment is of interest for much the same reasons. Schooling is assumed to impart valuable skills and thus to differentiate the rich from the poor. Accordingly, we may ask how well the existing income distribution reflects these criteria. Figure 8.3 provides the answer to this question.

The first thing to notice in Figure 8.3 is the different shape of the IQ, education, and earnings distributions. IQ tests are scored to conform to a smooth bell-shaped curve (the "normal" distribution). The distribution of educational attainments, however, is characterized by huge discontinuities at high school completion and college graduation. Finally, the income distribution looks like a disfigured bell with a long tail extending to the right. These differently-shaped distributions suggest that the links between ability and income are far from perfect. At the extremes of the distributions, the

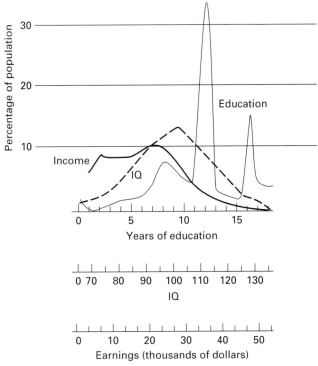

Source of data: Adapted from Lester C. Thurow, *Poverty and Discrimination* (Washington, DC: The Brookings Institution, 1969), p. 68; 1992 data from U.S. Census Bureau.

FIGURE 8.3 Distribution of Earnings, Education, and IQ for Males, 25 Years of Age and Over

differences are particularly evident. There is a higher concentration of low incomes than either low IQ or low education. At the other end of the scale, the opposite is true: High educational attainments are more common than high incomes or high IQ.

Some interesting implications follow from Figure 8.3 and our previous discussions of ability and education. We have already suggested that high IQ scores are not equally accessible to all individuals of similar genetic capacity (see Chapter 7). Black children, for example, have less of an opportunity to develop their capacities into performing abilities. This implies the income distribution is even less representative of innate capacities than is suggested by its observed relationship to IQ. Similarly, we should note that educational attainments depart considerably from the IQ distribution, suggesting that access to, and the quality of, education are not uniform.[8] These observations are considered further in Chapter 9.

---

[8]Richard Herrnstein and Charles Murray assign a more prominent role to IQ, suggesting that IQ differences create a meritocracy in which high-IQ individuals uniformly excel; see their *The Bell Curve: Intelligence and Class Structure in American Life* (New York: Free Press, 1994). Among the many critiques of their work, see Claude S. Fischer et al., *Inequality by Design: Cracking the Bell Curve Myth* (Princeton, NJ: Princeton University Press, 1996).

SUMMARY

Individuals with greater educational attainments unquestionably earn more money, on average, than persons with less education. Persons with highly valued abilities also tend to earn larger incomes. Accordingly, it is hardly surprising to discover that the poor tend to have less education and fewer marketable skills than the nonpoor. While the evidence reviewed in this chapter demonstrates that these relationships are not perfect, they do have a general validity. More important than the question of association, however, is that of causality. What we really seek to discover is not whether the poor are undereducated or underskilled, but whether a lack of education or skills is responsible for their poverty.

Education does operate as a powerful mechanism in determining the distribution of poverty. Where only a limited number of income opportunities are available, they will be reserved on a "least-educated last" basis. That is, the person with educational credentials will have a competitive edge in the labor market, at least within racial or sexual population groups. There is, therefore, some basis for attributing the poverty of individuals to educational deficiency. This link may have even strengthened in recent years as the wage gap between high school and college graduates has widened.

The relationship between education and poverty is not so simple on an aggregate basis, however. The competitive position of all workers cannot be raised simultaneously; if one individual's relative educational position rises, someone else's falls. Education cannot be a cause of aggregate poverty unless low levels of schooling preclude employment at wages that would prevent poverty. There is little evidence that such structural unemployment is severe enough to explain a substantial amount of poverty.

The relationship of ability to poverty is also more complex than commonly assumed. Because we lack unambiguous definitions and measurements of ability, there is no firm basis for declaring that the poor are less able. At most, such an observation means only that the poor make less money. Even when confined to measures of performance, such as IQ, we find that the relationship of ability to income is oblique. The distribution of incomes diverges considerably from educational or IQ distributions and even further from the distribution of innate talents.

FURTHER READING

Brittain, John A., *The Inheritance of Economic Status.* Washington, DC: The Brookings Institution, 1977.

Hauser, Robert M., and Thomas N. Daymont, "Schooling, Ability, and Earnings: Cross-sectional Findings 8 to 14 Years After High School Graduation," *Sociology of Education* (July 1977).

Herrnstein, Richard J., and Charles Murray, *The Bell Curve: Intelligence and Class Structure in American Life.* New York: Free Press, 1994.

Jencks, Christopher, et al., *Who Gets Ahead? The Economic Determinants of Success in America.* New York: Basic Books, 1979.

Jensen, Arthur, *The g Factor.* Cambridge, MA: Harvard Graduate School of Education, 1996.

Levy, Frank, and Richard Murnane, "Earnings Levels and Earnings Inequality: A Review of Recent Trends and Proposed Explanations," *Journal of Economic Literature* (September 1992), pp. 1333–1381.

Markey, James P., "The Labor Market Problems of Today's High School Dropouts," *Monthly Labor Review* (June 1988).

Murnane, Richard J., "Education and the Well-Being of the Next Generation," in *Confronting Poverty,* eds. S. Danziger, G. Sandefur, and D. Weinberg. Cambridge, MA: Harvard University Press, 1994.

Murray, Charles, "IQ and Economic Success," *The Public Interest* (Summer 1997), pp. 21–35.

Vroon, P. A., J. De Leeuw, and A. C. Meester, "Distribution of Intelligence and Educational Level in Fathers and Sons," *British Journal of Psychology* (1986).

CHAPTER

Discrimination in Education

9

Education appears to have a major impact on the distribution, if not necessarily the extent, of poverty. Anyone denied equal opportunity to education has an increased probability of being poor. In other words, discrimination in education helps determine who will be poor.

Discrimination in labor markets has similar effects. To achieve nonpoverty status, an individual must be able to employ his or her abilities in the labor market. Acquisition of acceptable characteristics alone is no guarantee of escape from poverty. If there exist forces that prevent or limit access to the labor market, the rewards to demographic achievements are never realized.

Barriers to either the development or utilization of human capital are the subject of this and the following chapter. The discussion in this chapter begins with a consideration of the meaning and nature of *discrimination* and ends with an examination of discriminatory barriers in the educational system. Chapter 10 focuses on discrimination in the labor market.

DISCRIMINATION

The terms *discrimination, prejudice,* and *racism* are widely used. Seldom do they fail to evoke emotional, often heated responses. While most people do not always understand what is meant by these concepts, they stand forever ready to deny or proclaim the significance of each. The report of the National Advisory Commission on Civil Disorders (the "Riot Commission") in early 1968 provided a striking example of this volatility. In searching for an explanation of the urban strife that was becoming characteristic of American cities, the commission concluded that white racism was a principal source of injustice and unrest. Very few white Americans, President Johnson included, were ready to accept the commission's sweeping indictment. White Americans generally felt neither significantly prejudiced nor sufficiently involved in the ghetto to be responsible for the conditions therein. After the 1992 Los Angeles riots some of the same questions about racial injustice and its consequences were again fiercely debated.

One of the obstacles to meaningful debate is the highly charged content of the term *racism*. For many people, racism means burning school buses, racial taunts, or protesting equal opportunity. Relatively few Americans identify easily with such characterizations. Racism, however, has other meanings. In fact, as used by the Riot Commission, the concept transcends the attitudes and behavior of individuals. The commission's indictment referred to entire patterns of racial interaction and the institutional character of much discrimination. A survey of students at Stanford University revealed that black students easily identified with this institutional definition of racism while white students thought of racism primarily in interpersonal terms. In other words, whites thought people but not institutions could be racist, while blacks felt institutions could be racist even if individuals were not.[1]

Attitudes versus Action

To understand the nature of racism, we must begin by distinguishing between attitudes and actions. People often think differently than they act. As a result, they may adopt patterns of behavior that are injurious to others without consciously wishing to inflict injury. Conversely, they may harbor hostile feelings toward particular individuals or groups but refrain from acting them out due to personal, moral, or legal inhibitions. The term *prejudice* refers to the unfavorable feelings and attitudes that people harbor against others, especially other population groups. These are to be distinguished from unfavorable actions or behavior, which fall under the heading of discrimination. Prejudiced individuals may or may not discriminate, and discrimination does not necessarily imply the existence of prejudice.

While people's prejudices are often the origin of discriminatory behavior and may be appropriate targets for public policy, they are relevant to our discussion only insofar as they find expression in behavior. Accordingly, we focus on the nature of discrimination. We may note here, however, that the broader term *racism* encompasses the concepts of both prejudice and discrimination.

The concept of discrimination need not convey notions of injustice or injury. In general, it refers only to the differential treatment of persons. Thus, we discriminate when we assign the tallest boys to the basketball team or when we cheer for the local football team. Yet we hardly think of these phenomena as being related in any meaningful way to, say, the exclusion of blacks from higher-status jobs or classrooms. Clearly, a general concept of discrimination encompassing both situations is too anemic for practical use. But how, then, are we to identify the kind of discriminatory treatment that we regard as the proper concern of public policy?

The Relevancy Standard

We can move closer to a relevant concept of discrimination by recognizing the criteria on which differential treatment is based. Assigning taller boys to a basketball team, for example, serves a very specific and productive function. In this case, the criterion of selection is directly relevant to the task at hand. The same cannot be said for the selection of a less qualified white competing with a more qualified black. Here the basis of selection—color—is irrelevant to the task at hand, and the resultant choice is actually

---

[1] John H. Bunzel, "Black and White at Stanford," *The Public Interest* (Fall 1991), pp. 61–77.

counterproductive. Hence, we could refine our concept of discrimination by incorporating the relevancy of selection criteria. The kind of discrimination that is based on irrelevant or nonproductive criteria must be considered as injurious to the public welfare.

The U.S. Supreme Court employed this relevancy concept of discrimination when it restricted the use of aptitude tests for job seekers. The Court observed that intelligence tests and other hiring criteria used by the Duke Power Company were not related to job performance. That is, the tests performed no useful economic function. Yet they were effective in screening out black job seekers. In *Griggs* v. *Duke Power Company* (1971), the Court ruled that such practices were unfairly discriminatory.

Unfortunately, even this refinement of the concept of discrimination does not provide a completely workable definition. There remain many choices we would consider socially injurious that are still not identifiable by the criterion of relevancy. The choice of one's neighbors is an example: The only obviously relevant criterion in choosing neighbors is one's own desires and satisfaction. Thus, the choice of a white neighbor over a black one conforms to a certain standard of relevancy. Nevertheless, we have come to regard racial discrimination in housing as a socially pernicious practice. On what grounds do we distinguish this kind of individual choice from others? Are there fundamental differences between the situation where a homeowner chooses a white neighbor and, say, the situation where you choose to listen to a rock singer rather than an opera singer?[2] Both situations reflect the free expression of individual choice.

There are few objective grounds for distinguishing between the choice of the selection decision: The opera singer loses potential income and the black home seeker loses a potential residence. Our distinction between the two situations rests instead on more subjective grounds. Racial discrimination in housing is singled out for special attention because it violates common notions of social justice. Against a combined background of religious, moral, legal, and historical considerations, we have collectively determined that racial discrimination is a particularly deleterious form of individual choice. It is on the basis of this subjective determination that racial discrimination has become a pressing public concern.

An important factor in our subjective judgment about the nature of racial discrimination is our perception of its effects. Where all whites discriminate against all blacks, the expression of free choice becomes especially pernicious. The black home seeker is denied not one potential home, but all potential homes in white areas. Free choice for whites thus implies restricted choice for blacks and, hence, violates a basic dimension of freedom. Other choices that are less uniform or pervasive are not equally worthy of public concern. Racial discrimination itself would cease to be a public concern were it the practice of only a relatively few, scattered whites. Yet most black Americans believe they are denied equal opportunity in housing, education, and employment. Even a substantial number of whites believe discrimination persists (see Table 9.1).

Costs and Benefits of Discrimination

While it is obvious that blacks, Hispanics, and other targets of discrimination suffer real and intangible losses from the practice of racial discrimination, it is not so apparent whether or how the white community gains. Psychologically, many whites may feel bet-

---

[2]This analogy was put forth by Milton Friedman in *Capitalism and Freedom* (Chicago: University of Chicago Press, 1962), Chapter 7.

TABLE 9.1   Do Black Americans Have the Same Opportunities as Whites?

	Responses of	
	Blacks *(percent)*	*Whites* *(percent)*
In Housing		
Same opportunity	22	48
Not the case	75	47
In Education		
Same opportunity	38	73
Not the case	59	24
In Employment		
Same opportunity	27	30
Not the case	70	66

Source: Public opinion polls reported in The Gallop Poll, monthly, October 1993 and *TIME*, February 2, 1987, p. 21.

ter off for having subordinated someone else. And if majority white individuals actually feel uncomfortable around minorities, on the job, in school, or at home, we may conclude that they are even happier as a result of discrimination.[3] But the economic costs and benefits that may accrue to the white community are our immediate concern.

Many whites do reap tangible benefits from the practice of discrimination. When blacks and Hispanics are discriminated against in the labor market, for example, they will receive lower wages than white workers who possess equal qualifications. As a result, two groups gain. White workers who are immunized against competition from minority workers obtain higher wages than otherwise. In addition those employers (laundries and hotels, for example) who actually hire minority workers benefit by getting higher-quality labor than they are, in fact, paying for. In the educational field, white children gain from discrimination by monopolizing better facilities and teachers. As long as racial discrimination is practiced, white children of lesser ability are also released from the necessity of competing with more able minority children in the quest for admissions.

Not all whites gain directly, however, from racial discrimination; some, in fact, actually lose. White workers who cannot escape menial occupations suffer from increased competition from minority workers. The wages of white laundry and hotel workers, for example, will be held down by the large number of blacks, Hispanics, and Asians excluded from other occupations. This relationship is illustrated in Figure 9.1. Some employers, too, will suffer losses. In a segregated community employers will often incur higher labor costs through the use of lesser-qualified whites. In the field of education, many whites will suffer from racial discrimination. Not all whites can flee the inner city. Those left behind, primarily the poorest, will be trapped in increasingly inferior educational systems, unable to enjoy the fruits of suburban white monopolies.

---

[3]The perception of psychological benefits may, of course, rest on prejudices, in which case the nature of benefits could be altered by illuminating and reducing racial stereotypes.

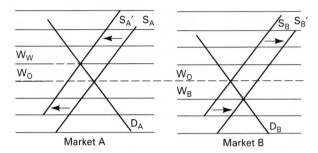

Suppose there are only two kinds of jobs, those in Market A and those in Market B. If everyone is allowed to move freely from one market to another, the equilibrium wage will end up at W_O in both markets. Why? Because if wages were higher in A than B, people would move out of B and into A, thus lowering wages in A while raising them in B. Hence, freedom of movement between Markets A and B assures an equality of average wage rates.

But now suppose black workers in A are kicked out and sent to Market B, making A a "whites only" preserve. This has the effect of shifting the labor supply curve in A to the left (to S_A') and the labor supply curve in B to the right (to S_B'). The net result indicated by the new supply and demand intersections is to raise wages in A (to W_W) and to lower wages in B (to W_B). Thus, black workers and any white workers trapped in Market B suffer lower wages, while the white workers in Market A end up with higher wages.

FIGURE 9.1   Wage Effects of Discrimination

They, like their black and Hispanic neighbors, will find their human capital potential underdeveloped.[4]

On an individual basis, then, some whites gain and some lose as a direct result of discrimination, making it difficult to calculate the net microeconomic gain or loss to the white community. No such ambiguity attaches to the indirect losses that are incurred on an aggregate, or macroeconomic, level, however. Where discrimination against minorities is pervasive, society as a whole loses potential human capital. The abilities and creativity of the minority communities remain underdeveloped and underemployed. Hence, total output of goods and services is less than it would be in the absence of discrimination. Estimates of the size of this loss run into tens of billions of dollars a year. In addition, much of the output we do produce is directed to relatively unattractive uses such as the surveillance of homes, streets, jails, and welfare caseloads. Thus, whatever direct gains or losses individual whites incur are overwhelmed by the very large indirect losses to the economy as a whole.[5]

---

[4]Some whites may also suffer from policies designed to eliminate vestiges of discrimination against blacks; where blacks are given *preferential* (not just equal) access to schools or jobs, some whites suffer reverse discrimination. Reverse discrimination is discussed in Chapter 14.

[5]White workers as a class may also lose if racial discrimination weakens worker solidarity, reducing labor's share of total income. See Michael Reich, "Who Benefits From Racism? The Distribution Among Whites of Gains and Losses From Racial Inequality," *Journal of Human Resources* (Fall 1978); and his "Changes in the Distribution of Benefits from Racism in the 1960s," *Journal of Human Resources* (Spring 1981).

Proving Discrimination

Given the potential socioeconomic cost of discrimination, it is clearly in society's interest to recognize its existence and eliminate it. The identification of discrimination is not always easy, however. Consider a situation where a white worker and a Hispanic worker both apply for the same job. The white applicant is accepted, and the Hispanic applicant claims that he was unfairly discriminated against. What grounds do we have for accepting the charge of discrimination, as opposed to, say, the charge that the Hispanic applicant is simply a poor loser?

The easiest cases of discrimination to prove are those that involve blatant discrepancies in treatment. If the Hispanic applicant was required to take special tests or possessed identifiably superior qualifications, the issue is readily resolved. The same simplicity exists where black children are confined to dilapidated schools or a prospective black home buyer is turned down after offering to pay the full retail value of a house.

But the practice of discrimination is not always so apparent. Indeed, with the public eye focused on discrimination, those who engage in discriminatory practices are likely to develop great subtlety. Accordingly, evidence of discriminatory treatment may have to rest on the observation of end results. If a metropolitan area company has 4,000 employees, none of whom is black, there exists a strong presumption that its hiring procedures are not impartial. So it is with the schools: If blacks and whites go into the educational system comparatively equal but come out with gross disparities in achievement, we may conclude that they were treated differently somewhere along the line. Evidence of discriminatory treatment may be gathered by direct observation of treatment or by inference from results. Both types of evidence will be considered in our discussion of the educational and labor-market systems.

RACIAL DISCRIMINATION IN EDUCATION

Discrimination in the American educational system was once both blatant and pervasive. In the eighteenth and early nineteenth centuries, the teaching of slaves was barred in most southern states. In 1885, California adopted a school segregation law allowing the exclusion of Chinese and Mongolian children from white public schools. A county school superintendent in Texas proclaimed that "our Mexicans" were better off transplanting onions than going to school. In 1876, a black student admitted to the University of Pennsylvania Medical School was asked to sit behind a screen in the classroom, so as not to offend the white students. White students at Harvard University simply ejected the black entrants.[6]

The U.S. Supreme Court effectively condoned all this behavior by declaring in 1896 that "separate, but equal" education was constitutional (*Plessy* v. *Ferguson*). Even separate but unequal was tolerable, as long as the inequalities were not motivated by racial hostility (*Cumming* v. *Richmond County Board of Education*, 1899).

---

[6]These and other historical examples are cited in U.S. Commission on Civil Rights, *Toward Equal Educational Opportunity: Affirmative Admissions Programs at Law and Medical Schools* (Washington, DC: U.S. Government Printing Office, 1982).

Disparate Outcomes

Discrimination still exists in American schools, even though it is much less pervasive or blatant than in the past. While this assertion will surprise very few readers, it is worthwhile to review the evidence on which it is based. Blacks and whites go into the educational system comparatively equal but come out of the system very different. By the time they are nine years old, black and Hispanic students are about 25 percent behind majority white students in reading, science, and math. These disparities continue to grow, so that by age 17 black students are over 30 percent behind white students in measured performance.[7]

Strong as these grounds are for believing that the education provided whites and blacks is not equal, they tend to understate disparities in black and white educations. The ability comparisons of black and white high school seniors, for example, necessarily exclude those students who dropped out of school before reaching the twelfth grade. Yet, the decision to quit school may itself reflect inferior educational opportunities and recognition of widening achievement disparities.[8] Seen in this light, black dropout rates are especially disturbing. While over 90 percent of white students now graduate from high school, only 87 percent of black students and 70 percent of Hispanic students graduate.[9]

Perhaps the most complete statement of black educational deficiencies is the rate of functional illiteracy among black youth. In 1975, the U.S. Office of Education sponsored a survey of the nation's 17-year-olds still in school. Students were asked to respond to 86 questions on reading items encountered in everyday life (for example, street signs, telephone directories, store coupons). Ninety-two percent of all white 17-year-olds were rated as functionally literate, having answered correctly at least three-fourths of all the questions. By contrast, only 58 percent of the black 17-year-olds were considered functionally literate.[10]

Figure 9.2 offers one final perspective on the outcomes of the educational process. This figure shows the percentage of different groups that complete at least four years of college. One-fourth of all whites graduate from college. Only 17 percent of blacks and even fewer Hispanics attain that much education. If minorities and whites really do enter the educational system with equal potential, these differences in educational outcomes require further explanation.

---

[7]National Center for Education Statistics, *Digest of Education Statistics, 1982* (Washington, DC: U.S. Government Printing Office, 1982). For more recent evidence, see John F. Kain and Kraig Singleton, "Equality of Educational Opportunity Revisited," *New England Economic Review* (May–June 1996).

[8]Congressional Budget Office, *Inequalities in the Educational Experiences of Black and White Americans* (Washington, DC: U.S. Government Printing Office, 1977), pp. x–9. Recent studies suggest that these disparities are shrinking; see Lyle Jones, "White-Black Achievement Differences: The Narrowing Gap," *American Psychologist* (November 1984), pp. 1207–1213.

[9]See U.S. Department of Education, *Dropout Rates in the United States: 1995* (Washington, DC: U.S. Government Printing Office). For further analyses of dropout rates, see Jonathan Crane, "Effects of Neighborhoods on Dropping Out of School and Teenage Childbearing," and Susan E. Mayer, "How Much Does a High School's Racial and Socioeconomic Mix Affect Graduation and Teenage Fertility Rates?" both in *Urban Underclass,* eds. C. Jencks and P. Peterson (Washington, DC: Brookings, 1991).

[10]The U.S. Department of Education now computes disaggregated indices of prose, document, and quantitative literacies rather than a composite index of functional literacy. See U.S. Department of Education, *Adult Literacy in America* (Washington, DC: U.S. Government Printing Office, 1992).

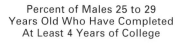

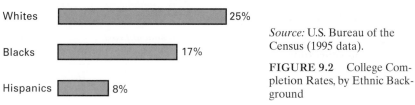

Source: U.S. Bureau of the Census (1995 data).

FIGURE 9.2   College Completion Rates, by Ethnic Background

School Segregation

The indirect evidence indicating discriminatory treatment in the educational system is highly suggestive. In fact, the observed disparities in achievement between white and black students are so great that direct evidence of discrepancies in educational opportunity should be easy to find. Segregation of facilities provides one such example: Where separate schools are maintained for whites and blacks, the documentation of inequalities is simple.

Before looking at the extent of continuing racial segregation in American schools, we need to establish some perspective on the meaning of segregation. When most people refer to *integrated schools,* they are encompassing all schools serving both whites and blacks. Such a definition is deceptive, however. Consider the case of a city with only two high schools: School A has 2,000 students, only one of whom is black; School B's 1,000 students, on the other hand, are all black. By the usual criterion of biracial enrollment, School A would be regarded as integrated, yet the racial isolation common to both schools is surely of greater significance than School A's dubious claim to biracial enrollment.

A more meaningful concept of integration must refer to the *proportion* of students attending school with children of another race. Complete integration would be a situation where all black students attended school with white children, and vice versa. By this stricter definition of integration, the distinction between School A and School B disappears. For the city as a whole, we may say that only 0.1 percent of the black population attends school with whites. This is far more descriptive than saying that 50 percent of the city schools are integrated.

This broader concept of integration has tremendous significance for our perceptions of educational desegregation. Ten years after the Supreme Court's historic order to desegregate, the state of Florida boasted that nearly a third of its schools were integrated. Closer scrutiny revealed, however, that only 2.65 percent of Florida's black pupils were attending school with whites. Progress was even slower in other southern states.

Table 9.2 summarizes the extent of school segregation in American schools for both black and Hispanic students. The table shows the percentage of black or Hispanic students attending schools that are either predominantly (over 50 percent) or exclusively (over 90 percent) attended by other minority students. The first thing to notice is that most black students and even a higher proportion of Hispanic students attend

TABLE 9.2   Segregation in Public Schools

PERCENT OF BLACK AND HISPANIC
STUDENTS IN SEGREGATED SCHOOLS

	School at Least 50% Minority		School at Least 90% Minority	
Year	Blacks	Hispanics	Blacks	Hispanics
1968–69	76.6	54.8	64.3	23.1
1980–81	62.9	68.1	33.2	28.8
1991–92	66.0	73.4	33.9	34.0
1994–95	67.1	74.0	33.6	34.8

Source: Gary Orfield et al., *Deepening Segregation in American Public Schools* (Cambridge, MA: Harvard Project on School Desegregation, 1997).

schools that are predominantly minority in enrollment. A third of all black and Hispanic students attend schools that are virtually all-minority institutions. Although segregation of black students has diminished since 1968, the segregation of Hispanic students has intensified. Even for black students there was a trend reversal in the 1980s that increased school segregation. Whether he or she lives in the North or the South, in the city or on a farm, a black, Hispanic, or other minority child is very unlikely to attend a truly integrated school. Racial isolation in the schools is still the hallmark of the American educational system.

Even if *schools* were more integrated, *classrooms* might not be. The concept of integration we have offered goes no further than the outer walls of the school, but even an ostensibly integrated school may be severely segregated within. Students may be assigned rooms, teachers, and facilities within the school on an explicitly racial basis. An extreme illustration of such internal segregation was encountered in Milwaukee. Like most other cities, Milwaukee was prodded by the courts to integrate its schools. In part, integration was achieved by busing black pupils to previously white schools. The substance of educational opportunity was little changed, however. The bused-in black pupils were maintained in separate classrooms and bused back and forth to their old schools for lunch. Black students who lived close to the white schools were even required to proceed to the more distant black schools for bus transportation to the receiving schools!

Not all internal school segregation is as explicit and extreme as was the case in Milwaukee. Nevertheless, *classrooms* remain more segregated than *schools*.[11] A popular and subtle form of classroom segregation is embodied in the so-called *tracking systems,* under which the more able students are separated from the rest and provided special opportunities to advance, while the least able students are held back for intensive remedial work. What makes the system so racially discriminatory is the fact that black pupils have received inferior education prior to integration, so that using IQ tests

[11]See Office of Civil Rights, U.S. Department of Education, 1986 Elementary and Secondary School Civil Rights Survey: National Summaries (December 1987).

or other achievement examinations to allocate pupils serves to perpetuate racial separation.[12] A still subtler form of segregation within the classroom may prevail where teachers or white students regard black pupils as innately or culturally incapable of attaining success.[13]

Equality of Facilities

The statistics of Table 9.2, together with our observations on the nature of integration, provide a sobering view of our efforts to provide equal opportunity "with all deliberate speed." In light of that background it may be argued that blacks and other minorities still attend school separately from majority whites. How equal, then, are their separate opportunities?

A comparison of educational opportunities at the local level is easily made: Visit any black (or Hispanic) school and any white (Anglo) school in the same city. You can readily detect enough qualitative differences in their educational environments to judge the relative attractiveness of the minority school. These local observations of school quality cannot be expanded across the country, however. It would be too expensive and time consuming to visit all the school districts across the nation in order to assess the average quality of black and white schools. Even if we had enough time and money, our judgments would depend on the perspectives and standards of many different observers. Finally, any conclusions we reached would be limited to such statements as "white schools are better (or very much better)," with no clear indication of how great existing inequalities are. Accordingly, we are compelled to seek more objective, easily quantified measures of school quality.

In the most comprehensive survey of educational facilities ever undertaken, the U.S. Office of Education employed 67 separate measures of school quality. These measures ranged from the number of books in the school library to the education of the teachers' mothers. They represented a concerted effort to capture and measure every dimension of the educational environment that might distinguish white schools from black schools. What the Office of Education discovered is that black and white schools differ on a multitude of separate measures but that such individual differences were relatively small. The only clear pattern to emerge from their mountain of statistics was that black schools tended to be most deficient in primarily academic facilities such as science labs, textbooks, and debate clubs.

In assessing these results, the Office of Education recognized many limitations in their approach. They reported that:

> The school environment of a child consists of many things, ranging from the desk he sits at to the child who sits next to him, and including the teacher who stands in front of his class. Any statistical survey gives only the most meager evidence of these environments, for two reasons. First, the reduction of the various aspects of the environment to quantitative measures must inherently miss many elements, tangible and more subtle, that

---

[12]See Angelia Dickens, "Revisiting *Brown* v. *Board of Education*: How Tracking has Resegregated America's Public Schools," *Columbia Journal of Law and Social Problems* (Summer 1996).

[13]The impact of more subtle racism on the college experiences of black students is examined in Joe R. Feagin, "The Continuing Significance of Racism: Discrimination Against Black Students in White Colleges," *Journal of Black Studies* (June 1992), pp. 546–578.

are relevant to the child. The measures must be comparable from school to school; yet the elements which are experienced as most important by the child will likely differ from one school to another, and may well differ among children in the same school.

Second, the child experiences his environment as a whole, while the statistical measures necessarily fragment it. Having a teacher without a college degree may indicate an element of disadvantage; but in the concrete situation, a schoolchild may be taught by a teacher who is not only without a college degree, but who has grown up and received his schooling in the local community, who has never been out of the State, who has 10th-grade vocabulary, and who shares the local community's attitudes.

For both these reasons, the statistical examination of difference in school environments for minority and majority children will give an impression of lesser differences than actually exist.[14]

More recent studies have used better measures of school inputs to quantify the dimension of school quality. One such study tracked 1.8 million elementary pupils in 4,500 Texas elementary schools for five years (1990–1994). Like the earlier Coleman study, the Kain-Singleton study documented racial achievement gaps that increased with years of school. Unlike the Coleman report, however, the Kain-Singleton study identified differences in school quality that contributed to those achievement disparities. Specifically, the study found that minority-dominated schools had teachers with lower achievement test scores, education, and experience than those in predominantly white (Anglo) schools.[15] The minority schools also had higher student/teacher ratios. Hence, the separate schools of white and minority children were demonstrably unequal.[16]

Even the Kain-Singleton study failed, however, to provide a summary measure of school quality, much less a definitive assessment of how much differences in school quality explain achievement disparities. All we can say with certainty is that our everyday observations agree with more formal surveys that find tangible (and intangible) differences in black and white educational facilities. We have no summary measure, however, of how large or how important those differences are.[17]

Inherent Inequalities

The Supreme Court provided a way out of this statistical ambiguity in 1954 by determining that segregated facilities were *inherently* unequal. The Court declared that "to separate them [black children] from others of similar age and qualifications solely because of their race generates a feeling of inferiority as to their status in the community that may affect their hearts and minds in a way unlikely ever to be undone."[18] The

[14]U.S. Office of Education, *Equality of Educational Opportunity* (The Coleman Report) (Washington, DC: U.S. Government Printing Office, 1966), p. 37.

[15]See John F. Kain and Kraig Singleton, "Equality of Educational Opportunities Revisited," *New England Economic Review* (May–June 1996).

[16]For differing views on the importance of school inputs for educational achievements, see Christopher Jencks et al., *Inequality* (New York: Basic Books, Inc., 1972); and Anita A. Summers and Barbara L. Wolfe, "Do Schools Make a Difference?" *American Economic Review* (September 1977).

[17]Michael A. Boozer, Alan B. Kruger, and Shari Wolkon, "Race and School Quality Since *Brown* v. *Board of Education*," *Brookings Papers on Economic Activity*, Special Issue on Microeconomics (1992), pp. 269–326.

[18]*Brown* v. *Board of Education*, 347 U.S. 483 (1954).

Court thus relegated the issue of tangible facilities to one of distinctly secondary importance. Even ostensibly "equal" schools for blacks and whites could never generate equal educational opportunity.

There were several specific considerations that led the Supreme Court justices to their landmark decision. They recognized that black pupils in segregated schools would have low self-esteem, knowing they were surrounded by failures and in schools regarded as inferior. Moreover, they would acquire a personal sense of futility knowing that, regardless of their individual attainments, they would always be identified by the community as members of a group viewed as less able, less successful, and less acceptable. Hence, the individual black child would see little reason to develop his or her individual talents. Community views would also affect the attitudes of teachers. Aware of, and probably sharing, the white community's low regard for blacks, teachers attached to black schools would tend to accept and transmit low expectations. They would not teach as much, or as well, to children deemed less teachable.

Impressive evidence in support of the Court's judgment was assembled by the U.S. Commission on Civil Rights in 1967. The commission discovered that black pupils of similar backgrounds performed quite differently in varying racial situations. In particular, it found that black educational achievements increased substantially where schools were more thoroughly integrated. In addition to the fact that white schools were generally better, it was observed that black pupils benefited from integration by believing that their opportunities had improved and by seeing others succeeding around them. Discrimination, then, and more especially school segregation, were seen to be major determinants of black achievements and status.[19]

CLASS DISCRIMINATION IN EDUCATION

While blacks do suffer from serious discrimination in the educational system, there is no reason to believe that they alone are singled out for substandard treatment. On the contrary, it is clear that other minority groups, among them Mexican-Americans, Puerto Ricans, and American Indians, confront barriers at least as formidable as do blacks. Accordingly, nearly everything we have said about racial discrimination against blacks applies with equal force to all minority group members. But including other minority groups in our discussion does not completely cover the subject of discrimination. As we are just beginning to perceive, racism has its counterpart in what has become known as *classism*. Poor individuals as a group, irrespective of their ethnic origin, are provided substandard facilities and opportunities in America.

We have already noted that many whites lose out as a result of racial discrimination in education, namely those who are not able to escape predominantly black neighborhoods and schools. But even where minority groups are not present, poor whites may be confined to separate and substandard schools. Neighborhoods are even more

---

[19]More recent evidence confirms the Court's view. See Congressional Budget Office, *Inequalities in the Educational Experiences of Black and White Americans* (Washington, DC: U.S. Government Printing Office, 1977), pp. 10–11.

likely to be homogeneous by income classes than by race; that is, poor families will be located in distinct areas of any city. Moreover, because school expenditures and decisions are determined by administrative bodies composed largely of the nonpoor, schools in low-income neighborhoods are likely to receive less than equal facilities.

School Finances

Inequality of educational opportunities across income classes tends to be reinforced by the way schools are financed. Slightly over half of all elementary and secondary school expenditures are financed by local property taxes, with most of the remainder financed out of state revenues (only 10 percent of elementary and secondary school expenditures are financed out of federal revenues). This implies that children in poorer states and poorer school districts are provided with fewer resources. And so they are: In 1994, for example, average per pupil expenditure varied across states by more than $6,000 (from a low of $3,439 in Utah to $9,677 in New York). Within states, disparities across school districts have often been just as large. In Georgia, Connecticut, Massachusetts, and California, high-spending school districts spent more than twice as much per pupil as did the school districts with lowest per pupil expenditure. Because expenditures within a school district may also be distributed unequally, educational opportunities are unlikely to be the same for all income classes.

Jonathan Kozol has described in vivid terms how these differences in spending affect the school environment. Schools in poor districts have ill-equipped labs, erratic heating and cooling, broken playground equipment, and a shortage of textbooks. Students in those schools are often taught by uncertified teachers and frequently by substitutes. By contrast, schools in wealthier districts have new equipment, computer labs, attractive environments, and certified teachers. As a result of these "savage inequalities" the quality of a child's education depends on the wealth of his or her parents and neighbors.[20]

The analogy of class discrimination to racial discrimination goes beyond differences in school facilities. Like minority children, poor white children tend to be surrounded by families that have failed to achieve material success. Poor white children see few demonstrations of personal aspiration and talent leading to higher socioeconomic status. Furthermore, they are aware that society regards material success as a mark of personal worth and thus see themselves and their families as stigmatized by the larger community. They know, too, that their schools are inferior and that completion of their studies will leave them ill prepared to compete in the labor market. As a consequence, they are likely to internalize a sense of futility and inferiority.

Educational Attainments

The cumulative impact of class discrimination is apparent in the educational attainments of lower-class children. Poor children drop out of high school at over twice the rate of nonpoor children. Even more startling is the fact that a substantial number of poor children leave the educational system even *before* they enter high school. And those relatively few lower-income children who do manage to make it through until

---

[20]Jonathan Kozol, *Savage Inequalities: Children in American Schools* (New York: Crown, 1991).

high school graduation cannot depend on their abilities to get them into college. College admissions are still reserved primarily for those who can support themselves or can afford to forego several years of employment income.

Table 9.3 provides some perspective on the barriers to higher education imposed by low incomes. This table includes all families with at least one child 18 to 24 years old. Within this group of families, the table indicates the percentage of families within each income class who have at least one child attending college full-time. For example, 56 percent of all high-income ($50,000 plus) families have at least one child in college. Among the lowest-income families (under $10,000), only 21 percent have a child in college. As the first row of Table 9.3 reveals, the likelihood of attending college increases markedly with family income.

Another notable feature of Table 9.3 is the absence of significant racial differences *within* income classes. Look at the group of families with incomes of $40,000–49,999, for example. Within this income class, Hispanic youth are actually *more* likely to attend full-time college than (Anglo) white youth. Within other income classes, racial differences are also relatively small. This suggests that *racial* differences in educational opportunity may, in fact, reflect *class* differences. From this perspective, blacks and other minorities do worse than whites in the educational system because their families' incomes are generally lower.

The Question of Ability

It is generally assumed by the nonpoor that poor children do not attain higher educational status because they are uniformly less able, but there are some very obvious weaknesses in this assumption. For example, very talented poor youngsters have no control over family finances. Hence, if the family cannot afford either to forego their earnings or even to supply them with school clothes and lunches, they will not be able to take advantage of "free" high school education. Furthermore, there are no scholarship or loan programs for high school students. So, we may anticipate that many talented poor children will never complete high school. Even for those who do attain high school diplomas, college admission will be barred by similar financial obstacles and by a legacy of inferior schooling.

TABLE 9.3   Percent of Families with Children in College Full-Time, by Family Income and Race (1992)*

		Family Income					
	Total	*Under $10,000*	*$10,000– $19,999*	*$20,000– $29,999*	*$30,000– $39,999*	*$40,000– $49,999*	*$50,000– and Over*
All	41.2	20.9	26.3	32.9	41.4	45.4	56.4
White	42.9	18.6	25.7	34.3	42.4	44.6	59.5
Black	28.1	17.9	24.1	25.2	33.5	39.2	50.0
Hispanic	24.3	15.3	17.3	20.0	34.0	45.6	40.1

*Children ages 18–24.

Source: U.S. Department of Education.

It is not easy to determine how many bright, poor children are denied higher education because of their poverty. IQ tests remain our only standardized measure of ability, and those tests create problems for poor whites similar to those for blacks. Because their schools are substandard, poor whites fall increasingly far behind the nonpoor in educational performance. Hence, they demonstrate decreasing IQs over time, and it is difficult to discern how many originally bright children existed among the poor. And yet, even on the restrictive criterion of IQ tests, we can identify a large number of poor and able high school graduates who never attained a college degree.

As Table 9.4 reveals, the socioeconomic status of one's family has tremendous impact on a child's chances for college education. For any demonstrated level of twelfth-grade IQ, children from higher-status families are far more likely to reach college graduation. What is especially noteworthy here is the comparatively small proportion (20 percent) of very able poor students who graduate from college. Children of lesser ability but more prosperous families take the places of the more gifted among the poor. Educational opportunity is distributed neither equally nor evenly on the basis of demonstrated ability.[21]

Class discrimination in education, then, is a strong force in the educational system and helps to determine the distribution of poverty. Whatever aggregate level of poverty exists, we may confidently predict that the children of the poor will be heavily overrepresented in the poverty statistics. It is also possible that class discrimination has become a stronger force in American society than racial discrimination. The U.S. Commission on Civil Rights, for example, found that schools were severely segregated by socioeconomic class and that the social class composition of schools is a stronger determinant of achievement than race.[22] Moreover, there is mounting evidence that middle-class whites, if forced to choose, would prefer as neighbors middle-class blacks to poor whites. Poor persons, of whatever color, are least accepted by the larger society. This will be of little comfort to poor blacks and other minorities, of course, who are likely to be the subject of both racial and class discrimination.

TABLE 9.4   College Graduation Rates, by Socioeconomic Status and IQ

| | IQ Score | | |
Socioeconomic Status	Low	Middle	High
Low	1.8	5.4	19.6
Middle	2.1	9.5	27.4
High	2.9	17.9	46.7

Source: Bruce Eckland and Louis Henderson, *College Attainment—Four Years after High School* (Durham, NC: Research Triangle Institute, June 1981).

[21]Richard Herrnstein and Charles Murray claim that such class discrimination has all but disappeared, so that a meritocracy based on intelligence now determines access to education; see their *The Bell Curve: Intelligence and Class Structure in American Life* (New York: Free Press, 1994). Their view is challenged in Claude S. Fischer et al., *Inequality by Design: Cracking the Bell Curve Myth* (Princeton, NJ: Princeton University Press, 1996).

[22]Similar evidence is presented in S. Mayer, "How Much Does a High School's Racial and Socioeconomic Mix Affect Graduation and Teenage Fertility Rates?" Table 4.

SEX DISCRIMINATION IN EDUCATION

The educational handicaps of minority and lower-class groups are reasonably easy to document, but the disadvantages that women confront in the educational system are more subtle, at least in the early grades. The sex barriers that characterize primary and secondary educational systems consist of sex-typing certain kinds of curricula. Girls are encouraged to take home economics, foreign languages, and typing, while gently discouraged from taking manual crafts, business courses, and science. The barriers emanate both from school counselors—who want to be "realistic" about occupational goals—and, perhaps more importantly, from parents and peers attuned to certain expectations with respect to male and female roles in society. As the Carnegie Commission on High Education noted:

> Almost from the moment of birth, boys and girls are subject to a wide variety of cultural influences that tend to prepare them for differentiated roles in life. Little girls are typically given dolls or miniature cooking utensils for toys; boys are generally given trucks and electric trains and mechanical toys. School readers show pictures of father going off to work and mother waving good-bye at the window, or of father playing baseball with his sons while mother bakes cookies. Girls play jump rope or tag on the school playground, while boys play ball. At about the seventh or eighth grade, boys take a course in manual training, while girls are taught cooking and sewing.
>
> We are not suggesting that matters ought to be reversed, or that little girls should be forbidden to play with dolls, but rather that there ought to be more freedom of choice. Girls who show signs of a mechanical bent should be given an opportunity to play with mechanical toys and to enter the course on manual training. Boys should not be barred from courses on cooking and sewing if they are interested.[23]

Gender Segregation

This kind of acculturation—what the Sadkers call "educational sexism"[24]—tends to restrict the educational aspirations of female students and to frustrate them when they challenge those restrictions. One of the manifestations of this educational sexism is the "glass wall" that partitions women from men in college curricula. Although women are a bit more likely than men to attend college, they are not likely to be found in science or engineering classes. Only 30 percent of the students who major in physics, chemistry, or computer science are women. In engineering, the female presence drops to 15 percent. College coeds are more likely to major in home economics (89 percent of all degrees go to women), health sciences (78 percent), or general liberal arts (67 percent). This gender segregation reflects not only the persistent reinforcement of gender stereotypes from childhood, but also the gender bias in instruction and testing.[25]

---

[23]Carnegie Commission on Higher Education, *Opportunities for Women in Higher Education* (New York: McGraw-Hill Book Company, 1973), pp. 42–43; see also American University of University Women, *How Schools Shortchange Girls* (Washington, DC, 1992).

[24]Myra and David Sadker, *Failing at Fairness: How America's Schools Cheat Girls* (New York: Scribners, 1994).

[25]*Ibid.,* for extensive documentation.

Graduate Degrees

Equally explicit manifestations of sex discrimination in education have been apparent at the post-college level. As suggested earlier, female college graduates have had difficulty gaining access to the professional schools that confer the necessary credentials for many desirable jobs. Secretarial schools have always been easy to get into, but law schools, medical schools, and business schools have often been a different story. Figure 9.3 depicts the proportion of different educational degrees awarded to women in 1994–95. As is evident, women accounted for a very substantial percentage of graduate enrollments in education schools, but were poorly represented in law or medicine, and virtually nonexistent in engineering schools.

To a large extent, this pattern of graduate education is the consequence of sex-differentiated roles and expectations nurtured from the crib to the campus. But these forces are reinforced at the graduate-admissions level by a tendency to reject female applicants with superior qualifications in favor of male applicants with lesser qualifications. Together these forces result in the fact that as of 1995 only 30 percent of female college graduates had gone on to complete graduate school, as compared with 37 percent of male graduates.

FIGURE 9.3   Women in Education, 1994–95

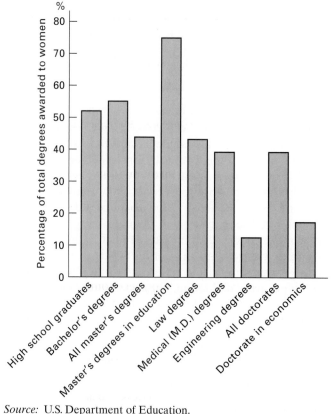

Source: U.S. Department of Education.

The same kind of observation has been made by the Council of Economic Advisers. In a special study on the economic role of women, the Council noted that although fewer women receive college and post-college degrees:

> Even more striking are the differences in the courses taken. At both the undergraduate and advanced levels, women are heavily represented in English, languages, and fine arts—the more general cultural fields. They are poorly represented in disciplines having a strong vocational emphasis and promising a high peculiar return. In 1970, 9.3 percent of the baccalaureates in business and 3.9 percent of the masters in business went to women. In the biological sciences, women had a larger share, taking about 30 percent of the bachelor's and master's degrees and 16 percent of the doctorates. But only 8.5 percent of the M.D.s and 5.6 percent of the law degrees went to women. Most of these percentages, low as they are, represent large gains from the preceding year.
>
> The situation is quite different in the so-called women's occupations. In 1971, women received 74 percent of the B.A.s and 56 percent of the M.A.s given in education. In library science, which is even more firmly dominated by women, they received 82 percent of all degrees in 1971. And in nursing 98 percent of all the degrees went to women.[26]

The implication of this pattern of sex discrimination is that women will enter the labor market with less valuable human capital than men.[27] As a consequence, we anticipate that a disproportionate number of women, especially those trying to raise families on their own, will end up in poverty.

SUMMARY

Discrimination on the basis of race, income class, or sex violates commonly accepted standards of social justice. Where discrimination is pervasive, the freedom of minority groups is severely restricted, as are their opportunities for achievement. Such limitations harm not only those discriminated against, but also the larger community. Talents go undeveloped, potential output is irrevocably lost, and markets are unnecessarily restricted.

In the American educational system, racial discrimination has resulted in a pattern of segregated and inferior schools for blacks and other minorities. Over one-third of all minority students continue to attend virtually all minority elementary and secondary schools. The inferiority of the education these children receive derives not only from disparities in school facilities but, more importantly, from a sense of isolation and subjugation imposed by the white community. The consequences of this discrimination are manifest in the low educational attainments of minority youth.

As serious and pervasive as discrimination against minorities is, it is not the only kind of discrimination practiced in the educational system. Poor children, in particular, are maintained in schools segregated largely by socioeconomic class and provided with substandard facilities. They and their families are also stigmatized by the larger community for failure to attain material success. As a result, children of poor families

---

[26]*Economic Report of the President* (Washington, DC: U.S. Government Printing Office, 1973), pp. 101–102.

[27]This point was underscored by a 1975 report of the Carnegie Council on Policy Studies in Higher Education that identified underrecruitment of women to appropriate graduate programs as the major obstacle to greater equality of jobs in higher education. Although women still lag behind men in many graduate degrees, the enrollment gap has narrowed substantially in the last decade.

drop out of school at alarming rates and generally lag behind nonpoor children in demonstrated achievement. Even those relatively few poor children who do demonstrate high levels of achievement are denied high levels of education. Class discrimination, then, is directly analogous to discrimination against racial or minority groups.

Finally, we must recognize that women are discriminated against in the educational system as well, even if such discrimination is more subtle. To the extent that such discrimination restricts later job opportunities, particularly for those women who end up as heads-of-household, it too contributes to the level and distribution of poverty.

Because educational attainments are a prime determinant of the distribution of poverty, those discriminated against in the schools are most likely to be among the poor. For whatever level of aggregate poverty exists, the children of yesterday's poor, blacks, and female-headed families will be grossly overrepresented in the poverty statistics. Children of poor black families headed by women will be the most disadvantaged, as they may be subject to all forms of discrimination.

FURTHER READING

On the Nature of Discrimination

Albelda, Randy, Robert Drago, and Steven Shulman, *Unlevel Playing Fields.* New York: McGraw-Hill, 1997.

Bunzel, John H., "Black and White at Stanford," *The Public Interest* (Fall 1991), pp. 61–77.

Darity, William S., ed., *Economics and Discrimination.* Lyme, NH: Edgar Reference Collection, 1995.

Dollard, John, *Caste and Class in a Southern Town.* Garden City, NY: Doubleday and Company, Inc., 1957.

Hacker, Andrew, *Two Nations: Black and White, Separate, Hostile, Unequal.* New York: Scribners, 1992, Chapters 1–2.

Kluegel, James R., and Eliot R. Smith, "Affirmative Action Attitudes: Effects of Self-Interest, Racial Effect, and Stratification Beliefs on Whites," *Social Forces* (March 1983).

Massey, Douglas S., and Nancy A. Denton, *American Apartheid: Segregation and the Making of the Underclass.* Cambridge, MA: Harvard University Press, 1993.

Tuch, Stephen A., and Michael Hughes, "Whites' Racial Policy Attitudes" (and responses thereto), *Social Science Quarterly* (December 1996), pp. 723–788.

On Discrimination in Education

Boozer, Michael A., Alan Kruger, and Shari Wolkon, "Race and School Quality Since *Brown* v. *Board of Education*," *Brookings Papers on Economic Activity,* Special Issue on Microeconomics (1992), pp. 269–326.

Gotteredson, Denise C., "Black-White Differences in the Educational Process: What Have We Learned?" *American Sociological Review* (October 1981).

Kain, John F., and Kraig Singleton, "Equality of Educational Opportunity Revisited," *New England Economic Review* (May–June 1996).

Kozol, Jonathan, *Savage Inequalities: Children in American Schools.* New York: Crown, 1991.

Orfield, Gary, et al., *Deepening Segregation in American Public Schools.* Cambridge, MA: Harvard University Press (April 1997).

Sadker, Myra and David, *Failing at Fairness: How America's Schools Cheat Girls.* New York: Scribners, 1994.

CHAPTER

Discrimination in the Labor Market

I n 1927, a clothing manufacturer in New York City advertised for help with the following wage offer: "White Workers $24; Colored Workers $20."[1] His offer embodied one of the most flagrant forms of racial discrimination in the labor market; namely, the payment of unequal wages for equal work. Few employers are so blatant today, and certainly no one advertises such discriminatory practices in print anymore. Nevertheless, as we observed in Chapter 9 (Table 9.1), most blacks and even one out of every three whites believe that blacks do not receive equal treatment in the labor market.

If minority workers are discriminated against in the labor market, they are denied full use of their productive abilities. As a consequence, their incomes will be depressed, and they will be heavily represented in the ranks of the poor. Hence, racial discrimination in the labor market tends to affect both the distribution and extent of poverty. In this chapter, we examine the consequences, forms, and practices of discrimination in the labor market. As in Chapter 9, we begin with a discussion of racial discrimination and then consider the phenomena of class and sex discrimination.

RACIAL DISCRIMINATION IN THE LABOR MARKET

We know that there are tremendous disparities between the incomes of blacks and whites. In Chapter 2 we noted that one out of three blacks is poor compared to only one out of ten whites. In Chapter 7, we observed that average black family incomes are $17,000 less than white family incomes. Hispanic families fall even further behind. Moreover, we have observed that racial or cultural theories cannot explain these inequalities. Thus, there are strong grounds for assuming that blacks and Hispanics continue to be the subject of discrimination, despite the lack of advertising to that effect.

It would be mistaken, however, to conclude that all existing income inequalities can be explained by discriminatory practices in the labor market. We know, for instance,

---

[1]Cited by Orley Ashenfelter, "Changes in Labor Market Discrimination Over Time," *Journal of Human Resources* (Fall 1970), pp. 403–430.

that blacks and Hispanics enter the labor market with less human capital than whites as a result of racial discrimination in the schools. Accordingly, a labor market that rewarded all individuals only on the basis of demonstrated achievement would still provide less income for blacks than whites. A very high proportion of blacks also continue to live in the South, where employment levels and wages are generally lower. Hence, income disparities alone do not prove the existence of racial discrimination in the labor market; they simply create a presumption that discrimination will be discovered if sought.

Even if we find that income disparities continue to exist after we have accounted for educational and geographic differences, we cannot assert conclusively that discriminatory practices are rampant in the labor market. If discrimination against minority workers ceased altogether, they would still be handicapped by past labor-market discrimination. They would be less skilled and experienced and lower on seniority ladders, for example. As in the area of education, minority workers would remain disadvantaged by past discrimination, even if present discrimination were eliminated.

The observed income disparities between white and minority workers, then, are potentially the result of three forces: nonmarket discrimination, past labor-market discrimination, and present labor-market discrimination. What we seek to identify in this section is that portion of existing income disparities attributable solely to continuing racial discrimination in the labor market.

Disparities in Earnings

White families have accumulated vast amounts of wealth in the form of property, savings accounts, bond holdings, and stock ownership. Stockholders' equity alone now amounts to over $4 trillion, while another $10 trillion is tied up in savings, cash, government bonds, and other financial assets. Black families have comparatively little access to this wealth, as they have been denied equal opportunity to earn and accumulate money in the past. Thus, the average white family has over ten times as much wealth as the average black family. Such disparities in wealth tend to overwhelm differences in income.

For the most part, these differences in wealth do not reflect current labor-market discrimination. They do, however, tend to distort comparisons of current white and black incomes. Current income includes money derived from accumulated wealth, especially money received in the form of dividends, interest, and capital gains. Accordingly, *total* income differences between blacks and whites are much larger than differences in *earnings,* that is, income derived from labor-market activity. To assess the impact of racial discrimination in the labor market, then, we need to focus on racial disparities in earnings alone.

In 1995, the mean earnings of white male workers over age 15 were $33,406. For black workers, the average was only $23,374, just two-thirds of white earnings. The earnings of Hispanic workers were lower still, as Figure 10.1 illustrates. In absolute terms, the earnings gap between (Anglo) white and minority workers was $10,000–$12,000 per year.

How much of this earnings difference was due to discrimination in the labor market? To isolate the impact of racial discrimination on this disparity, we need to

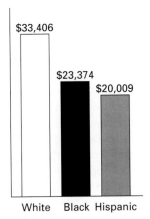

Source: U.S. Bureau of the Census (1995 data for males 15 years old and older).

FIGURE 10.1   Mean Male Earnings, by Race

identify the influence of other earnings determinants. Education, skills, age, and geographic location all influence a person's earnings. Only by controlling for these other factors can we perceive the independent influence of racial discrimination in the labor market.

Educational Differences

We have already noted the tremendous importance of educational attainments for income. Therefore, we must control for the influence on earnings of the nonmarket discrimination suffered in schools. This may be done by observing the comparative earnings of workers with equal educations. If there were no racial discrimination in the labor market, blacks, Hispanics, and whites with equal education should command approximately equal incomes.

As Table 10.1 shows, this isn't the case. However, the earnings of white, black, and Hispanic men with equal years of schooling are closer than the unadjusted comparisons. As Figure 10.1 illustrates, the "raw" median Hispanic earnings are only 60 percent of median white earnings. However, Hispanic college graduates earn 75 percent of what white college graduates earn. Hence, once schooling differences are taken into account,

TABLE 10.1   Male Earnings, by Race and Education

| | *Average Earnings of* | | |
Education	*White Workers*	*Black Workers*	*Hispanic Workers*
High school dropout	$17,600	$15,353	$15,037
High school graduate	27,467	19,514	20,882
Some college	29,206	24,894	21,705
College graduate	47,016	36,026	35,109

Source: U.S. Bureau of Labor Statistics (1995 data for males 18 years old and older).

the earnings gap between Hispanics and whites is cut nearly in half. The same kind of schooling adjustment reduces the black and white gap by roughly a third. This reduces the potential explanatory power of pure labor-market discrimination considerably.

Further adjustments in the gross earnings comparisons are needed to identify white, black, and Hispanic workers possessing equal human capital. Table 10.1 adjusts only for the *quantity* of schooling. But what about the *quality?* As we observed in Chapter 9, years of schooling do not have the same educational significance for blacks and whites. A complete adjustment for nonmarket discrimination would have to control for the significant differences in the *quality* of education received by each group. We must recognize that a typical black high school graduate comes to the job with as little educational preparation as the typical white high school dropout. When this additional control for nonmarket discrimination is imposed, observed labor-market disparities shrink further. Black workers of equivalent educational backgrounds, including both quantity and quality of schooling, earn incomes approximately 90 percent as large as their white counterparts.[2]

It appears, then, that most of the earnings disparity between whites and blacks can be attributed to prior (nonmarket) discrimination in the schools. This means that only about a third of the observable earnings disparity can be explained by present labor-market discrimination. Indeed, the combined influence of other factors, including skills, age, and region, reduce the disparity further. Recent studies of discrimination have estimated that only about one-fourth of existing earnings disparities are directly attributable to discriminatory labor-market practices.[3] As a rough approximation, then, we may say that two-thirds of the $10,000–$12,000 earnings disparity is due to nonmarket discrimination (education, residence); one-sixth due to past market discrimination (work skills and experience); and one-sixth to current labor-market discrimination.[4]

While nonmarket discrimination apparently overwhelms other types of discrimination, some caution is necessary in interpreting these conclusions. Clearly, these are only rough approximations to the relative impact of various handicaps. They are best viewed as orders of magnitude, not precise estimates. Even if the allocation of the gross racial earnings gap is correct, current labor-market discrimination still exacts a significant toll: One-sixth of the gross earnings gap amounts to a "tax" of $1,600–$2,000 on the annual earnings of minority workers. Racial discrimination in the labor market is,

---

[2]This conclusion is reinforced by the finding that black and white workers with similar literacy skills—an outcome of the quantity and quality of education—have similar employment probabilities; see Francisco L. Rivera-Batiz, "Quantitative Literacy and the Likelihood of Employment Among Young Adults in the United States," *Journal of Human Resources* (Spring 1992), pp. 313–328.

[3]See Derek Neal and William Johnson, "The Role of Premarket Factors in Black-White Differences," *Journal of Political Economy,* 1996, 104.5, pp. 869–895; Nan Maxwell, "The Effect of Black-White Wage Differences in the Quantity and Quality of Education," *Industrial and Labor Relations Review* (January 1994), pp. 249–264; David Card and Alan K. Krueger, "School Quality and Black-White Relative Earnings: A Direct Assessment," *Quarterly Journal of Economics* (February 1992), pp. 151–200; June O'Neill, "The Role of Human Capital in Earnings Differences between Black and White Men," *Journal of Economic Perspectives* (Fall 1990), pp. 25–45.

[4]Richard Herrnstein and Charles Murray claim that measured IQ accounts for the entire earnings gap between white and black workers employed year-round, leaving no discriminatory residual; see their *The Bell Curve: Intelligence and Class Structure in American Life* (New York: Free Press, 1994). Among the many critiques of their argument are Claude S. Fischer et al., *Inequality by Design: Cracking the Bell Curve Myth* (Princeton, NJ: Princeton University Press, 1996).

thus, a large and important racial barrier, even if outstripped by discrimination in education. Furthermore, it cannot be assumed that these proportions are fixed. If, in fact, the quality and quantity of schooling for blacks and Hispanics increase—as they have in recent years—we have no assurance that minority educational attainments will continue to be rewarded at the same rate. As more educated black and Hispanic workers emerge, racial discrimination in the labor market may intensify. Much potential discrimination in the labor market is now averted due to the fact that relatively few blacks and Hispanics are able to compete directly with whites. As minority educational attainments—and thus labor-market competition—increase, the situation may change dramatically.[5] Accordingly, we have no firm basis for predicting a linear reduction of earnings disparities as educational opportunities become more equal. These calculations illustrate where the locus of discrimination is now; they cannot predict where it will be in the future.

Components of Earnings Disparities

While the image is provocative, it is mistaken to picture a thief called Discrimination openly robbing minority workers of $10,000–$12,000 each year, even though the effect may be the same. Instead, we must realize that this earnings loss emerges from several dimensions of the labor-market process. Minority workers are not robbed of their earnings outright. Very little of the discrimination that takes place in the labor market is of the sort exemplified by the New York garment manufacturer who paid different wages to white and black workers. Aside from being illegal, the visibility of such practices makes them especially vulnerable to public scrutiny and civil rights action. In addition, such overtly inequitable treatment violates the consciences of most employers. Rather, minority workers are hired less often, for fewer hours, for less desirable jobs, and at lower wages (see Figure 10.2). They are also offered less training on the job. The sum total of these different forces leaves the minority worker poorer. A more thorough understanding of discrimination is attained by considering the relative importance of each of these forces.

Because minority workers are less educated, less experienced, and less attractive to most employers than available white workers, they are least likely to be hired. In any given job situation white workers will be hired first and laid off last. Hence, the frequency of employment and the number of hours worked will differ for minority and white workers as the combined result of nonmarket and market racial discrimination. Indeed, a significant part of the observed earnings disparity derives not from the decision to pay minority workers lower wages but from the decision to employ them less often.[6] Table 10.2 shows that black workers are more than twice as likely to be unemployed as are white workers. Black workers also tend to remain unemployed for a

---

[5]Asian men apparently experience this kind of higher-level discrimination; see Harriet Orcutt Duleep and Seth Sanders, "Discrimination at the Top: American-Born Asian and White Men," *Industrial Relations* (Fall 1992), pp. 416–432. A similar pattern has been observed for black women in Deborah Anderson and David Shapiro, "Racial Differences in Access to High-Paying Jobs and the Wage Gap Between Black and White Women," *Industrial and Labor Relations Review* (January 1996), pp. 273–286.

[6]Supply effects are relevant also. Confronted with discrimination in the labor market, minorities may choose to drop out of school or withdraw from the labor market. See M. Baldwin and W. G. Johnson, "The Employment Effects of Wage Discrimination Against Black Men," *Industrial and Labor Relations Review* (January 1996), pp. 302–316.

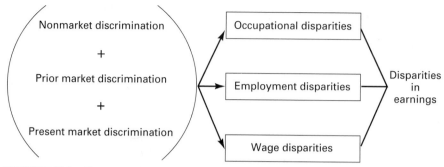

FIGURE 10.2 Components of Earnings Disparities

longer time. Hispanic workers also experience unemployment more frequently, although for shorter periods of time.

Of still greater significance to the observed earnings disparity is the decision to employ black and Hispanic workers at different kinds of jobs. Once again, all forms of discrimination take their toll. Minority workers are denied entrance to many occupations because they lack necessary educational attainments or credentials. They also often lack required work skills and experience. And finally, whites regard many jobs as being inappropriate for blacks and therefore exclude them. Garbage collection and bus driving are regarded as acceptable black or Hispanic occupations; retail sales, management, or even teaching are less appropriate. And few whites could imagine trusting themselves to the services of a black doctor or lawyer (not to mention a female one of any race). Accordingly, most minority workers are largely excluded from full participation in the more pleasant and remunerative occupations. Table 10.3 indicates the general nature of existing occupational patterns.

White workers of either sex are much more likely to hold white-collar jobs than are minority workers. The very small percentage of black and Hispanic workers in managerial and administrative jobs is especially noteworthy. Apparently, minority workers seldom have the opportunity to be the boss. Indeed, black and Hispanic men are more likely to be nonfarm laborers than white-collar professionals. Yet white men are nearly three times as likely to be in a professional occupation (15.6 percent) as in nonfarm labor (5.4 percent).

Occupational disparities are further aggravated by the fact that minority workers who do gain access to the better occupations end up in the lowest and least desirable jobs *within* each occupational group. Within the professional, technical, and managerial

TABLE 10.2 Unemployment of Male Workers, by Race

	Whites	*Blacks*	*Hispanics*
Unemployment rate (percent)	5.3	11.6	8.3
Average duration of unemployment (weeks)	14.7	21.0	16.2

Source: U.S. Bureau of Labor Statistics (data for first quarter of 1997).

TABLE 10.3　Occupational Status, by Race and Sex

Occupational Status	Male Workers			Female Workers		
	White	Black	Hispanic	White	Black	Hispanic
White collar	47.7	32.7	27.9	73.2	58.2	55.8
Professional and technical	15.6	9.6	7.0	20.7	16.0	11.4
Managers and administrators	14.5	7.8	7.2	12.3	8.0	7.9
Sales workers	11.9	6.4	7.4	13.0	9.1	11.5
Clerical workers	5.7	8.9	6.3	27.2	25.1	25.0
Blue collar	38.4	44.6	47.4	9.0	14.0	16.7
Craftspeople	19.6	14.0	20.0	2.0	2.5	2.8
Operatives	6.7	9.6	11.0	4.7	8.4	11.1
Transport drivers	6.7	10.6	7.3	0.8	1.1	0.5
Nonfarm laborers	5.4	10.4	9.1	1.5	2.0	2.3
Service workers	9.2	19.4	16.2	16.7	27.5	25.6
Farm workers	4.5	3.2	8.4	1.0	0.3	1.7

Source: U.S. Bureau of Labor Statistics (1993 annual averages). See also Barbara H. Woofton, "Gender Differences in Occupational Employment," *Monthly Labor Review* (April 1997), pp. 15–24.

class, for example, white workers tend to be lawyers, doctors, engineers, and social scientists. Black workers, on the other hand, are more likely to be funeral directors, welfare workers, and teachers in segregated schools. The same situation exists in the other occupational categories, sometimes in even more extreme forms. For example, among clerical workers are grouped both white insurance adjusters and black postal clerks, among sales workers both white stockbrokers and Puerto Rican sales clerks. In other words, the tremendous disparities evident in occupational distributions reveal only a relatively small proportion of the job barriers that actually confront minority workers.

At the bottom of the occupational ladder, the respective concentrations of blacks and whites are, of course, reversed. As Table 10.3 reveals, two-thirds of all black workers are concentrated in the lower occupational categories, and, again, the disparities in actual jobs are great. Black women are maids in private homes or maids in hotels and office buildings. Black men are day laborers, porters, and janitors. The better service and blue-collar jobs, including firefighters, police, bartenders, and teamsters, are largely reserved for whites. The fact that minority workers are employed less often and for fewer hours is of relatively little significance in comparison with this uneven distribution of occupational opportunities.

Job disparities *within* occupational categories are reflected in earnings. Table 10.4 displays the weekly earnings of whites, blacks, and Hispanics working in the same occupational category. Within professional occupations, for example, the typical majority white worker earns $868 per week, substantially more than blacks ($634) or Hispanics ($674) working in the same broad occupational category. These disparities reflect the

TABLE 10.4   Weekly Earnings, by Occupation and Race

	Median Earnings ($) of Male Workers		
Occupational Status	*White*	*Black*	*Hispanic*
White collar			
Professional	868	684	733
Managers and administrators	871	643	626
Sales workers	603	421	447
Clerical workers	500	415	391
Blue collar			
Craftspeople	573	467	409
Operatives	453	381	319
Transport drivers	499	413	375
Nonfarm laborers	348	317	288
Service workers	375	307	288
Farm workers	303	263	264

Source: U.S. Bureau of Labor Statistics (1996 data for full-time wage and salary workers).

fact that minority workers hold different *jobs* within a given occupation, are likely to be more concentrated in certain *industries,* and may be paid less for the same work.

Another disparity between majority and minority workers relates to training. Workers in the U.S. economy get most of their skill training on the job. This on-the-job training provides the basis for both job security and later advancement. In general, the more training an employer "invests" in a worker, the faster the worker is likely to advance on the job. The additional human capital acquired also makes a worker more attractive to other employers.[7]

The amount of training actually received by whites is nearly double that received by minority workers. White workers report that they are more likely to receive on-the-job training and to get it for a longer period of time.[8] As a consequence, observed disparities in occupations and earnings may understate eventual income differences.

Who Discriminates?

It is not easy to visualize so much discrimination taking place in the labor market. It is even more difficult to picture those persons or groups who actually engage in discrimination. Very few of us can readily identify anyone as an outright racist. The whole notion of purposeful maltreatment simply runs counter to the way we are accustomed to

---

[7]For the theory and experience of training programs, see Orley Ashenfelter and Robert LaLonde, eds., *The Economics of Training* (2 vol.) (Lyme, NH: Edgar Reference Collection, 1996).

[8]Saul D. Hoffman, "On-the-Job Training: Differences by Race and Sex," *Monthly Labor Review* (July 1981). For more recent estimates, see Jonathan Veum, "Training Among Young Adults: Who, What Kind, and For How Long," *Monthly Labor Review* (August 1993), pp. 27–32.

viewing ourselves or the marketplace. Nevertheless, employers, unions, employees, employment agencies, and training programs are all implicated in the charge of labor-market discrimination. To understand how so many individuals and groups are involved, we must return to the nature of discrimination.

Much market discrimination is unintended. Even persons free of prejudice or animosity may engage in discriminatory patterns of behavior. While such unintentional practices make fewer headlines, their impact on minority employment opportunities is no less important. Traditional company recruitment practices provide a simple illustration. Most companies, large or small, rely heavily on existing employees for new recruits. If new jobs open up, present employees usually are able to locate friends or relatives who want the new positions, and a word-of-mouth recruitment system is remarkably efficient. Present employees know the company, the jobs, and the applicants; therefore, they are in a position to match jobs and people accurately. Word-of-mouth recruitment is also inexpensive; no outside agencies need be contacted, and advertisement costs are kept to a minimum. Large companies are so impressed with this recruitment system that they offer bonuses to employees who bring in new workers.

Word-of-mouth recruitment practices, although efficient, tend to exclude minority workers from better jobs. Would-be minority applicants do not have a network of friends in better employment positions. Accordingly, they are seldom aware of developing opportunities and are rarely brought to the attention of recruitment personnel. Even in the absence of willful discrimination, they are effectively cut off from new jobs.

Recruitment outside the firm does not always yield much better results. Companies are generally unfamiliar with the people and skills available in minority residential areas, especially ghetto areas. They do not know who, how, or where to recruit. As a result, they tend to rely on traditional sources and agencies of recruitment more readily accessible to whites.[9] Would-be minority applicants also experience a certain hesitancy in approaching unfamiliar companies or employment agencies. Knowing that prejudice exists and having possibly confronted explicit discrimination themselves, minority job seekers are often reluctant to risk embarrassment or harassment. They rely, instead, on familiar sources and companies with established reputations in the community for fair treatment. Recent converts to equal employment opportunity have difficulty communicating their new intentions.

While these institutionalized patterns of behavior constitute a barrier to truly equal employment opportunity, we cannot ignore the impact of overt discrimination. Not all discriminatory practices are innocent. Some persons and groups willfully exclude minority workers from employment opportunities. Here we can only review the most obvious and widespread examples.

Labor Unions

Labor unions are a popular target for attack on many fronts, the subject of racial discrimination included. Labor unions are often large and highly visible. They also tend to control access to the better-paid jobs in crafts or industries for which minority job

---

[9]See Kathryn M. Neckerman and Joleen Kirschenman, "Hiring Strategies, Racial Bias, and Inner-City Workers," *Social Problems* (November 1991), pp. 433–447, for more discussion of how blacks and low-income job seekers are disadvantaged in the hiring process.

seekers are presently most qualified. High-status employment areas of lesser union strength, among them clerical, technical, and professional work, tend to require higher educational credentials. Hence, unions are sometimes in a position to provide a fast route to improved economic status.

The history of labor unions is not very encouraging. While the American Federation of Labor (AFL) was founded on the principles of racial and worker solidarity, its practices quickly departed from that philosophy. As early as 1895, nine years after its inception, the AFL compromised on the issue of racial equality by admitting deliberately discriminatory unions. By 1899 the AFL was even admitting unions whose constitutions explicitly forbade black membership, thereby forsaking even the pretense of racial equality. This development was particularly damaging to black workers because the AFL was strongest in those areas where black employment skills were concentrated, namely the crafts, such as carpentry, blacksmithing, and mechanical arts. Indeed, at the time of the Civil War black workers dominated craft employment in the South, outnumbering white craftspeople five to one. As the craft union movement grew, however, blacks lost their foothold in the job market. Black craftspeople were forced out of their jobs and denied access to new ones. Apprenticeship programs were also closed, thereby eliminating future opportunities for employment.

While racial prejudice was clearly at the root of much union discrimination, there is abundant evidence that economic motivations were dominant. The nascent unions knew that their strength and welfare depended on their ability to control job entry. Any potential craftsperson was viewed as a direct economic threat. The AFL unions not only sought to eliminate existing and potential competition from blacks but also worked vigorously to restrain all immigration from abroad. The Chinese were viewed as "people of vice and sexual immorality who were incompatible with our moral concepts."[10] Japanese and Koreans were no less undesirable. Even European immigrants were viewed as a threat to economic security and organizational strength. Hence, it is probably fair to conclude that the AFL was egalitarian in its discriminatory practices; that is, it discriminated against all potential competition with little regard to race, creed, or color! Where racial arguments were employed, their primary purpose was to camouflage narrower economic interests. Nevertheless, black workers were most abused, since they were the largest and closest competition.

The Congress of Industrial Organizations (CIO) emerged in 1935 in a changed economic climate and with a different constituency. Whereas the AFL had focused on craft labor, the CIO directed its attentions to the mass of workers on assembly lines and in less skilled jobs. These jobs generally required less training and experience and were concentrated more in the North. Not only were blacks significantly represented in these jobs, they also constituted an enormous threat to future union strength. If excluded from the industrial unions, black workers could be used by employers as strikebreakers to undercut union power. The same possibility did not exist in craft unions because specific skills were required for available jobs. Hence, the CIO had a powerful economic incentive to lower racial barriers to union entry. This combined with the

---

[10]Cited by Herbert Hill in *Employment, Race, and Poverty,* eds. Arthur M. Ross and Herbert Hill (New York: Harcourt Brace Jovanovich, Inc., 1967), p. 389.

egalitarian outlook of its leaders, especially John L. Lewis, led the CIO to establish nondiscriminatory membership policies.[11]

The AFL–CIO merger in 1955 did not revolutionize union practices. While the new union was founded on stronger antidiscrimination principles, it did little to alter the actual practices of local affiliates, especially the older AFL locals. Local unions retain a broad range of autonomy, and the national leadership has little power or incentive to discipline them on the subject of racial equality. Consequently, black workers continue to be excluded from many unions and relegated to inferior jobs or separate seniority lines when admitted. Experienced black workers are often required to undergo long and low-paid apprenticeship courses as a condition for union entry; inexperienced black workers find that they cannot enter apprenticeship programs at all.

Employers

Like unions, business management tends to reflect the interests and attitudes of its members: Some employers harbor racial prejudices and stereotyped views of minority workers. Even more prevalent, however, is a general reluctance to engage in actions that are controversial or merely tangential to primary business pursuits. Employers are hesitant to challenge traditional hiring practices or to confront what they regard as the community's racial attitudes. Hence, employers will often ignore potential minority workers, not as a result of their own prejudice, but because they fear that such hiring will trigger the prejudices of white employees or existing customers.[12] Employers have very little incentive to stir up racial troubles or even to bother determining whether such troubles would actually emerge. Profits, politics, recreation, and even the community chest command more attention and commitment. As a result, only the most cautious antidiscriminatory actions are undertaken, and then usually only as a result of economic or social pressures, such as boycotts or legal action.[13]

Another barrier to more affirmative action on the part of business management arises from the nature of collective bargaining. Where management does, in fact, decide to hire minority workers on a more equal basis, the unions are likely to demand reciprocal concessions. Unions tend to view management's initiatives as an encroachment on their own prerogatives. Altered hiring practices are interpreted as a concession to management, so the union seeks compensation in other areas, chiefly in wages or working conditions. Thus, the cost of affirmative action escalates, and management is even less likely to press for the elimination of discriminatory employment patterns.

---

[11]The tendency of craft unions to be more discriminatory was also documented in the 1970s; see Orley Ashenfelter, "Racial Discrimination and Trade Unionism," *Journal of Political Economy* (May 1972); and Duane E. Leigh, "Racial Discrimination and Labor Unions," *Journal of Human Resources* (Fall 1978). The general impact of unions on racial inequality is examined in E. M. Beck, "Labor Unionism and Racial Inequality: A Time-Series Analysis of the Post-World War II Period," *American Journal of Sociology,* vol. 85 (1980).

[12]The productivity of white males may also decline if newly hired minority upset traditional on-the-job social relations; see Barbara Bergmann and William Darity, Jr., "Social Relations, Productivity, and Employer Discrimination," *Monthly Labor Review* (August 1981).

[13]Evidence of direct employer discrimination in the hiring process is offered by Genevieve M. Kenney and Douglas A. Wissoker, "An Analysis of the Correlates of Discrimination Facing Young Hispanic Job-Seekers," *American Economic Review* (June 1994), pp. 674–683.

Finally, even "objective" hiring practices of employers may have discriminatory effects. We have already observed how word-of-mouth recruitment and traditional advertising may tend to exclude minority workers. Another obstacle emerges from the use of employment tests and other credentials as hiring criteria. All too often, test and educational credentials used to screen out prospective employees exclude a disproportionate number of minority workers. Moreover, such tests may have no direct relationship to job performance. Under such circumstances, the tests simply reduce an employer's hiring costs by reducing the number of extended interviews. In the process, however, many minority workers lose potential job opportunities. Such nonfunctional tests were outlawed by the U.S. Supreme Court in 1972 (*Griggs* v. *Duke Power Company*) but have not been eliminated completely.

Even if all such tests were eliminated, minority workers would still suffer from *statistical discrimination*. In reality, employers do not know for sure which job seekers will turn out to be the best employees. Tests and educational credentials are used to help reduce such uncertainty. If all such screening criteria are eliminated, employers may rely more on racial characteristics. Because white workers have, on average, more education, skill, and experience than minority workers, an employer is statistically "safer" in hiring white workers. In other words, screening out minority workers on the basis of their lower *average* qualifications may be an efficient recruitment technique, particularly if no surer screening mechanisms are available. In this case, minority workers are excluded from equal consideration on statistical grounds, not because of employer prejudice.[14] Of course, to the minority job seeker, the end result is the same.

Finally, it must be noted that managers tend to hire people like themselves. This may be human nature. It becomes discrimination, however, when managers are predominantly white males.

CLASS DISCRIMINATION IN THE LABOR MARKET

Minority racial groups are not the only workers who suffer discrimination in labor markets. Racial discrimination has a counterpart in class discrimination. In this case, individuals from low-income backgrounds are consistently denied equal access to better jobs and pay.

Employers, like the larger society, tend to have low estimates of the capabilities of job applicants who are poorly dressed or from "bad" neighborhoods. There is an underlying conviction that poverty reflects personal inadequacy (flawed characters). As a result, poor applicants are viewed differently than others and must exhibit exceptional talents to obtain competitive jobs. As a result, if their talents are only equal to, say, middle-class applicants, then prejudice is likely to deny employment to the poor. Prejudices are reinforced, of course, by the use of academic achievement tests that often have little or no relation to the content of the available job.

---

[14]The concept of *statistical discrimination* is discussed in Edmund S. Phelps, "The Statistical Theory of Racism and Sexism," *American Economic Review* (September 1972); and Dennis J. Aigner and Glen G. Cain, "Statistical Theories of Discrimination in Labor Markets," *Industrial and Labor Relations Review* (January 1977). More recent evidence is examined in Gerald S. Oettinger, "Statistical Discrimination and the Early Career Evolution of the Black–White Wage Gap," *Journal of Labor Economics* (Winter 1996), pp. 52–78.

These discriminatory practices are often institutionalized in the recruitment procedures of companies. As we noted earlier, corporations tend not to recruit in poverty areas. They know virtually nothing about available talent in poor neighborhoods and expend little effort to increase their knowledge. As a consequence, poor job seekers and company recruiters seldom make contact. The same kind of isolation results from the word-of-mouth recruitment practices previously mentioned. Like blacks in general, poor whites tend to have comparatively few friends or acquaintances employed at higher-status jobs. They thus have little knowledge of or access to good jobs that are opening up. What jobs they hear of are those they have always encountered: dirty, low-paid, and menial.

Class discrimination in the labor market, then, means that poor job seekers have less chance to obtain employment than nonpoor job seekers of equal ability. Racial discrimination has the same effect for blacks and other minority groups, sex discrimination the same effect for women. In all cases, discrimination takes place as a result of individual prejudices and institutionalized practices. The poor, like blacks, have many personal characteristics and backgrounds unfamiliar to middle-class employers, employment agencies, and even unions. Conduct, speech, and dress are among those factors that create communication barriers. Employers tend to see these differences as indicators of ability rather than as the result of socioeconomic environment. It is assumed that the poor will not be as able or dependable on the job. Workers are not sought from poorer areas and, when they come forth, are unfavorably considered.[15]

SEX DISCRIMINATION IN THE LABOR MARKET

The same forces that tend to constrain the earnings of minorities and lower-income classes also operate to limit the employment and income opportunities of women. Here again, we must take into account the fact that women enter the labor market with less human capital than men do, especially when measured in terms of advanced degrees. They also tend to be trained for different kinds of work, as a result of both societal pressures and overt discrimination in the educational system. These handicaps help explain why women exhibit less labor force participation, inferior occupations, and lower pay. But such handicaps do not provide a complete explanation because female workers additionally suffer from limited access to jobs for which they are otherwise qualified.

Occupational Segregation

As we noted in our discussion of racial discrimination (see Table 10.3), occupational segregation is a major source of earnings disparities. This tendency is especially important for women as well, as they tend to be relegated to a limited number of occupations and an even more limited number of jobs within each occupation. According to

---

[15]These kinds of class barriers may help explain the handicap of low-income backgrounds on later income, as observed in Mary Corcoran, R. Gordon, D. Laren, and G. Solon, "The Associations Between Men's Economic Status and Their Family and Community Origins," *Journal of Human Resources* (Fall 1992), pp. 575–601.

estimates by Heidi Hartmann and Donald Treimann, occupational segregation accounts for over a third of the wage gap between men and women.[16]

The statistics in Table 10.5 provide a clue as to how high the sex barriers are when one begins to examine the labor market in detail. Within the "professional and technical" occupational category, for example, we discover that there are clearly "female jobs" and "male jobs": 95 percent of all registered nurses are women, while only 7 percent of our engineers are women. The same kind of imbalance is evident throughout the list.

Nor is this the end of the story. Even within the more detailed occupations of Table 10.5, men and women tend to be employed at different kinds of jobs, in different industries, or in different work settings. Consider just one example, that of waiters and waitresses. Women comprise a whopping 85 percent of that category, but how many of them are employed in the best restaurants (where prices and tips are highest, incidentally)? Very few.

TABLE 10.5 A Nonliberated Labor Force

	Traditional Jobs for Women	Percent of Jobs Held by Women	Nontraditional Jobs for Women	Percent of Jobs Held by Women
Professional and technical	Librarians	86	Engineers	7
	Registered nurses	95	Lawyers and judges	20
	Elementary		Doctors	20
	teachers	85	Clergy	7
	Dietitians	90		
Managers and administrators	Restaurants, cafeterias, and bars	34	Public agencies	6
Sales workers	Demonstrators	69	Sales representatives	40
Clerical and kindred workers	Secretaries	99	Mail carriers	21
	Bank tellers	90	Shipping clerks	30
	Telephone operators	92	Dispatchers	46
Craftspeople	Bookbinders	58	Electricians	1
	Decorators	58	Telephone lineworkers	8
Operatives	Dressmakers	93	Taxicab drivers	11
	Laundry and dry cleaning	64	Truck drivers	15
Service	Practical nurses	96	Police officers	11
	Waitresses	85	Bartenders	50

Source: U.S. Bureau of Labor Statistics, unpublished data (1987).

---

[16]Heidi Hartmann and Donald Treimann, eds., *Women, Work, and Wages: Equal Pay for Jobs of Equal Value* (Washington, DC: National Academy Press, 1981). For an analysis of *why* female-dominated occupations pay lower wages, see David A. Macpherson and Barry T. Hirsh, "Wage and Gender Composition: Why Do Women's Jobs Pay Less?" *Journal of Labor Economics* (1995). Aggregate measures of occupational segregation are discussed in Mary C. King, "Occupational Segregation by Race and Sex, 1940–88," *Monthly Labor Review* (April 1992), pp. 30–36.

These male-female job disparities *within* occupational groups result in sharply different wages for men and women. The median weekly earnings of full-time female workers ($427 in 1997) is only three-fourths of male workers ($582). The same kind of differential exists within most occupations.[17] Like minorities, women are also less likely to receive OJT training that will increase their responsibilities and wages.

A popular explanation for these job and pay disparities is the lesser labor force attachment of women. Most women who do work either start their careers after having children or interrupt their careers for that purpose. The job interruption that typically accompanies childbirth translates into lost job experience and thus less human capital development, at least from a labor-market point of view. Can this "natural" barrier to female productivity explain occupational and income differentials? Partially, but *only* partially. As the President's Council of Economic Advisers observed:

> One important factor influencing the (earnings) differential is experience. The lack of continuity in women's attachment to the labor force means that they will not have accumulated as much experience as men at a given age. The relatively steeper rise of men's income with age has been attributed to their greater accumulation of experience, of "human capital" acquired on the job.
>
> (But) a differential, perhaps on the order of 20 percent, between the earnings of men and women remains after adjusting for factors such as education, work experience during the year, and even lifelong work experience.[18]

More recent estimates, using panel data and improved methodology, suggest that the discrimination differential is considerably smaller.[19] However, the existence of a sex-based differential is undisputed. Accordingly, we cannot dismiss occupational and earnings differentials between men and women on the basis of the "natural" responsibilities of childbirth. Discrimination is clearly at work here: The pay and job status of women workers are being constrained by exclusionary employment practices. Moreover, we must take care to note that the same kind of negative feedbacks that constrain the human capital development of blacks affect women, too. Why should a woman postpone childbirth or pursue a lengthy and difficult course of study if it appears that she will not receive commensurate rewards in the labor market? Role differentiation and labor-market discrimination tend to reinforce each other.[20]

---

[17]Within-occupation segregation may actually be increasing, according to William E. Spriggs and Rhonda M. Williams, "A Logit Decomposition Analysis of Occupational Segregation," *Review of Economics and Statistics* (May 1996), pp. 348–355.

[18]*Economic Report of the President* (Washington, DC: U.S. Government Printing Office, 1973), pp. 104–106.

[19]Sharmila Choudhury, "Reassessing the Male-Female Wage Differential: A Fixed Effects Approach," *Southern Economic Journal* (October 1993), pp. 327–340.

[20]For an analysis of feedback effects, see David Neumark and Michele McLennan, "Sex Discrimination and Women's Labor Market Outcomes," *Journal of Human Resources* (Fall 1995), pp. 713–746. A study of business-school seniors, however, found no negative feedback effects on women's labor supply; see Francine D. Blau and Marianne A. Ferber, "Career Plans and Expectations of Young Women and Men," *Journal of Human Resources* (Fall 1991), pp. 581–607. The theoretical problem of assessing causation in similar situations is discussed in Glen G. Cain, "The Uses and Limits of Statistical Analysis in Measuring Economic Discrimination," in *Essays on the Economics of Discrimination,* ed. E. Hoffman (Kalamazoo, MI: Upjohn Institute, 1991).

SUMMARY

Minority racial groups, women, and the poor generally start out in the labor market at a distinct competitive disadvantage, largely as a result of discrimination in the educational system. Their handicaps do not end there, however. In the labor market itself, these groups do not even have an equal opportunity to make the best of their disadvantaged beginnings. Prejudice and institutional employment practices combine to handicap them still further.

Racial and class discrimination in the labor market takes many forms. Some employers and unions willfully exclude blacks, Hispancis, and other minority workers. Others, perhaps less prejudiced, rely on recruitment procedures that have the same effect on minority racial groups, women, and the poor. Doubts about the capabilities of individuals who fall into any of these categories also limit employment and promotional possibilities. Notions of what kind of work is "proper" for minority workers and fear of employee or community disapproval restrains even unprejudiced, but profit-maximizing, employers from providing equal opportunity. The cumulative impact of these practices is evident: Members of minority or poor populations end up working less often, for fewer hours, at less attractive jobs—and, ultimately, for less income.

FURTHER READING

Bergmann, Barbara R., *In Defense of Affirmative Action.* New York: Basic Books, 1996, Chapters 2–3

Blau, Francine D., Marianne A. Ferber, and Anne E. Winkler, *The Economics of Women, Men, and Work,* 3rd ed. Upper Saddle River, NJ: Prentice-Hall, 1998.

Darity, William, Jr., ed., *Economics and Discrimination* (2 vols). Lyme, NH: Edgar Reference Collection, 1995.

Gill, Andrew M., "Incorporating the Causes of Occupational Differences in Studies of Racial Wage Differentials," *Journal of Human Resources* (Winter 1994), pp. 20–41.

Hoffman, Emily P., ed., *Essays on the Economics of Discrimination.* Kalamazoo, MI: Upjohn Institute, 1991.

Jacobsen, Joyce P., "Trends in Work Force Sex Segregation, 1960–1990," *Social Science Quarterly* (March 1994), pp. 204–211.

Kirschenman, Joleen, and Kathryn M. Neckerman, "'We'd Love to Hire Them, But . . .' : The Meaning of Race for Employers," in *The Urban Underclass,* eds. C. Jencks and P. Peterson. Washington, DC: Brookings, 1991.

Nakamura, Alice, and Kathryn Shaw, eds., "Women's Work, Wages, and Well-Being," *Journal of Human Resources* (Spring 1994).

C H A P T E R

Welfare Programs

Public policy toward the poor has been plagued by a persistent dilemma. Should we provide poor people with enough income to buy essential shelter, food, and clothing, or should we instead focus on improving opportunities for the poor to *earn* more income? In a nutshell, should public policy emphasize *welfare* or *work?*

The choice of policy emphasis is rooted in views of poverty causation. If the poor have Flawed Characters, then welfare benefits might be viewed as an inappropriate "reward" for moral turpitude and shiftlessness. Indeed, the Big Brother view of poverty contends that more generous welfare provisions actually *encourage* socially destructive behavior, thus increasing the incidence of poverty. President Ronald Reagan went so far as to assert that welfare is "a cancer that is destroying those that it should succor and threatening society itself."

Others have a more benign view of welfare. They contend that a lack of jobs, good education, and training prevents the poor from achieving financial independence. Until the fetters of Restricted Opportunity are eliminated, the poor will need direct financial support.

There is plenty of room between these opposing views to "fine tune" welfare policies. Indeed, it is in this broad middle ground that most of the details of welfare policy are settled. Even the historic welfare reforms of 1996—the reforms that President Clinton had promised would "end welfare as we know it"—reflected elements of the Flawed Character, Restricted Opportunity, and Big Brother perspectives. The Flawed Character perspective led to time limits on welfare eligibility and toughened work requirements. Increased funding of child care and medical assistance were motivated by the concern over Restricted Opportunity. A sense that Big Brother was getting in the way prompted Congress to turn more program and funding decisions over to the states.

This chapter examines the motivations for these and earlier welfare reforms. We first look at how welfare is distinguished from other income transfer programs, then describe the major cash and in-kind programs that comprise the welfare system. As we will see, the many federal, state and local progams that provide income assistance to the poor are less a welfare "system" than a collage of overlapping activities. The 1996 welfare reforms accentuated this diversity by reducing the federal role in program design and funding. The reforms themselves were a response to the conflicting goals that make all public assistance initiatives so complex and controversial.

WELFARE VERSUS SOCIAL INSURANCE

An important starting point for any discussion of welfare policy is a clear delineation of what constitutes a "welfare" program. The federal government spends over $800 billion a year on income transfers, and state and local governments spend billions more. Not all of these transfers are "welfare" payments, however.

What distinguishes welfare programs from other income transfers are the eligibility conditions for benefit receipt. Eligibility for welfare benefits is based on income and assets; only poor people qualify. That is to say, all welfare programs are *means-tested* income transfers.

The Social Security program is 1.5 times larger than all the welfare programs combined. Unlike welfare, however, Social Security retirement benefits are not conditioned on current income or assets: Both rich people and poor people get Social Security benefits. The only conditions for benefit receipt are age and work history. Once a person with at least ten years of work experience reaches retirement age, he or she can start collecting monthly Social Security benefits.

Other transfer programs that are conditioned on *events* rather than *means* are Medicare and unemployment insurance. Once individuals reach age 65, they automatically qualify for Medicare assistance. Individuals who lose their jobs qualify for weekly unemployment benefits if they satisfy specific work-experience requirements. Generally, all event-conditioned transfers are referred to as *social insurance* programs because they insure against income losses that result from specific events. As Figure 11.1 illustrates, social insurance programs overwhelm welfare programs in the federal budget.

Although welfare programs are generally smaller than the major social insurance programs, they are far more numerous. In 1996, there were at least eighty different

FIGURE 11.1 Federal Income Transfers: Welfare versus Social Insurance

WELFARE
Food Stamps
TANF
SSI
Housing aid
Child nutrition
Medicaid

SOCIAL INSURANCE
Social Security
Medicare
Unemployment Insurance

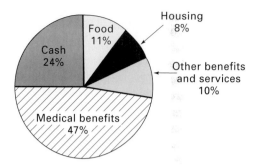

Note: Includes federal, state, and local spending on means-tested benefits and services.

Source: U.S. Congress, House Ways and Means Committee, *1996 Green Book,* Appendix K (Washington, DC: U.S. Government Printing Office, November 1996).

FIGURE 11.2   Welfare Spending by Type of Benefit

means-tested programs. One way to fashion some order out of this array is to distinguish among programs by the type of benefit they provide. Some programs provide outright *cash* assistance ("welfare checks"), while others provide *in-kind* assistance—items like housing, food, and medical assistance—rather than cash. Figure 11.2 shows that only a fourth of all public assistance is conveyed in cash. Most federal, state, and local welfare spending is on in-kind benefits, particularly medical assistance (e.g., Medicaid), food (e.g., food stamps), and housing (e.g., rent subsidies). We will first examine the major cash welfare programs, then turn to means-tested programs that offer in-kind benefits and services.

WELFARE: THE CASH ASSISTANCE PROGRAMS

Table 11.1 provides a summary view of the major programs that provide cash assistance to the poor. The three programs listed in the table are directed to very different population groups. The federal Supplemental Security Income (SSI) program was established for the aged, the blind, and the permanently disabled. It was introduced in July 1973, taking the place of three previous programs.[1] As of 1997 it was providing cash assistance to about 6 million people at an estimated annual cost of approximately $29 billion. By contrast, the federal-state Temporary Aid to Needy Families (TANF) program (formerly the Aid to Families with Dependent Children (AFDC) program) was serving more than 11 million people in the spring of 1997, at an annual cost of roughly $19 billion. The third program, General Assistance (GA), is operated solely under state and local auspices to provide help to those who are poor but do not fit one of the other two categories.

Inadequacies

The statistics provided in Table 11.1 suggest that we are giving a lot of money to a lot of people. Hence, it is not too surprising that in the minds of most hard-working taxpayers welfare conjures up visions of the easy life—a can of beer on a hot afternoon, color

---

[1]The SSI program was enacted as part of the 1972 Social Security Act Amendments and consolidated the Old Age Assistance (OAA), Aid to the Blind (AB), and the Aid to Permanently and Totally Disabled (APTD) programs.

TABLE 11.1 Cash Assistance Programs (1997)			
Program Target Group	Number of Current Recipients (millions)	Average Benefit per Recipient ($ per month)	Total Annual Payments ($ billions)
Supplemental Security Income (SSI) Aged and disabled poor	6.6	375	29
Temporary Aid to Needy Families (TANF) Poor families with children	11.4	134	19
General Assistance (GA) Poor people not covered elsewhere	1.4	190	3
Total	19.4		51

Source: U.S. Department of Health and Human Services (1997 data).

television at night. Former Treasury Secretary William Simon characterized welfare programs as a "haven for the chiselers and rip-off artists," while former President Nixon referred to welfare as a "free ride." But it is clear from actual welfare experience that very few welfare families are even tolerably comfortable, much less riding high. The typical TANF family (mother and two children), for example, received only $4,800 of cash assistance in 1997. That was less than half the amount the government had determined such families need. A budget that small simply does not go far, no matter how thinly it is spread. Just recall how little food, shelter, and clothing are provided by the much larger poverty budget. It would be a strange individual who forsook any but the poorest paying and most loathsome job for such a "free ride."

In light of the pittance available to TANF recipients, it seems unlikely that wage earners, even low-paid ones, would rush to the welfare rolls. To guard against this possibility, however, stringent property limitations have been established for those who seek public assistance. You cannot turn to welfare, at least not for long, just because you run out of money. To enter and remain on the welfare rolls, you must also dispose of nearly all property. A welfare family may possess no more than $1,000 in personal property exclusive of home and car.

A discussion of welfare programs must begin, then, from the observation that financial dependence on public assistance is not comfortable. Families turn to public assistance only after they are impoverished and no other support is available. Families that depend on cash welfare benefits as their sole source of income will have a standard of living well below levels society otherwise deems minimally adequate.

Inequities

In addition to providing inadequate levels of income maintenance, the welfare system is also beset with inequities. Less than 20 million people received cash assistance in 1997, even though over 36 million people were counted as poor in that year. Clearly, the welfare system provides some help to many, but none at all to others. The question is: Who is denied help and for what reasons?

Conspicuously missing from the welfare rolls in nearly every state are male-headed poor families. As we noted earlier, the SSI program aids the aged, the blind, and the disabled, while the TANF program is supposed to provide help to families with children. But of the 24 million poor people in families with children in 1997, only 11 million were receiving TANF assistance (Table 11.1). Thus, being poor in a family with children was not sufficient qualification for receiving welfare support; a further distinction was made between the deserving and the undeserving poor. In this case, the deserving are those whose fathers or husbands are dead, deserted, or otherwise absent from the home. The presence of a male adult in the home is taken as prima facie evidence that the family is capable of its own support. TANF payments are largely reserved for fatherless homes, regardless of whatever needs male-headed poor families may have.

Poor families with both parents present may receive welfare benefits under the TANF program. However, limitations on owned property and earnings exclude most intact families counted as poor. Prior to 1989, the individual states could elect not to provide welfare benefits at all and half of the states chose that option. In 1988 Congress passed legislation that requires all states to provide benefits. Most intact families remain ineligible for benefits, however, due to asset and earnings limitations. The states can also limit benefit receipt to six months and require one parent in the family to perform community service. These restrictions further limit the participation of two-parent families in the TANF program.

Even among those families poor enough to receive welfare payments, there are tremendous disparities in the amount of support provided. Notice in Table 11.1, for instance, how differently recipients of SSI and TANF are treated: SSI recipients receive on average nearly three times as much aid as TANF recipients. This disparity arises in part from taxpayers' sympathy for the aged and disabled, combined with their distrust of younger poor families. The distrust of TANF families stems largely from the assumption that they could support themselves if they so chose. Not only are the adults who benefit from TANF relatively young but their marital status—which the program itself constrains—is suspect. Public distrust of the program is heightened by the fact that large numbers of blacks, Hispanics, families headed by women, and illegitimate children participate in the program. Even more distressing to taxpayers is that the program's growth appears impervious to advances in the economy. Thus, provision of TANF benefits usually begins against a background of public mistrust and resentment.

Further inequities in the cash assistance programs arise from the different levels of benefits received by families in identical situations. Although the "average" TANF family of three received approximately $4,800 in cash assistance in 1997, actual benefits varied widely across states: Some families in Alaska, California, and Connecticut received over $8,000 per year in welfare payments, while similar families in Mississippi received less than $1,500. Table 11.2 indicates how actual and maximum benefits varied in other states.

Differences in state benefit levels not only imply unequal treatment of poor people, but may also alter residence decisions. People in high-benefit states may be reluctant to seek job opportunities elsewhere. Conversely, families in low-benefit states may

TABLE 11.2   TANF Payments in Selected States, 1996

	Monthly Benefit for 3-Person Family	
	Maximum Allowed	*Average Payment*
High-benefit states		
Alaska	$923	$721
Connecticut	636	520
California	607	555
Vermont	656	511
Low-benefit states		
Tennessee	185	172
Texas	138	159
Alabama	164	148
Mississippi	120	120

Source: U.S. Department of Health and Human Services.

be induced to migrate in search of higher benefits. Although the evidence on such immigration effects is mixed, the issue sparks considerable concern in high-benefit states.[2]

Disparities in support reflect far more than differences in the cost of living. In essence, they reflect the ability and willingness of taxpayers in each state to provide for the needy. Welfare payments in Mississippi, for example, are low, both because there is little public or private money in the state and because white Mississippians do not want to spend what little there is in providing for the poor, many of whom are black.[3]

Family Disincentives

While the low and uneven level of welfare benefits clearly limits their antipoverty effectiveness, those benefits also threaten family stability. As we observed, cash welfare benefits are largely reserved for female-headed families. This targeting of benefits may affect family decisions in ways that increase the number of such families. Specifically, the number of female-headed families may increase if:

- Fathers in intact poor families leave in order to make the remaining family members eligible for welfare;
- Wives view welfare as an alternative source of economic support and so are more likely to divorce or separate in the wake of marital discord;
- Unmarried women view welfare as a source of economic support after childrearing and so are less reluctant to become mothers;
- Unwed mothers who previously lived with relatives use welfare benefits to establish their own households.

[2]See Paul E. Peterson and Mark C. Rom, *Welfare Magnets* (Washington, DC: Brookings Institution, 1990); for a different view, see Russell L. Hanson and John T. Hartman, "Do Welfare Magnets Attract?" (Madison, WI: Institute for Research on Poverty, 1994).

[3]See Larry Orr, "Income Transfers as a Public Good," *American Economic Review* (June 1976); and Bradley R. Schiller, "Income Transfers as a Public Good: Comment," *American Economic Review* (December 1978).

Critics of cash welfare have argued that such family disincentives are at the heart of America's welfare crisis. They contend that welfare has undermined the family stability of low-income families and created a growing population of female-headed families that remain impoverished and dependent. By one estimate, some 2.5 million additional children have been added to the poverty rolls by such behavioral changes—what Lowell Gallaway calls "poverty by choice."[4]

Despite the evident inducement for female-headed families, there is little concrete evidence that welfare payments actually change family behavior. As Ellwood and Summers point out, the number of female-headed families has grown much faster than the number of welfare families. Furthermore, the real value of benefits has been *declining* while welfare rolls have been increasing. They argue that the feminization of family structures is more a product of social values than welfare rules.[5]

Although the evidence is mixed, a consensus of expert opinion appears to agree that welfare does have some effect on family stability.[6] Of greatest concern is the encouragement that welfare gives to unwed mothers to establish their own households—households that are most likely to be poor and dependent for a long time.[7]

Work Disincentives

Family disincentives are not the only problem associated with welfare. Welfare benefits also create disincentives for working. In the absence of welfare benefits, a family would have to work or seek assistance from family, friends, or community charities. The pressure to find a job would be enormous. The availability of welfare benefits relieves that pressure. A family that does not participate in the labor market won't forsake all income: Welfare benefits will provide financial support. While not exactly the "good life," the assured flow of welfare benefits may kill the desire to find a job.

The work disincentive implicit in any offer of welfare benefits is compounded by the way in which a family's welfare benefits are calculated. When a family applies for welfare, it is obliged to report any income at its disposal. A woman with small children, for example, might earn $150 a month by babysitting for neighbors. Up until 1967 welfare authorities subtracted any such income from the family's needs, as determined by those same authorities, and provided the difference. Suppose the welfare authorities

---

[4]Lowell Gallaway and Richard Vedder, *Poverty, Income Distribution, the Family, and Public Policy,* a study for the Joint Economic Committee, U.S. Congress (Washington, DC: U.S. Government Printing Office, December 19, 1986). Charles Murray also highlights this family disincentive as a root cause of increased dependency; see "Does Welfare Bring More Babies?" *The Public Interest* (Spring 1992), pp. 17–30.

[5]David Ellwood and Lawrence Summers, "Is Welfare Really the Problem?" *The Public Interest* (Spring 1986).

[6]For research summaries, see Robert Moffitt, "Incentive Effects of the U.S. Welfare System: A Review," *Journal of Economic Literature* (March 1992), pp. 1–61; Kevin R. Hopkins, ed., *Welfare Dependency* (Alexandria, VA: Hudson Institute, 1987); and William Julius Wilson and Kathryn M. Neckerman, "Poverty and Family Structure," in *Fighting Poverty,* eds. S. Danziger and D. Weinberg (Cambridge, MA: Harvard University Press, 1986).

[7]Philip K. Robins and Paul Fronstin found evidence that young women were more prone to having a first child when they knew AFDC benefits were available; see their "Welfare Benefits and Family-Size Decisions of Never-Married Women" (Madison, WI: Institute for Research on Poverty, 1993). T. Paul Schultz also emphasizes the importance of distinguishing the responses of various welfare subgroups to different kinds of benefits. The *average* effect of welfare on family structure may not be that meaningful. See his "Marital Status and Fertility in the United States: Welfare and Labor Market Effects," *Journal of Human Resources* (Spring 1994), pp. 637–669.

concluded that Ms. Jones and her three children needed $400 a month: They paid her only $250, knowing that she could provide the rest.

Although the foregoing procedure for calculating welfare benefits might appear reasonable, it destroyed all monetary incentives to work. To appreciate the dynamics of this situation, imagine that Ms. Jones was offered regular part-time employment—as a nurse's aid, for example—at $5 an hour for ten hours a week. Ms. Jones may be reluctant to leave her small children in the care of others, but she could certainly use the money. Consequently, she is inclined to accept the new job rather than continue babysitting, especially if transportation problems (she has no car) and child-care arrangements can be worked out. But what will happen to her actual income if she takes this step toward self-improvement? Absolutely nothing. The welfare authorities simply noted that she is earning $200 a month rather than $150, reckoned that she is better providing for her own needs, and reduced her welfare payment to $200. Her family's income remained at $400 whether or not the family head found employment and regardless of how hard she strove for self-improvement. From Ms. Jones's perspective, work clearly did not pay.

The reduction in welfare benefits that took place when Ms. Jones accepted the nurse's aid job amounted to an implicit tax on her earnings. Indeed, the *marginal tax rate* turns out to be 100 percent in this case: Ms. Jones loses one dollar in welfare benefits for every additional dollar she earns. Faced with such a high tax rate, how many people would seek additional employment? Very few, which is the heart of the work incentive problem.

The Social Security Amendments of 1967 alleviated the work incentive problem somewhat by reducing the marginal tax rate. The significance of this change is illustrated in Figure 11.3. Consider the case of Ms. Jones again.

If she does not work at all, she will receive $4,800 a year ($400 a month) from welfare, a situation designated by point A. Now suppose she is offered the nurse's aid job, for 500 hours a year (ten hours a week). If she accepted the job under the old AFDC system, she would move to point E, working more but with no change in total income. Under the 1967 regulations, however, she moved to point D and increased her well-being by working. Point D is obviously more desirable than E, as it represents more income for the same amount of effort. Hence, whatever Ms. Jones's feelings about work, she was more likely to take a job under the post-1967 system than the old one. In this sense, the revised system provided a greater incentive to work.

How did Ms. Jones get to point D under the post-1967 system? First, the welfare authorities recognized that there are certain costs associated with working, such as transportation expenses, additional clothes, and added meal costs. In Ms. Jones's case, these expenses amounted to $60 a month (or $720 a year). To assure that Ms. Jones took home at least enough income from her new job to cover these costs and thus to eliminate the possibility of her incurring a net loss from working, the welfare department "disregarded" that much income in calculating her welfare benefits. Whereas they would have deducted $720 from her welfare checks under the old system, they now deducted nothing, thus enabling her to receive both the $4,800 in welfare benefits and the first $720 she earned. To give Ms. Jones still more incentive to work, the welfare authorities also disregarded an additional $30 per month ($360 per year). Ms. Jones could then earn a total of $1,080 in wages before experiencing any reduction in welfare benefits. In effect, the marginal tax rate, the rate at which welfare benefits are reduced

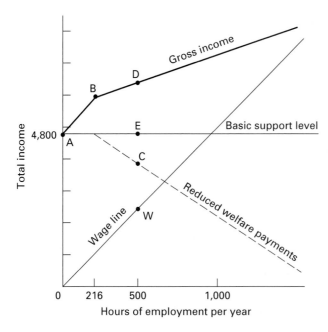

FIGURE 11.3 Work Incentive Provisions under 1967 AFDC Reforms

as earnings increase, on the first $1,080 of earnings dropped from 100 percent to 0 percent. As a result, Ms. Jones could work 216 hours per year earning $1,080 and move to point B without welfare department interference.

Only as Ms. Jones's earnings exceeded $1,080 a year did the welfare department begin to take notice of her added income and reduce her welfare check. Accordingly, beyond point B, Ms. Jones's total income rose more slowly than her increased earnings. But it did rise, because the welfare department no longer reduced her benefits by a dollar for every additional dollar she earned. That is, they no longer imposed a 100 percent marginal tax on earnings beyond point B, but instead allowed her to keep something for herself. Under the revised AFDC system the marginal tax rate was 67 percent, so that the welfare department reduced her benefit check by only 67 cents for every additional dollar she earned. The remaining 33 cents increased Ms. Jones's total income, thus providing a financial incentive to work. The incentive was still modest, to be sure, but nevertheless greater than the one that existed prior to the 1967 reform.

The total income of Ms. Jones and her family at point D is easily computed. The post-1967 welfare benefit formula was:

$$\text{Welfare benefit} = \$4{,}800 - (0.67 \times \text{Earnings in excess of } \$1{,}080)$$

If Ms. Jones worked all year (500 hours) at her new job, she received the following amount: her wages ($2,500 at point W) plus a welfare check reduced by two-thirds of her wages in excess of $1,080. In this case, she received a welfare check in the amount of $3,853 (point C). Her total income at point D was thus $2,500 from working plus $3,853 from welfare, or $6,353. By her own modest efforts, then, she managed to substantially increase her family's economic status.

Conflicting Welfare Goals

It is comforting to know that Ms. Jones could increase her family's income from $4,800 to $6,353 a year by working ten hours a week as a nurse's aid. It might, however, be nicer still if the welfare department would let her keep a little more of the money she earns from making beds, emptying bedpans, and sterilizing bandages. After all, the life of a nurse's aid is not exactly glamorous and Ms. Jones obviously needs the money. So why not lower the marginal tax rate from 67 percent to, say, 25 percent, or even zero? That would clearly solve the work incentive problem while giving Ms. Jones a real chance to make a few bucks.

The difficulty with this solution to the work incentive problem is that it conflicts with other goals. Three distinct goals are commonly associated with welfare systems:

- income provision
- work incentives
- cost minimization

To the extent that we want to protect people from the indignities of poverty, we should provide a high income floor (or guarantee). If we also desire to encourage employment and self-improvement, we must impose low marginal tax rates (allow recipients to keep a substantial share of their earnings above the minimum). And if we desire to hold program costs down to a reasonable level, we must limit the coverage of the program to those in need. All these objectives are worthwhile, just as the means for achieving them are clear. Nevertheless, they are mutually exclusive. We cannot move in all three directions at once.

Suppose that we actually eliminate the marginal tax rate on Ms. Jones's earnings, thus allowing her to keep everything she earns. In that case, her total income would rise to $7,300 ($4,800 in benefits plus $2,500in wages). Still no life of luxury, but improving. Now suppose that the hospital technicians form a union and pay scales are increased. Ms. Jones is offered a raise to $6 an hour, provided that she works 1,500 hours a year (30 hours a week). Because we no longer reduce her welfare benefits as her earnings increase, this stroke of good fortune will give Ms. Jones the opportunity to take home a total income of $13,800. Terrific! But should we still be providing $4,800 in welfare payments to someone who earns $9,000 on her own? How about someone earning $15,000? $20,000? Or, to make a long story short, where should we draw the line?

The crux of the problem here is a trade-off between work incentives and program costs. A marginal tax rate of 100 percent destroys the incentive to work. On the other hand, a marginal tax rate of zero makes everyone eligible for full welfare benefits. If we let people keep receiving all welfare benefits after they start working, program costs soar.

The conflict between the goals of income provision, work incentives, and cost minimization can be summarized in a simple equation:

$$\text{Breakeven income level} = \frac{\text{Income floor}}{\text{Marginal tax rate}} + \text{Disregarded income}$$

The breakeven income level refers to the amount of money a person can earn before losing all welfare benefits. In Ms. Jones's case, the breakeven point under the post-1967 AFDC system was:

$$\$8,280 = \frac{\$4,800}{0.67} + 1,080$$

Beyond that level of earnings, she would have been on her own. If the marginal tax rate were 100 percent as under the pre-1967 system, the breakeven point would be $4,800 ($4,800/1.00), meaning that people who earned $4,800 on their own would get no assistance from welfare. Under our aborted proposal to lower marginal tax rates to zero, the breakeven point would rise to infinity ($4,800/0), and we would all be on welfare.

As is apparent from this arithmetic, a lower breakeven income level can be achieved only by sacrificing a high income floor or low marginal tax rates. Hence, cost minimization can be fulfilled only by sacrificing income provision or work incentives. More generally, fulfillment of any two objectives necessitates sacrificing the third.

The Goal Compromise

Whatever compromise we strike between the goals of income provision, work incentives, and cost minimization, it is not going to please everyone. More important, however, we should note that the same compromise is not necessarily appropriate for all population groups. For those people incapable of working, a sacrifice of income provision for the sake of enhancing work incentives would be ridiculous. On the other hand, high-income guarantees for those who are capable of working might seem unnecessary. Hence, it would make sense to strike a different compromise of welfare goals for two distinct groups, those who can work and those who cannot.

Unfortunately, it is not always possible to draw such a neat distinction. A 92-year-old woman confined to a wheelchair would seem to have very few employment opportunities; for her, income provision would be more appropriate than work incentives. But what about the father of four children who loses his job? Or the mother who is left with a five-year-old child when her husband skips town with the next-door neighbor? Or what about the teenager who got pregnant and is now trying to raise a child on her own? Are work incentives irrelevant in these cases? Our collective response, as reflected in welfare regulations, has been "no."

Although it is often difficult to distinguish the potentially employable from the rest of the poor, we attempt to approach this distinction by segregating needy families into different welfare classifications. This is why we have a separate welfare program (SSI) for the aged, the blind, and the handicapped, a program that provides higher income guarantees and smaller work incentives. In the process, of course, many younger families temporarily unable to find or accept employment end up at the margins of deprivation.

President Reagan introduced another welfare rule to help alleviate these goal conflicts. He argued that once welfare recipients got a foothold in the job market, they would advance up the income ladder. Most jobs offer more than just entry wages; they also offer opportunities for training, promotion, and pay increases. Even entry-level jobs can provide contacts and experience that lead to better-paying opportunities. The key to success, therefore, is to get welfare recipients into jobs quickly. From that perspective, work-incentive provisions need not be permanent. Accordingly, the rules were changed to eliminate work-incentive provisions after a four-month period of employment. Since 1982 AFDC recipients have confronted a 67 percent marginal tax rate only for the first four months of employment. Thereafter they face a total loss of benefits. In principle, the implied marginal tax at the end of four months could exceed 100 percent (if the benefit loss exceeded the wage gain). This was a great disincentive to working, especially for welfare recipients who were not likely to advance up the wage scale quickly. Given the risk of unexpected job loss and the inevitable delay in reestablishing welfare, many recipients concluded that work simply did not make sense. After the 1982 rules went into effect, fewer families combined work and welfare.[8]

WELFARE: THE IN-KIND PROGRAMS

The goal conflicts of cash welfare programs are magnified by the many programs that provide in-kind benefits. As we noted in Figure 11.2, spending on in-kind programs exceeds spending on cash assistance programs by a three-to-one margin. All of these in-kind benefits substantially raise living standards among the poor. At the same time, however, the availability of so many in-kind benefits makes welfare more attractive. The *combination* of cash and in-kind benefits tends to diminish further the economic incentive to work and to create additional inducements for single parenthood.

In the following paragraphs, we review a few of the major in-kind programs, then look at their impact on welfare adequacy, cost, and work incentives.

Food Stamps

Food stamps are the most familiar in-kind welfare benefit. Food stamps are simply coupons ("stamps") that allow a person to buy food. The stamps are "spent" at the grocery store, where they are accepted at face value. The grocer, in turn, cashes the stamps in at a local bank, and the bank redeems them at face value from the government. In effect, then, food stamps are a direct substitute for cash. Food stamps are not fully equivalent to cash, however, since they may be used only for food purchases.

Food stamps are distributed to poor families on the basis of need. The value of stamps given to a family depends on its income and family size. The maximum monthly benefit in 1997 was $315 for a three-person family without other income. Average benefits are much lower—around $220 per month (about 80 cents per meal per person). The value of food-stamp transfers is automatically increased each year to account for higher food prices.

Medicaid

Even larger than the food-stamp program is Medicaid, the program that provides medical services to the poor. Under Medicaid an eligible person can use the services of a doctor or hospital just like anyone else. The difference is that the Medicaid patient simply passes the bill on to the government, rather than paying for it directly or submitting it to a private insurance company. Obviously, the amount of benefit a poor family gets from Medicaid depends on how often it requires medical treatment. Nearly all public welfare recipients make some use of Medicaid, as do many others who have incomes just above the poverty standard. The average value of the services received varies

---

[8]Alternatively, welfare families may have responded by simply reporting less of their labor-market activity; see S. Mayer and C. Jencks, "Recent Trends in Economic Inequality in the United States: Income versus Expenditures versus Material Well-Being," in *Poverty and Prosperity in the U.S.A. in the Twentieth Century,* eds. D. Papadimitriou and E. Wolff (New York: St. Martin's, 1993).

tremendously, however. Most Medicaid assistance goes to the aged, blind, and disabled recipients of supplemental security income; they have average medical costs in excess of $8,000 per year. Less than a fifth of Medicaid benefits go to younger families with children, most of whom also receive cash benefits. A typical three-person welfare family receives about $3,000 a year in Medicaid benefits.

Housing Assistance

In addition to food and medical services, a poor family can also receive housing assistance. In many cases, such assistance is provided in the form of public housing, usually large housing projects owned and operated by the government. In a public housing project the tenants enjoy cheap (subsidized) rents, although not a great deal more in terms of quality of environment. Nevertheless, the fact that they are paying less than the market value of their apartments means that they are effectively receiving an income transfer, which on average works out to approximately $2,000 a year.

In addition to public housing projects, there are also housing assistance programs for low-income people who are renting or even buying their apartments and homes in the private market. In these programs, the rent or mortgage payment is reduced, with the government (the Department of Housing and Urban Development, or HUD) making up the difference.

Nutrition Programs

In addition to the "big three" in-kind programs—food stamps, Medicaid, and housing assistance—there are scores of other means-tested programs. Table 11.3 displays two more, both intended to assure greater nutrition for low-income children. The school lunch and breakfast programs provide free or subsidized meals. The WIC program provides food vouchers (like food stamps) to pregnant women and infants.

The Welfare Package

As Table 11.3 documents, we spend a lot of money on in-kind welfare programs. Spending on just the five programs listed in Table 11.3 exceeded $200 billion in 1997, far more than was spent on cash benefits (Table 11.1).

TABLE 11.3   In-Kind Welfare Programs, 1995

Program	Number of Recipients (millions)	Average Benefit per Recipient per Month ($)	Total Annual Cost ($ billions)
Food stamps	28	71	26
Medicaid	35	279	156
Housing assistance	6	131	21
School lunch program	25	17	5
Women, Infants, and Children (WIC)	7	30	3
Total			211

Source: U.S. Congress, Committee on Ways and Means, *1996 Green Book* (Washington, DC: U.S. Government Printing Office, 1996).

When in-kind benefits are combined with cash benefits, the value of the "welfare package" increases substantially. As we noted earlier, a typical welfare family of mother and two children gets less than $5,000 a year in welfare checks (cash). But food stamps can bring in another $3,000 and housing subsidies another $4,000 of benefits. Medicaid can cover all medical expenses, and the nutrition programs can supply a lot of free meals. If a welfare family got all of these benefits, it would have a standard of living worth at least $15,000 a year. They wouldn't be rich, but they wouldn't be nearly as destitute as their cash income ($5,000) implied.

Few welfare families get all of these benefits. And virtually none get the *maximum* value of each benefit. However, most welfare families do get two or more benefits. As Table 11.4 reveals, 87 percent of AFDC recipients also get food stamps; nearly all of them make use of Medicaid. The median value of the resulting welfare package is about $12,000.

Revisiting the Goal Conflict

Tables 11.3 and 11.4 clearly demonstrate that in-kind welfare programs substantially raise the standard of living for the poor; they do so, however, at the expense of certain identifiable costs. Obviously, they involve a substantial amount of public expenditure—over $200 billion in 1996. This was four times more than was spent on the major cash assistance programs in that year (Table 11.1). Less obvious, but perhaps more important, is the impact of these in-kind programs on the goal compromise we observed earlier. As we noted, cash assistance programs tend to sacrifice more of the income-provision goal in order to better fulfill the work-incentive and cost-minimization goals. That compromise has been altered by the introduction of food stamps, Medicaid, and housing assistance.

Although it might seem that the in-kind programs are a way of meeting all three of our welfare goals simultaneously—of filling in the gaps left in our earlier compromise—that is only an illusion. The three goals remain irreconcilable, and the provision of in-kind assistance serves only to strike a new compromise, not to render the three competing welfare goals more compatible.

The impact of in-kind programs on our policy compromise can be seen in Figure 11.4. In this figure we reconstruct the opportunities available to Ms. Jones under the AFDC program. As we noted earlier, Ms. Jones had an incentive (albeit limited) to

TABLE 11.4 Multiple Benefit Receipts

Percentage of AFDC Households Receiving:

Food stamps	87%
Medicaid	97
Housing Assistance	31
School Lunch Program	63
WIC	25

Source: U.S. Congress, Committee on Ways and Means, *1996 Green Book* (Washington, DC: U.S. Government Printing Office, 1996), p. 654.

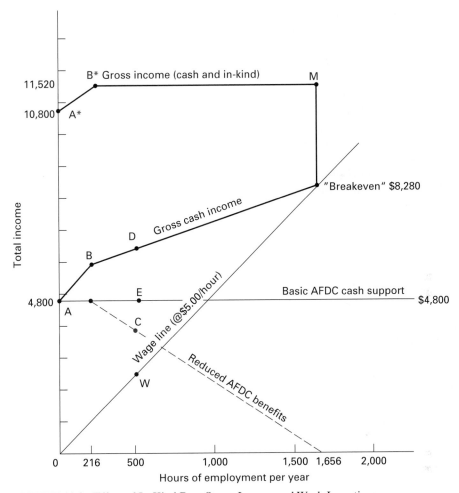

FIGURE 11.4 Effect of In-Kind Benefits on Income and Work Incentives

take a job under AFDC, as she could increase her standard of living (move to points B and D) by so doing.

The new and higher line in Figure 11.4 represents the opportunities available to Ms. Jones and her family from the combined provisions of AFDC, food stamps, Medicaid, and housing assistance. We will assume Ms. Jones qualifies for $2,000 each of food stamps, housing subsidies, and medical payments. As is evident, Ms. Jones's family enjoys a much higher standard of living when it gets not only welfare checks, but lives in subsidized housing and gets free medical services and food stamps as well. Even if Ms. Jones chose not to work at all, her total real income would be $4,800 in welfare benefits plus $6,000 in in-kind benefits. This combined income of $10,800 is represented by point A* in Figure 11.4. This is far superior to the cash (AFDC) income available at point A.

There is another change in Figure 11.4. Notice what happens to her total gross income as she works more hours. Her gross income rises slowly at first, then not at all. From point A* to B* her gross income is rising, but beyond point B* the gross income curve flattens out. Ultimately (at point M), her gross income actually *falls* as her work effort increases! Not only does Ms. Jones now feel less *need* to work as a result of her greater public subsidy, but she now confronts less *incentive* to work. The attainment of greater income provision has been achieved at the sacrifice (opportunity cost) of work incentives. That is not to say that the new compromise is any better or worse than the old one, but simply to point up the fact that the old goal conflict still exists.

The reduction in work incentives comes about from an increase in the implicit marginal tax rate. The rules for AFDC benefits haven't changed: Ms. Jones can still keep 100 percent of the first $1,080 she earns (the disregards) and 33 percent of any additional wages. Now, however, she loses some of her in-kind benefits when her earnings increase.

Recall that the value of a family's food-stamp allotment depends on a family's income. Families with higher incomes get fewer stamps. Hence, part of what Ms. Jones earns is effectively taken away in the form of food-stamp losses; this acts as a tax on earnings. The same is true of housing assistance: When Ms. Jones's earnings increase, she will have to pay a larger share of the market value of her rent. These provisions are perfectly compatible with the equity concept of reserving welfare assistance for the neediest. However, they also diminish the net rewards associated with employment.

In Figure 11.4 it is assumed that the *combined* "tax" on earnings imposed by food-stamp and housing subsidy regulations amounts to 33 percent. When Ms. Jones worked 216 hours, she earned $1,080. AFDC authorities disregarded these initial wages by imposing no "tax." Now, however, Ms. Jones loses $360 worth of food stamps and housing assistance when she earns $1,080. Her gross income increases more slowly than her wages. As a result her gross income is only $11,520 at point B*.

To the right of point B* work incentives diminish further. Once her wages exceed $1,080, Ms. Jones starts losing AFDC benefits. The *combined* marginal tax rate is now 100 percent—67 percent in AFDC "taxes" and another 33 percent from food stamps and housing assistance. The gross income line flattens out to the right of B*; further work effort does not result in higher real income. There is no financial incentive to work more than 216 hours per year (point B*) in this case. More generally, there is no incentive to earn more than $1,080 per year (even during the first four months of employment). In other words, the benefit-reduction rules associated with food stamps and rent subsidies eliminate even the small work incentive that AFDC alone contained.

A still greater blow to work incentives occurs at point M. At point M, Ms. Jones has achieved the breakeven point for AFDC and so no longer qualifies for cash benefits. When she stops receiving AFDC benefits, however, her Medicaid eligibility is at risk as well. Persons receiving AFDC are automatically eligible for Medicaid. If they leave the (cash) welfare rolls, however, families may lose their Medicaid benefits. This may happen immediately or may take as long as a year, depending on why AFDC benefits cease. In any case, the loss of Medicaid eligibility means that this family loses $2,000 of in-kind benefits if its wages reach the AFDC breakeven level. At the margin this means that $1 of additional wages *reduces* family income by $2,000. An experience like that could seriously diminish a person's desire to work![9]

---

[9]Significant impacts of Medicaid on employment behavior are estimated in Anne E. Winkler, "The Incentive Effects of Medicaid on Women's Labor Supply," *Journal of Human Resources* (Spring 1991), pp. 308–377; and Robert Moffitt and Barbara Wolfe, "The Effect of the Medicaid Program on Welfare Participation and Labor Supply," *Review of Economics and Statistics* (November 1992), pp. 615–626.

WELFARE REFORM

In view of the inadequacies, inequities, and disincentives associated with a mix of cash and in-kind welfare programs, welfare reform has been the eternal quest of social policy. The various strategies employed in that quest have included guaranteed income support (negative income taxes), guaranteed jobs, education, and training (Edfare), mandatory employment (workfare), and time limits on welfare receipt. Each of these strategies is reviewed briefly in the following paragraphs. Then the landmark welfare reforms of 1996 are described and assessed.

Guaranteed Income

The simplest alternative to the present welfare system is a universal guaranteed income, popularly referred to as a negative income tax (NIT). A negative income tax (NIT) is a tax system wherein people automatically receive transfers ("negative taxes") from the government if their incomes fall below established levels. The system consists of (1) a guaranteed income floor, and (2) a marginal tax rate. Together, these two parameters determine who will receive income transfers and how much. What distinguishes such systems from current welfare programs are two features: universality and simplicity.

The universality of NIT plans arises from the fact that their benefits would be available to everyone on the same basis of need; their simplicity derives from the consolidation of all welfare programs. As we have noted, the current patchwork of public assistance programs necessitates a case-by-case determination of eligibility, need, and grant levels. Not only is such a determination expensive and frustratingly slow; it often leads to administrative abuse. Under a negative income tax program, case-by-case determinations would be unnecessary and administrative abuse unlikely.

Another consequence of present administrative arrangements is that welfare regulations are confusing and vary by state. Recipients have little access to information regarding the rules that govern them or the benefits to which they are entitled. Generally, they are compelled to rely on caseworkers for this information, making them totally dependent on the capability and benevolence of local authorities.

NIT programs would overcome these deficiencies by standardizing eligibility criteria and by making assistance available as a matter of right. Every poor family would receive identical aid based on the number of family members. Access to financial assistance would be as simple and direct as income taxes now are, and similar verification procedures would be utilized to certify eligibility. Local authorities would have no discretionary control over the behavior of recipients, whose identities would be confidential.

The universality of an NIT would reduce but not eliminate the family disincentives embedded in the current welfare system. Intact low-income families would be eligible for welfare, and thus have no incentive to split up. However, the universality, simplicity, and anonymity of an NIT might also make the prospect of sole parenthood more attractive for unwed mothers and unhappy wives.

An NIT also fails to resolve the work disincentive problem. An NIT guarantees minimum income support for those who don't work or even seek work. It also "taxes" wages at the NIT recovery rate (marginal tax rate), lessening the net reward for working.

An NIT therefore does not dissolve the conflict between the goals of income adequacy, work incentives, and cost minimization; it simply alters the goal priorities. NIT programs generally appeal to people who worry more about income adequacy or work incentives than about program cost.

While the *theoretical* trade-off among welfare goals is evident, the *empirical* dimensions of that trade-off need to be assessed from actual behavior. To do this, the federal government has sponsored several NIT experiments. The experiments offered recipients various combinations of income guarantees and tax rates, then observed recipient behavior. In general, the experiments have shown that recipients reduce their work effort when offered high income guarantees or are confronted with high marginal tax rates. The effects are modest, however, especially for male household heads. On average, the labor supply of husbands declined by 5 percent as a result of the experimental NIT, while the labor supply of wives fell by 22 percent. The work effort of female heads of families was reduced by 11 percent.[10] Although modest, these effects underscore the potential conflict between the goals of income adequacy and work incentive.[11]

Another problem that NIT-type programs must confront is the immediacy and variability of families' income-maintenance needs. Families whom we count as poor aren't necessarily in need of income maintenance all year round. Their low income for the year may reflect adequate income part of the year and no income for the rest. By the same token, families whose *annual* income ranks them above the poor may experience short-term deprivation and need assistance. One of the reasons our present welfare system is so complex and costly is that it is responsive to such variation; thousands of families move on and off welfare every month. By contrast, NIT-type systems, modeled after our regular tax system, envision longer accounting periods and less responsiveness. Unfortunately, families who experience sudden income losses can neither eat last year's income nor afford to wait until assistance comes later, on a retroactive basis. Hence, NIT-type proposals are likely to end up with more administrative complexities than their proponents envision.

Guaranteed Jobs

An alternative approach to welfare reform is to guarantee jobs rather than income. Everyone who is able to work will be provided with a job, thus minimizing the need for welfare. A job guarantee eliminates the work incentive problem and might even strengthen family stability by assuring that fathers will be able to support their families.

---

[10]Michael C. Keely et al., "The Estimation of Labor Supply Models Using Experimental Data," *American Economic Review* (December 1978).

[11]For a discussion of the NIT experiments and their significance, see U.S. General Accounting Office, *Income Maintenance Experiments: Need to Summarize Results and Communicate the Lessons Learned* (April 1981). Other studies include Joseph Pechman and P. Michael Timpane, eds., *Work Incentives and Income Guarantee* (Washington, DC: The Brookings Institution, 1975); the symposium published in the *Journal of Human Resources* (Spring and Fall 1974); and John L. Palmer and Joseph Pechman, eds., *Welfare in Rural Areas* (Washington, DC: The Brookings Institution, 1978). For alternative models, also see Mark Killingsworth, "Must a Negative Income Tax Reduce Labor Supply? A Study of the Family's Allocation of Time," *Journal of Human Resources* (Summer 1976); Ronald Hoffman and Bradley R. Schiller, "Work Incentives of the Poor: A Reconsideration," *Review of Economics and Statistics* (August 1970); and Frank Levy, "The Labor Supply of Female Household Heads," *Journal of Human Resources* (Winter 1979).

President Jimmy Carter proposed a guaranteed jobs program in 1977. In his view, the low-income population could be separated into two distinct groups, employable families and unemployable families. The former would be guaranteed jobs with minimal welfare assistance. The latter group would be guaranteed decent income support.

There are two inherent problems with this approach—feasibility and expense. A guaranteed jobs program depends on two critical assumptions: (1) that the employable poor can be distinguished from the nonemployable poor, and (2) that the employable families will be able to find jobs. We have already observed that the first assumption is doubtful in many cases. Poor families move in and out of the labor force repeatedly and for a variety of reasons (see Chapters 3 and 4). Employability is not a permanent characteristic of a family or its members. Hence, the classification of poor families into employable and unemployable groups requires high administrative costs and invites subterfuge.

The assumption that all employable families will find work—and thus survive with minimal welfare support—is potentially even more troublesome. Millions of individuals are poor because too few jobs are available (see Chapter 3). For his welfare reform to succeed, President Carter had to guarantee jobs. To do so, he proposed to create 1.4 million jobs in public service employment, a very costly proposition. Worried about the cost and the feasibility of distinguishing between employable and nonemployable families, Congress rejected the Carter guaranteed jobs approach.[12]

Workfare

President Reagan proposed a very different approach to welfare reform. Rather than guaranteeing paid jobs to poor people, Reagan proposed to require welfare recipients to "work off" their benefits. Under this *workfare* concept, adult recipients of welfare would be required to perform community service. The number of required hours of service would depend on the size of the welfare benefit. Those who refuse to perform community service would lose their welfare benefits.

The workfare approach has several advantages. First, it eliminates the work-incentive problem. Instead of choosing between work and welfare, poor people would confront the choice of working without welfare or working with welfare. There would be no "free ride" for people who preferred welfare to working.

The second attraction of workfare is that it generates valuable community services. Welfare recipients end up as hospital aides, library aides, crossing guards at schools, and on clean-up crews. These additional services enhance the community and give taxpayers a tangible service for their welfare dollars. In the process, welfare recipients also acquire job experience and employment habits that may increase their chances of attaining better jobs and financial independence.

Finally, workfare is a very inexpensive welfare-reform option. There are no wages to pay since recipients are "working off" their benefits. The only added costs are administrative due to additional personnel needed to implement and monitor work sites and recipient performance. Even these costs may be offset, however, by reduced welfare caseloads as more people move from welfare to self-support.

---

[12]For a detailed analysis of President Carter's plan, see Sheldon Danziger, Robert Haveman, and Eugene Smolensky, "The Program for Better Jobs and Income—A Guide and Critique," a study prepared for the Joint Economic Committee of the U.S. Congress, October 1977.

Critics of workfare claim that mandatory community service is an unfair burden to poor families. They see it as a form of punishment ("slavefare") for impoverishment. Others question the appropriateness of compelling welfare mothers to perform community service rather than caring for their own children.[13] Critics also doubt the feasibility of finding enough community service jobs for all welfare recipients. Many also worry that workfare requirements could be imposed unfairly, particularly when the number of adult welfare recipients exceeds the number of workfare jobs. In such circumstances, local caseworkers would have a lot of discretion to decide who has to "work off" their benefits, and who doesn't.

In view of these criticisms, Congress in 1981 chose to experiment with workfare rather than adopt it on a national basis. Specifically, Congress gave the states the authority to implement workfare requirements on a demonstration basis. Between 1982 and 1988, over half of the states decided to take this approach. In most cases, however, the state legislatures simply passed the buck to their respective counties, letting them decide whether to impose a workfare requirement. Relatively few counties implemented the program, and participation rates were always low. As a consequence, only 1 to 2 percent of the national AFDC caseload participated in workfare.[14] In most cases, mandatory community service (called the Community Work Experience Program or CWEP) was one of many employment-related options recipients confronted.

Despite the low level of workfare utilization, there are indications that the program was effective in reducing caseloads. In addition, the program proved to be popular not only among taxpayers but also among welfare recipients as well.[15]

Although workfare appears to be a viable welfare-reform option, it is not a solution to welfare. Mothers of preschool children are generally exempt from mandatory community service. This exemption alone excludes roughly two-thirds of the AFDC caseload from participation. Other recipients are precluded from participation by illness, lack of transportation, or simply a shortage of work sites.

Edfare

A fourth path to welfare reform emphasizes education and training services that increase a recipient's job prospects. By investing in human capital, such programs seek to move people off the welfare rolls more slowly, but also more permanently. So-called *Edfare* programs make some form of human capital investment mandatory. Thus, recipients are obligated to do something that will help them move off of welfare. This may entail education classes for those with little schooling or vocational training programs for recipients with little job experience. Rather than simply offering these services to recipients who want them, Edfare programs *require* recipients to participate or

---

[13]The potential of workfare to increase family problems is discussed in Patricia Spakes, "Mandatory Work Registration for Welfare Parents: A Family Impact Analysis," *Journal of Marriage and the Family* (August 1982).

[14]Bradley R. Schiller and C. Nielson Brasher, "Workfare in the 1980s: Successes and Limits," *Policy Studies Review* (Summer 1990).

[15]See Bradley R. Schiller and C. Nielson Brasher, "The Effects of Workfare Saturation on AFDC Caseloads," *Contemporary Policy Issues* (January 1993).

risk losing welfare benefits. The experience with these and other employment-related programs will be examined in Chapter 13. At this juncture, we will simply note that the effectiveness of such programs has been very limited.[16]

The Family Support Act of 1988

Many of these welfare-reform approaches were incorporated in the Family Support Act (FSA) of 1988. After a decade of state experiments with various welfare initiatives, Congress came to two conclusions. First, welfare recipients had to assume more responsibility for achieving financial independence. Second, an eclectic mix of services was more likely to succeed than any unidimensional intervention.

Child Support   The increased self-responsibility envisioned by the FSA was manifest in provisions for child support and program participation. Title I of the act strengthened procedures for obtaining child support from noncustodial parents. States were required to establish paternity for AFDC children, to enforce guildelines for support awards, and to withhold support payments from the paychecks of noncustodial parents. Taken together, these provisions were designed to emphasize the responsibilities of parenthood while reducing the need for public assistance.

JOBS Program   To "encourage and assist" AFDC recipients to get off of welfare, the Family Support Act also imposed greater activity requirements on adult recipients. A major premise of the FSA was that welfare should be a short-term transition rather than a long-term solution. To help assure this, the FSA created the Job Opportunities and Basic Skills (JOBS) training program. While the educational and vocational services offered by JOBS are similar to those of previous programs, the provisions for participation were different. Participation in some JOBS activity was *mandatory* for most adult AFDC recipients without children under age three. States could even extend that participation requirement to parents of children at least one year old.

The JOBS program also included a workfare component. States were required to demand at least 16 hours of community service per week from one parent in two-parent households. Single parents who failed to find a regular job after completing training could also be required to perform community service.

Work Incentives   The "stick" of mandatory activity requirements was accompanied by a "carrot" of enhanced work incentives. As we observed earlier, the loss of benefits that accompanies increased employment is a financial disincentive to working. The severest disincentive occurs at that juncture (point M in Figure 11.4) where Medicaid coverage ceases. The FSA addressed this concern by extending Medicaid eligibility for one full year after an AFDC recipient left welfare and went to work. The FSA also guaranteed child care for recipients who participated in JOBS or became employed.

AFDC-UP   The FSA also required all states to offer AFDC benefits to *two*-parent families. Prior to 1989, states could choose whether to implement the AFDC-UP (unemployed parent) program. Only about half of the states did so, thereby leaving a gap

---

[16]For a brief summary of Edfare and workfare programs, see Evelyn Ganzglass, *Research Findings on the Effectiveness of State Welfare to Work Programs* (Washington, DC: National Governors' Association, 1994).

in welfare eligibility that encouraged single-parent families. Congress closed that gap by making AFDC-UP a required program. However, more stringent eligibility rules and limits on benefits kept the AFDC-UP program very small.

Funding Limitations The ambitions of the Family Support Act were constrained by budget considerations. Congress appropriated relatively little money for the program and many services were dependent on cost-sharing by the states. When the economy slipped into the 1990–91 recession, the states could not afford their share of program costs. As a result of these funding limitations, participation in the JOBS program remained below legislative targets.

State Waivers

Neither the provisions nor the funding levels of the Family Support Act (FSA) satisfied the quest for welfare reform. Many critics were particularly concerned that the FSA gave individual states so little authority to tailor programs to their own needs. In response to this concern, the U.S. Department of Health and Human Services granted "waivers" to individual states. The waivers permitted states to ignore, amend, or supplement the provisions of federal welfare law (FSA).

Between 1991 and 1995, 35 states obtained federal waivers. These waivers spawned a diverse array of state welfare "demonstrations." The demonstrations set time limits on welfare dependency, added new eligibility conditions, altered work requirements, restricted benefits for children born to welfare mothers ("family caps"), and modified work incentives.

At the same time that states were conducting their welfare demonstrations, welfare caseloads dropped sharply. Between January 1993 and January 1997, the national AFDC caseload plunged by 20 percent—the largest decline ever. Lots of governors were quick to credit their state-initiated reforms. However, the economy was growing steadily and unemployment rates were declining sharply. Hence, the economy, not the state reforms, was the principal cause of caseload declines.[17] Nevertheless, the apparent contribution of state reforms to the caseload decline rekindled the demand for more comprehensive federal reform. President Clinton responded to that demand, promising to "end welfare as we know it."

THE 1996 WELFARE REFORMS

After four years of intense debate and negotiations, Congress passed a truly historic welfare-reform law in 1996. The Personal Responsibility and Work Opportunity Reconciliation Act of 1996 ended a 60-year federal entitlement and turned the primary responsibility for welfare over to the states.

---

[17]For an analysis of the 1992–96 caseload decline, see Council of Economic Advisors, "Explaining the Decline in Welfare Receipt, 1993–1996" (Washington, DC: The White House, May 1997); and Bradley R. Schiller, "State Welfare Reform Impacts: Content and Enforcement Effects" (Washington, DC: American University, May 1997).

The End of AFDC

The 1996 reforms terminated the AFDC program. Since its inception in 1935, AFDC had been a federal *entitlement*. Anyone who satisfied its eligibility requirements was issued a welfare check. As a result, the amount spent on welfare each year was unforeseeable, since it depended on the flow of welfare applicants and recipients.

Temporary Assistance for Needy Families (TANF)

TANF Block Grants   In place of the AFDC entitlement, Congress created block grants to help finance the welfare system. Congress authorized a fixed amount ($16.4 billion per year) to be turned over to the states, who would then deliver whatever benefits and services they felt appropriate. The new program is called Temporary Assistance for Needy Families (TANF).

State Flexibility   TANF gives the states much more flexibility in designing their own welfare programs. Congress set a "maintenance of effort" rule that forbids states from reducing their own welfare spending very much. But it gave states wide discretion to decide who is eligible for welfare, how much aid they get, and what services and work requirements accompany a welfare check.

Time Limits   Although states enjoy unprecedented program authority with TANF, Congress did set some national rules. One of these is a time limit on welfare dependency. TANF has a *lifetime* elegibility cap of five years. This time limit is intended to break the cycle of dependency. However, Congress gave the states a couple of loopholes. States can exempt 20 percent of their welfare caseload from the five-year limit. They can also continue to use *nonfederal* funds to extend welfare benefits beyond the threshold.

Work Requirements   Congress also laid down new work requirements for welfare recipients. Within two years of welfare receipt, adult recipients must engage in some work-related activity. In addition, states are required to have a rising percentage of recipients in work programs for at least 30 hours per week. The work participation requirement began at 25 percent in 1997 and rises 5 percentage points a year. Thus, by 2002, half of adult recipients are supposed to be in some form of work activity (a job, job search, education, or training).

Child Care   To facilitate work activity, the 1996 reforms substantially increased funding for child care. Indeed, the legislation created *two* block grants, one for welfare benefits and a second for child care. The Child Care and Development Block Grant (CCDBG) provides for over $20 billion in federal support over the first six years of the TANF program (1997–2002). With such funding, states can virtually guarantee child care for any welfare parent who wants to go to school, work, or participate in training.

Nonmarital Births   The Personal Responsibility and Work Opportunity Reconciliation Act of 1996 also created new incentives and rules to reduce nonmarital births. The law requires teenaged mothers to live in a home with a responsible adult. This provision closes off the use of welfare by teenagers to establish their own households. Teen moms are also required to attend school. All unmarried welfare mothers are required to help identify fathers and establish paternity responsibilities. To prod states to enforce these edicts, Congress set up various financial incentives and penalties for state performance.

Noncitizens   Last, but not least, the 1996 reforms sharply limit noncitizen access to welfare. Illegal immigrants were always ineligible for welfare. The 1996 law extended that exclusion to most *legal* immigrants as well. All noncitizens are barred from Supplemental Security Income (SSI) and food-stamp benefits. In addition, states can deny TANF benefits to legal immigrants as well.

The Controversy

The 1996 welfare reforms were so comprehensive that it will be many years before their full impact is known. Indeed, many critics protested that Congress was creating a gigantic social experiment, pushing welfare policy into uncharted areas. In the process, they feared, the well-being of poor children and their families might be jeopardized. Liberals were particularly concerned about the five-year limit on welfare dependency and the two-year limit on nonwork. What might happen to the children in such families when welfare benefits were reduced or eliminated? And what would happen to immigrant children whose families were cut off the welfare rolls? Although states have the authority to provide *state*-funded assistance in such cases, there is no longer an *entitlement* safety net. Indeed, states might be persuaded by political and budgetary considerations to *reduce* their welfare services rather than augment them. Such a "race to the bottom" might deprive needy children and adults of even minimally-adequate income support.

Conservative critics of the 1996 legislation emphasized other flaws. The strengthened work requirements still have lots of loopholes. States are free to define the nature of "work," and can automatically exempt a large portion of adult recipients from any work requirement. States can also use their own funds to continue benefits to nonworking recipients. Conservatives also wanted "family caps" that would deny benefits to children born to mothers already on welfare. Congress didn't establish such caps but did give states the authority to do so.

Various observers also wondered if enough jobs could be formed to employ a substantial number of (former) welfare recipients. Were there enough job vacancies in the labor market? Do those jobs pay enough to support a family? Do they provide access to better jobs as experience accumulates? What will happen when the economy falters? Will welfare recipients who have hit the time limits be left high and dry?

Despite all these criticisms and uncertainties, the 1996 welfare reforms were a political success. As Figure 11.5 illustrates, the public overwhelmingly applauded the reforms.

THE LIMITS OF WELFARE

The reality of welfare reform is that it begets no simple answers. We won't know all the effects of the 1996 reforms for several years. Even as more experience with TANF accumulates, there will be continuing debates about what "worked" and what didn't. To a

A 1996 *New York Times* opinion poll revealed the following responses to the 1996 welfare reforms:

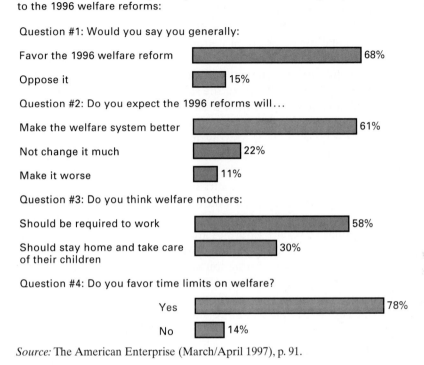

Question #1: Would you say you generally:

Favor the 1996 welfare reform — 68%

Oppose it — 15%

Question #2: Do you expect the 1996 reforms will...

Make the welfare system better — 61%

Not change it much — 22%

Make it worse — 11%

Question #3: Do you think welfare mothers:

Should be required to work — 58%

Should stay home and take care of their children — 30%

Question #4: Do you favor time limits on welfare?

Yes — 78%

No — 14%

Source: The American Enterprise (March/April 1997), p. 91.

FIGURE 11.5   Public Support for Welfare Reform

large extent, the continuing controversy will reflect the diverse goals that people have for welfare reform. The effects of the 1996 reforms are also certain to vary with the unique circumstance of different welfare families; some families will be better off, others worse off.

Despite the complexity of the welfare problem, the American people continue to prod elected officials to fashion a "silver bullet" that will end the welfare problem. Welfare reform is a politically appealing position, particularly when it promises a reduction in welfare caseloads and associated costs. As reformers soon learn when they try to grapple with the complexities of welfare, however, few reforms come cheaply.

In the midst of this frustration, simpler visions have a certain appeal. One of the most extreme suggestions is simply to eliminate welfare altogether. Charles Murray asserts that the very existence of a welfare system has nurtured the socially destructive behavior that traps people in poverty. If the promise of welfare support were withdrawn, teenagers would exercise greater birth control. Without the option of welfare support, teenage women who did have children would have to look to the child's father or their own families for support. Fathers would not feel they needed to abandon their families so they could get welfare and would be reluctant to leave if no benefits were available. The abolition of welfare could spark a revolutionary change in family relationships that restores the two-parent family to social and economic primacy. The elimination of welfare would also put an end to the work-incentive issue, since publicly supported nonwork would no longer be an option.

Some people could not cope without welfare, of course. Some families and parents are so dysfunctional for a variety of cultural, psychological, or physical reasons that they cannot achieve economic security even when the opportunity exists. Without a welfare system, the children in such families would be particularly vulnerable. Rather than keeping the welfare system intact "for the sake of the children," however, Murray proposes that society assume direct responsibility for such children by placing them in orphanages or nonparental adoption. If parents cannot or will not provide a safe and secure environment for their children, Murray argues, the children would be better off in nonparental care. This severing of parental rights would break the intergenerational cycle of underclass behavior that breeds dependency.

According to a 1992 public opinion survey, less than one out of ten Americans would be willing to take the gamble that Charles Murray proposes.[18] His suggestions, however, help underscore the limits of welfare reform. Modest adjustments in eligibility rules, benefit formulas, or service offerings are unlikely to transform the parameters of the welfare problem. People enter and exit welfare rolls for a variety of reasons, most of which are related to family formation and (re)marriage rather than narrower economic considerations like marginal tax rates and eligibility rules.[19]

The only lasting solution to the welfare problem will have to come from outside the welfare system. The solution lies in more and better jobs, more and better schooling, more stable families, and reduced teenage pregnancy. These are enormous challenges that must be approached from a much broader platform than welfare policy. What welfare reform can best accomplish in these circumstances is to encourage and assist individuals to move in these directions. In the limited context of welfare policy, modest expectations for piecemeal reform may be the most appropriate stance.

SUMMARY

Welfare programs are part of a much larger collection of income transfers. What distinguishes welfare transfers is the use of means-testing as a condition of eligibility. By contrast, social insurance programs are conditioned by events and thus available to rich and poor people alike.

There is no single welfare system in the United States. What is referred to as the welfare system is actually a conglomeration of diverse means-tested programs offering cash and in-kind assistance. Since the reforms of 1996, which gave states greater program authority, the welfare "system" has become even more diverse.

Prior to 1997, the largest cash welfare program was Aid to Families with Dependent Children (AFDC). AFDC was a federal entitlement, jointly financed by the federal and state governments. AFDC has been replaced with Temporary Assistance for

---

[18]Clancy Shulman Yankelovich, poll results reported in *The American Enterprise* (September/October 1993), p. 86.

[19]The interaction of personal, economic, and administrative variables on welfare behavior is explored in C. Michelle Piskulich, "Toward a Comprehensive Model of Welfare Exits: The Case of AFDC," *American Journal of Political Science* (February 1993), pp. 165–185.

Needy Families (TANF). TANF provides federal block grants to the states, which then fashion their own welfare programs. Federal TANF rules include a five-year limit on welfare dependency, stricter work requirements, and stepped-up child support enforcement. An accompanying block grant assures child-care availability.

In addition to cash benefits, most welfare families also get in-kind benefits like food stamps, Medicaid, nutrition programs, and housing assistance. These in-kind programs have expanded rapidly and now pay out far more in benefits. The combined "welfare package" of benefits has a median value of at least $12,000 per year for a mother and two children.

The central dilemma of welfare policy is the conflict among goals of adequacy, work incentives, and cost containment. As welfare benefits rise, the incentive to work is reduced and program costs increase. Low marginal tax (benefit-reduction) rates encourage work but raise program costs. Recent welfare reforms have used various rules (i.e., time limits, work requirements, denial of aid to teen moms living alone) to forge a politically acceptable compromise of the three policy goals. The general thrust of the reforms has been to require more self-help by recipients and limit society's income assurances.

It is unlikely that any single welfare reform will solve the welfare problem. People are driven onto the welfare rolls by a variety of social, demographic, and economic forces and exit welfare for as many diverse reasons. The "big" solutions to welfare are likely to lie in these larger socioeconomic dynamics rather than in the details of welfare rules and services. In this context, welfare reforms are likely to generate only modest changes in welfare caseloads and costs.

FURTHER READING

Bane, Mary Jo, and David Ellwood, *Welfare Realities.* Cambridge, MA: Harvard University Press, 1994.

Besharov, Douglas, and Karen N. Gardiner, "Paternalism and Welfare Reform," *The Public Interest* (Winter 1996), pp. 70–84.

Blank, Rebecca M., *It Takes A Nation: A New Agenda for Fighting Poverty.* Princeton, NJ: Princeton University Press, 1997, Chapters 3–4.

Coughlin, Teresa, Leighton Ku, and John Holahan, *Medicaid Since 1980.* Washington, DC: Urban Institute, 1994.

Hopkins, Kevin R., ed., *Welfare Dependency.* Alexandria, VA: Hudson Institute, 1987.

Katz, Michael B., *In the Shadow of the Poorhouse: A Social History of Welfare in America.* New York: Basic Books, 1986.

Mead, Lawrence M., *The New Politics of Poverty: The Nonworking Poor in America.* New York: Basic Books, 1992.

Moffitt, Robert, "Incentive Effects of the U.S. Welfare System: A Review," *Journal of Economic Literature* (March 1992), pp. 1–61.

Murray, Charles, *Losing Ground: American Social Policy 1950–1980.* New York: Basic Books, 1984.

Ohls, James C., and Harold Beebout, *The Food Stamp Program.* Washington, DC: Urban Institute, 1993.

Rank, Mark R., *Living on the Edge: The Realities of Welfare in America.* New York: Columbia University Press, 1994.

CHAPTER

Social Insurance Programs

12

T he welfare system is designed to provide financial assistance to people who have fallen into poverty. By contrast, the social insurance system is designed to *prevent* families from falling into poverty. Social insurance is intended to cushion income losses from specific events that might otherwise push people below poverty thresholds.

As we noted in Chapter 11, expenditures on social insurance programs vastly exceed welfare expenditures. They are also vastly more effective in reducing poverty. This is hardly surprising, given the failure of welfare programs to provide income support in excess of poverty thresholds and the unique mission of social insurance in preventing poverty. It is instructive, however, to consider how much poverty might exist if the United States had no social insurance programs.

In this chapter three major social insurance programs—Social Security, Medicare, and unemployment insurance—are examined. The major features of each program are described and their special impacts on poverty are assessed. Proposals to expand the government's role in child support are also discussed.

SOCIAL SECURITY

Social Security is by far the largest income transfer program in the United States. Unlike welfare, however, Social Security benefits are not reserved for those in need. Tax contributions rather than need establish eligibility for benefits. Anyone who has paid Social Security payroll taxes for a prescribed number of years is eligible to receive Social Security benefits at retirement age. Thus, the program is neither intended nor operated as an antipoverty mechanism. The majority of the 45 million individuals who receive Social Security benefits have never experienced poverty. Yet they receive over $400 billion in annual payments, triple the size of combined annual expenditures on cash welfare, food stamps, and rental assistance.

OASDHI Programs

Social Security is really a mixture of three distinct programs that share a common source of financing. The original Social Security Act of 1935 created only one program for older Americans—the Old Age Insurance (OAI) program. The purpose of OAI was to assure a basic floor of retirement income after older workers left the labor force. Four years later, Congress amended the act to authorize payment of benefits to survivors and dependents of workers who died (survivors' insurance). The combination of old age and survivors' coverage (OASI) is the essential *retirement* program of Social Security.

In 1956 the coverage of Social Security was extended to disabled workers, creating a second major benefit program (disability insurance) for American workers. A third program of health insurance (HI) was added in 1965, creating the Medicare program.

Financing

All three major Social Security programs are financed by a common payroll tax levied on wages and salaries—a tax euphemistically referred to as a "contribution" toward Social Security benefits. Most people mistakenly believe that their "contributions" accumulate in their accounts during their working years. They envision a savings "balance" from which retirement, disability, and health benefits are later paid. In reality, people do not accumulate any savings in the Social Security program. There is no huge pool of savings being set aside for future retirees. Instead, the Social Security system is a pure income transfer program, financed on a pay-as-you-go basis. The system uses the *current* contributions of workers to pay *current* benefits to retirees. By contrast, a conventional savings program uses *current* income to finance *future* payments. Accordingly, the availability of benefits for retirees depends on the continued ability and willingness of workers to make Social Security contributions.

The FICA Payroll Tax   The contributions of current workers to benefits for Social Security recipients are actually a tax on payrolls. The Social Security tax is deducted directly from employee paychecks, along with income tax withholding. This special payroll tax is popularly known as the FICA deduction in recognition of the law (Federal Insurance Contributions Act) that requires employers to withhold these Social Security contributions.

In addition to the employee's contribution, employers are taxed as well. Employers not only withhold the FICA tax from employee paychecks but also make an additional contribution of equal size. Thus, the revenues of the Social Security program come from payroll taxes on both employers and employees. Self-employed persons must pay both sides of the tax.

Tax Rates   The FICA tax covers not only contributions to the Social Security retirement (OASI) and disability insurance programs (DI), but also to health insurance (HI) programs (primarily Medicare) authorized by the Social Security Act. In 1997, the total FICA payroll tax was 7.65 percent. This included:

Program	Tax Rate
OASI (old age and survivors' insurance)	5.60%
DI (disability insurance)	0.60
Subtotal, OASDI	6.20
HI (health insurance)	1.45
Total FICA tax	7.65%

The OASI and DI tax receipts pay for retirement and disability benefits; HI tax receipts fund Medicare. To a taxpayer, the bottom line is a total Social Security tax of 7.65 percent.

The Wage Base   The FICA tax is a tax on wages. However, not every dollar of wages is taxed. Congress sets a *ceiling* to taxable wages; only wages below the ceiling are taxed. For the OASDI programs in 1997, the wage ceiling—called the wage base—was $65,400. Accordingly, the *maximum* OASDI tax an individual paid was:

$$\text{Maximum annual contribution for OASDI programs} = \text{OASDI tax rate} \times \text{wage base}$$
$$= .062 \times \$65,400$$
$$= \$4,054.80$$

The FICA tax also includes a contribution for health insurance (at a rate of 1.45 percent). There is no ceiling on taxable wages for HI, however; all wages and salaries are taxed to pay for Medicare. Recall that the employer pays an identical amount and a self-employed worker pays both parts (15.3 percent) of these taxes.

Benefits

The Social Security payroll tax brings in over $400 billion a year for the retirement and disability programs, most of which is paid out immediately in benefit checks to over 45 million recipients.[1]

Early versus Normal Retirement   The basic retirement benefits of Social Security are available under two age-related options:

- *Normal retirement*—a worker born before 1937 who retires at age 65 is eligible for full retirement benefits. For workers born after 1960, the normal retirement age will be 67.[2]

- *Early retirement*—a worker may retire at ages 62 to 64 and receive smaller monthly benefit checks.

The early retirement alternative is designed to pay just as much in lifetime benefits. Because the expected retirement period is longer, however, the monthly benefit checks are smaller. Despite this disadvantage, most Americans choose the early retirement option.

Benefit Levels   The size of the benefit check depends on a worker's employment history. Workers receive a credit for every calendar quarter they are employed. To be eligible for retirement benefits, a worker must accumulate at least 40 credits, or the equivalent of ten years of employment.[3]

---

[1]Since the early 1990s annual receipts have exceeded benefit payments by a wide margin. The resulting surpluses are intended as a bulwark against a projected upsurge in payments when the baby boomers of the 1950s start retiring after 2010. Then the U.S. Treasury will have to start repaying the Social Security Trust Fund from general revenues.

[2]The normal retirement age will increase by two months each year, beginning in the year 2000 until it reaches age 67 in the year 2022. Early retirement will still be available at age 62 but at proportionately reduced benefit levels.

[3]Quarterly credits are actually based on annual earnings. In 1996, a worker got one quarter of credit for every $640 earned during the year (up to a maximum of four credit quarters).

The amount of benefits a retired worker receives depends on the wages he or she earned. The relationship between wages and benefits is not linear, however. Workers with low wages get *proportionately* higher benefits. The benefit award in 1996 was calculated as:

- 90 percent of the first $437 of monthly earnings, plus
- 32 percent of the next $2,198 of monthly earnings, plus
- 15 percent of any earnings over $2,635.

A private insurance program would pay benefits in proportion to wages. The Social Security system instead uses a *progressive* benefit formula. The formula shown above gives low-wage workers a higher ratio of benefits to contributions. The progressivity of the system is reinforced with a limit on maximum benefit awards ($1,248 per month in 1996).

The benefit formula and maximum benefit amount are increased automatically each year at the rate of inflation. Congress also changes the formula and age thresholds on occasion. In the 1960s and early 1970s Congress made the formula more generous, causing Social Security benefits to rise much faster than inflation.

Benefit Adjustments   The benefits computed by the foregoing formula are "full" benefits for a worker retiring at age 65. A worker who chooses early retirement at age 62 would get only 80 percent of the full benefit amount. As noted earlier, this reduction is due to the fact that the retirement period is lengthened by early retirement.

Social Security also provides benefits to nonworking spouses. A 50 percent supplement is added to the monthly benefit check if the retiree has a spouse who is not eligible for his or her own benefits (or whose own benefits would be less than the 50 percent supplement). Widow(er)s and children of workers who die may also receive survivor benefits.

Beneficiaries   Over 45 million individuals receive some form of Social Security benefits. Nearly three out of four beneficiaries are retired workers or their survivors (old age and survivors' insurance). In 1997, the average benefit for a worker retiring at age 65 was approximately $900 per month.

Workers who become disabled before reaching retirement age can also receive Social Security benefits. In this case, benefits are paid from the DI (disability insurance) part of the program. Nearly 6 million individuals were receiving DI benefit checks in 1996. Once DI recipients reach retirement age, they start getting regular (OASI) retirement benefits.

Poverty Impact

The lion's share of Social Security benefits goes to people who are not poor. Even though the benefit formula is progressive, individuals who earned higher wages when in the labor force also receive larger benefit checks when they retire. Table 12.1 shows how benefit amounts vary by income class. Retirees whose *total* income places them in the top quintile of aged households got median Social Security benefits of $13,281 per year in 1994. This was more than twice as much as retirees in the lowest income quintile received. Although the Social Security benefit formula is progressive, it clearly doesn't equalize retirement benefits.

TABLE 12.1   Median Social Security Benefits by Income Quintile

Income Quintile	Median Social Security Benefits (per year)
Top fifth	$13,281
Second fifth	12,364
Third fifth	10,359
Fourth fifth	8,500
Bottom fifth	5,397

Source: Susan Grad, *Income of the Population 55 or Older, 1994* (Washington, DC: U.S. Government Printing Office, January 1996).

Despite the high proportion of benefits paid to the nonpoor, Social Security is still a highly effective antipoverty mechanism. Its antipoverty effectiveness results from the massive amount of income that is transferred and from the fact that virtually all older people receive Social Security benefits.[4] Even though most of the money goes to people who were never poor, there is still enough to keep millions of others out of poverty.

Income Dependence   The first indicator of Social Security's pivotal antipoverty role is the proportion of *total* income that comes from that source. As we first observed in Chapter 5 (Figure 5.2), Social Security benefits account for nearly 40 percent of all the income received by aged households. That dependence on Social Security grows even larger as retirees get older. As Figure 12.1 illustrates, over half of the income of

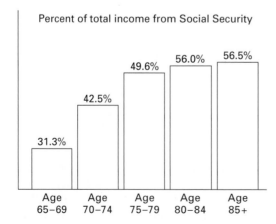

Percent of total income from Social Security

Age 65–69	Age 70–74	Age 75–79	Age 80–84	Age 85+
31.3%	42.5%	49.6%	56.0%	56.5%

Source: Susan Grad, *Income of the Population 55 or Older* (Washington, DC: U.S. Government Printing Office, January 1996), Table VII.1.

FIGURE 12.1   Dependence on Social Security, by Age

---

[4]Over 90 percent of older Americans receive Social Security benefits. Those who don't are either still working or receiving retirement benefits from another public pension program (federal, state, or local government; railroad retirement).

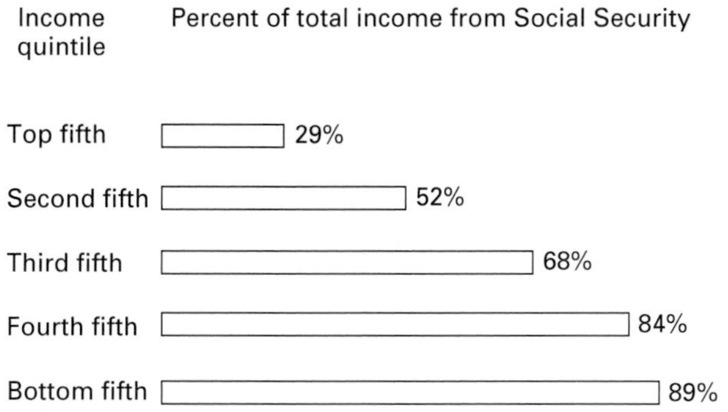

Income   Percent of total income from Social Security
quintile

Top fifth   ⬜ 29%

Second fifth   ⬜ 52%

Third fifth   ⬜ 68%

Fourth fifth   ⬜ 84%

Bottom fifth   ⬜ 89%

Source: Susan Grad, *Income of the Population 55 or Older,* Table VII.5.

FIGURE 12.2 Dependence on Social Security, by Income Quintile

people over age 75 comes from Social Security. As other income sources (e.g., earnings) disappear, Social Security benefits become ever more important.

The importance of Social Security for preventing poverty is even more apparent when the distribution of benefits across income classes is considered. In the lowest income quintile of aged households, Social Security benefits represent nearly 90 percent of total income. In the fourth quintile, Social Security dependence is nearly that high as well, as Figure 12.2 illustrates. For these lower-income aged households, Social Security benefits are the mainstay of financial support.

Table 12.2 illustrates how critical Social Security is in preventing older Americans from falling into poverty. In 1994, one out of eight older Americans was poor even while receiving Social Security benefits. Were Social Security benefits to cease, more than half of all older Americans would fall into poverty. Hence, for four out of ten older Americans—nearly 13 million individuals—Social Security benefits provide the margin of financial security that keeps them out of poverty. Table 12.2 shows how this margin of security becomes increasingly important as people age. Two-thirds of all individuals over age 85 would be poor without Social Security benefits.

TABLE 12.2 Antipoverty Impact of Social Security

	Percent in Poverty	
Subgroup	*With Social Security*	*Without Social Security*
All aged households	12	54
White	10	53
Black	29	69
Hispanic	21	61
Households aged 65–74	11	46
aged 75–84	13	61
aged 85+	17	66
Married couples	3	42
Nonmarried persons	18	62

Source: Susan Grad, *Income of the Population 55 or Older, 1994,* Table VIII.5.

Behavioral Responses   Although the Social Security program is undoubtedly the foremost safety net for older Americans, 13 million people would not necessarily fall into poverty if benefits ceased. Table 12.2 illustrates how many older people would be poor if they lost their Social Security benefits and *nothing else changed.* In reality, people would behave differently if there were no Social Security program. Without Social Security, people would stay in the workforce longer. When a worker becomes eligible for Social Security benefits, work is much less a necessity. Moreover, continuing payroll and income taxes, together with the implied sacrifice of retirement benefits, sharply reduce the *incentive* to work. Workers aged 62–64 who continue working lose $1 in benefits for every $2 they earn over a specific limit (roughly $8,600 in 1998). This benefits reduction is akin to a 50 percent marginal tax rate. When combined with income and payroll taxes, the implied burden on an older worker's wages exceeds 75 percent. This makes continued work unprofitable. Like welfare recipients, older workers opt for more leisure rather than more work when confronted with such work disincentives.[5]

In the absence of Social Security people might also save more during their working years so as to accumulate larger nest eggs for retirement. Fewer retirees would live on their own, choosing instead to live with relatives or friends in order to reduce expenses. These behavioral changes might not make up for the loss of Social Security benefits, but they would lessen the poverty impact. To the extent that Social Security benefits now *substitute* for these income alternatives, their antipoverty impact is exaggerated.

Reform Proposals   However different the country might look without Social Security, the program is now viewed as a permanent feature of the American political system. Accordingly, most reform proposals focus on modest changes in the program rather than its wholesale elimination.

The Social Security program has done a remarkable job of reducing the number of aged poor and of alleviating the condition of those who remain poor. Nevertheless, there are many observers who argue that we could further reduce poverty by increasing Social Security benefits. Across-the-board increases in benefits would extend to the poor and nonpoor alike, of course. Thus, if we wanted to aid the aged poor while holding down program costs (and payroll taxes!), minimum benefit levels would have to be raised faster than average benefit levels.

There are strong objections to raising minimum benefit levels faster than average benefit levels or, for that matter, raising any benefit levels at all. The primary objection is that the Social Security system should retain as much of its insurance character as possible, and not become a straightforward welfare program.[6] What is feared is that the further substitution of welfare (income redistribution) objectives for insurance objectives will undermine the popular support that the Social Security system enjoys. Thus,

---

[5]This appears to be particularly true for men; see Cordelia Reimers and Marjorie Honig, "Responses to Social Security by Men and Women," *Journal of Human Resources* (Spring 1996), pp. 359–382.

[6]In reality, the redistributional component of Social Security overwhelms its annuity component; see Edward N. Wolff, "Social Security Annuities and Transfers" in *Poverty and Prosperity in the U.S.A. in the Late Twentieth Century,* D. Papadimitrou and E. Wolff, eds. (New York: St. Martins, 1993).

Congress walks a thin line when it seeks to aid the aged poor while maintaining broad public support.

A second objection to increased benefits arises from fears about the system's financial viability. As we have noted, current benefit payments depend on current payroll taxes. Higher benefits thus require higher tax rates or an alternative source of financing. Critics argue that tax rates are already so high that they are eroding work incentives and inflating production costs. Critics also fear that dependence on alternative financing sources (e.g., general revenues) would destroy Social Security's unique character and its political credibility.

In 1996, Congress addressed the problem of work incentives by raising the earnings limit for workers aged 65–70. In 1998 an older worker could earn $14,500 without any reduction in Social Security benefits. That earnings ceiling rises each year, reaching $30,000 in 2002. Only earnings above those ceilings are "taxed" via benefit reductions, and then at a rate of only 33.3 percent. Fearful that such enhanced work incentives might drive up program costs (the now familiar goal conflict), however, Congress refused to extend these incentives to workers aged 62–64. They still confront much lower earnings limits and a higher benefit-reduction rate (50 percent).

MEDICARE

Older Americans receive not only *cash* transfers from Social Security but also *in-kind* transfers. The most important of these come from the Medicare program. Like other forms of social insurance, the benefits of Medicare are available to all older Americans without consideration of income or wealth. Medicare benefits come in two forms: basic hospital insurance and a supplemental medical insurance option.

Hospital Insurance

The core of the Medicare program is universal hospital insurance (HI) for people over age 65 (and younger disabled recipients of disability insurance). The HI program provides for

- inpatient hospital care
- skilled nursing care
- home health care
- hospice care

Although its scope is broad, the HI program provides full coverage of related expenses for very limited time periods. After 20 to 30 days of care, patients must pay a significant share of their own bills ($85 to $350 a day, depending on the nature of service provided). After 90 to 100 days, all HI coverage ceases.

Supplemental Medical Insurance

Because HI coverage is so limited, Medicare gives older Americans the option of purchasing subsidized insurance for additional medical costs. The supplemental medical insurance (SMI) program offers very broad coverage for a low monthly premium

($44 in 1997). With SMI coverage, an older person pays a small annual deductible ($100 in 1995) and 20 percent of covered medical expenses. Virtually all older Americans enroll in the SMI program.

Poverty Impact

In 1996, the Medicare program paid out $180 billion in benefits. Only $20 billion was collected from older Americans in the form of SMI premiums. Hence, Medicare generated a net transfer to the aged that was worth over $160 billion. About two-thirds of this transfer was financed by the FICA payroll tax; the rest came out of the federal government's general revenues.

The in-kind Medicare transfer of $160 billion amounts to roughly $5,000 per year for every older American. Although the amount of benefits actually received depends on an individual's health status, the average transfer puts perspective on the relative importance of Medicare for financial security. The total *money* income of the average older couple was approximately $36,000 in 1996; for aged persons living alone the average was just under $12,000. Accordingly, the in-kind Medicare transfer increased real incomes of the aged by 20 to 30 percent.

Because Medicare is an in-kind benefit, it does not directly affect the official poverty count, which focuses exclusively on *cash* income. The Medicare subsidy, however, reduces the expenses of the aged and so allows them to stay above poverty living standards even if their cash income falls short of official poverty thresholds. According to Census Bureau estimates, approximately 1 million older people now officially counted as poor would not be so if the value of Medicare benefits were taken into account. Millions more older Americans enjoy a higher living standard due to Medicare as well.

UNEMPLOYMENT INSURANCE

The Social Security and Medicare programs are principally sources of social insurance for retired workers. For younger individuals still active in the labor force, social insurance against income loss is far less extensive. To a large extent, this gap reflects the conviction that people should work to support themselves (work incentives).

There are two major programs for active workers: unemployment insurance and workers' compensation. As Table 12.3 indicates, the combined benefits of these two programs amount to less than one-sixth of benefits paid to older Americans.

Despite the relatively small amount of money set aside for unemployment insurance (UI), that program could be an important factor in preventing poverty. As we observed in Chapter 3, unemployment is a major cause of poverty. By replacing some of the income lost during spells of unemployment, the UI program reduces slippage into poverty. How effective the UI program is in preventing poverty depends on how much it offers in benefits and to whom.

Eligibility Conditions

The UI system created in 1935 was not designed to provide benefits for everyone who experiences unemployment. Rather, the program was targeted more narrowly on experienced workers who lose their jobs through no fault of their own. Graduating stu-

TABLE 12.3   Major Social Insurance Programs

Program	Benefits Paid in 1997
Social Security	
Old Age and Survivors' Insurance	$317 billion
Disability Insurance	$ 44 billion
Medicare	
Hospital Insurance	$137 billion
Supplemental Medical Insurance	$ 76 billion
Unemployment Insurance	$ 24 billion
Workers' Compensation	$ 49 billion
Veterans' Benefits	$ 39 billion

Source: U.S. Congress, Committee on Ways and Means, *1996 Green Book* (Washington, DC: U.S. Government Printing Office, 1996).

dents just looking for their first full-time job don't qualify for UI benefits. Nor do workers who quit their jobs or who get fired for cause.

Because each state runs its own UI program, there is no uniform set of eligibility conditions for UI benefits. However, all states require that UI applicants

- have certain amounts of recent work experience and earnings,
- demonstrate an ability and willingness to seek and accept suitable employment, and
- have lost their jobs through no fault of their own.

Over 95 percent of the *employed* workforce is covered by UI. However, only about a third of all *unemployed* persons are covered due to the work experience and job-loss conditions.

Benefits

If eligible for UI insurance, an unemployed worker can collect a weekly UI benefit check. Generally, the UI benefit amounts to 50 to 70 percent of the former wage, up to a specified maximum. There is tremendous variation among the state programs, however. An unemployed worker in Hawaii could have gotten as little as $5 a week in 1996. In Massachusetts, an unemployed worker could have received as much as $521 per week. Table 12.4 illustrates some of this variation in benefit levels.

Although there is great interstate variation in weekly benefit levels, the duration of benefit eligibility is more uniform. Federal legislation authorizes a basic 26-week program, funded completely out of state payroll tax receipts. Federal law also authorizes an additional 13-week period of benefits when state unemployment rates exceed certain thresholds. The second period of eligibility is jointly funded by the federal and state governments.[7] In severe national recessions, Congress has also authorized a third period of extended benefits, paid exclusively out of federal revenues.

---

[7] All state and regular federal extended benefits are financed by a payroll tax of 6.2 percent on the first $8,000 of annual wages.

TABLE 12.4 Variations in State UI Benefits

State	Minimum Benefit	Maximum Benefit	Average Benefit
High benefits:			
Hawaii	$ 5	$347	$262
Massachusetts	14	521	239
New Jersey	60	362	245
District of Columbia	50	359	223
Low benefits:			
South Dakota	28	180	140
Alabama	22	180	135
Mississippi	30	180	130
Louisiana	10	181	119

Source: U.S. Congress, Committee on Ways and Means, *1996 Green Book*
(Washington, DC: U.S. Government Printing Office, November 1996).

Poverty Impact

Most UI benefits are not paid to poor people or even to people who are at high risk of becoming poor. This is hardly surprising, given our earlier observation (Chapter 3) that most people who experience unemployment are not poor.

The family income of UI recipients is typically kept substantially above poverty levels by the presence of other workers in the household. Nearly two-thirds of all UI recipients are married, and most of these married recipients have a working spouse.

The financial security of many UI recipients is also buttressed by the nature of their job loss. A sizable proportion of UI recipients is employed in industries where recurrent layoffs are common. Typically, the jobs are in manufacturing or construction and are often unionized. Over a third of all UI recipients end up getting recalled to their former jobs in a relatively short amount of time.

As emphasized in Chapter 3, unemployment poses the greatest risk of poverty if it continues for a long period of time. Most of the people who receive UI benefits don't stay unemployed very long. In 1996, the median duration of UI receipt was only 15.6 weeks. During that period, the average UI recipient received nearly $3,000 in benefits.

The UI recipients most likely to be at risk of poverty are those who remain unemployed until their UI eligibility is exhausted. About 30 percent of all UI recipients exhaust their regular benefits. Although nearly half of these exhaustees find employment shortly after their UI benefits run out, their post-UI jobs often pay less than their former employment. Even more at risk are those UI exhaustees who remain unemployed for months longer after their UI benefits cease. Even among this small minority of UI recipients, however, few end up in poverty. Only 7 percent of all UI exhaustees end up on welfare.[8] Accordingly, the UI program is more appropriately viewed as a middle-class safety net rather than as a major factor in preventing poverty.

CHILD-SUPPORT ENFORCEMENT

Child support has long been viewed as a family law issue to be resolved by local courts. Over time, however, state and federal governments have taken an increasingly aggressive role in the establishment and enforcement of child-support obligations. Prior to 1984, state and federal governments largely restricted their enforcement efforts to welfare (AFDC) cases. Since 1984, however, states are *required* by federal laws to offer child-support enforcement to *all* parents who request it. Further federal legislation in 1988 (the Family Support Act) promulgated mandatory wage withholding for child-support obligations and established national guidelines for child-support awards. With these and other changes, child-support enforcement has evolved from a means-tested welfare service to something more akin to social insurance.[9] In the process, it has also become a more effective mechanism in preventing poverty.

Child-Support Gaps

The impetus for public child-support initiatives comes from the recognition that more and more children grow up in single-parent families, often with no financial support from the absent parent. In 1970, only 12 percent of all children (under age 18) lived in a one-parent family; today, nearly 30 percent do so. As discussed in Chapter 6, this revolutionary change in family structure has affected rich and poor and all racial and ethnic groups.

The financial security of single-parent families often depends on support contributions from the absent parent. It is widely believed that absent parents also have a moral and social obligation to provide child support even in cases where financial insecurity is not present. This societal expectation for child support is often not met, however. In 1989, there were 10 million women raising children in the absence of their natural fathers. Fewer than 4 million of these mothers received any child-support payments from absent fathers. Accordingly, over 6 million mothers—and their 10 million children—had to get along without child-support payments. (Another 2 million children live with their custodial father, but few statistics are collected on them.)

Table 12.5 shows how the gap in child support affects both poor and nonpoor families. Just over half of all nonpoor custodial mothers and just over one-third of all poor custodial mothers are supposed to receive child support from noncustodial fathers, either by court order or agreement. In both income groups, child-support entitlement is common among remarried and divorced mothers but rare among never-married

---

[8]For more information on the characteristics and experiences of UI recipients, see Walter Corson and Mark Dynarski, *A Study of Unemployment Insurance Recipients and Exhaustees* (Princeton, NJ: Mathematica Policy Research, 1990).

[9]The evolution of child support into social insurance is summarized in Irwin Garfinkel, "The Child-Support Revolution," *American Economic Review* (May 1994), pp. 81–85.

TABLE 12.5   Child-Support Payments, by Marital Status of Poor Mothers

Marital Status	Number (%)	Percent Entitled to Support	Percent Receiving Support	Average Payment	Average Income
All poor mothers	3,513,000	39	22	$1,992	$5,683
Remarried	338,000 (5%)	55	41	$1,433	$3,708
Divorced	837,000 (26%)	55	38	$2,424	$6,889
Separated	836,000 (19%)	39	27	$1,736	$4,917
Never married	1,449,000 (50%)	25	18	$1,515	$5,725

Source: U.S. Congress, Committee on Ways and Means, *1996 Green Book,* Table 9-6.

mothers. Indeed, the low child-support entitlement among poor women is largely due to the fact that half of them never married the father of their children.

Only about three out of four custodial mothers who are supposed to get child support actually receive any payments. Only two out of four receive the full amount due. This gap is particularly evident among poor families, where only one out of four custodial mothers gets any child support. Here again, the likelihood of actual support depends greatly on marital status, with never-married mothers least likely (18 percent) to get *any* child support. Even when they do get some support, the amount of money is very low (average of $1,515 per year).

Table 12.5 documents that millions of custodial mothers are raising their children without any financial support from absent fathers. These unsupported women and children are at high risk of poverty and have swelled welfare caseloads in every state.

Enforcement Policies

To increase parental support, government at all levels has expanded the government's role in child-support enforcement. The 1975 amendments to the Social Security Act (Title IV, part D) strengthened enforcement mechanisms by providing the states with federal matching funds for:

- enforcing child-support obligations
- locating absent parents
- establishing paternity
- obtaining support awards

Any custodial parent who applies for federally-funded welfare must agree to help collect child support and also assign all rights to support payments to the welfare agency. In return, the state is required to initiate a paternity investigation (including mandatory genetic testing), to seek and enforce support obligations, and to implement guidelines for support awards. Since 1994 states have also been required to impose automatic withholding of support payments from the paychecks of noncustodial parents. To find absent parents and enforce support obligations, the states are authorized to access all government databanks including tax records, motor vehicle registrations, Social Security records, and the Selective Service System.

As noted earlier, federal law has required the states since 1984 to make these child-support enforcement services available to *all* custodial parents, regardless of income. The states can charge a fee of no more than $25 to nonwelfare parents. Even this fee can be charged to the noncustodial parent or paid by the state itself if it chooses.

Poverty Impact

In theory, child-support payments could be an important antipoverty mechanism. In practice, however, they are more effective in preventing slippage into poverty than facilitating poverty exits. More than $10 billion a year in child-support payments is received by nonpoor mothers.

Single mothers already in poverty clearly don't fare as will. To some extent, their poverty reflects the failure to collect support payment from absent fathers. The gap between collections and entitlement is not wide enough, however, to explain much poverty. In 1991 there were 1.26 million single-parent families in poverty entitled to a child-support award. If *full* payment had been made on those awards, only 140,000 of those families—one out of nine—would have had incomes above the poverty threshold. Hence, child-support enforcement is a fairly ineffective mechansim for reducing poverty; it serves, however, as a substantial safety net for keeping low-income families from falling into poverty. [10]

Reform Proposals   The primary weakness of child-support enforcement as an antipoverty mechanism originates in the status of the poor child's parents. The problem starts with never-married mothers and fathers. Nearly 60 percent of the poor women who don't receive child support are never-married mothers, typically in their late teens and early twenties. Without a marital union, they confront greater obstacles to obtaining child support. They must be willing and able to identify the father and, if necessary, to establish legal paternity in the courts or administrative agencies. Many young mothers may be hesitant to do so. They may be hopeful of maintaining a household with the father, and reluctant to antagonize him. Alternatively, they may regard the father as a poor marital or parenting prospect and prefer to avoid further contact with him.[11] Since the welfare agency gets any support payments collected, the economic incentive to pursue paternity and child support is also weak.

Regardless of the mother's feelings or incentives, there is also little expectation of substantial support in many cases. The sexual partners of teenage mothers are typically teenage boys with little work experience, modest education, and little income.[12] While they may have a moral and social obligation to support their children, it is not evident

---

[10]There is evidence that the prospect of enforcement may deter low-income couples (especially fathers) from divorcing; see Lucia A. Nixon, "The Effects of Child Support Enforcement on Marital Dissolution," *Journal of Human Resources* (Winter 1997), pp. 159–181.

[11]An experiment in Ohio revealed that nearly half of all unmarried welfare mothers refused to identify their children's fathers; see Charles Adams, David Landsbergen, and Larry Cobler, "Welfare Reform and Paternity Establishment," *Journal of Policy Analysis and Management* (1992), pp. 665–687.

[12]See Ronald Mincy and Elaine Sorensen, "Deadbeats and Turnips in Child Support Reform," *Journal of Policy Analysis and Management* (Winter 1998); Maureen Piroq-Good and David Good, "Child Support Enforcement for Teenage Fathers: Problems and Prospects," *Journal of Policy Analysis and Management* (1994, 14), pp.15–42; Robert Lerman and Theodora Ooms, eds., *Young Unwed Fathers: Changing Roles and Emerging Policies* (Philadelphia, PA: Temple University Press, 1993).

how that obligation can or should be enforced. Should a teenage father be compelled to quit school and take a job? Should he be imprisoned if he can't or won't pay? Aside from abstinence, there are no easy answers for the economic security of children born to teenage parents.

Child-support collections are also inhibited by the tangle of red tape. There are substantial administrative costs associated with child-support enforcement. Even though such activities appear to be highly cost-effective, limited public budgets typically require a rationing process. As administrative delays lengthen, the probability of establishing and enforcing child-support obligations diminishes. If a noncustodial parent moves to another state, the process of enforcement becomes much more costly and success much less likely.

Professor Irwin Garfinkel and others have urged that the present system of child-support *enforcement* be replaced with a system of child-support *assurance.* In effect, the federal government would guarantee a certain threshold of child support to children of absent parents. Just as Social Security insures against the death or disability of a breadwinner, so would a child-support assurance system insure against the absence of a parent. With such a system *all* single parents would receive assured child support. The government would assume full responsibility for collecting child-support obligations from noncustodial parents, according to fixed guidelines (e.g., 17 percent of gross income for one child, 25 percent for two children, and so on) and using mandatory wage withholding.

A child-support assurance system could have a dramatic effect on poverty rates and welfare caseloads. According to simulation estimates, assured annual support of $1,000 to $3,000 per child would reduce the poverty gap by 13 to 24 percent and reduce welfare caseloads by 12 to 32 percent.[13]

Although a child-support assurance system might significantly *reduce* poverty among single-parent families, such an approach is not universally welcomed. One objection emerges from cost considerations. Universal child-support assurance could cost up to $5 billion per year. Costs would come down only if the government could substantially increase collections from absent parents. Since most of the absent parents of poor children are poor themselves, the prospects for increased collections (and lower net costs) are not good.

Another objection is based on family values. Many critics fear that further government intrusion into family matters will weaken already tenuous family bonds. The administrative and legal procedures entailed in public child-support assurance may antagonize parents and diminish chances of reconciliation. Public resources would be better spent, they say, in promoting parent access, family formation, and employability than in focusing on financial collections.[14] Finally, critics fear that assured child-support

---

[13]Irwin Garfinkel, "Child Support Assurance: An Addition to Our Social Security Menu," in *Security for America's Children,* eds. P. Vande Water and L. Schorr (Dubuque, IA: Kendall/Hunt, 1992), pp. 57–70. Lower estimates of potential welfare reduction (including observations on welfare *reentry*) are contained in Daniel R. Meyer, "Child Support and Welfare Dynamics: Evidence from Wisconsin," *Demography* (February 1993), pp. 45–62.

[14]Another alternative is to assure quality child care rather than direct financial support; see Barbara Bergmann, "Curing Child Poverty in the United States," *American Economic Review* (May 1994), pp. 76–80. Bergmann compares the French and American systems of child support in *Saving Our Children from Poverty* (New York: Russell Sage, 1996).

payments would increase the incentives for childbirth already associated with the more onerous welfare system.

As the larger issues entailed in a child-support assurance system continue to be debated, incremental changes in the present system are advocated. Given the demonstrated efficacy of child-support enforcement efforts, proponents want enforcement budgets increased. They also want to increase the efficiency of enforcement efforts by requiring more coordination across state boundaries. If child-support enforcement became more certain, voluntary support payments might increase. There might even be a greater reluctance to have children one didn't plan to support.

SUMMARY

Social insurance programs are the largest component in the U.S. income transfer system. They are distinguishable from welfare programs by the absence of income or wealth eligibility conditions (means-testing).

The Social Security programs of retirement, survivors', and disability insurance are the largest expenditure item in the federal budget. Social Security is a pay-as-you-go system, with current benefits financed by current payroll taxes. Eligibility and benefit levels are determined by age and earnings history. Social Security is the nation's most effective antipoverty program, providing nearly 40 percent of all retirement income.

The Medicare program also provides substantial in-kind income to older Americans. The health insurance subsidies of Medicare substantially reduce the cash expenses of older Americans, eliminating real poverty for close to 1 million older Americans and raising real living standards for millions more.

Unemployment insurance (UI) is available to workers with recent work experience who lose their jobs because of layoffs, plant closings, and other nonpersonal reasons. Although benefits vary widely across states, they average from 50 to 70 percent of previous wages. Because most experienced workers who have a spell of unemployment are not poor, the UI program is not a major antipoverty mechanism. Most at risk of poverty are individuals who remain unemployed for several months after their UI benefits cease.

Child-support enforcement has evolved into a quasisocial insurance program. In principle, any single parent can access government services to establish and enforce child-support obligations. Present child-support payments fall far short of universal coverage, however, leaving millions of single parents and their children in poverty. More aggressive enforcement activity has significant potential to increase payments. However, its antipoverty potential is limited by the youth and low income of absent fathers who were the sexual partners of never-married mothers. Reform proposals range from a child-support assurance system that guarantees support payments to more modest administrative changes that would increase support collections.

FURTHER READINGS

Beller, Andrea, and John W. Graham, *Small Change: The Economics of Child Support.* New Haven, CT: Yale University Press, 1993.

Congressional Budget Office, *Reduced Entitlement Spending.* Washington, DC: U.S. Government Printing Office, September 1994.

Garfinkel, Irwin, Sara S. McLanahan, and Philip Robins, *Child Support and Child Well-Being.* Washington, DC: Urban Institute, 1994.

Hungerford, Thomas L., "The Distribution and Anti-Poverty Effectiveness of U.S. Transfers, 1992," *Journal of Human Resources* (Winter 1996), pp. 255–273.

Moon, Marilyn, *Medicare Now and In the Future.* Washington, DC: Urban Institute, 1993.

Schiller, Bradley R., *Social Security: The Economics of an Aging Population.* New York: Mc-Graw-Hill, 1992.

Schulz, James H., *The Economics of Aging,* 5th ed. Westport, CN: Auburn House, 1992.

Steurle, C. Eugene, and John M. Bakija, *Retooling Social Security for the 21st Century.* Washington, DC: Urban Institute, 1994.

U.S. Congress, Committee on Ways and Means, *Green Book.* Washington, DC: U.S. Government Printing Office, annual.

CHAPTER

Employment Policies

13

If meaningful and long-term solutions to the problem of poverty are to be implemented, public policy will have to venture beyond income maintenance. Simply providing money to the poor has little potential for stimulating financial independence. The only possible lasting solution to the problem of poverty is to assure that decent jobs are available to all who seek them. Under such circumstances, poverty and the need for income maintenance will be at a minimum.

The government has several alternatives at its disposal for expanding employment opportunities. At the most general level, it may seek to increase the demand for labor by stimulating aggregate demand. A variety of fiscal and monetary measures are available for that purpose. Rather than raise the general demand for labor, the government might instead try to increase the demand for specific groups of workers (e.g., low-income workers; welfare recipients). This may entail tax credits or other financial incentives for hiring target groups. Or the government might take still more direct action by creating jobs itself via public emplyment programs.

The government can also influence the *supply* of labor. Rather than stimulate new demand, government policy may focus on training unemployed workers for jobs already available. Still another possibility is to make labor markets more efficient in matching available workers with vacant jobs.

To some extent, each of these policy alternatives has been implemented, but they have received markedly different degrees of attention. In the 1930s a heavy emphasis was put on public employment. After World War II the government placed primary reliance on aggregate economic policies to provide the necessary job opportunities. Only in the late 1950s and early 1960s did an awareness emerge that other approaches were also necessary to provide a requisite number of jobs; at that time, a variety of training programs was introduced. The whole sequence started again in the 1970s. First there was an expansion of public employment programs, especially in the mid-1970s. Then the primary importance of aggregate demand policies was emphasized, along with an increasing concern for aggregate supply. This concern led to a preference for training over public jobs and a search for new ways to improve the match between job seekers and job vacancies. In the 1980s there was an increasing emphasis on the obligation of welfare recipients to work or improve their employability prospects (e.g., via human capital investment). The recession of 1990–91 helped shift attention back to the adequacy of the social safety net. As the economy recovered, greater emphasis was directed toward the nature of available jobs and government policies that, in President Clinton's words, would "make work pay." This chapter reviews the nature, history, and potential of these many different dimensions of employment policy.

AGGREGATE DEMAND POLICIES

Most people believe that the United States could have averted the Great Depression were we as knowledgeable in 1930 as we are now about the workings of the economy. This belief stems from the conviction that economists can now manage the economy to a degree formerly unheard of. Present-day arguments between economists concentrate not on the issue of whether the level of demand can be affected, but on how much success can be achieved by such policies.

The claims of modern economists inspire hope for the plight of the poor. If we really can manage aggregate demand, we can provide enough jobs for the unemployed, the underemployed, and the discouraged poor. Anyone who has even skimmed through an introductory economics textbook can provide an outline for action. Fiscal policies can expand demand through increased government expenditures, consumer tax cuts, or enhanced tax incentives for investment. Monetary policy may provide a stimulus to demand by making access to credit easier and cheaper. Together, such policies could potentially move millions of persons out of poverty.

As enticing as the notion of complete demand management might appear, it is evident that the economy has not performed as well as such management capability would imply. The economy continues to suffer periodic recessions. Unemployment rates linger above policy targets. And millions of people remain in poverty. What explains this gap between the promise and performance of (macro) aggregate economic policy?

Full Employment versus Price Stability

One explanation for the shortfall of aggregate demand is the perceived conflict between the goals of full employment and price stability. As the economy approaches full employment, there is less and less available capacity. New employees are harder to find and more expensive to recruit. Supplies take longer to be delivered and often come only at premium prices. As inventories of unsold goods and services decline, producers begin to charge higher prices. These kinds of pressures threaten to push price levels higher, frustrating the goal of price stability.

The politics of the unemployment-inflation trade-off don't favor the poor. Inflation tends to hurt the middle class and older Americans depending on fixed-income sources (e.g., interest on bonds, private pensions). They will favor policies that shield them from the threat of inflation. Even when the national unemployment rate is relatively high, the number of *employed* individuals far exceeds the number of *unemployed*. Accordingly, the commitment to full employment may waver once prices start rising.

In the late 1950s full employment was defined as the attainment of less than 5 percent unemployment. When Walter Heller, President Kennedy's economic advisor, publicly aspired to reach full employment of 4 percent, he was chided for recklessness.

As unemployment sank below even 4 percent in the mid-1960s, some began to wonder whether we had not previously underestimated our abilities and unnecessarily relegated millions of individuals to poverty. The public never became wholly convinced, however. When the rate of inflation did spurt at the end of the 1960s, it was concluded immediately that the rise in prices was due to our efforts to create full employment. Indeed, both the Nixon and Ford administrations argued repeatedly that full employment should be redefined as an unemployment rate of 5 or 5.5 percent. The Carter administration first adopted 4.9 percent as its definition of full employment, then raised it to 5.5 percent. The Reagan administration made full employment appear still more attainable by setting it at 6.5 percent. When the employment rate dropped below this level in 1987–1988, efforts were undertaken to "cool" the economy. In 1993–1994, a similar scenario unfolded when the Clinton administration backed off its commitment to "jobs, jobs, jobs" and supported monetary policies designed to quell any threats of inflation. Such repeated U-turns in economic policy have slowed the growth of new jobs and with it, the exodus from poverty.

The Quality of Jobs

Fear of inflation has not been the only obstacle to more effective aggregate demand policies. In the general euphoria of our discovery that we could manipulate aggregate demand, we neglected some simple truths. The way in which aggregate demand is stimulated has significant impact on the economy. A large reduction in interest rates, for example, will stimulate the housing and lumber industries, where interest charges are a major component of total cost. Investment credit allowances, on the other hand, benefit manufacturers of steel, airplanes, and heavy machinery with little impact on housing production. More generally, tax cuts expand the private sector while increases in government spending expand the public sector. Indeed, every fiscal or monetary action will affect the distribution of output, as well as its volume.

Some observers claim that the content of our economic growth has actually worsened job prospects for the poor. They see the manufacturing sector declining and the service sector expanding. In the process, they assert, "good" jobs are disappearing and "bad" jobs are proliferating. Without access to the higher-wage jobs in manufacturing, more workers are likely to be poor at any given level of aggregate unemployment.[1]

Paradoxically, other observers assert that recent job growth has been disproportionately in "good" jobs. As they see it, the jobs created in today's economy require advanced education and technical skills. Middle-class workers have the prerequisites, but poor people don't. As a consequence, college graduates quickly and easily get on the financial fast track. By contrast, job seekers with few skills and little education get left at the starting gate. Hence, the proliferation of good jobs widens wage inequalities and does little to reduce poverty.[2]

---

[1]For discussion of the "good" versus "bad" jobs issue, see Bennett Harrison and Barry Bluestone, *The Great U-Turn* (New York: Basic Books, 1988); Gary Loveman and Chris Tilly, "Good Jobs or Bad Jobs?" *International Labor Review,* 129 (1988), 593–611; Gary Burtless, ed., *A Future of Lousy Jobs?* (Washington, DC: Brookings, 1990).

[2]For analyses of widening wage inequalities, see the symposium in the Spring 1997 *Journal of Economic Perspectives;* also S. Danziger and P. Gottschalk, *America Unequal* (Cambridge, MA: Harvard University Press, 1995).

Although these two perspectives on the labor market are very different, they come to similar policy conclusions. In etiher case, low-skilled job seekers face bleak prospects. Either they confront an abundance of bad jobs (the first view) or no jobs at all (the second view). To remedy this problem, more attention must be paid to the *structure* of demand, rather than simply its *level*. Some policies provide more jobs for the poor with little effect on prices, while others do just the reverse. The trick is to find the right ones. This will require that policy makers explicitly incorporate antipoverty objectives into their budget plans and look more closely at the impact of alternative policy strategies on the distribution of job opportunities.[3]

However, even truly enlightened full employment policies will not provide decent jobs for all who need them. As unemployment levels drop, it becomes increasingly difficult—and socially expensive—to reach those who still need employment. Accordingly, expansionary fiscal and monetary policies alone cannot wholly eliminate poverty among those who are presently or potentially in the labor force. But it is even more important to emphasize that without determined full employment policies all other efforts to eliminate poverty are rendered impotent. In 1991–92, for example, more money was spent on welfare, training, education, and other antipoverty efforts than in earlier years. Nevertheless, the number of people in poverty grew by 4.5 million because unemployment levels rose sharply. The demand for labor, especially labor provided by the poor, must be kept at high levels if the poor are to gain financial independence. All other efforts are secondary.

TRAINING PROGRAMS

As every freshman economist knows, both supply and demand forces operate in the labor market. Hence, to many observers it seems as logical to adapt supply to demand as to proceed the other way around. Indeed, training programs for unemployed workers enjoy much greater acceptance than policies designed to expand and redirect labor demand toward the poor. What accounts for their popularity and how effective are they?

Job Vacancies

The potential of training programs to increase total employment is suggested by the persistence of job vacancies. Help-wanted ads continue to appear even in periods of high unemployment. People move from job to job with great frequency, creating a kind of musical chairs situation in the labor market. In addition, there are always businesses either expanding or contracting, thereby creating or eliminating available jobs. As a result, some jobs are always vacant and employers must advertise that fact. How fast those vacancies are filled depends on how many workers are looking for jobs and what their talents are. Where millions of workers are unemployed, vacancies are quickly filled. In periods of lower unemployment, employers must wait longer and look further before obtaining needed labor.

---

[3]This kind of industrial policy is advocated by Richard Caputo, "Family Poverty, Unemployment Rates, and AFDC Payments: Trends Among Blacks and Whites," *Families in Society* (November 1993), pp. 515–526.

Almost as important as the number of available workers are the skills they possess. If employers are seeking skilled craftspeople, millions of unemployed day laborers will contribute little to the fulfillment of job vacancies. Skills possessed by job seekers must bear some resemblance to the requirements of available jobs. Nevertheless, it should not be concluded that an existing mismatch of job requirements and skills of the unemployed constitutes an insurmountable barrier to full employment. On the contrary, rarely is a worker hired who is ready to perform his or her job with no orientation or training. Employers can and do provide available workers with needed skills.

Even though private employers frequently provide some form of orientation or training, they seek to keep training expenses to a minimum. They much prefer to hire persons who are already skilled and experienced. That option is not always available. Those who are not yet hired are likely to possess fewer skills. The amount of training employers will have to provide thus varies inversely with the level of unemployment. If aggregate demand is strong, employers will incur the added expenses willingly.

Government programs to train the unemployed have a slightly different orientation. To some extent, they merely relieve private employers of the burden and expense of training. This may be done by providing training directly or by subsidizing the training efforts of private industry. But training programs directed at the poor have an additional objective: They seek to improve the competitive position of the poor in the labor market. Although the two training functions overlap, they have very different implications. Training designed to create skills in demand leads directly to increased employment; training designed to increase the competitive position of the poor also serves to redistribute existing unemployment.

The first full-scale government training program was established in 1962 under the Manpower Development and Training Act (MDTA). Persistently high rates of unemployment in the period 1958–61 coupled with fears of advancing automation led many observers to conclude that a basic mismatch existed between people and jobs. The only way to approach fuller employment, it seemed, was to provide the unemployed with the new skills demanded by advancing technology. Accordingly, Congress provided for a national effort to retrain displaced and unemployed workers in new skill areas.

In the years since the establishment of the MDTA program, the federal government has introduced and operated scores of training programs, with various services and for different target groups (the young, the old, the skilled, the unskilled, welfare recipients, high school dropouts, and so on). Several of those programs are particularly significant because they illustrate different approaches to skill training.

The CETA Program

The Comprehensive Employment and Training Act (CETA) of 1974 was the centerpiece of employment policy in the 1970s. A unique feature of CETA was its transfer of program responsibilities from the federal government to state and local governments. Local *prime sponsors* received CETA funds from the federal government to run employment and training programs tailored to local needs.

The CETA program included a broad range of employment and training services. In part, this reflected the decentralized nature of the program. Even more important, however, is the fact that CETA funds were allocated by Congress under six different subprograms, defined by target group and type of service. The subprograms (separate titles of the act) gave Congress continuing control over the content of the overall CETA program. When President Carter, for example, decided that public service employment (PSE) should be expanded, he was able to do so by persuading Congress to allocate more funds to the appropriate titles. Local prime sponsors then had the choice of expanding PSE or foregoing some federal grants. In its peak years of operation, CETA was spending over $4 billion a year on PSE programs.

Another feature of CETA was its increasing focus on disadvantaged (low-income and minority) workers and youth. In its final year (fiscal 1983) over 95 percent of CETA participants were disadvantaged. This focus maximized the program's antipoverty effectiveness. To further assure that disadvantaged workers could participate in CETA, the program paid participants a stipend while enrolled in education and training classes. Although small, these stipends enabled people with little other income to acquire needed skills.

From 1974 to 1982 the CETA program served over 30 million people. In 1981 alone, nearly 4 million participants were enrolled at a cost of $8 billion. One-third of this cost was associated with the public sector employment part of the program.

The CETA program was terminated in 1983, at the urging of the Reagan administration. In part, the cutbacks and subsequent termination of CETA were simply part of the Reagan administration's general retrenchment of social spending. There were additional motivations for the termination of CETA, however.

The chief criticism of CETA was its heavy emphasis on public sector employment. These PSE jobs were viewed as extraordinarily expensive "make-work" jobs that taught few skills, seldom led to private sector employment, and were too easily corrupted by local political interests. Critics also argued that CETA undermined the work ethic by paying people to rake leaves or attend classes. Although defenders of the program pointed to its success in serving the truly needy, they were unable to demonstrate that the public service employment programs were having any lasting impact on skills or employment.[4]

JTPA Programs

CETA was replaced by the Job Training Partnership Act (JTPA) of 1982. Like CETA, JTPA provides for a variety of employment and training services. There are important differences, however, in JTPA's focus, content, and administration.

Under CETA, employment and training funds were allocated to local prime sponsors, often bypassing state governments. In the process, a whole new bureaucracy was created. JTPA eliminated this level by distributing funds directly to governors to allocate within their own states. At the same time, JTPA gave local private industry councils veto power over JTPA expenditures. This cemented the "partnership" dimension of the program, and provided some assurance that the program would be responsive to business needs.

---

[4]For a review of CETA performance, see Sar Levitan and Garth Mangum, eds., *The "T" in CETA* (Kalamazoo, MI: Upjohn Institute, 1980); and Laurie Bassi, "The Effect of CETA on the Post-Program Earnings of Participants," *Journal of Human Resources* (Fall 1983). A review of these and other studies with an emphasis on methodological evaluation issues is contained in Burt Barnow, "The Impact of CETA Programs on Earnings," *Journal of Human Resources* (Spring 1987).

Whereas CETA provided a mix of training and public sector employment, JTPA focused more on training. The only potential job creation occurs in the summer jobs program for youth (which enrolls around half a million youth aged 14–18). Regular PSE for adults cannot be funded with JTPA appropriations and no more than 15 percent of program funds may be spent on administration costs. Furthermore, the U.S. Labor Department established performance standards for training programs and must demonstrate to Congress every two years that the training programs are cost-effective. JTPA is seen more as a long-term solution to subemployment, rather than as a short-run response to cyclical unemployment.

The focus of JTPA was broadened to include dislocated workers as well as the disadvantaged workers who were the target of CETA. Dislocated workers are those who have lost jobs because of plant closings and permanent layoffs, and who have little chance of returning to their old jobs. They need not be low-income or minority status, as are disadvantaged workers. The act tries to get dislocated workers back into employment by providing skills, (re)training, job search assistance, and other services. If successful, these services can help prevent dislocated workers from slipping into poverty.

In 1996 approximately half a million people participated in JTPA training programs at a cost of roughly $1.5 billion. Most of these participants were disadvantaged and about a fifth were on welfare.

The WIN Program

A frequent criticism of JTPA and other mainstream programs is that they fail to serve adequately the neediest individuals. The number of available training and employment slots is always less than the number of unemployed workers. Hence, some deliberate choices must be made about whom to serve. Under these circumstances, program administrators often prefer to serve those individuals who are most job-ready. The least needy individuals are likely to provide the greatest success stories for program administrators. Unfortunately, this tendency to cream from the pool of potential program participants leaves many of the neediest job seekers to fend for themselves.

The failure of mainstream training programs to provide adequate help to the neediest led to the creation of another major training program, the Work Incentive Program (WIN). What distinguished WIN from the outset was the fact that it served only those receiving public assistance: Program participation was specifically limited to adult recipients of AFDC assistance. Moreover, all adult recipients were *required* to register for WIN services, unless exempted for reasons of health or the care of preschool children. This provision resulted from the widespread conviction that welfare recipients avoid employment (see Chapter 7). On a more positive note, the program attempted to provide the supplemental services necessary for successful program completion. These ranged from day-care services and work orientation to medical examinations, transportation allowances, counseling, and job placement. In addition, because of WIN's link to welfare, there were no financial barriers to program participation. WIN enrollees continued to receive the same public assistance they had prior to entry. Thus, the program offered a fairly comprehensive package of services designed to move people from welfare to employment.

Although WIN seemingly offered all the ingredients for successful movement into employment, the program has not been regarded as a success. Four major problems constrained program performance. The first constraint was a lack of funding. Funding levels fell far short of program requirements, rendering the promise of comprehensive services impossible to fulfill. As a result, only welfare recipients without child-care, transportation, or training needs were likely to get through the program.

A second problem was that welfare recipients were required to *register* for the program but not required to *participate*. This created a mass of paper shuffling and fostered widespread cynicism about program goals. In 1986, 1.6 million welfare recipients were registered for WIN services but only around 220,000 individuals actually received any services.[5]

The WIN program also exempted from registration and participation welfare mothers with preschool children (under age 6). This effectively meant that young women just turning to welfare wouldn't get any employment-related services for years.

Finally, there was too much federal direction. The flexibility of state and local programs was constrained by voluminous regulations and guidelines handed down by the federal government. This limited the kinds of services that could be offered, the way services were delivered, and which clients got served.

The JOBS Program

After 21 years of activity, the WIN program was replaced in 1989 by the Job Opportunities and Basic Skills (JOBS) training program. Like the earlier WIN program, the JOBS program offered an array of employment and support services to hasten the movement from welfare to work. There were important differences in the design of JOBS, however. To begin with, there was much greater emphasis on the obligation of welfare recipients to participate and on the obligation of states to enforce participation requirements. At least one adult in every two-parent welfare family (AFDC-U) was required to participate. Mandatory participation was also extended to mothers whose children were at least three years old (versus six years old under WIN). States could even stretch that requirement to mothers whose youngest child was only one year old. Under JOBS, the requirement was to *participate* in some self-help activity (e.g., education, training, work experience), not just register for the program.

Because the potential number of participants would overwhelm available resources, Congress foresaw that participation requirements would have to be phased in. Congress set specific thresholds for that phase-in process. By 1995, states were to have enrolled at least 20 percent of the nonexempt AFDC caseload. By 1997 at least 75 percent of the AFDC-U caseload was to be enrolled. To enforce this timetable, Congress threatened to reduce federal cost sharing for states that failed to meet these participation thresholds.

The JOBS program also put more emphasis on mandatory community service (workfare) than earlier programs. State demonstrations of alternative program activities during the 1980s had revealed that workfare and job-search assistance activities

---

[5]Mary Jo Bane and David T. Ellwood, *Welfare Realities* (Cambridge, MA: Harvard University Press, 1994), p. 20. For more description of WIN services and outcomes, see Bradley R. Schiller, "Lessons from WIN: A Manpower Evaluation," *Journal of Human Resources* (Fall 1978).

were effective in reducing welfare caseloads.[6] JOBS not only authorized all states to implement workfare programs but made that activity one of four employment options from which states had to choose at least two. (The other work-related options were on-the-job training, job search, and wage subsidies.)

Like earlier efforts, JOBS has been hobbled by funding constraints. Congress offered the states $1 billion in initial matching funds. The 1990–91 recession squeezed state budgets so tightly, however, that the states were unable to allocate enough of their own funds to secure the federal matching grants. Even if they had, a billion dollars in matching funds would not have stretched very far.

State Block Grants

The welfare reforms of 1996 (see Chapter 11) terminated the JOBS program. Rather than specify a federal program design for the states, Congress decided instead to give the states block grants that they can use for training, job placement, or other services for welfare (TANF) recipients. Since July 1997 states have had much greater flexibility in deciding how much money to spend on training programs and what kind of training services to provide.

Generic Problems

As states try to fashion their own training programs for the poor, they confront some hard realities. As good as the concept of skill training sounds, the actual experience with government-funded training programs has been disappointing. Traditional skill training programs are expensive and their performance is marginal, particularly for disadvantaged participants. Typically, successful graduates of such programs earn only a few hundred dollars more than they would have without training.[7] That isn't enough to get most off welfare, much less to raise their living standards significantly. Rarely are such programs cost-effective.[8]

The performance of traditional training programs is inherently constrained by information gaps. The administrators of government training programs often have limited knowledge of job opportunities in the private sector. They simply respond to offers of training services from vocational schools and other institutions whose business is to train people, not hire them. Program participants are also ill-informed about the kinds of jobs that are available, what skills they require, or how much they pay. Accordingly, the training decision is often the outcome of an agreement between two individuals (a trainee and program administrator) who are acting on the basis of incomplete information.

---

[6]See Bradley R. Schiller and C. Nielson Brasher, "Workfare in the 1980s: Successes and Limits," *Policy Studies Review* (Summer 1990) and "The Effect of Workfare Saturation on AFDC Caseloads," *Contemporary Policy Issues* (January 1993); also Judith M. Guerron and Edward Pauly, *From Welfare to Work* (New York: Russell Sage, 1991).

[7]See Howard S. Bloom, et al., "The Benefits and Costs of JTPA Title II-A Programs," *Journal of Human Resources* (Summer 1997), pp. 549–576; also June O'Neill, "Can Work and Training Programs Reform Welfare?" *Journal of Labor Research* (Summer 1993), pp. 265–279; and Gueron and Pauly, *From Welfare to Work.*

[8]Stephen H. Bell and Larry L. Orr, "Is Subsidized Employment Cost Effective for Welfare Recipients?" *Journal of Human Resources* (Winter 1994), pp. 42–61.

Job-search and workfare programs help address this problem by exposing participants (and administrators) to real jobs. Ideally, a job-search program will find someone a job. Even if it doesn't, however, it will give program participants a better sense of what jobs are available and the kinds of skills employers seek. Workfare programs give participants not only work experience but also expose them to a variety of specific jobs. If the workfare experience is successful, it can also generate a job reference—a valuable asset in competitive labor markets. Job-search and workfare activities can be particularly beneficial for individuals with little or no work experience. A 1995 evaluation of the JOBS program concluded that programs that emphasized labor force attachment (e.g., work experience) were much more successful than programs that emphasized human capital development.[9]

TAX CREDITS

All of the employment programs discussed so far entail direct government expenditure and administration. As a result, they are highly visible and inevitably viewed as part of the public sector. The tax system, however, offers alternative approaches for employment and training policy. Rather than using the tax system to fund *government* training programs, we can use the tax system to subsidize *private*-sector training. The policy mechanism here is tax credits. By offering tax credits to employers, the government can encourage the training and hiring of low-income workers. The govenment can also use tax credits to increase the *supply* of low-income workers by increasing the reward for working.

Employer Credits

The Targeted Jobs Tax Credit (TJTC) of 1978 illustrates the potential of the credit approach. The TJTC was designed to increase the employment and training of specific (targeted) groups, including disadvantaged youth, ex-convicts, veterans, and welfare recipients. Companies hiring from these groups could claim a tax credit equal to 40 percent of the first $6,000 of wages paid. Thus, the implicit subsidy for hiring a disadvantaged targeted person was $2,400. An employer could also get credit for hiring disadvantaged targeted youth in summer jobs. These credits reduce the cost of hiring labor and thus encourage more hiring and training of the poor.

Although tax credits have a lot of appeal, they have important limitations. To be effective, the tax credits must stimulate a net increase in the employment and training of disadvantaged workers. Otherwise, the credits become just a general subsidy to firms that were already employing disadvantaged workers. This was the case in the early years of the TJTC program, as indicated by the fact that three-fourths of the credits were certified retroactively, after employment decisions had already been made.

Tax credits are also weakened by an inherent goal conflict. The more specifically tax credits are targeted on certain groups or activities, the more complex they become. This increases the administrative cost of using them, especially for small firms. Work-

---

[9]See S. Freidman and D. Friedlander, *"The JOBS Evaluation: Early Findings on Program Impacts at Three Sites,"* New York, NY., Manpower Demonstration Research Corp., 1995; also U.S. Government Accounting Office, *Welfare to Work: Most AFDC Training Porgrams Not Emphasizing Job Placement* (Washington, DC: GAO, 1995).

ers, too, are often reluctant to reveal their disadvantaged status to prospective employers.[10] Nevertheless, as many as 1 million credits were used in a single year, mostly for youth and welfare recipients. Because there was little evidence of net employment growth, however, Congress let the TJTC credit expire at the end of 1994.

Despite the apparent failure of the TJTC to increase employment, a similar tax credit was introduced in 1996. The Work Opportunity Tax Credit offered employers $2,000 or more in tax credits for hiring and retaining welfare recipients and other high-risk employees.

Employee Credits

Employer tax credits are intended to increase the *demand* for low-skilled labor. An alternative approach is to encourage a greater *supply* of labor. As we observed in Chapter 11, welfare benefits create a work disincentive by offering an alternative source of financial support and imposing high marginal tax rates. A low-wage worker who not only pays payroll and income taxes, but also loses 30–70 cents of welfare benefits for every dollar earned, doesn't have much incentive to work. The implied marginal tax rate is so high that supplying additional labor makes little sense. To help overcome these disincentives, the government can reward low-income workers with favorable tax treatment. That is the basic idea behind employee tax credits.

The Earned Income Tax Credit (EITC) was first authorized in 1975. The unique feature of the EITC is that it is a *refundable* tax credit. If the tax credit exceeds an individual's tax liability, the individual gets a check for the difference.

The EITC was expanded greatly during the Clinton administration. A low-income worker with two or more children is eligible for $4 of tax credits for every $10 he or she earns. Thus, the federal government supplements a low-income worker's paycheck with a tax check at the subsidy rate of 40 percent. A worker employed for $5 an hour gets an additional $2 an hour from Uncle Sam. This subsidy makes low-wage jobs much more appealing and helps reduce working poverty. In 1997 18 million households received EITC tax credits averaging $1,500. With total credits now exceeding $27 billion a year, the EITC is the largest cash transfer program directed at the poor.[11]

Although the EITC provides a substantial work incentive for low-income workers, it also has negative supply effects. The maximum credit in 1996 was $3,566 for workers earning up to $11,610 per year (see Table 13.1). Once earnings rise above that threshold, the EITC credit begins to shrink. The phase-out rate is 21.06 percent. Thus, the phase-out of the EITC resembles a marginal tax rate of 21 percent. The implicit tax of 21 percent comes on top of regular (explicit) payroll and income taxes. This increased tax burden may induce people in the phase-out range of income to work *less*. EITC thus has two contrary effects on labor supply. It encourages people with very low incomes to work more. But it also encourages workers earning higher wages to work less. The net effect therefore depends on how these two incentives compare. Because there are more than twice as many eligible households in the phase-out range ($11,610

---

[10]The conflict between general and targeted tax credits is discussed in Dave M. O'Neill, "Employment Tax Credit Programs: The Effects of Socioeconomic Targeting Provisions," *Journal of Human Resources* (Summer 1983).

[11]It is not a pure welfare program, however, since benefits depend not only on *means* (i.e., low income) but also *events* (i.e., working).

TABLE 13.1 EITC Provisions, 1996

Number of Children	Credit Rate	Wage Ceiling for Maximum Credit	Maximum Credit	Phase-Out Rate*	Breakeven Wage
0	7.65%	$4,220	$ 323	7.65%	$ 9,000
1	34.00%	$6,330	$2,152	15.98%	$25,078
2	40.00%	$8,890	$3,556	21.06%	$28,495

*Phase-out rates begin at $5,000, $11,290, and $11,610, respectively.

Source: U.S. Congress, Committee on Ways and Means, *1996 Green Book* (Washington, DC: U.S. Government Printing Office, 1996), p. 805.

to $28,495) than the subsidy range ($1 to $8,890), negative labor-supply effects outweigh the positive effects. The General Accounting Office came to such a conclusion after estimating that "phase-out households" would work 70 hours less a year, while "subsidy" households would only work an additional 48 hours per year.

Another concern relates to the enhanced incentives for tax fraud created by the more generous EITC. Usually the Internal Revenue Service worries that people *understate* their incomes. The EITC, however, creates an incentive to *overstate* income. A nonworker with two children who claims to have earned $8,890 is eligible for a $3,556 EITC payment. Even if a person paid Social Security payroll taxes on this nonexistent income, the net return would exceed $2,000. Neighbors could even collude, paying each other $8,890 a year to care for each others' children. *Reported* income and employment could increase significantly, even if low-income workers chose to work less.

While both liberals and conservatives have supported the EITC, the program is not faultless. Like all other antipoverty programs, the EITC must confront trade-offs between goals of income security, work incentives, and program cost. As the EITC becomes the largest cash or near-cash antipoverty program, those trade-offs will come under renewed scrutiny.

A COORDINATED APPROACH

Aggregate demand policy, training programs, public service employment, and tax credits are not mutually exclusive alternatives. Instead, they must be perceived and implemented as complementary dimensions of a single, coordinated employment policy. High aggregate demand reduces the need for, and improves the outcome of, training programs. By the same token, training programs make expansionary macroeconomic policy more effective by reducing skill bottlenecks. The two approaches are complementary, not contradictory. Likewise, tax credits may do little to reduce poverty unless ample training and job opportunities exist.[12]

---

[12]A demonstration program in Washington state revealed that work incentives may not be an adequate substitute for mandatory participation in work-related programs; see S. Long, D. Nightingale, and D. Wissoker, *The Evaluation of the Washington Family Independence Program* (Washington, DC: Urban Institute, 1994).

In attempting to assess the potential effectiveness of employment policies for eliminating poverty, then, one must perceive the whole spectrum of policy options. We must recognize that no single approach will bring about full employment or eliminate poverty—at least not without enormous social costs. Government training efforts illustrate the point most vividly. Government training programs enrolled over 4 million individuals in 1991, at a federal cost of nearly $10 billion. Nevertheless, they failed to make a significant dent either in unemployment or poverty. Restrictive fiscal and monetary policies undercut all employment programs and plunged the economy into recession. Even in more favorable economic conditions, however, the potential of training programs to reduce poverty is limited by the tangle of forces that affect family structure and employment. Moreover, training programs may need to be accompanied by a mix of education and support services to be fully effective for some target groups.[13] This implies a level of budget expenditures that taxpayers may not support.[14] This makes it all that much more important to maintain job-creating aggregate demand policies that both reduce the need for training and increase the effectiveness of such training.

The end product of a coordinated employment policy should be an abundance of jobs that provide decent wages and advancement opportunity. The benefits of such jobs are as obvious as is the necessity for them. They will provide the incomes necessary to lift families out of poverty, to keep them together, and to give them promise of a secure future. Their benefits will reach to the children of the poor, who will have the means and incentive for staying in school. Employment policy has the potential, then, of at least minimizing both present and future poverty.

SUMMARY

The major components of employment policies are macroeconomic fiscal and monetary actions, training programs, public service employment, and tax credits. While each of these components has its own character and purpose, they are all interdependent. No one component can succeed alone. At the same time, effective action in any one area enhances the potential for success in the others. One reason government employment policy has not been more effective in the past is that these components have been viewed more as alternatives than as complements.

The track record of government training programs is not impressive. The prerequisites for successful training efforts are (1) a strong economy, with ample job vacancies, and (2) efficient matches between participant skills and employer needs. All too often, neither prerequisite is fulfilled. As a result, even programs that offer a comprehensive array of incentives and support services (e.g., WIN, JOBS) typically generate only modest employment gains and minimal welfare reduction.

Job-search assistance and mandatory community service (workfare) activities have become more common in welfare-to-work and other training programs. One advantage

---

[13]For a review of different employment-service configurations and their impact, see U.S. Department of Health and Human Services, *Evidence from Employment, Education, and Training Programs for Welfare Recipients* (Washington, DC: Office of Assistant Secretary for Planning and Evaluation, December 1994); and S. Freedman and D. Friedlander, *The JOBS Evaluation, op. cit.*

[14]James Heckman estimates the cost of a true antipoverty training effort to exceed $200 billion; see "Is Job Training Oversold?" *The Public Interest* (Spring 1994).

of these activities is that they expose participants to the job market, thereby encouraging more informed decisions on training and employment. These activities are also far less expensive than vocational training.

Public service employment has been regarded as the unwanted stepchild of employment policy. It suffers from distorted memories of the 1930s and widespread fears of make-work and government expansion. Workfare programs overcome some of these fears by requiring welfare recipients to perform community service, at little additional taxpayer cost. More explicit programs (e.g., the CETA) entail potentially unacceptable budget outlays or, if underfunded, the certainty of unfulfilled promises.

Tax credits can be used as subsidies for labor supply or demand. The Earned Income Tax Credit (EITC) offers a substantial wage supplement to low-income workers but creates a work disincentive (an additional 21 percent marginal tax rate) for workers with two children earning more than $11,610 a year.

While no employment policy offers a perfect solution, employment policies are the key to poverty reduction. Coordinated and comprehensive employment policies could sharply diminish existing and future poverty. Jobs—in abundance and of good quality—are the most needed and most permanent solution to the poverty problem.

FURTHER READING

Ashenfelter, Orley C., and Robert J. LaLonde, eds., *The Economics of Training* (2 vols.). Lyme, NH: Edgar Reference Collection, 1996.

Blank, Rebecca M., "The Employment Strategy: Public Policies to Increase Work and Earnings," in *Confronting Poverty,* eds. S. Danziger, G. Sandefur, and D. Weinberg. Cambridge, MA: Harvard University Press, 1994.

Edin, Kathryn, and Laura Lein, *Making Ends Meet.* New York: Russell Sage, 1997.

Gueron, Judith M., and Edward Pauly, *From Welfare to Work.* New York: Russell Sage, 1991.

Heckman, James J., "Is Job Training Oversold?" *The Public Interest* (Spring 1994), pp. 91–115.

Kaus, Mickey, *The End of Equality.* New York: Basic Books, 1992, esp. Chapters 8 and 9.

Lalonde, Robert, "The Promise of Public-Sector Training Programs," *Journal of Economic Perspectives* (Winter 1995).

Lane, Julia, and David Stevens, "Family, Work, and Welfare History: Work and Welfare Outcomes," *American Economic Review* (May 1995).

Levitan, Sar, D. Gallo, and I. Shapiro, *Working But Poor.* Baltimore: Johns Hopkins University Press, 1993.

Nightingale, Demetra S., and Robert Haveman, eds., *The Work Alternative.* Washington, DC: Urban Institute, 1994.

Orr, Larry, et al., *Does Training for the Disadvantaged Work?* Washington, DC: Urban Institute, 1996.

Scholz, John Karl, "The Earned Income Tax Credit: Participation, Compliance, and Antipoverty Effectiveness," *National Tax Journal* (March 1994), pp. 63–85.

CHAPTER

Equal Opportunity Policies

14

arlier chapters have documented the disadvantaged status of minority groups in America. Not only do such groups command fewer resources now, but they have less chance to acquire resources in the future. They have less opportunity to attain higher educational levels or even good-quality schooling at lower levels. Even with appropriate educational credentials, they are not permitted to make maximum use of their attainments in the labor market. Such discrimination—both in schools and in the labor market—creates institutional barriers between people and jobs. Those barriers, in turn, alter both the size and composition of the poverty population.

In Chapter 10, a distinction was drawn among three different categories of discrimination. These were present market discrimination, prior market discrimination, and nonmarket discrimination. These disparate sources of inequality create a fundamental dilemma for corrective policy. Can we create "equal opportunity" just by eradicating all overtly discriminatory behavior from present-day job and educational markets? Or would minorities still be so disadvantaged by *past* discrimination in schools and jobs that they still could not reasonably "catch up" in a race- and gender-blind marketplace?

If minorities still carry the burden of past discrimination, how can the government reduce that burden? Should the government fund special training programs to provide skills and education earlier denied? Should it create new job opportunities? Should it redistribute access to schools and jobs via affirmative action or even rigid quotas?

Public opinion on the limits of "equal opportunity" policy is sharply divided. On the one hard, the vast majority of Americans favor the principle of equal opportunity. On the other hand, nearly as many people oppose programs that seem to give special preference to past or present victims of discrimination. This "principle-implementation gap" makes the design of equal opportunity policy particularly difficult. In this chapter we review past and present government policies and try to develop a sense of their potential effectiveness.

EQUAL EMPLOYMENT OPPORTUNITY POLICIES

Public concern with the employment status of black workers came to the forefront just prior to World War II. Frustrated with their inferior employment status in a generally depressed labor market, black workers threatened to march on Washington, DC, in the spring of 1941. To forestall that march, President Roosevelt issued an executive order creating the first federal Fair Employment Practices Committee (FEPC). The stated purpose of the FEPC was to provide the machinery necessary to enforce the general provisions of the Thirteenth, Fourteenth, and Fifteenth Amendments to the Constitution, amendments which were thought to forbid discrimination in the labor market. The FEPC was to monitor and correct any such discriminatory practices.

Although Roosevelt's FEPC had little power or authority, it confronted persistent and decisive opposition in Congress. Congress twice dismantled the FEPC, finally burying it in 1945. Despite the FEPC's quick demise, its members nevertheless saw great potential for meaningful action. In their final report, the FEPC staff claimed that racial discrimination in employment could be ended if and when the federal government took decisive action.

No further equal employment opportunity action was taken until 1951. At that time, President Truman created a committee similar to the FEPC. That committee, too, had few powers and continued to exist quietly throughout the eight years of the Eisenhower administration.

The federal effort to promote equal employment opportunity first began to look serious in 1961. That was the year President John Kennedy issued an executive order committing the government to action. According to Kennedy's executive order, the federal government assumed specific responsibility to "promote the full realization of equal employment opportunity." The government pledged not only to eliminate discrimination within its own agencies and departments but to assure equal opportunity in all private firms that performed work for the federal government. Failure to eliminate discrimination, the government warned, would result in the termination of federal contracts. This threat was the first real power such a committee attained. An Office of Federal Contract Compliance—now called the Office of Federal Contract Compliance Programs (OFCCP)—was established to carry out the executive order.

The EEOC

A parallel move toward equal employment opportunity took place in Congress shortly afterwards. The historic Civil Rights Act of 1964 incorporated provisions to forbid discrimination in the labor market. Title VII of that act explicitly outlawed discrimination by corporations, unions, or any other labor market participants. The enforcement of that prohibition was delegated to the newly created Equal Employment Opportunity Commission (EEOC).

The enforcement machinery and effectiveness of the EEOC and the OFCCP differ greatly. The Equal Employment Opportunity Commission has only limited enforcement power. It is directed by Congress to "endeavor to eliminate any discriminatory employment practice by informal methods of conference, conciliation, and persuasion." It may not impose sanctions, issue cease and desist orders, nor even make public the fact that discrimination is being practiced. It depends largely on the goodwill of the offender to bring about equal employment opportunity once a complaint is filed. Punitive or remedial action is rarely sought through the courts, and until 1972 it required the initiative of the victims of discrimination.

The potential effectiveness of the EEOC is limited by its procedural orientation. Before the EEOC can take any action at all, it must receive a sworn complaint from an individual. Once the complaint is received, the commission seeks to determine whether the allegation is reasonable. If the complaint appears well founded, the commission then approaches the offending employer, union, or employment agency for "conference, conciliation, and persuasion." If conciliation is not attained, the complainant and the EEOC may seek redress in the courts.

This dependence of the EEOC on individual complaints has several drawbacks. First, it is tremendously expensive and time consuming to review and process each complaint (over 60,000 complaints are filed each year). This results in a backlog of unprocessed complaints that saps the morale of the complainants and staff. A second procedural drawback is the lack of incentive: An aggrieved person has to report discriminatory actions. The complaint procedure subjects an individual to potential union or employer retaliation, costs him or her time and money, and yields little practical benefit. At best, a complaining individual is apt to gain employment, promotion, or back pay with a chastened and resentful employer.

Much more effective action would be possible if the EEOC had the power to initiate broader investigations and seek more comprehensive resolutions. Realizing this, a former chairman of the EEOC, Lowell Perry, argued that "the one-to-one approach is not going to make a dent in our problem" and initiated investigations of "systemic" discrimination. What this means is that the EEOC would study the hiring and promotion policies of an entire company vis-à-vis minority groups, rather than just the experiences of individual complainants. In this way one action could bring relief or compensation to a much larger number of workers. In one of the first suits developed for this purpose, the EEOC was successful in persuading American Telephone and Telegraph Company (AT&T) to pay nearly $50 million in compensation to its female employees who had been denied equal job opportunities.

The OFCCP

Stronger powers of initiative and enforcement have always been available to the Office of Federal Contract Compliance Programs. The OFCCP may itself initiate investigations to determine whether discriminatory practices exist. It may also impose sanctions, such as contract termination, where discrimination is discovered. Furthermore, OFCCP may require employers to take affirmative action to remedy past discrimination. These sanctions may be applied to all businesses that sell or service products to the government. Thus, the potential power of the OFCCP is as vast as the government's position in the economy.

While the potential power of the OFCCP to eliminate discriminatory practices and rectify past injustices is great, that power has been used rarely. The first constraint on OFCCP is a lengthy administrative process. Once complaints are filed, they are adjudicated by administrative law judges within the U.S. Department of Labor. The decisions of these judges can then be appealed to the U.S. Secretary of Labor. Politically sensitive cases can lay buried in the secretary's office for years. When Robert Reich,

President Clinton's first Labor Secretary, tried to clear up the backlog of cases in his office, he discovered that two dozen cases had been on appeal for an average of 7.5 years. In one case he turned down an appeal from Honeywell, against whom complaints had been filed 16 *years* earlier (when Reich himself had still been a student at Yale Law School). Even that ruling didn't end the case, since Honeywell could appeal Reich's decision in federal court.

Politics are largely to blame for these endless delays. Employers beset by the OFCCP always have recourse to other authorities. Should they command the attention and sympathy of Congressmen or other executive offices, OFCCP sanctions may be delayed or suspended. Bureaucratic interests also undermine the OFCCP's power. The Department of Defense, for example, regards weapons procurement as more vital to its mission than guidelines for equal opportunity. Hence, it may devote relatively little attention to compliance with OFCCP edicts and may even inveigh against contract cancellations that threaten orderly procurement. Accordingly, the power of the OFCCP remains largely on paper. Until 1979, not a single contract had been terminated or canceled to enforce equal opportunity. Moreover, the first big enforcement case against Uniroyal (the nation's third largest rubber manufacturer, with $36 million in federal contracts in 1978) was based on the company's failure to cooperate with an OFCCP investigation of discrimination (begun in 1968!), not because of discrimination per se.

Quotas and Guidelines

A more affirmative kind of action has been taken by the government with regard to the nation's labor unions, especially the construction unions. As we saw in Chapter 10, blue-collar unions have the potential to provide immediate access to remunerative employment. In addition, the government is a major force in the construction industry, purchasing up to one-third of total output, and could exert considerable leverage to break down discriminatory barriers. In pursuing such an effort, the Nixon administration tried to establish guidelines for minority recruitment in the building trades. The first attempt, in Philadelphia, proposed to raise the proportion of new black recruits from 5 percent in 1970 to 25 percent in 1975. That attempt and later "Philadelphia plans" elsewhere were not notably successful, however. Unions have tremendous political strength and do not like interference. From their point of view, "plans" and "goals" look too much like quotas, especially when enforced by threats of contract termination. Furthermore, the slack economy of the early 1970s raised anxious questions about whose jobs would have to be sacrificed to make room for newly hired black workers, the same kind of "reverse discrimination" fear that later surfaced in other industries (including universities).

While there have been few stunning employment rights achievements from direct federal action, federal policy has had important indirect impacts. One of the most important side effects of federal legislation and pronouncements has been to stimulate private legal actions against discriminatory employers. Federal action has established a legal basis on which private individuals can build. Accordingly, much of the responsibility for implementing and enforcing equal employment opportunity has been taken over by individuals and the courts. And in a score of cases, including the major EEOC suit against AT&T in 1974, individuals have won substantial sums of money from their employers to compensate for the income they were denied as a consequence of discriminatory practices in hiring and promotion. More importantly, there is evidence that minority employment has risen as a direct and indirect result of affirmative action initiatives.[1]

Reverse Discrimination

The employment successes that have been achieved with various forms of affirmative action have not eliminated discriminatory barriers. They have been effective enough, however, to arouse growing hostility to any form of special opportunities for women and minority workers. Eight out of ten Americans oppose equal employment opportunity programs that give special preference (quotas, guidelines, and so on) to certain groups. In large part, this hostility arises from the threat that affirmative action poses for already privileged positions. But this is not the only basis for decrying reverse discrimination. Critics also point to the basic contradiction between special hiring preferences and equal opportunity. Others point out that the existence of affirmative action casts a shadow over the real achievements of minority workers. Such achievements are too easily dismissed as the outcome of affirmative action. Finally, there is concern that affirmative action will make the workplace less efficient, thereby slowing economic growth and reducing average incomes.[2] These kinds of considerations help explain why only a bare majority of minority and women workers favor special preferences.[3]

The critics of affirmative action have taken their case to court. In a landmark complaint, Brian Weber, a white male employee of Kaiser Aluminum, sued Kaiser and his union, the United Steel Workers, for reverse discrimination. Weber had been rejected by a craft training program that reserved half its places for minorities. In the absence of such a privileged "set-aside," Weber argued, he would have been accepted for training. Lower courts agreed with Weber, noting that Kaiser could not use racial quotas except as a remedy for past discrimination at Kaiser. Since Kaiser itself did not admit to such prior discrimination, there was no legal basis for the special quotas. In 1979, the Supreme Court overruled the lower courts, however, arguing that preferential access to training is permissible when used to remedy "manifest racial imbalance."

The Court broadened the basis for quotas in *Fullilove* v. *Klutznick* (1980). In this case a white contractor challenged a provision of the 1977 Public Works Act authorizing 10 percent of government funds to be "set aside" for minority employers. This provision clearly gave minority contractors preferential treatment even where neither past discrimination nor racial imbalance existed. The Court upheld the set-aside provision, however, arguing that such quotas were not an unjust burden to place on whites (even if they had not consciously committed discrimination) and were permissible ". . . as long as remedial classifications serve important governmental objectives, and are substantially related to the objectives."

[1]Jonathan S. Leonard, "The Impact of Affirmative Action and Equal Employment Law on Black Employment," *Journal of Economic Perspectives* (Fall 1990), pp. 47–63.
[2]For debates on this issue, see the symposium in the March 1996 issue of *Society;* also contrast Peter Brimelow and Leslie Spencer, "When Quotas Replace Merit, Everybody Suffers," *Forbes,* February 5, 1993 with Frank McCoy, "Rethinking the Cost of Discrimination," *Black Enterprise* (January 1994).
[3]For public-opinion trends on affirmative action, see Jack Citrin, "Affirmative Action in the People's Court," *Public Interest* (Winter 1996), pp. 39–58.

In another case the Supreme Court made a decision that seemed to stretch the concept of affirmative action to its limits. Winnie Teal, a black female employee of the Connecticut Department of Public Welfare, had applied for the post of permanent welfare supervisor. She was required to take a written examination, which she failed. In fact, 46 percent of the blacks who took the exam failed, compared with only 26 percent of the whites. The department then hired 11 blacks, or 22.9 percent of the total black applicants, and 35 whites, or 13.5 percent of the total white applicants. It appeared, then, that the department had given blacks a decided advantage in hiring. Nevertheless, Winnie Teal sued the department, arguing that she had been discriminated against on the basis of race. In July 1982, the Court agreed with her, ruling that no step in the hiring process could manifest "disparate impact." This ruling (*Connecticut* v. *Teal*) appeared to proclaim that blacks had to be guaranteed a proportional share of jobs, regardless of qualifications or seemingly fair hiring criteria.

These and other court decisions were challenged by the Reagan administration. In 1983, William Bradford Reynolds, chief of the Justice Department's Civil Rights Division, publicly characterized affirmative action as a "racial spoils system" that violated basic American concepts of fair play. As Reynolds saw it, "Thus we come full circle—fighting discrimination with discrimination . . . an urgent need has been pressed and those intent on finding a quick fix rather than a lasting solution have reached for the loaded weapon—the so-called remedial use of racial discrimination."[4] The Reagan administration rejected this approach, and sought to eliminate quotas as an affirmative action tool. In pursuing this policy, the Justice Department sided with white Boston firemen in their challenge to affirmative action. The case arose as a result of budget cuts that forced layoffs within the Boston Fire Department. Based upon the department's "last hired-first fired" seniority rule, minorities would have been laid off first and disproportionately. The NAACP argued, however, that a layoff of black firemen would destroy the gains of earlier affirmative action. When lower courts agreed to shelter the blacks from seniority-based layoffs, the white firemen took their case to the Supreme Court. The case was declared moot, however, when Boston provided the money needed to rescind the layoffs.

In 1989, the Supreme Court—dominated by Reagan appointees—again shifted the focus from disparate *outcomes* to discriminatory *processes.*. In *City of Richmond* v. *J.A. Crosen Co.,* it ruled that the governments could require hiring quotas and set-asides only if clear and precise evidence of past discrimination was apparent. Moreover, any subsequent affirmative action had to be "narrowly tailored" to that past discrimination. In that same year, the Court also ruled that individuals who complained of discriminatory treatment could not rely on statistical patterns of apparent inequality but had to offer evidence of discrimination in specific employment practices (e.g., hiring, promotion, or job-assignment procedures). In a third case, the Court ruled that whites could bring reverse discrimination claims against Court-approved affirmative action plans. Those three decisions made it much more difficult to implement affirmative action.

Congress curbed the Supreme Court's 1989 rulings with the 1991 Civil Rights Act. That legislation shifted more of the burden of proof back to employers, who must

---

[4]William Bradford Reynolds, "Legitimizing Race as a Decision Making Criterion: Where Are We Going?" lecture at Amherst College, April 29, 1983.

justify employment practices that have disparate effects on women or minorities. The 1991 act also extended to women the right to claim monetary damages in the wake of intentional discrimination.

Comparable Worth

The conflict between the goals of equal opportunity (nondiscrimination) and affirmative action (reverse discrimination) has not been confined to racial issues. The same conflict has arisen in attempts to eliminate both past and present sex discrimination in hiring, occupational status, pay rates, pensions, and maternity leave.

Until the Civil Rights Act of 1991, sex discrimination battles had been fought on different battlefields. The first was the field of "equal pay for equal work." The Equal Pay Act of 1963 required employers to pay men and women equal pay for equal work. The courts enforced this act by providing compensatory damages to women whose pay was below that of men performing "identical" work in "similar" conditions.

Critics have argued, however, that this concept of equal pay is too restrictive. Because of occupational discrimination, few women hold jobs identical to men's. To assess "fair" wages, it is argued, "comparable" jobs, not identical ones, should be considered. By this standard, women should get equal pay for jobs *comparable* to men's. Comparability is measured in various ways, including skills, responsibility, mental and physical effort, importance, and the extent of training required. The Supreme Court gave impetus to comparable worth cases when it ruled that female prison guards had the right to sue over pay discrimination even though they weren't performing tasks identical to male prison guards (*County of Washington* v. *Gunther,* 1981).

Although the concept of comparable worth has obvious appeal, it suggests a radical departure from market economics. The forces of supply and demand have a major impact on the wages for different jobs. Wage differentials also encourage people to take jobs that society values highly. To the extent that wages are set instead by computations of comparable worth, labor markets will be less efficient. Critics also question whether anyone really has the ability to make conclusive and objective computations of the "worth" of different jobs.[5]

Class-Based Preferences

Critics of both affirmative-action and comparable-worth policies have proposed a wholesale shift of focus for equal opportunity policy. They argue that any preferences extended to individuals should be based on economic class, not race or gender. Not all blacks, Latinos, or women suffer from discriminatory treatment. Why, then, critics ask, should all of these individuals have access to contract set-asides, preferential hiring, or lower employment standards? Moreover, whites who are trapped in the same blighted neighborhoods as poor minority groups are unfairly denied similar preferences solely because of their race or gender. Preferences based on economic class, rather than race

---

[5]For more views on comparable worth, see Paula England, *Comparable Worth: Theories and Evidence* (New York: Aldine de Gruyter, 1992); also Erica L. Groshen, "Comparable Worth: Is it a Worthy Policy?" *Journal of Economic Literature* (March 1996). The Canadian experience with comparable worth is discussed in Kenneth A. Kovach, "An Overview and Assessment of Comparable Worth Based on a Large Scale Implementation," *Public Personnel Management* (Spring 1997).

or gender, would provide more equal access to those who need it the most. In the process, affirmative action would become a more potent antipoverty tool. A class-based system of preferences might also defuse much of the sociopolitical tension that now envelops affirmative action policies.

While not opposed to greater inclusion of the poor in employment preferences, proponents of gender- and race-based preferences worry that the broader goals of social justice will be sacrificed by class-based preferences. The burden of discrimination isn't borne solely by the poor. Rather, its effects are apparent throughout the income distribution. The issue, therefore, isn't just the antipoverty effectiveness of affirmative action, but also the consequences for broader social justice.[6]

EQUAL EDUCATION OPPORTUNITY POLICIES

The controversies that accompany remedies for *employment* discrimination apply as well to *education* policies. Do minorities suffer from present-day discrimination within school systems, or do they bear the burden of past discrimination? What remedies might effectively relieve either burden? Can the goverrnment redress past or present wrongs without engaging in reverse discrimination? Who should pay the price, if any, for more "equal opportunity"?

Limits on Federal Policy

Governmental policy in the field of equal educational opportunity is more difficult to characterize than in the field of employment opportunity. Politics and bureaucracy again take their toll, of course, and there is, again, much complacency and inertia. What renders this subject especially complex, however, is the degree to which equal educational opportunity responsibilities are shared by different levels of government. Educational policy has traditionally been a prerogative of the separate states. The federal government provides less than 10 percent of all educational expenditures and administers no schools. Consequently, it has less power to create equal opportunity in the schools. It cannot terminate contracts or open new job slots as it may do in the labor market. In general, it must instead rely on, and cooperate with, the states and the courts to abolish discrimination in the schools. Only in higher education, particularly among large, research-oriented universities, does federal grant money account for a significant enough share of total income to make direct federal action a more serious threat.

The most obvious form of discrimination in the educational system is school segregation. While discrimination can take place even in the absence of segregation, not even a pretense of equal opportunity is possible as long as segregated schools are maintained. The Supreme Court itself made this observation, as we saw in Chapter 9. To what extent, then, are governmental bodies endeavoring to abolish segregation?

---

[6]For a lucid defense of gender- and race-based affirmative action, see Barbara R. Bergmann, *In Defense of Affirmative Action* (New York: Basic Books, 1996). The judicial shift to class-based preferences is examined in Richard D. Kahlenberg, "Class-Based Affirmative Action," *California Law Review* (July 1996). See also David B. Oppenheimer, "Understanding Affirmation Action," *Hastings Constitutional Law Quarterly* (Summer 1996).

De Jure versus *De Facto* Segregation

A distinction is commonly made between two kinds of segregation. The first, *de jure,* refers to a situation where blacks and whites are legally constrained to attend separate schools. The second, *de facto,* refers to a situation where school segregation results, not from edict, but from circumstance. Such a case occurs where blacks and whites live in different neighborhoods, thereby making school integration difficult.

While the distinction between *de facto* and *de jure* segregation is often useful, it creates a distinction that few victims of discrimination can appreciate. As Judge J. Skelly Wright noted in a 1967 ruling on District of Columbia schools: "Racially and socially homogeneous schools damage the minds of all children who attend them . . . whether the segregation occurs in law or in fact." The distinction between *de jure* and *de facto* also gives rise to a false aura of innocence. *De jure* segregation is commonly seen as the consequence of evil intent, while *de facto* segregation is seen as the innocent by-product of socioeconomic forces—especially in the housing market. Such a view obscures the fact that government bodies can and do set the pattern for much *de facto* segregation. Segregation of the schools is rarely, if ever, a completely natural and unplanned circumstance.

Governments have two avenues of influence on *de facto* segregation. They may directly affect residential housing patterns, thereby enlarging or diminishing the foundation for *de facto* segregation; or they may alter the distribution of schools within established housing patterns, thereby facilitating or obstructing greater integration of the schools.

Housing Patterns

To a large extent existing residential patterns are the outcomes of millions of individual housing decisions, but free choice is not the only force operating in the housing market. The government, through its building and loan programs, has also participated in the establishment of segregated neighborhoods, and thus, must bear a significant responsibility for the *de facto* school segregation that results from neighborhoods isolated by race and class.

The Federal Housing Authority (FHA) has been a major factor in the housing market since its creation in 1938. It had a particularly important role in establishing the housing patterns of the post-World War II housing boom, patterns that still predominate today. The power of the FHA to alter housing choices lies in its ability to insure or guarantee loans on residential construction. FHA support often determines whether a house can be purchased, at what location, and at what cost. During the housing boom of the late 1940s and 1950s, the FHA helped finance one-third of all new housing. Today's suburbs are, in large part, the product of FHA financing.

Given the power of the Federal Housing Authority in the housing market, its ability to foster or contain segregation is clear. For the most part, it has chosen to encourage and extend rigid racial and class segregation. The FHA Underwriting Manual of 1938 declared that "if a neighborhood is to retain stability, it is necessary that properties shall continue to be occupied by the same social and racial groups." Agency valuators, considering whether or not to make FHA loans, were warned to protect against "inharmonious racial groups." The FHA even composed and distributed a model racially restrictive covenant, prohibiting "the occupancy of properties except by the race for which they are intended." The FHA deemed it necessary and proper to create and maintain racially and socially homogeneous neighborhoods.

In 1962, President Kennedy issued an executive order that ended the explicitly segregationist practices of the FHA, but that order came too late and has too little force. The new FHA policy of nondiscrimination is limited largely to new housing. Thus, the established patterns of housing segregation are virtually unaffected.[7]

Poor families of whatever color are further handicapped by the FHA's focus on middle-class families. Because loan applicants must be eligible for commercial loans, FHA insurance and guarantees benefit few, if any, poor families.

Federal efforts designed explicitly to improve the living conditions of the poor have likewise failed to promote residential integration. Public housing is almost always located in the poorest areas and most often segregated by race. Thus, it tends to intensify racial and economic isolation. The U.S. Commission on Civil Rights reports that, of the quarter of a million public housing units built in the nation's 24 largest metropolitan areas, only 76 units had located outside the central city. The result is not only residential segregation but *de facto* segregation of schools as well.[8]

School Patterns

While public and private housing decisions have created a foundation for school segregation, residential patterns alone do not maintain segregated schools. School authorities have broad discretion in defining the number and nature of school boundaries to be superimposed on residential patterns. Hence, local school authorities have the power to combat the segregation that exists in housing. Once again, however, this power has often been employed to intensify rather than to combat racial and economic isolation.

The power of local school authorities to encourage or resist school segregation is embodied in a variety of public decisions. Housing patterns alone do not define neighborhoods, much less school zones. Instead, the definition of a neighborhood is partly determined by the decisions of where and how to locate public schools. The number of schools to build, their size, and their geographic location are all decisions that help to shape neighborhoods. Building one large school between racially segregated housing areas, for example, does more to promote school integration than constructing two separate schools within racially homogeneous communities. Also important for the pattern of school integration is the number of grades to be served by each school and the actual specification of attendance zones. These decisions, too, can abet or overcome residential segregation.

To a large extent, existing school patterns reflect historical, rather than current, decisions. This fact does not exonerate school authorities from responsibility, however. Residential patterns are continually changing and schools are continually being built or rezoned. Hence, school authorities have discretion to alter the distribution of pupils

---

[7]Local zoning ordinances can also enforce racial and class housing segregation and ultimately access to schools: see Raquel Fernandez and Richard Rogerson, "Keeping People Out: Income Distribution, Zoning and the Quality of Public Education," *International Economic Review* (Winter 1997).

[8]The need to coordinate housing and desegregation policies is highlighted in Gary Orfield et al., *Deepening Segregation in American Public Schools* (Cambridge, MA: Harvard Graduate School of Education, April 1997).

or facilities and to counteract past decisions. Some of the tactics used to promote or impede integration include:

- *Gerrymandering*   Gerrymandering refers to the purposeful restructuring of school attendance zones to foster specific attendance patterns. It is the oldest, simplest, and most blatant tactic available to local school authorities. Its visibility, however, has led to a decline in its use, especially where legal action has focused attention on the practice.

  The potential for gerrymandering is broadened when a school system is expanding or contracting. When a system is shrinking, some schools must be closed, and their students reassigned to other schools. In the process, entirely new attendance zones can be created. Those new zones can be designed either to foster or impede school integration.

- *Optional Zones*   A tactic not far removed from gerrymandering is the use of optional attendance zones. An optional zone is a limited geographical area in which students are permitted to choose the school they will attend. In effect, optional zones are a more subtle and flexible tool to achieve either greater integration or segregation.

  In the South, *free choice* provisions are the counterpart of optional attendance zones. Students are permitted or required to state a preference for the schools they wish to attend. Priority is given to those preferences, however, that are based on residential location, established school ties, or other correlates of race.

- *School Construction*   As noted earlier, the selection of a school site can have tremendous impact on the pattern of school segregation. Schools located within all-white or all-black residential areas solidify racial isolation. Schools located in fringe areas have the potential of accelerating integration. Unfortunately, site selection all too often conforms to segregationist practices. Of the 371 schools constructed in 16 cities from 1950 through 1965, over 80 percent opened nearly all white or all black.

- *Grade Structure*   Even when faced with established school locations and size, school authorities are not powerless to alter racial attendance patterns. One subtle but effective means for overcoming these obstacles is to redefine grade structures. Enlarging the number of grades a school will serve has the effect of shrinking its attendance zone. On the other hand, schools that serve only a few grades must reach out in all directions to include a sufficient number of pupils.

- *Selling the Schools*   School and government officials in Shaw, Mississippi, provide a final example of mechanisms for circumventing desegregation. In 1966, an all-white school board foresaw the inevitability of court-ordered desegregation in the public school system. To avoid this fate, the school board authorized the sale of selected public schools to private academies for a price of one dollar each. The private academies had more freedom to discriminate. This situation continued until 1983, when the school board acquired a 3–2 black majority, and voted 3 to 2 to buy back the schools.

  The many options local school boards have for creating or restructuring school attendance patterns greatly weaken the distinction between *de jure* and *de facto* segregation. In 1974, the federal courts explicitly noted the difficulty of maintaining this distinction in Boston. Boston had never been segregated by law. However, Judge W. Arthur Garrity, Jr., observed that in the purchase and construction of new facilities, the assignment of staff and students to individual schools, and the use of open enrollments, the Boston School Committee was "at all times displaying an awareness of the potential racial impact of their actions. . . . The defendants have, with awareness of the racial segregation of Boston's neighborhoods, deliberately incorporated that segregation into the school system."[9]

---

[9]Opinions of Judge Garrity in *Morgan* v. *Hennigan,* cited in U.S. Commission on Civil Rights, *Fulfilling the Letter and Spirit of the Law* (Washington, DC: U.S. Government Printing Office, 1976).

Busing

To reduce the segregation of Boston's school system, Judge Garrity ordered mandatory busing of pupils between white and black schools. In view of the extensive segregation of both neighborhoods and schools, busing was perceived as the shortest route to equality of educational opportunity. Proponents of busing argued that buses are the only sure access to equality of facilities and may help promote more complete social integration. The legal basis for using school buses to promote equal educational opportunity had been firmly established by the U.S. Supreme Court in 1971 (in *Swann* v. *Charlotte-Mecklenberg*).

The reaction to interracial busing in Boston and other cities was initially hostile and even violent. Visions of masses of white children being bused into black ghettos stir the fears of most white parents. Anxiety is also expressed for the stamina of children who must be bused daily to their classrooms. What is seldom realized is that busing of children to school is a common phenomenon in the United States. Nationally, slightly more than 50 percent of all schoolchildren are bused to school. Most are bused simply because such transportation is most convenient. Only 3.6 percent of all public school pupils are bused for desegregation purposes. Ironically, still others are bused to extend and enforce racial segregation.

The question of busing—especially when it is proposed for purposes of facilitating integration—touches a very sensitive nerve in most Americans. Three out of four Americans oppose mandatory busing, even though most still claim to support school integration. Indeed, the hostility to busing is so strong that many white families have fled the cities or schools where mandatory busing has been imposed.[10] In some cases, the court attempted to overcome the problem of "white flight" by forcing students to be bused between the central city and its suburbs. In June 1995, however, the United States Supreme Court ruled (*Missouri* v. *Jenkins*) that the Kansas City School system could no longer look beyond its borders for remedies to racial isolation.

Why is the opposition to busing so fierce? In part, the opposition to busing reflects fears for the safety and stamina of children. As noted earlier, however, this fear may be exaggerated. A more important concern may be the expectation that the quality of education will decline when mandatory busing is imposed. In part, this concern may simply manifest latent racial prejudices. In addition, however, white parents realize that their children already have a monopoly on better schools. To share these limited resources with bused-in black students implies a reduction in educational services. To be bused into a formerly black school implies an even larger reduction in educational services.

Finally, busing is almost always perceived as a direct threat to the cherished notion of a neighborhood school. Neighborhood schools are usually deemed desirable for two reasons. They are close to home and thus conveniently accessible. They also serve to foster community cohesiveness. Children who reside close together and attend a common school have more opportunity to interact and are thought to establish more enduring relationships. These two benefits, proximity and social integration, are the mainstays of neighborhood school support.

---

[10]See Lino A. Graglia, "The Triumph and Defeat of the Nondiscrimination Principle," *Society* (March 1996); also Charles T. Clotfelter, "School Desegregation, 'Tipping,' and Private School Enrollment," *Journal of Human Resources* (Winter 1976).

What is curious about arguments for neighborhood schools is not their potential benefits but their historical perspective. Arguments against economic or racial integration usually proceed from the assumption that integration is destroying the neighborhood school. There are three problems with this perspective. First, children have historically traveled quite far to school and continue to do so. More proximate schools have resulted from increasing population density rather than from an increased awareness of any "neighborhood" benefits. Second, we have already demonstrated that there is considerable flexibility in defining a neighborhood school. School attendance zones themselves can create neighborhoods, and deliberate manipulation of school zones can even affect residential choice. Families will want to live near the schools they know they can attend. Finally, the narrow neighborhood concept has been repeatedly sacrificed to other social objectives. Every major city, for example, has at least one citywide school reserved for students of outstanding ability. In these cases, productivity and individual development are deemed more important than neighborhood cohesiveness. No one has argued that the attending students are in any way deprived. A high percentage of white parents send their children to distant private schools for exactly the same reasons.

The opposition to busing, then, is firmly based in both prejudice and privileged position. To overcome this opposition, school authorities would have to provide credible evidence that busing does not reduce the quality of education. School authorities may even have to "bribe" white students to stay in the public schools with improved facilities and programs. In other words, busing for desegregation purposes is most likely to succeed when school authorities recognize the origins of white opposition and respond to them in tangible ways.

Fiscal Disparities

As we have observed, one of the arguments for school busing is that it will help reduce inequalities in educational facilities. Interestingly enough, the opponents of busing also argue that a more equal distribution of educational resources would eliminate the need for busing, and often offer to redistribute some resources, to provide "quality education for everybody," when pro-busing forces seem to be gaining strength. It seems reasonable to assume, then, that nearly everyone recognizes that educational resources are not equally distributed, that some children are provided with a lot more school resources than others.

Much of this problem derives from the way schools are financed. Local communities continue to provide the bulk of their own school resources. In 1996 the federal government supplied only 9 percent of all educational expenditures and the state governments contributed 48 percent; local governments provided the remainder. This means that the quantity and quality of educational resources in a community depends largely on the ability of the local populace to pay taxes. In substantive terms this means that wealthier white enclaves in the suburbs can provide educational opportunities for their children that few cities can ever hope to match.

It is easy to see how such disparities arise. In the suburbs the ratio of property values to school-age children is far higher than in the cities. Indeed, population density is ten times larger in urban ghettos than in surrounding areas. This means that residents of the city must support far more schoolchildren per square mile than people in the suburbs. Furthermore, the wealthier residents of the suburbs are better equipped to support public schools. They have the property and income on which school revenues depend.

The economics of local school financing encourages school districts to attempt to maximize their tax base while minimizing enrollment size. That is, they seek to include the wealthier and exclude the poorer, especially those with many children. The results are staggering. In California, for example, the poorest elementary school district had only $438 of assessed property per pupil in 1977. The richest district had over $2.4 million of property per pupil. This led to a lower tax rate for those most able to pay, an outcome of great benefit to the wealthier but of great disadvantage to the poor.

Given the nature of school financing, suburban communities have a tremendous incentive to insulate their school systems from the poor. They have little desire to impose higher tax rates on themselves to provide more educational opportunity for others. In some communities wealthier neighborhoods may even seek to incorporate independent school districts to dispose of responsibilities they already share. This tactic has taken on special significance as the courts have ordered opportunities to be equalized within, but not across, school districts.

To some extent, state and federal governments attempt to equalize the educational inequalities between richer and poorer communities. The Elementary and Secondary Education Act of 1965 is an example of such an attempt. Under this act the federal government distributes $5–6 billion a year to the poorest schools, but even this infusion of funds is inadequate. Only two-thirds of the students eligible to receive aid from Title I of the Elementary and Secondary Education Act are actually served. This reflects a number of problems, including inadequate funding, poor selection procedures, and the lack of Title I programs at certain grade levels. Even those served by Title I programs only receive an additional $500 to $600 in educational services per year.[11] The most absurd and distressing statistic of all is, perhaps, this: The wealthiest schools are more likely than the poorest schools to have subsidized milk or food programs. Many poor schools are denied such benefits because they cannot afford cafeterias, extra personnel, or their share of total costs. While the federal government is spending $5–6 billion in special aid, over $150 billion is being spent on education, with the biggest share still going to wealthier communities.

The subject of school financing highlights several important dimensions of the educational opportunity issue. The localized nature of school financing, for example, provides an independent motive for segregation. Even persons who harbor few racial prejudices are not immune to self-interest. On the contrary, most people seek to minimize their tax burden while providing well for their own children. Thus, they seek to exclude poor children, many of whom are black, from their school systems. This exclusionist tendency illuminates again the close ties of racial and class discrimination.

The class discrimination inherent in existing patterns of school financing has become a major judicial issue. In August 1971 the California Supreme Court acknowledged that fiscal disparities between school districts "make the quality of a child's education a function of the wealth of his parents and neighbors." Ruling that such discriminatory treatment violated the Fourteenth Amendment of the U.S. Constitu-

---

[11]U.S. Commission of Civil Rights, *Statement on the Fiscal Year 1984 Educational Budget* (Washington, DC: U.S. Government Printing Office, July 1983).

tion, the Court declared the state's entire system of financing public schools to be unconstitutional. However, the U.S. Supreme Court effectively overturned that decision in 1973 in a similar case originating in San Antonio, Texas. In its decision the Supreme Court admitted that the present basis for financing schools was "imperfect," but argued that it did not have the prerogative to interfere with the function of the legislative branch and overturn the wisdom and experience of state legislatures and educational administrators. Solutions to the inherent inequalities of school finance, the Court suggested, should be sought in state legislatures, not the courts.

Since then at least two dozen state school systems have been embroiled in legal disputes over disparate school finance. In 1994 a state judge ruled that New Jersey's methods of funding public schools was unconstitutional. The state had 611 school districts of widely varying size, wealth, and spending levels. Since the 1970s the state had tried to reduce fiscal disparities between these districts by supplementing local property tax revenues with state sales tax revenues. Even with supplemental funds, however, poor school districts were still spending half of what the richest districts spent per pupil. The state supreme court ruled that such disparities created a separate class of students that was undereducated and isolated; it ordered the state to achieve spending equality by 1997. To do this without reducing school quality in rich districts, the state will have to increase overall school spending by $500–600 million per year. This will require new taxes, a shift in budget priorities, or possibly even the merging of rich and poor school districts.

Compensatory Education

An approach to equal education opportunity that has aroused relatively little hostility is compensatory education, the provision of added educational resources to children from poor or minority homes. Indeed, most of the federal money spent on elementary and secondary education is distributed to the lower-income school districts either by federal statute (Title I of the Elementary and Secondary Education Act) or by allocation decisions made by the states that receive federal grants. The unspoken objective of these efforts is to improve the resources available to poor and minority groups without sharing those (via racial or class integration) available to upper-income groups. As we noted earlier, however, the total federal effort is small in relation to the size of the educational system.

Head Start   Perhaps the most important form of compensatory education has been the preschool program, particularly Head Start. As the designers of Head Start observed:

> . . . the early years of childhood are a most critical point in the poverty cycle. During these years, the creation of learning patterns, emotional development and the formation of individual expectations and aspirations take place at a very rapid pace. For the child of poverty, there are clearly observable deficiencies in these processes, which lay the foundation for a pattern of failure, and thus a pattern of poverty, throughout the child's entire life.

To help such children get a more equal start in the education system, Head Start was created to provide educational, health, nutritional, and social services to disadvantaged children in their preschool years. Since its creation in 1964, over 10 million children have participated in Head Start. In 1997, over 750,000 children participated, almost all of them from poor families.

Evaluations of Head Start have consistently documented its success in raising preschool children's capabilities, interest, and aspirations. At the same time, however, observers noted that the program's impact tended to be short-lived: After a year or two in their regular school systems, Head Start children performed no better than their similarly disadvantaged classmates.[12] Critics of the program were quick to cite this as evidence of the basic genetic or cultural deficiencies of minority children. More sympathetic observers argued, however, that ghetto schools operated as levelers, that the higher motivation and aspirations of Head Start children were not being reinforced by their regular schools. Indeed, the realities of ghetto schools, combined with the increased awareness and ambition fostered by Head Start, might well inculcate an irrevocable sense of defeat. Accordingly, the Follow Through program was created in 1967 to provide continuing services to Head Start children as they progress from kindergarten to the third grade. Unfortunately, the resources of the program have not been large enough to provide services to all needy Head Start graduates.

College Admissions

One very clear implication of our review of (un)equal opportunity in the preschool, elementary, and secondary school systems is that minority groups will be less prepared than others to enter colleges and universities. Because they are not provided full and equal opportunities to develop their skills earlier, they will not exhibit the required skills at the time of admission to higher education. This will be manifested not only in grade records, but even more clearly in standardized college entrance exams (the SAT, for example) that are a major screening mechanism for admissions applicants. Accordingly, if all college applicants were treated equally, we would expect a much lower proportion of blacks and other minorities to gain entrance to higher education. The effect of such an "equal opportunity" policy would be to widen educational disparities between whites and minority youth and ultimately increase income inequalities as well.

The vestiges of prior discrimination thus raise very serious policy questions about our concept of equality and the appropriate role of educational institutions in fulfilling equal opportunity goals. On the one hand, it can be (and is) argued that equal treatment is the only objective of policy and that schools should not be expected to exceed that mandate. From this point of view, the overriding goal of higher education is to enhance society's productivity by concentrating resources on the most able. So long as all applicants are treated equally, then the goals of efficiency and equality are both fulfilled.[13]

As we have noted, however, this "color blind" admissions policy effectively "writes off" the talents of individuals who have been discriminated against in the earlier components of the school system. Hence, an alternative viewpoint stresses the importance of achieving equality of status between whites and blacks, while suggest-

---

[12]For a review of the Head Start evidence, Edward Zigler and Sally J. Styfro, "Head Start: Criticisms in a Constructive Context," *American Psychologist* (February 1994), pp. 127–132.

[13]For a fuller discussion of this viewpoint, see the symposium on "Black Separation vs. American Integration," in *Society* (March 1996); and the symposium "On Equality" in *The Public Interest* (Fall 1982).

ing that black applicants will prove their worth (demonstrate their latent abilities) once they have an opportunity to catch up. Thus, it is argued, blacks and other minorities should be admitted to college and professional schools on a preferential basis (with lower test scores and grade point averages), a policy that will not only hasten the achievement of status quality, but will ultimately fulfill our goals of efficiency as well.

The Assault on Preferences   Clearly, there is considerable merit to the preceding argument, particularly if the preferentially admitted students do indeed catch up. But the merits of the case are not likely to impress those who end up paying the costs of such a policy—in particular, those white applicants who are denied admission to make room for minority groups. Such students have worked hard to meet college admission standards and are naturally resentful when others with fewer "qualifications" take their place. Indeed, such students argue that they themselves are being denied equal opportunity—as the victims of reverse discrimination—and have sought appropriate relief from the courts.

A landmark case concerns a rejected applicant to the University of California's Medical School at Davis (*Regents of the University of California* v. *Alan Bakke*). Under a special admissions program, sixteen of that school's one hundred admissions were set aside for minorities, a policy that was attacked on the basis of reverse discrimination. A superior court judge in the county ruled that the program did violate the equal protection clause of the U.S. Constitution, the corresponding provision of the California constitution, and Title VI of the U.S. Civil Rights Act of 1964. In June 1978, the U.S. Supreme Court also agreed with Bakke. The Court noted that race could be considered as one factor in the admissions process, but ruled that rigid quotas based on race were too discriminatory. Since then universities and courts have been compelled to differentiate quotas from less rigid preference policies. In 1994, the U.S. Department of Education ruled that the preferential admissions policies at the University of California at San Diego were legal, even though they gave minority and low-income applicants a decided (but not conclusive) advantage. Rejected law school applicants sued the University of Texas in 1994, claiming that the admissions threshold for minority applicants was far below the reject threshold for white applicants. The white students ultimately prevailed in court, forcing the University of Texas to abandon racial preferences in admissions.

In California, voters took to the polls, not the courts, to dismantle racial preferences. In 1996, Proposition 209 decreed that the state could not engage in any discrimination, including the reverse discrimination implied by preferential race policies. "Color-blind" admissions policies were mandated for the state's graduate schools in 1997 and for undergraduate admisisons beginning in 1998.

The end of racial preferences had a dramatic effect on minority enrollments. At the University of Texas—which had produced more minority lawyers than any other school in the country—black and Hispanic admissions plummeted by 75 percent in 1997. At the Berkeley and UCLA law schools, minority admissions fell by 50–80 percent.

The precipitous decline of minority admissions with "color-blind" programs has intensified the debate over the nature of "equal opportunity." Critics of affirmative action cite the admissions drop-offs as proof of how unfair and inefficient the racial double standard was. Defenders respond that the admisisons decline also demonstrates how disadvantaged minorities are by the racial and economic disparities that permeate the entire school system from preschool to college.

There is no simple way to resolve these competing claims for educational resources; there is clearly some degree of merit to each argument. Only by making admission available to everybody (a policy initiated at City University of New York) can everyone's claim to admission be satisfied. However, such a policy not only arouses serious concern for the quality of higher education but puts severe pressure on school budgets. In the absence of open admissions, some observers say, governments at all levels should at least commit far more resources to preparing minority students for college admissions. Even then, however, a delicate compromise must be struck between those claims to admission based on achievement and those based on denied opportunity (and thus potential achievement).

SUMMARY

Equal opportunity policies can help eliminate poverty in two ways: They may provide access to educational credentials; and they may dismantle artificial barriers between people and jobs. Access to educational credentials is important to the extent that it opens new employment opportunities or redistributes existing ones.

The federal government's effort to create equal opportunity in employment has not met with much success. Black workers continue to suffer inordinate levels of unemployment and to be relegated to undesirable jobs. A major reason for this continuing discrimination lies in the nature of government efforts. For decades the federal government has had the power only to exhort employers to create equal employment opportunities. It was not until the early 1960s that the government acquired some meaningful powers to enforce its proclamations. The Office of Federal Contract Compliance Programs may terminate contracts of discriminatory employers, while the Equal Employment Opportunity Commission may facilitate legal action. Those powers have been used rarely, however, and then mostly as a threat. Political, bureaucratic, and economic interests continue to impede the attainment of equal employment opportunity; what progress has been achieved is largely the result of private legal action, building on public legislation.

In the educational system, equal opportunity has been just as elusive. Local and state governments have not demonstrated a consuming ambition to open school doors to all. On the contrary, they have often employed a variety of manipulative techniques to forestall school integration for as long as possible. The localized nature of school financing also creates a tremendous incentive for wealthier white communities to exclude poor minority children from their schools. Federal authority to alter the pattern of segregation resides primarily in the power to bestow or withdraw funds under the Elementary and Secondary Education Act. But the amount of funds involved is relatively small and the political pressure to maintain their flow great. The quest for more equal educational opportunity has become focused on school finances, particularly disparities in per-pupil spending across school districts. At the college level, the focus is on the degree of exclusivity entailed in minority preferences.

FURTHER READING

Bergmann, Barbara, *In Defense of Affirmative Action.* New York: Basic Books, 1996.

Betsey, Charles, "The Role of Race-Conscious Policies in Addressing Past and Present Discrimination," *Review of Black Political Economy* (Fall 1992), pp. 1–35.

Burstein, Paul, ed., *Equal Employment Opportunity: Labor Market Discrimination and Public Policy.* New York: Aldine de Gruyter Press, 1994.

Clayton, Susan D., and Faye J. Crosby, *Justice, Gender, and Affirmative Action.* Ann Arbor, MI: University of Michigan Press, 1992.

Curry, George E., ed., *The Affirmative Action Debate.* Reading, MA: Addison-Wesley, 1996.

Donohue, John H., III, and James Heckman, "Continuous Versus Episodic Change: The Impact of Civil Rights Policy on the Economic Status of Blacks," *Journal of Economic Literature* (December 1991), pp. 1603–1643.

Massey, Douglas A., and Nancy Denton, *American Apartheid: Segregation and the Making of the Underclass.* Cambridge, MA: Harvard University Press, 1993.

Miller, L. Scott, *An American Imperative: Accelerating Minority Education Advancement.* New Haven, CT: Yale University Press, 1995.

U.S. Commission on Civil Rights, *With All Deliberate Speed, 1954–19??.* Washington, DC: U.S. Government Printing Office, 1981.

CHAPTER

Directions and Prospects

15

According to official estimates, over 35 million Americans remain in poverty. Although these estimates are exaggerated by the neglect of in-kind transfers, it is evident that millions of Americans are poor, either because their standard of living is below minimally adequate standards or because they depend primarily on public assistance (welfare) to maintain that poverty standard. Recognition of such widespread poverty has led to two simple questions: (1) Why are so many Americans poor? and (2) What policies will eliminate their poverty? The preceding chapters have provided much of the background material necessary to resolve these questions. This concluding chapter attempts to summarize the salient impressions of our inquiry and offer policy suggestions.

THE CAUSES OF POVERTY

The most popular diagnoses of poverty focus on the personal characteristics of those who are poor. The poor are viewed as less able, less motivated, overly reproductive, too aged or sick, or otherwise handicapped. By inference or declaration, they are thus assumed to be responsible for their own impoverishment. This Flawed Character view of poverty, as we have called it, is reinforced by statistical profiles of the poverty population. Very high percentages of the poor are in families that *are* aged, or female headed, or large, or headed by a nonworker.

There are two critical weaknesses in these demographic theories of poverty, however. Not all of the poor fit one or another of the various categories of misfits. Traditional married-couple families with children are one of the most prevalent groups in the poverty population. Furthermore, a substantial percentage of both single-parent and two-parent families does participate in the labor market, often on a year-round, full-time basis. It would be difficult to fit these profiles into the Flawed Character concept.

The Flawed Character generalization suffers not only from a narrowed focus but also from shortsightedness. Even those poor families who manifest distinctive demographic traits, such as broken homes, are not necessarily poor because of those traits.

On the contrary, most of the aged poor were poor before they became aged, many broken poor families were poor before they were fragmented, large poor families were poor when they were smaller, and sick poor families were poor even when they were well. Thus, theories of poverty causation that are based only on observations at a single point in time fail to perceive the dynamics of impoverishment. They confuse association with causality.

A broader, more dynamic perspective on poverty is achieved by focusing on the relationship of people to the labor market. For the most part, it is a person's relationship to the market that determines his or her economic, and even social, status. One immediate advantage of this perspective is that it draws attention to two critical questions: (1) What forces determine how many good income-earning opportunities are available? and (2) What forces determine who will obtain those opportunities? The myopic perspective of demographic theories of poverty encompasses only the second question. It assumes that good jobs are always available in sufficient quantity. But they are not, as history has repeatedly shown, and as we witnessed in the high unemployment rates of the early 1980s and again in 1990–92. To understand why so much poverty exists at any point in time, we must consider and resolve the first question. The answer to the second question tells us primarily how that poverty will be distributed.

In seeking to resolve the first question, we have put a heavy stress on the importance of aggregate (macro) economic policies in determining the extent of poverty. The number of available jobs is a phenomenon over which individual members of society have very little control. Similarly, they have little control over what kinds of jobs will be available or where they will be located. These decisions are made, instead, by the interplay of labor-market forces, among which government fiscal and monetary decisions are often decisive. Accordingly, we conclude that collective social decisions in the area of economic policy—especially those concerning the extent and structure of the demand for labor—are responsible for much poverty.

We should not conclude, however, that all available income-earning opportunities are taken. Even in relatively prosperous times, some families break up, others become sick or disabled, and some may even choose not to work. Still more children will be born to unwed teenagers and face a high probability of poverty regardless of labor-market conditions. Hence, even with prolonged full employment, not all families will participate fully in the economy. Sometimes the mismatch between the number of available jobs and potential workers originates in demographic forces, and we must include them as independent causes of poverty where appropriate. In this regard, the alarming increase in the number of unwed teenage mothers stands out as an independent cause of poverty and long-term dependency. Increasing rates of marital dissolution also increase the number of poor people in any given macroeconomic environment. Finally, age and disability tend to increase the incidence of poverty as well.

The third general set of causes are those related to discrimination, both in the schools and in the labor market. Minority groups, the offspring of the poor, and women are still deprived of an equal chance to acquire productive skills and to use those skills in the labor market. Racial, class, and sex discrimination has significant impact on both the distribution and extent of poverty. As long as discrimination persists, the children of the poor, blacks, Hispanics, and female-headed families will dominate the ranks of the poverty population. Even in a relatively prosperous economy, discrimination creates artificial barriers between workers and jobs, leaving some individuals poor.

Finally, we have recognized that government efforts to assist the poor may also play a role in perpetuating poverty. Although the welfare system is an essential source of income support, it also threatens family stability and work incentives. In extreme cases a job would actually reduce the income of a welfare recipient. Continued presence of the father could also reduce the family's total income. These dimensions of the welfare system create added barriers between people and economic security.

In assessing the causes of poverty, then, we may make the following generalizations: (1) Labor-market forces are primarily responsible for the extent of poverty, with demographic handicaps and discrimination of secondary importance; and (2) the distribution of poverty is determined by changing demographic patterns (especially unwed mothers, family breakups, and ill health) and discrimination. Public programs to alleviate poverty and discrimination, while successful in many respects, also contribute to the problem by distorting family and work incentives. This is a reflection of the goal conflicts inherent in all such programs. Because available knowledge and statistics about poverty and discrimination are not complete, there is room for argument on the precise dimensions of each relationship. Nevertheless, the broad outlines of causality are clear enough to provide a solid foundation for public policy.

POLICY DIRECTIONS

An understanding of the causes of poverty gives direction to the formulation of required public policy. To eliminate poverty, we must first expand the number of decent job opportunities and their availability. Harry Johnson of the University of Chicago summarized the point well: ". . . in the absence of a policy of raising the demand for labor to the stretching point, ad hoc policies for remedying poverty by piecemeal assaults on particular poverty-associated characteristics are likely to prove both ineffective and expensive. The most effective way to attack poverty is to attack unemployment, not the symptoms of it."[1]

A strong economy not only creates more job opportunities but also reduces discrimination barriers.[2] In a sluggish economy, the competition for available jobs fosters an "us versus them" mentality that resists *equal* opportunity, not to mention *preferential* opportunity for minority groups. When jobs are plentiful, white males are less threatened by the advancement of minorities and women and are more receptive to affirmative action.

To promote a stronger economy, the government has several options available. First and foremost, it must seek to maintain a high level of aggregate demand by the judicious use of fiscal and monetary tools. In addition, it must give special consideration to the structure of demand those tools stimulate. Aggregate economic policies have identifiable impact on different areas, industries, and labor-market groups. Accordingly, it is the responsibility of government policy makers to select that mix of public

[1]Harry G. Johnson, "Poverty and Unemployment," in *The Economics of Poverty,* ed. Burton Weisbrod (Englewood Cliffs, NJ: Prentice-Hall, Inc., 1965), p. 170.
[2]See Judith Fields and Edward N. Wolff, "The Decline of Sex Segregation and the Wage Gap, 1970–80," *Journal of Human Resources* (Fall 1991), pp. 608–622.

actions that maximizes impact on the unemployed and poor, while minimizing dislocations, such as inflation, elsewhere.

Aggregate economic policies must also incorporate clear supplyside incentives for employment and training of the poor. Tax, spending, or regulatory policies that raise the cost of hiring the poor will not reduce poverty. In developing macroeconomic policies, these potential supplyside effects must be addressed as well.

In addition to seeking full employment, government agencies must make a determined effort to equalize educational and employment opportunities. This will not only further reduce poverty and inequity, it will also make the attainment of full employment easier and less expensive.

Finally, the public must assume responsibility for those who are temporarily or permanently unable to participate in the labor market. Adequate income support must be available, both to alleviate hardship and to reduce intergenerational deprivation. Greatest priority should be placed, however, on reducing the need for public assistance to a minimum.

Viewed against this policy framework, the history of antipoverty policy appears misdirected. Only rarely has there been a sustained and determined effort to reach full employment, and even at those times, policy decisions stopped short of considering the structure of aggregate demand thereby created. Moreover, "poverty" policies have been treated as something separate and apart from "employment" policies. This approach seems to be motivated by the mistaken belief that poverty can be eliminated without full employment. As a consequence, public antipoverty activities often have the aura of a bread and circus kind of gesture. We have allotted—grudgingly, to be sure—huge sums of money to feed, clothe, and house the poor, in the hope, perhaps, of achieving social tranquility. At the same time, we have subjected the poor to a kaleidoscope of training and educational activities, holding out false promises of job opportunity. Yet we have done too little to create the job opportunities that are our most pressing need.

Welfare Reform

At the beginning of 1997 there were nearly 30 million individuals receiving, in the aggregate, more than $200 billion of public assistance (cash and in-kind). Translated into tax dollars, this means that the average nonpoor individuals in the United States contributed nearly $1,000 in 1997 to provide the poor with cash benefits, food stamps, housing assistance, and medical services. While these amounts are a small fraction (under 15 percent) of all government expenditures, they are large enough to stir public anguish. Indeed, the cry for welfare reform has been strident.

In Chapter 11, we reviewed the character of recent welfare reforms. Beginning with the Reagan reforms of 1981, policymakers have adopted an increasingly "get tough" set of welfare policies. The welfare reforms of 1996 completed this policy evolution by ending the federal entitlement to welfare and emphasizing the obligations of welfare recipients to improve their own lot. The new Temporary Assistance to Needy Families (TANF) program sets limits on annual federal welfare outlays and the amount of time a family can receive benefits. More exacting requirements to work, to attend school, and to establish paternity were also imposed by the 1996 reforms.

The underlying theme of these recent welfare reforms sounds strikingly similar to the Flawed Character refrain. Even those legislators who didn't embrace the Flawed

Character perspective were likely frustrated and perplexed by the seeming intractability of the "welfare problem." Time limits and outlay ceilings at least offered a sure solution to the fiscal dimensions of the welfare problem.

The decision of federal lawmakers to turn more welfare responsibilities over to the states was also an admission that Congress didn't know how to solve the larger welfare problem. Since July 1997 the states have taken much greater control over who gets welfare, for how long, and under what conditions. As a consequence, cash welfare is now much less of a national program.

The 1996 welfare reforms were introduced at a time of rising economic prosperity. As unemployment rates fell across the country, so did welfare caseloads. Although welfare reformers were quick to claim credit for the sharp drop in welfare caseloads (1994–1997), the strong economy deserved most of the credit.

The real test for the 1996 welfare reforms will occur when the macro economy again slows down. When jobs begin to disappear, the transition from welfare to work won't be so easy. Then state and federal lawmakers are likely to discover that they haven't yet "solved" the nation's welfare problem. In reality, there may be no permanent "fix" for welfare. Restructured incentives, stronger behavioral strictures, and expanded employment services can all foster welfare exits. But the dynamics of dependency are painfully slow. The most visible payoffs to fundamental reform—reform that changes expectations and behavior—may not be apparent for years after implementation.

Social Insurance

The most powerful antipoverty programs have been broader social insurance policies. While not designed as antipoverty mechanisms, Social Security and Medicare transfer so much income that they greatly reduce poverty among the aged, the disabled, and survivors of deceased workers. The explicit redistributive emphasis of Social Security is also vital to its antipoverty effectiveness.

Unemployment insurance is presently less of an antipoverty mechanism than a middle-class safety net. To increase its poverty impact, benefits would have to be available to a broader spectrum of unemployed workers. Such an expansion would be very costly, however, especially in relation to its poverty impact.

Child-support enforcement is virtually a failsafe policy option as it not only reduces poverty and welfare but also appeals to a broader social consensus on parental obligation. Its antipoverty impact is not likely to be large, however, unless tougher enforcement reduces the rate of illegitimate births, particularly among teenagers. A child-support assurance program could have much greater poverty impact but faces substantial budgetary and social opposition.

Education and Training

Education and training initiatives typically rank high in most antipoverty agendas. Administrative and congressional spokespersons exhort the young to stay in school and the unemployed—especially those on welfare—to undertake further training. There are always suggestions to expand government training programs and political support for educational outlays is easy to muster.

No general case against educational and training expenditures has been presented here. Again, the focus is only on the effectiveness of those expenditures as antipoverty tools. The issue is important because educational and training programs gather much of their support on the basis of their reputed antipoverty effectiveness. What we have sought to demonstrate is that this belief bears very little resemblance to the causal roots of poverty. Lack of formal training or education, by itself, is not a very significant cause of poverty. Thus, programs to provide more education and training are not particularly well suited to reduce the incidence of poverty. What impact they have is dependent on general economic conditions. Ironically, they are most effective when least needed (in a strong economy) and least effective when the need for them seems most apparent (in a weak economy with high rates of unemployment). Low skill levels are a major concern for broader issues of inequality but by themselves are not very compelling explanations for poverty.

Even if skill deficiencies were identified as a basic cause of poverty, it is not evident that expanded government programs would remedy the problem. Public training programs have rarely attained noteworthy net impact, much less cost-effectiveness. Most training takes place on the job. Hence, it is more important to get people into real job settings than into formal training programs. Once individuals have some job experience, they can make better training decisions.

Training and education programs can still be improved, of course. Of particular interest is the potential to target training services more directly on the poor. CETA did this by focusing almost exclusively on the disadvantaged, and most JTPA expenditures are similarly targeted. Available evidence suggests that mandatory participation requirements help bring these services to those who need them but might otherwise not participate. Early exposure to real-world job situations—via job-search or workfare-type programs—can also increase the efficiency of training decisions and outcomes. Tax credits can also encourage low-skill workers to take low-wage jobs and encourage employers to hire them.

Macroeconomic Policy

The single most important observation of this book is the causal significance of aggregate demand policies for the incidence of poverty. High unemployment and sluggish economic growth are the most certain and forceful agents in perpetuating poverty. Nevertheless, public policy in the mid-1970s and early 1980s can be characterized as a deliberate return to the slower growth and higher unemployment rates that characterized much of the 1950s. The recovery from the 1990–91 recession was also deliberately slowed to avoid any increase in actual or expected inflation. Only after the economy again approached full employment in 1995–97 did poverty rates begin to recede once more.

The lesson of these repeated experiences is clear: Fighting inflation is politically more important than fighting poverty. Whenever a trade-off between full employment and inflation is apparent or imagined, our employment goals are quickly abandoned. This forestalls any real prospect of eliminating poverty.

Equal Opportunity

Recent activity in the area of civil rights has largely been a retreat from aggressive affirmative action. It is important to realize, however, that even complete enforcement of civil rights legislation will not lead to equal status for whites and blacks. The desegregation and affirmative action activities of the last several decades have narrowed the gap between white and minority Americans, but the results are agonizingly slow to appear. Even if all racially based barriers to achievement fell tomorrow, blacks would continue to be handicapped by past discrimination. Black and Hispanic schoolchildren would still be far behind their white peers in educational attainments. Equal opportunity to attend college would thus still exclude most minorities. In the labor market, too, the enforcement of nondiscrimination would be of relatively little use to a person who has been denied 20 years of training and experience.

To achieve equal economic status between whites and minority groups, we must do more than enforce equal opportunity; we must also compensate for the heritage of previous discrimination. This means providing compensatory education and training. It also means providing preferential opportunities in some situations. Minority schoolchildren with fewer attainments will have to receive special consideration, while job requirements, in terms of qualifications, experience, and credentials, will have to be set aside for many black workers. As we noted in Chapter 14, such extreme affirmative action inevitably conflicts with the claims of those whites who feel they have "earned" admission to desired schools or jobs and thus necessitates difficult and delicate compromises. But to forsake any such action is to perpetuate second-class status.

CAUSES, ATTITUDES, AND POLICY

While present policy directions are unlikely to achieve equality or eliminate poverty, there is some prospect for future change. Both the nonpoor and the poor are becoming increasingly frustrated with policies that provide more income maintenance and fewer opportunities. While nearly two out of three Americans feel that "we are spending too little on assistance to the poor," only one out of five thinks we are spending too little on welfare.

Although public demands for less welfare and more jobs are persistent, an undercurrent of hostility and distrust remains. Over 80 percent of the public agrees that "too many people on welfare could be working" and that "too many people on welfare cheat by getting money they are not entitled to." With respect to minority concerns, 41 percent of white America believes that black unemployment rates are high because blacks don't want jobs. In addition, one out of four whites believes blacks have less native intelligence. Only 4 percent of all whites believe that job discrimination is a major barrier to black employment. White perceptions of Spanish-speaking minorities are comparable. Finally, a majority of Americans opposes preferential access to jobs or schools for either poor people or minorities, preferring to let "merit" determine access to schools and jobs.

These perceptions of poverty and discrimination are major determinants of public policy. If we are going to eliminate either poverty or discrimination, public perceptions must reflect reality more closely. Then those perceptions must be reflected in public policy.

Index